A Short History of
the West Indies

A Short History of the West Indies

J. H. Parry
P. M. Sherlock
A. P. Maingot

FOURTH EDITION

MACMILLAN
CARIBBEAN

First published 1956
Reprinted once
Reprinted (with alterations) 1960
Second edition 1963
Reprinted twice
Third edition 1971
Reprinted 12 times
Fourth edition 1987
Published by
MACMILLAN EDUCATION LTD
London and Oxford
Companies and representatives throughout the world
www.macmillan-caribbean.com

ISBN 0–333–40954–X

21 20 19 18 17 16 15 14 13
08 07 06 05 04 03 02 01

This book is printed on paper suitable for recycling and
made from fully managed and sustained forest sources.

Printed in Malaysia

A catalogue record for this book is available from the
British Library.

Cover: painting of Portuguese Carracks attributed to
Cornelius Anthonizoon, reproduced by courtesy of The
National Maritime Museum, London. Photograph by
Michael Holford.

Contents

Contents

List of Illustrations

Introduction

One of the most significant and least recognized of recent Caribbean achievements has been the creation by Caribbean scholars of a common body of knowledge about the societies of the region.

The seeds were planted in the Spanish colonies with the founding of the University of Santo Domingo in 1511 and the University of Havana in 1721. These universities gave to the intellectual a place of respect in the society, enabled him to keep in touch with European thought, to examine ideas in a local setting and to establish within the society a capability for intellectual analysis and philosophical thought. Gordon Lewis, in *Mainstreams in Caribbean Thought*, has described the first flowering in Cuba, in the 1840's, and has shown the significance of Jose Antonio Saco and other Cuban thinkers of that period.

A larger region-wide movement developed in the 1930's, one of the great watershed periods in Caribbean history. It grew out of a combination of explosive ideas which propelled the Caribbean into the twentieth century. Generating ferment and discontent, they powered the rise of nationalist and labour movements, impelled intellectuals to champion the working class and inspired in Caribbean blacks a vision of Africa as symbol and mother. Voices from the four major language groups of the fragmented Caribbean proclaimed common themes. Caribbean blacks found in Garvey's Pan Africanism links with a past and promise of a future. Fernando Ortiz pioneered Afro-Cubanism and 'set the drums beating in Cuban music'. In Haiti, Jean Price Mars affirmed the enriching value of the African heritage and Jacques Roumain prepared the way for negritude and Aimee Cesaire. Two West Indian historians, C. L. R. James with *Black Jacobins* and Eric Williams with *Capitalism and Slavery* pioneered the writing of Caribbean history from a Caribbean point of view and opened new perspectives that compelled European historians to revise some of their historical judgments.

Up to that time, though many West Indians had migrated to Panama, the coastlands of Central American and to Cuba in search of employment, the English-speaking Caribbean, blinkered by an educational system that perpetuated European rivalries, was virtually cut off from intellectual contacts with other Caribbean countries. James and Williams removed the blinkers and beckoned the West Indian intellectual to be a Columbus to the world that lay around and to the whole new continents and worlds within the various Caribbean societies. They revealed the inner coherence in the history of Caribbean societies which differed in culture and political organization but had been moulded by the same powerful forces of colonialism, the sugar plantation, African slavery and miscegenation, and they revealed the strength and courage with which the folk had responded to the harsh penalization of slavery.

With the founding, in 1948, of the University of the West Indies and its Institute of Social and Economic Research, the English speaking Caribbean gained a permanent point of intellectual contact with other Caribbean scholars. In a relatively short time West Indian scholars working within the Caribbean became members of the larger Caribbean intellectual community and began to add to the expanding body of Caribbean research. The story of new Caribbean universities such as those of the West Indies, Puerto Rico and the Dominican Republic, vividly illustrates how essential it is for Third World countries to develop their own centres of excellence and to enlarge their capability in research.

The authors have drawn on this body of new knowledge in preparing the fourth edition of the *Short History of the West Indies*. They have rewritten the Introduction and, within the narrow limits of available space, have amended the original text where this appeared to be necessary. They have rewritten the final chapter of the third edition and added two new chapters.

The purpose remains the same: to give an account of the recorded history of the islands in the Caribbean Sea; the four large islands of Cuba, Hispaniola, Jamaica and Puerto Rico and the hundreds of smaller islands which form an arching breakwater against the Atlantic, from the scattered peaks of the Virgin Islands in the north, to Curaçao and Aruba lying off the coast of South America. These make up a sub-region of what it has become fashionable to call the Caribbean Basin, a faceless term that should not be permitted to mask the fact that the Basin is lop-sided, the mainland sectors being part of a continent, the northern and eastern sectors no more than a thin fissured rim. This book treats the story of the islands as a connected whole and is not directly concerned with the history of the mainland countries except for areas such as Belize and the Guyanas, whose development was closely connected with that of the islands.

The recorded history of the West Indies does not grow gradually, as most Old World histories grow, out of a more remote mythological or archaeological past. It begins abruptly with a definite event: the arrival of the first European discoverers in Columbus's fleet in 1492. The present aspect of the islands has been shaped largely by events which took place after that date.

The peoples who inhabit the islands — with a dwindling handful of exceptions — migrated or were deliberately transplanted from the Old World. They came from Europe, Africa and Asia, bringing with them their religious beliefs, their languages, their social habits. Today the evidence of this transplanting of social institutions can be seen on every hand in the Caribbean. Not only the people, but their physical surroundings, are largely transplanted. All the domestic animals and most of the useful plants came from the Old World. Sweet potatoes, squashes, cassava, tobacco, beans, cocoa, pumpkins, maize and groundnuts were introduced also from tropical America. Even the wild animals and the wild plants were, many of them, introduced, and have driven out or modified the native plants and animals.

The West Indians, then, are imported people in a largely imported environment. There is nothing unique about this. The same is true, in varying degrees, of many other peoples in the New World. But they were much slower than most American peoples to grow away from their Old World origins and to form characteristic communities of their own. This difference was due partly to economic dependence: the early settlers set themselves deliberately to produce precious metals and tropical crops for sale in Europe, and their economy developed accordingly. Partly the difference was due to the deep divisions between the immigrants: divisions of language, religion and political allegiance between the European groups who settled in the various islands; and divisions in each island between European, African and Asian. These divisions were complicated and emphasised by the separateness of the islands themselves, small as most of them are, and scattered in a great expanse of sea. Until the steamship and the aircraft brought them some measure of freedom, the island people were at the mercy of the winds and currents which governed the movement of sailing ships. For sailing ships, the Caribbean is easy to enter from the east, but hard to leave. Almost any gap in the Antillean break-water will serve for a west-bound ship; but one east-bound must beat out against the north-east trade wind, which blows steadily for most of the year, and relatively few exits are safe and convenient for that purpose. For the early settlers, bound to their respective origins in Europe by sentiment, by political discipline and by economic dependence, the most useful harbours were naturally those which lay near the best exits. The principal settlements therefore grew up along well-defined sea-lanes to Europe. To this day, sea-borne communications between the islands are difficult and haphazard, while inter-island air travel is limited by high cost.

The Caribbean has sometimes been likened, in its historical role, to the Mediterranean; but the likeness is superficial. The Mediterranean is an enclosed sea which for millennia linked, in peace or war, the cities, the empires, the cultures of the peoples living round its shores; and for millennia those peoples had no need to look far beyond the boundaries of their sea.

The Caribbean has been less of a meeting place than a corridor. The islands were occupied by colonists who were tied to Europe. The gravitational pull of Europe to the east was balanced by a corresponding pull to the west. The Caribbean waterways have linked Europe with Latin America, Spain with the Phillipines, New England with California, South America with the United States and Canada. They have divided the Caribbean countries shore from shore, island from island.

Three waves of colonizers founded three types of settlements in the islands; Spanish colonies based on ranching and mining; English and French 'plantations' to produce exotic crops, manned by a white labour force of owners and indentured servants; and Dutch trading posts. The sugar revolution of the mid-seventeenth century and the massive introduction of African slaves split the society into two groups. In Elsa Goveia's words: 'The slave society of the Leeward Islands at the end of the eighteenth century was divided into separate groups, clearly marked off from each other by their differences of legal and social status, of political rights and economic opportunity, and of racial origin and culture. The existence of these separate groups is so striking that it tends to obscure the existence of the community of which they were a part. But this community did exist, and its fundamental principles of inequality and subordination based on race and status were firmly impressed upon the lives of all its members. It was these basic principles embodying the necessities of the West Indian slave system which determined the ordering of the separate groups as part of the community and held them all together within a single social structure.'

The privileged resisted change. They usually do. Change threatens them. There was among the West Indian proprietors no Bolivar, no Toussaint, no Jefferson with a vision of a nation guided by a bright constellation of moral principles. It was among the mass of African slaves in the Caribbean and in AfroAmerica that the passion for freedom and justice manifested itself — in the founding of Maroon communities wherever forests and mountains offered protection, in sabotage on the estates, in risings, rebellions and wars of independence. The story of the rejection of slavery by blacks throughout AfroAmerica is a remarkable one.

Those who remained on the estates, and the great majority did, also have a remarkable record of achievement. They had been uprooted from their native land, torn from family, kinsfolk, tribe, transported as individuals amongst other black strangers, subjected to the cruelties of the terrible Middle Passage, set to work at unaccustomed tasks in a strange environment under the control of men of another race who spoke an unknown language. Some pined away and died. The majority survived and slowly, out of courage, memory and what lay at hand, fashioned a way of life. Their efforts to communicate with others gave birth to a family of vivid Creole languages. Striving for that communion with the ancestors and the gods which had been a part of their lives, they created Shango, Vodun and, later in Cuba, Santeria. At night, in stolen hours, they entertained each other with tales of the Spider God Anansi, of the hare and tortoise. One generation handed on to another songs and music. But they had no tradition of oral history. Their past had been taken from them. Dispossessed of homeland, they had been cast adrift in time. This was psychologically the severest deprivation of all. The story of how these folk created the seed bed for the various Caribbean cultures and struggled continually for freedom and justice forms the core of Caribbean history.

The societies and cultures of the Caribbean were further enriched and diversified in the nineteenth century by the importation of indentured labourers from India, Madeira, Liberia, the Canary Islands, Hong Kong and Canton. Again the story is of the exploitation and degradation of human beings and of a process of painful adjustment in a strange environment.

The importation of large numbers of East Indians into Trinidad and Guyana over a period of 80 years resulted in the division of the community into two groups whose cultures were fundamentally different and who, in the early years, distrusted and despised each other. As time passed they learned to live with each other, and in some areas of life the cultures blended. It was not so much a matter of one group accepting or tolerating the other, since this implies that something had to be accepted or tolerated. It was more of a symbiotic relationship in which each group learns that people of different cultures see things differently and at the same time discovers that it is possible to contain these differences within a framework of shared loyalties and values. In the process Caribbean society gained immeasurably from the talents and skills of the East Indians as well as of the other smaller groups of imported people.

Few things in the world of today hold out greater promise for mankind than the growth of mixed societies that are free from the tensions and violence that have attended the determination of one race to dominate others. The history of the Caribbean, which for so long was a record of discrimination and social injustice, has become, not without travail and agony, a record of diverse peoples in which the key words are those which Haitian peasants use to greet each other, honour and respect.

The book which follows begins with the name of Christopher Columbus in recognition of the quinquennial anniversary of his first Trans Atlantic crossing of 1492. Time, which often relegates the great to obscurity, continually enlarges the stature of the explorer whose practicality, knowledge and courage changed the history of mankind.

We close this introduction with an affectionate and respectful tribute to two distinguished historians: the late Dr. Elsa Goveia, Guyana Scholar and first Professor of Caribbean History at the University of the West Indies and to the late Dr. John Parry, co-author the Short History, the first Chairman of the Department of History of the University of the West Indies and latterly Professor of Oceanic Studies at Harvard University. Their scholarship and gift of exposition lit candles of understanding in the minds of the Caribbean people.

Discovery

Christopher Columbus, while in Lisbon studying Portuguese records of their exploration of the West African coast, conceived the idea of reaching China and the Indies by sailing westwards across the Atlantic. According to his son Ferdinand 'it was in Portugal that the Admiral began to think that if men could sail so far south, one might also sail west and find land in the same quarter'.

Columbus soon moved from surmise to certainty. The basic facts were not in dispute: that the world was a sphere, that the Altantic was the world's only great ocean and that it separated Europe from Asia. Some geographers calculated the distance between the two continents as 5000 miles; Columbus reckoned it was of the order of 3500 miles. His study of Ptolemy and of the most eminent georgraphers of his time, his examination of the charts and maps of Portuguese Atlantic exploration, his experience as a sailor in the North Atlantic and down the coast of West Africa confirmed him in his opinion. That question having been settled, the task was to obtain royal funding and to secure a royal commission that established his position as commander of the expedition and representative of the Crown. Through six frustrating years of rejection he was sustained by his natural tenacity of purpose and by a growing conviction that God had called him to this mission.

Portugal seemed the most likely prospect. She stood on the threshold of greatness, her economy greatly strengthened by an infusion of Italian capital and financial expertise, her capital city Europe's chief centre for the study of Atlantic navigation, and the spirits of her people lifed by the triumphs of her explorers and seamen. In 1419 she occupied and settled Madeira, and later the Azores, the Cape Verde islands, Fernando Po and São Thomé. In 1443 Nino Tristao reached Senegal and opened up a trade in ivory, gold, malaguetta and African slaves. While her explorers thrust south in search of an ocean route to the Indies, she established a flourishing sugar industry in the islands, making use of a technology transferred by the Genoese and Venetians from the Eastern Meditteranean to Sicily and thence to Spain and

1

Portugal. African labour made possible the spread of sugar production in the Algarve and in the Portuguese island colonies. In this way there were gathered together in the womb of time the people, the crop, the technology that were to shape the history of a vast and as yet unknown region that lay beyond the Atlantic.

After some hesitation Portugal turned down the proposal. So did England, France and, first time around, Spain. At last success came. In January 1492 Columbus was granted audience by Isabella of Castile, whose marriage with Ferdinand of Aragon had unified Spain. The time was right. In the journal of this first voyage Columbus wrote: 'In this same year I saw the royal banners of Your Highnesses placed by force on the towers of the Alhambra — and I saw the Moorish King come out of the gates of the city and kiss the royal hands of Your Highnesses'. In that moment of triumph Ferdinand and Isabella commissioned Columbus 'to go by way of the West to India', appointed him high admiral of the Ocean Sea and made him Viceroy and perpetual governor of any lands he discovered. By this act the rulers of newly unified Spain secured a vaster and richer New Spain beyond the Atlantic.

Columbus set sail from Palos on August 3 and landed on Guanahani, which he named San Salvador, on October 11. The recorded history of the Caribbean begins with his arrival. To say that Columbus discovered America is a misuse of words. Columbus revealed to Europeans the existence of continents and islands which were inhabited already, and had been so for many centuries. Columbus did not discover a new world; he established contact between two worlds, both already old. More important, he did so at a time when the peoples of western Europe had recently developed ships and navigating instruments good enough to maintain that contact in regular voyages, so that people, plants and animals began to flow in a steady stream from the world of Europe to the world of America. In most parts of Latin America, and even to some extent in North America, the two worlds met and mingled. In the West Indies, however, there was little or no mingling, because the shock of conquest proved too much for the weaker race. In the larger islands the native peoples soon dwindled before the impact of an aggressive alien culture. They could not adapt themselves to living beside Europeans; they could not retreat, as the Plains Indians were to retreat centuries later, with the dwindling buffalo herds; there was nowhere for them to go. Within a century they were extinct, and a new society of immigrants from Europe and Africa had taken their place.

Today the Arawaks are hardly even a memory. They had no

writing; their only records took the forms of carving in wood and stone and of rude graffiti on natural rock faces. Our knowledge of them is derived partly from the accounts of sixteenth-century Spanish writers, and partly from examination of burial caves and middens. All the witnesses agree that they were a kindly and peaceful people. They had no reason to be otherwise. Except in eastern Puerto Rico they had little or no contact with warlike enemies; and though they got some of their food by hunting, their quarries — the aguti and the iguana — were not beasts which put much tax upon the courage and endurance of the hunter. Fishing was more important to them than hunting. They rarely went far from the sea. Their sites are often marked by great mounds of conch shells. For more adventurous kinds of fishing they fashioned dug-out boats of considerable size from the trunks of silk-cotton trees. They had some agriculture. Oviedo says that they used maize, though the absence of grinding-stones from their pre-Columbian sites suggests that they knew only a soft variety; hard types of maize, from which bread flour could be made, came later from the mainland. Their only bread-stuff was cassava; the discovery of a method of leaching out the poisonous juice of this root must have been, for so primitive a people, an economic event of the first importance. Cassava will flourish where little else will grow; it has spread from the Americas to parts of the Old World, in particular to West Africa, but has never commended itself greatly to European taste. Today, in remote and arid parts of Jamaica, 'cassava without salt, coffee without sugar' is proverbial diet in times of drought and hardship. In addition to food crops, the Arawaks grew tobacco, which they used as a drug, as an ingredient in ritual, and as a means of exchange. Tobacco is the only native crop which became an important article of export from the West Indies after the European occupation. It has made more fortunes than all the silver of the Indies.

The Arawaks made good baskets and serviceable pottery, which has a rough and distinctive beauty and is often decorated with incised patterns. They made polished stone tools — knives, scrapers, axes and adzes — which compare with the neolithic artefacts of the Old World. They had no knowledge of hard metals, but in some of the islands used gold, washed from the streams and hammered into trinkets, for personal ornament. Like most New World peoples they had no beasts of burden and no wheeled vehicles. Though they used caves for burial purposes and probably sometimes for shelter, they made their own dwellings of thatch and lived in settled villages. They slept in hammocks made either of woven cotton or of string open-work. This habit much impressed the Spaniards and was one of the few Arawak contributions to European material culture as it developed in the West Indies and elsewhere. Of Arawak government and religion relatively little is known; but some of the chiefs reigned over considerable tracts of country and seem to have kept some state. The Spanish writers often remarked on the loyalty and devotion which these *caciques* drew from their people.

In Columbus's time the Arawaks occupied all the greater islands of the Caribbean; but in the easternmost island, Puerto Rico, they were already suffering from the raids of an intrusive and far more warlike people, to whom the Spaniards gave the name of Caribs. Carib means cannibal; and cannibalism, whether for ritual purposes or merely for food, was one of the characteristics of these canoe-borne marauders who were pushing north along the line of the lesser Antilles and enslaving or destroying the earlier inhabitants in their way. Though a handful of Caribs still survive in Dominica, even less is known of their early culture than of that of the Arawaks, from whom, probably, many of their skills were originally derived. They were dangerous enemies, and after the first few encounters the Spaniards left them and their islands alone, to their own great disadvantage, as later appeared; for other Europeans were to seize the islands which the Spaniards had passed by.

The world which these simple peoples inhabited had two characteristics which it still retains — breath-taking physical beauty and, in parts, great fertility. Columbus wrote to his king from Cuba: 'The banks of the rivers are embellished with lofty palm trees, whose shade gives a delicious freshness to the air, and the birds and the flowers are uncommon and beautiful. I was so delighted with the scene, that I had almost come to the resolution of staying here for the remainder of my days; for believe me, Sire, these countries far surpass all the rest of the world in beauty and conveniency.' Many later travellers, in different parts of the West Indies, have echoed his words. Geographically and geologically the islands fall into two great groups, the division corresponding almost exactly with the ethnographical division at the time of the conquest. The Greater Antilles rest on a common submarine bed and form parts of a partially submerged continental tract which once extended continuously from Cuba to the Virgin Islands. They are traversed by an abrupt and lofty mountain range, of which the peaks are nearly 12 000 feet high, culminating in Hispaniola and falling off on either side in Cuba, Jamaica and Puerto Rico. They are composed mostly of limestones, with outcrops of other rocks, all much older than the eruptive rocks of the Lesser Antilles, and nowhere showing traces of recent volcanic activity.

The Lesser Antilles in the north form two parallel chains, of which the outer, terminating in Marie-Galante, represents an area of upheaval on the seaward slope. Except for Antigua, its members are of marine origin, coral below and limestone above. The inner chain, which runs through to Grenada, is a partly submerged peninsula. The existing islands represent old volcanic cones, culminating in Dominica at a height of 5340 feet. Trinidad and Tobago, and probably Barbados, belong geologically to Venezuela. The nomenclature of these island groups is confusing. Today the name Leeward Islands is applied to the northern portion of the chain, from the Virgins to Guadeloupe; the Windward group includes Dominica, Martinique, St. Lucia, St. Vincent, the Grenadines and Grenada. In early Spanish times the whole chain from the Virgins to Trinidad was called the Windward Islands — Islas de Barlovento — the name Leeward being confined to the other islands off the South American coast; a logical and descriptive distinction, considering the prevailing north-east wind.

Vegetation is exuberant in all the islands, and most of them in Columbus's time must have been covered in forest to the water's edge, except perhaps on the south-east coast of Cuba, where early voyagers reported the same harsh xerophytic plants — cactus and the like — which grow there today. Now the islands are largely deforested except in the higher mountains. The larger fauna is poor in species, except for birds. Most native species differ from those of the mainland, owing to the length of time that the islands have been separated from the continent, but the fauna of Trinidad and Tobago, as might be expected, is South American in character. Fish and turtles abound everywhere, and land reptiles, including crocodiles, are common in the larger islands; but, except for the fer-de-lance in Martinique and St. Lucia, and for the Trinidadian species, there are no poisonous snakes.

As if to compensate for their great beauty and for their comparative freedom from animal pests, the West Indies are peculiarly subject to natural cataclysms: hurricanes, earthquakes, and, in some of the Lesser Antilles, volcanic eruptions. These recurrent disasters have played a considerable part in the history of all the islands, and are still a serious danger. Columbus on his first voyage escaped the evidences of these visitations; but he was to have his full share of hurricanes later.

Columbus's first irruption into the terrestrial paradise of the Arawaks was a mere reconnaissance, though a well-planned and ably executed one. He set sail from Palos on August 3 and, making the best of the North Atlantic wind system — it was not the least important of his discoveries — he sailed from the Canaries to the Bahamas before the north-east trades, and later returned to the Azores in the zone of the westerly winds of winter. His first West Indian landfall was at San Salvador in the Bahamas. But which island? At one time nine competed for the honour. In 1926, though there was no consensus, Watling Island was awarded the prize and renamed San Salvador. The debate was re-opened in 1986 by a National Georgraphic Research team which, on the basis of five years research, claimed that Samana Cay, 65 miles south-west of Watling Island, was the island on which Columbus landed.

During his stay in the West Indies he explored Santa María de la Concepción, which later and less pious sailors renamed Rum Cay; the north-east coast of Cuba; and part of the north coast of Hispaniola — La Isla Española — modern Haiti. Almost everywhere the newcomers were received by the natives with hospitality and respect — respect due, it may be, to belief in their divine origin. In Hispaniola they obtained by barter a number of gold nose-plugs, bracelets, and other ornaments; small trinkets, but valuable enough to attract fresh expeditions and to seal the fate of their over-trustful owners.

Columbus claimed, and believed until his death, that he had found islands lying off the coast of eastern Asia, and possibly part of the mainland too. The name West Indies is testimony to his belief. We cannot be sure whether these claims agreed with Columbus's original intentions and promises, nor whether Ferdinand and Isabella entirely accepted them. Some intelligent contemporaries certainly did not; and doubt in the minds of Columbus's own men is suggested by the alternative name of Antilles, from Antilla or Atlantis. But beyond doubt Columbus had found an extensive archipelago of hitherto unknown islands which yielded some gold and were inhabited by a peaceful and tractable, though primitive, people. These islands might prove to be merely another Atlantic group, like the Canaries, over which Spain and Portugal had been bickering for many years; they might prove easy stepping-stones to India. In any event, they were worth careful investigation.

The first voyage, though successful, had been expensive. Columbus had lost his flagship and had been compelled to leave half his men behind in Hispaniola to face an uncertain fate. The plunder he had secured was negligible in proportion to the cost of the enterprise. It was now essential to follow up the discovery and to produce a return on the investment. Immediately upon receipt of Columbus's first report, the sovereigns commanded him to begin his preparations for a second voyage. Shortly afterwards they embarked on negotiations with the Papacy and with Portugal in order to secure a monopoly of navigation and settlement in the seas and lands which Columbus had discovered.

The negotiations with the Papacy presented little difficulty. Alexander VI was himself a Spaniard, already under heavy obligations to the Catholic monarchs and looking to them for support in his endeavour to create a principality in Italy for his son. His predecessors had conferred on Portugal the monopoly of exploration and missionary activity in West Africa, and Alexander was willing to do as much for Spain. He issued a series of four bulls, each successively strengthening and extending the provisions of the previous ones, in accordance with successive demands made by Ferdinand and Isabella, upon Columbus's advice. The first two granted to the sovereigns of Castile all lands discovered, or to be discovered, in the regions explored by Columbus. The third, the famous *Inter Caetera*, drew an imaginary boundary from north to south a hundred leagues west of the Azores and Cape Verde Islands, and provided that the land and sea beyond the line should be a Spanish sphere of exploration. The fourth, *Dudum Siquidem*, extended the previous grants to include 'all islands and mainlands whatever, found or to be found...in sailing towards the west and south, whether they be in regions occidental or meridional and oriental and of India'; further, all grants previously made in the regions mentioned were cancelled, even if they had been followed by actual possession.

Whatever the international force of these enactments — and Catholic opinion was divided in the matter — the four bulls constituted for Spaniards the basic legal claim of the Spanish Crown to the lands of the New World. As instruments regulating relations with Portugal they were superseded, it is true, by the Treaty of Tordesillas in the following year. By that treaty the Spaniards unwittingly signed away their claim to the real route to India, the imaginary land of Antilla, and (as later appeared) the real land of Brazil; but the treaty did not affect the West Indies, and Columbus was back in the islands long before it was signed. He left Cadiz in September 1493 in command of a large fleet, ships, caravels and pinnaces, seventeen sail in all. The composition of the fleet, no less than the instructions which the admiral carried, indicated the purpose for which it was sent. It contained no heavily armed fighting ships; it carried no trade goods, other than small truck for barter with savages. Its chief cargo was men — priests, gentlemen-soldiers, artisans, farmers, twelve hundred people in all — and agricultural stock —

tools, seeds and animals; a whole society in miniature. The immediate object of the voyage, then, was not to open a new trade or to conquer oriental kingdoms, but to settle the island of Hispaniola, to found a mining and farming colony which should produce its own food, pay for the cost of the voyage by remitting gold to Spain, and serve at the same time as a base for further exploration in the direction of India or Cathay. There had been no lack of volunteers. For men-at-arms, unemployed through the decline of private war and the fall of Granada, the Indies offered adventurous service, plunder, and the possibility of landed ease; for humbler folk there was the hope of escape from the harsh uplands of Castile, overrun by the privileged flocks of Mesta, to a place where soil and climate were kind and native labour cheap and plentiful; and who knew what golden dreams might lie beyond?

The fleet made a prosperous passage and a good landfall, at Dominica; and passed along the beautiful arc of the lesser Antilles, through the Virgin Islands, past Puerto Rico, to the north coast of Hispaniola. There Columbus's good fortune ended. The settlement of Navidad, planted on the first voyage, had been wiped out; in selecting as a site for his second settlement the unprotected, unhealthy shore which he named Isabela, Columbus made his first serious blunder. Isabela never prospered. It would have taken a leader of commanding genius to maintain discipline among those early Spanish settlers — touchy, adventurous and greedy as they were — to compel them to clear the forest, build houses, and plant crops instead of roaming about the island in search of gold or of slaves. Great explorer and sea commander, brilliant navigator though he was, Columbus had neither the experience nor the temperament of a successful colonial governor. He was, moreover, a foreigner and the son of an artisan tricked out with an empty title and a new coat of arms. It soon became a question whether he and his officers could keep his men in hand until the relief fleet arrived.

The search for India could not be delayed, however, and after sending some of the most troublesome away to explore the interior, Columbus again set sail with three caravels, to explore the south coast of Cuba and to discover Jamaica. On his return to Isabela, he found his people weakened by sickness and at open enmity with the natives. The peaceful Tainos had been exasperated to the point of war by the incessant demands for food and women. Columbus turned upon the Indians, hunted them through the forest with armed men and savage dogs, and imposed upon them a poll-tax of gold dust which they could not pay. The captives in this pitiful warfare were enslaved. Columbus shipped some hundreds to Spain, where most of them died. The remainder were released and sent back by the orders of the queen, so that even the slave trade brought no profit. Meanwhile, at Isabela, the surviving Indians left their land untilled. Columbus's fleet had brought a stock of food from Spain, but not enough to feed the colony for any length of time. Over-optimism about the extent to which Europeans could live off the country in the tropics was a common feature of all these early explorations. War with the Indians caused a scarcity of local food supplies; and famine threatened the Spaniards in their fever-ridden camp.

Matters were in this state when, in the spring of 1496, Columbus sailed for Spain to deal with the complaints which had been carried there by malcontents from Isabela. In his absence, but with his approval, his brother Bartolomé, whom he left in charge, organised the removal of the settlement from Isabela to a better site on the south coast. There, in 1496 or 1497, the colonists began to build the town of Santo Domingo, which was to be for half a century the capital of the Spanish Indies, and which survives as a thriving city today.

The Catholic monarchs still trusted Columbus. With their support and at their expense he returned to the Indies in 1498; but this time there were few volunteers, and men had to be pressed or released from prison to sail with the admiral. Columbus sailed to the south of his former course, to discover the island of Trinidad and the mouths of the Orinoco, by far the largest river then known to Europeans, whose great volume of fresh water proved the new-found coast to be part of a mighty continent. By ill-luck he missed the pearl-bearing oyster-beds off the Venezuelan coast, but sailed directly north from Margarita, by a remarkable feat of navigation, to Hispaniola, to the new city which his brother had founded.

At Santo Domingo Columbus found half his settlers, under the *alcalde* Francisco Roldán, in open revolt against the authority of Bartolomé. Columbus could not — or did not — suppress the revolt by force, but bought off Roldán and his followers by concessions — pardon, restoration to office, and free land grants. Besides consenting to these humiliating terms, the admiral made at this time another and more significant concession to the rebels — the division of the Indians of the island among the Spanish settlers as servants and estate labourers. This *repartimiento* system later became general in modified form throughout the Spanish Indies. For a time, the arrangement served its turn in pacifying the leaders of the rebellion, and Columbus was able to suppress subsequent minor Spanish revolts with a severity probably overdue. The damage was done, however. Where

Columbus's policy had been weak, malcontents returning to Spain were able to represent it as tyrannical. In the spring of 1499 the sovereigns appointed Francisco de Bobadilla to supersede Columbus and to investigate the complaints against him. Bobadilla sent the admiral home in irons. Though his sovereigns restored his titles and property and treated him with all courtesy to the end, Columbus was never again allowed to exercise his offices of admiral and viceroy or to interfere in the government of his island of Hispaniola; but time continually enlarges his achievement. By establishing transatlantic shipping routes he set in motion forces that shifted Europe's centre of gravity from the Mediteranean to the Atlantic, transferred primacy in trade from Venice and Genoa to Antwerp, Amsterdam and London, and transformed the western periphery of Europe into the eastern seaboard of the North Atlantic basin. By taking possession and establishing settlements he secured control of the western terminal of the new trading system, facilitated a rapid diffusion of people, animals, plants, food crops and precious minerals, transformed Europe's picture of the world and profoundly altered the mainstreams of European thought.

The real beginnings of settled government in the Indies date from the arrival of Bobadilla's successor, Frey Nicolás de Ovando, Knight Commander of Alcántara. It was characteristic of the time that this task should be entrusted to a high officer of an order founded to garrison Christian outposts in Spain against the forces of Islam. Ovando arrived with a great fleet of thirty ships and brought 2500 people to reinforce the 300 or so surviving settlers. He governed Hispaniola for six years with a severity far harsher than Columbus had ever dared to exercise. Discipline, indeed, was what the settlers chiefly needed. As for the Indians, Ovando secured a royal decree in 1503 giving legal form to the *repartimientos* begun by Columbus. From the subjugated Indians the invaders exacted tribute and forced labour in return for conversion and protection. Against the wild Indians they waged relentless war. Probably the Tainos were doomed already and Ovando's severities only hastened their extinction. Forced labour drove some of them to despair and suicide; European diseases, smallpox especially, killed many; and the Spaniards loosed against them yet other destructive enemies. A primitive agricultural people, tilling unfenced clearings in the forest, cannot live close to an aggressive pastoral community, such as the Spaniards formed in both the Old World and the New. The Indians were defeated not only by armies of down-at-heel swordsmen, but by greater armies of wandering beasts which rooted up their cassava and trampled and grazed their corn. The Spaniards, for their part, achieved a modest prosperity, pasturing great herds of pigs and horned cattle upon open range and washing for gold in the streams. The production of gold increased steadily, and reached by the second decade of the sixteenth century a quantity sufficient to attract the interest and the cupidity of Ferdinand and his advisers. It reached a peak in 1518, but thereafter declined sharply. By the middle of the century the silver of New Spain and Peru had become the main interest of government, and the gold of the islands was relatively insignificant.

Lack of labour was the chief hindrance to the development of Hispaniola. The settlers resorted to slave-raiding in the Bahamas to replace the dying Tainos, but the captured Lucayos also died or killed themselves rather than face the harsh conditions of forced labour in mines and fields. To men of the temperament of the early Spanish settlers land was useless without hands to work it; even gold-mining was tedious work which called for unskilled labour. It was lack of labour as much as greed for gold, missionary zeal, or simple rest-lessness which drove many Spaniards on from Hispaniola to settle in other islands and mainlands, where the native population might prove more numerous and more hardy. Hispaniola became, as its founder had intended, the base for further exploration and the source of bacon, dried beef and cassava bread to victual the exploring expeditions which sailed out in ever-increasing numbers during the government of Ovando's successor, the old admiral's son, Diego Colón.

In 1509 Juan de Esquivel began the settlement of Jamaica, or at least of the area round New Seville, near what is now St. Ann's Bay, where Columbus had beached his worm-riddled caravels five years before. Jamaica yielded no precious metals. It supported a small population of Spaniards who lived by cattle-ranching, but was never of much importance in Spanish times. The much larger enterprise of settling Cuba was undertaken shortly after. Sebastián de Ocampo, sent out by Ovando to reconnoitre in 1508, circumnavigated Cuba and proved it to be an island, contrary to what Columbus had asserted. In 1511 Diego Velázquez, who had been lieutenant-governor of Hispaniola under Ovando, began the work of settlement, as a pri-vate investment, but with official approval. Oviedo, who knew Veláz-quez, has related the story of the conquest in detail. Like Ovando, Velázquez was a disciplinarian and an administrator of considerable ability. With a small force of personal followers he put down native resistance and occupied the whole island — or, at least, desirable sites throughout the island — within three years. He showed remarkable foresight and skill in selecting the best localities for the establishment of Spanish settlements; during the first five years of his governorship he founded seven towns, and though both the names and the precise sites of several of them changed more than once, they all survived in the districts where they were founded. Santiago in the south-east was the first, and remained, by virtue of its proximity to Hispaniola, the chief settlement, until a shift in Caribbean trade routes brought Havana into prominence. Cuba produced considerable quantities of gold; and being more fertile and less mountainous than Hispaniola, it offered better opportunities for ranching, tobacco-farming and sugar-planting. As in Hispaniola, the labour for mines and farms was procured in the early years by *repartimientos* of the native population. Cuba attracted many settlers from Hispaniola, and for a time at least Velázquez succeeded in making himself practically independent of the governor of the older colony.

The fourth major island settlement, that of Puerto Rico, which began in 1512, was less immediately successful. Intrusive groups of Caribs from the Lesser Antilles had already established themselves in Puerto Rico, and offered a much more formidable resistance to the Spaniards than the natives of Hispaniola had done. The attention of the first governor, Juan Ponce de León, was, moreover, divided between the island itself and the peninsula of Florida, where he made an unsuccessful attempt to settle in 1514. The settlement of Puerto Rico, in consequence, was slower, more sanguinary and less complete than that of the other islands, and the colony did not attract large numbers of Spaniards in the sixteenth century.

Hispaniola had been the base for the conquest of Cuba and for all subsequent settlements down to 1519. In that year Cuba in its turn became the base for a greater conquest. Ever since Columbus's fourth voyage, expeditions, sailing either from Hispaniola or from Spain itself, had been exploring and settling in Castilla del Oro, as the Isthmus of Darien was called. Balboa, the first of the great *conquistadores* of the mainland, was a soldier of fortune from Hispaniola. In 1513, following up an Indian report, he led an expedition through the dripping forests of the Isthmus to the shores of the Pacific. Balboa's discovery not only revealed to Europeans the existence of the 'South Sea'; it revealed also how narrow a strip of land separated the two oceans, and so gave a new encouragement to those who hoped to find a strait through Central America and a westward all-sea route to India. It was partly that hope which prompted the exploration of the coastline of the western Caribbean and the Gulf of Mexico. The conquest of Central America was thus in a sense an incident in the race between Spaniards and Portuguese to reach the East. In the same year — 1513 — that Balboa crossed the Isthmus, the first Portuguese ships reached the true Indies, the Moluccas, whence the spices came. In the same year — 1519 — that Cortés sailed from Cuba to conquer Mexico, Magellan left Spain on the voyage which was to reveal both the true western route to the East and the daunting size of the Pacific. Magellan's voyage also revealed that the Spaniards had lost the race; but in tropical America they had a reward of a different sort. Though they failed to find a strait, they founded a great empire. The Caribbean was the highway to that empire, Cuba and Hispaniola its gatehouse towers.

CHAPTER II

The Spanish Indies

The expeditions which sailed from Hispaniola to settle Golden Castile, and from Cuba to conquer Mexico, made heavy demands upon the resources of the islands. Cortés' departure in particular, with 600 armed men, eleven ships and sixteen horses, weakened seriously the fighting strength of the Spaniards who stayed behind; and the victualling of so large a force must have imposed a severe strain on the economy of the island. In the following year a hurricane destroyed trees and crops on the south coast of Cuba; a smallpox epidemic swept both Cuba and Hispaniola, killing some Spaniards and many thousands of Indians. The process of depopulation went on, as tales of plunder and high adventure drew settlers in a steady stream from the islands to Mexico. The mainland provinces soon overshadowed the islands in population, wealth, and royal estimation, especially when the small quantities of alluvial gold in Cuba and Hispaniola showed signs of becoming exhausted. The islands, however, were not deserted. Spanish settlement had struck deep roots. Santo Domingo was already a place of some importance, by virtue of its early settlement and its central position. It was, and for some years remained, the administrative centre for the Caribbean area, including the mainland coast of South America. Other towns were useful as ports of call for shipping. Outside the towns, undeveloped estates and great ranges of wild pasture, deserted by their owners in the rush to Mexico, were bought cheaply by less adventurous but more business-like people who were content to produce relatively humdrum commodities: provisions for sale to passing ships, hides and tallow, sugar and tobacco, for export to Spain. Settlers continued to come to the West Indies, and made a modest living. Most of them were relatively humble folk; the great *conquistadores* went elsewhere. A few Portuguese came from Madeira and the Azores, and a sprinkling of German artisans settled in Hispaniola in Charles V's time, when the Welsers maintained an agency at Santo Domingo; but the great majority of settlers were, of course, Spaniards. Of the four larger islands, Cuba, Puerto Rico, and the larger part of Hispaniola remain Spanish in character and language to this day.

The Spanish communities in the West Indies lived by a predominantly pastoral economy. In the arid uplands of Castile, from which most of them came, pastoral pursuits, the grazing of semi-nomadic flocks and herds, had long been preferred to arable farming. The preference was social and military as well as economic; it was the legacy of centuries of intermittent fighting, of constantly shifting frontiers. The man on horseback, the master of flocks and herds, was well adapted to such conditions, whether in the Old World or the New; the peasant, conversely, was economically vulnerable and socially despised. The labour of tilling the soil in Spain was left, wherever possible, to the *moriscos*. In America it was left to the Indians, so long as there were Indians to do it.

The raising of cattle, though it called for daring horsemanship and occasional bursts of great energy, required no careful or sustained effort. The beasts were turned out on the virgin savannahs and multiplied prodigiously. Cattle-grazing properties were very loosely defined, usually in terms of a radius from a fixed spot, and little attempt was made to survey boundaries. Cattle were sorted, and calves branded, at periodic round-ups, but many escaped the branding and took to a completely wild existence in the forests. These *cimarrones* were so numerous that *monteria* — the hunting of wild cattle — became an established right held in common by the settlers in each locality. The chief value of the beasts lay in the hides. Leather was in constant demand in Europe, both for saddlery and for protective clothing, for an ox-hide jerkin would turn a knife-thrust. Tallow also was a marketable commodity, for making candles and for coating the hulls of ships as a protection against marine borers. When hides and tallow had been removed, the carcasses of slaughtered cattle were often left to rot where they lay. Much of the fecklessness of the early settlers throughout Spanish America can be attributed to these circumstances; whatever the economic difficulties of the time, no Spaniard need starve, when beef could be had in abundance for the trouble of slaughtering it.

Grants of grazing land for cattle went chiefly to the wealthier settlers, who could afford to stock them; though lesser people sometimes sought and obtained grants merely in order to sell them. The Crown itself operated ranches in Hispaniola, by means of overseers, down to the middle of the sixteenth century. The ranchers, with the owners of gold-mines, were the principal capitalists in the early days. Agriculture — until sugar became important — was the recourse of those who lacked capital to undertake more lucrative enterprises. Of course beef was not the only subsistence of the settlers, nor leather and gold their only exportable products. Cassava remained the principal breadstuff throughout the sixteenth century, with maize occupying second place, for the islands were too poor to import wheat flour from Europe in any quantity. Tobacco, the other important native crop, was also taken over to some extent by Spaniards. It was characteristically the small planters' crop. Its production and export did not reach significant proportions in any of the islands until the last quarter of the century.

Both Columbus and Ovando during their respective governments had tried to settle European farmers in Hispaniola, and had introduced Old World crops to supplement tobacco and cassava. Their efforts met with varying success. Vines, olives and European cereals all failed; rice did moderately well in suitably wet areas. Fruit trees were an immediate success. Spaniards are fond of orchards and skilled in their management — one of the gracious characteristics, perhaps, inherited from the Moors. They introduced bananas from the Canary Islands, figs, oranges and lemons from Spain, all in the first two decades of the sixteenth century. All these trees flourished in cultivation, and soon no monastery, and few private houses of any size, lacked the amenity of a walled orchard.

The most important crop introduced by the Spaniards, however, was sugar. The story of sugar is a continuous thread running through the whole history of the West Indies. In later years the fortunes of the islands were to rise and fall with the price of sugar, and the requirements of the sugar industry were to determine the nature of their population. In the Spanish Islands the story of sugar began modestly. Hispaniola was the only island which produced an exportable surplus in the sixteenth century, partly because it had very much better communications with Spain than had the other islands, partly because it obtained, at government expense, the services of a number of Canary Islanders who understood the peculiarities of sugar culture. Sugar-cane is highly perishable, and must be milled within forty-eight hours of cutting. The sugar producer, therefore, must be a manufacturer as well as a cultivator; or at least cultivator and manufacturer must be in very close touch. The planting and the reaping of cane are both heavy undertakings demanding considerable labour. The manufacture of sugar — even by the crude small-scale methods of the sixteenth century — required a crushing mill, and power to turn it. A small mill might be turned by a mule or an ox, or even by man-power; a larger one needed a water-wheel or windmill. Coppers and furnaces were needed for boiling, and pots for crystallising the juice. Carts, and beasts to pull them, were necessary for transporting cane; and the manufactured product, being full of molasses, had to be shipped in casks. The production of sugar in quantities large enough for export, therefore, required considerable initial capital and a large labour force, including unskilled hands for field work and skilled men for the processes of manufacture.

Shortage of capital does not seem to have been the main difficulty of the Hispaniola planters. A sugar estate was a good investment, provided that the crop could be shipped to Europe, where demand was high; and the government itself was prepared to make loans for the construction of mills. The first mill was built in 1508 or 1509, and the first samples of sugar sent to Spain about 1515. Oviedo says that by 1523 there were twenty-four mills of various types working in the island, which must have represented a considerable capital investment.

Shortage of labour was the critical problem. The settlers solved it by subjecting the Indians to forced labour and slavery; a solution with its origins in ancient times among the societies and tribes of Africa, Asia and Europe. Trade routes from the Crimea through the Caspian to Istanbul, from the Elbe south to Italy and Spain, from black Africa across the Sahara, fed slaves into the production systems of the Mediteranean, where slavery was regarded as 'a condition and institution made in antiquity,' not limited to any particular race or religion. It embraced Jew and Gentile, Muslim and Christian, black, brown and white. In its more barbarous forms it was used punitively, by consignment to the galleys and salt mines and in its more humane forms, for producing goods and supplying services. Tradition, custom, laws and religious instructions limited the powers of masters and preserved rights of personality for slaves; they were part of society, not apart from it; in Catholic countries they had access to the sacraments of the Church, could own property, had open to them various ways of changing their status from slave to free, could marry and raise children. Slavery as an institution was viewed as an economic necessity and not as an evil to be abhorred. When the King of Spain raised the question of ethics the Council of the Indies after consulting theologians and jurists, assured him that 'there cannot be any doubt as to the necessity of those slaves for the support of the Kingdom of the Indies'; slavery and trading in slaves were 'long-lived and general custom in the Kingdom of Castile, America and Portugal, without any objection on the part of His Holiness or eccesiastical state, but rather with the tolerance of all of them'.

Eric Williams, in *Capitalism and Slavery* emphasized the close relationship between slavery and serfdom in the Americas and the rise of capitalism in Europe, and he showed how, as one form of slavery proved inadequate, another took its place — whether Indian or white or black. In the lesser Antilles, as we will see, black slavery took the place of white serfdom; in Hispaniola Indian slavery gave way to black slavery.

The central question for the state was not whether to permit black slavery in the Indies but how to ensure that importing slaves did not mean importing the heresy of Judaism or of Mahommedanism. In 1501 Nicolas Ovando was permitted to take in only 'ladinos', black Christianised slaves from Lisbon. In 1510 the government in Spain ordered its agents at Seville to send out 250 slaves for the gold mines of Hispaniola. Events compelled a change of policy, however, with provision for the Christianisation of slaves after arrival; from 1518, in order to forestall Portuguese smuggling, the Crown began to grant licences to private traders for the import of slaves into the West Indies. In this way the third racial element was added to the West Indian mixture. By the late fifteen-twenties all the disciplinary problems of plantation slavery had made their appearance: shortage of European supervisors — partly due, in this instance, to the exodus to Mexico; servile mutinies; bands of runaways hiding in the mountains and emerging at intervals to attack the settlements. Even so, the planters constantly clamoured for more slaves. There were never enough. Import was by individual licence, though sometimes a monopoly for a period of years might be granted, with the right to sell individual licences to sub-contractors. The licensees had to buy their slaves from Portuguese dealers; the supply was haphazard and irregular; and the island buyers had to compete with larger producers of sugar on the mainland. The only satisfactory solution, from the settlers' point of view, lay in a firm contract for a regular annual supply; and such a contract did not become possible until the union of the Spanish and Portuguese crowns later in the century. Labour shortage, and the difficulty of shipping to a distant market, combined to limit the development of sugar production. Though important in the sixteenth century, it did not become the predominant occupation of West Indians until a much later date; and for the same reason Africans never came to outnumber Europeans in the Spanish Indies as they did elsewhere.

The main economic undertakings of Spanish West Indians all required intermittent supervision rather than constant personal attention. Cattle-ranching and sugar-making were both to some extent seasonal occupations. Even the mines were left by their owners largely in the care of overseers. The leading settlers did not care to live permanently in the country, among the sullen, resentful Indians or the mutinous Africans, whose labour they employed. They preferred to live, for most of the year, in the towns. Spanish life, in the colonies as in Spain, was strongly urban in character, and the corporate town rather than the great country house was the characteristic stronghold of the ruling class. The contrast with the later English settlements is obvious even to a casual observer today; for English wealth, in the West Indies as in England, liked to keep its state in the country. The towns of the Spanish islands are well planned, dignified, and often architecturally distinguished, unlike the haphazard and often mean collections of buildings in the British colonies; but Cuba and Puerto Rico have nothing comparable with the Georgian 'great houses' of Jamaica and Barbados.

The foundation of towns was always the first care of the leader in charge of a new Spanish conquest or settlement. The business of foundation was attended with considerable ceremony. After the selection and formal marking of the site, the first step was to trace the lines of the central square and the main streets, which were laid out usually with the rectilinear rigidity of a Roman camp, even though the buildings might for years be mere huts of adobe or thatch. The next step — subject to eventual royal confirmation — was the creation of a municipal governing body — a *cabildo*. The towns of Hispaniola first secured the formal privilege of municipal incorporation in 1507. *Cabildos* exercised administrative and judicial authority over wide tracts of surrounding country, and in the early days were the only formal institutions of law and order in newly settled areas. The *cabildos* of large towns could become very powerful bodies. They corresponded directly with the Crown, either by letter or by accredited representatives (*procuradores*) and were at times both outspoken and effective in their criticism of royal policy. The members of a *cabildo* — the *regidores* — might vary in number from four in a small place to twenty-four or more in a great provincial capital. They were appointed initially by the commander of the settlement, the governor, from among his own associates, and the officers of the conquest; thereafter they usually appointed their own successors annually, subject to the governor's approval. In some small towns some or all of the *regidores* might be elected by the whole body of householders; in Havana, for instance, popular election was the rule at the beginning and survived intermittently until about 1570. To many sixteenth-century Spaniards, however, popular election was a dangerously

anarchic proceeding, and the Crown discouraged it. Even where it
existed it appeared in practice to make little difference to the character
of municipal bodies. Respectable citizens understood, and expected,
that offices should circulate among the heads of the leading families
of the neighbourhood. The concentration became narrower still when,
in the fifteen-twenties, persons who had claims on the royal gratitude
began to ask, and to obtain, appointments to membership of colonial
cabildos for life. Such life appointments might, with further royal
permission, be sold or bequeathed; and in the last decade of the
sixteenth century the Crown itself began to sell life *regimientos* by
public auction. These practices, of course, put an end to any form of
election. There was, therefore, nothing democratic about the constitution of the *cabildos*. Municipal government was the perquisite of
local magnates, who, in most places, formed a close and jealous
oligarchy.

The *cabildos* supplied the means whereby groups of associates
— who, it must be remembered, had undertaken conquests and
settlements at their own risk and expense — recouped themselves for
the hardships they had undergone. *Regidores* received no salary, but
might have many unofficial perquisites. For example, the leading
settlers, as private individuals, required land; as *regidores* they were
responsible for distributing land. As ranchers they produced the beef
and other provisions with which the towns were fed; as *regidores* they
fixed the prices at which those provisions were to be sold. As landowners and mine-owners they needed labour; as *regidores* they were
responsible — at least in the early days — for the administration of
native labour under the *repartimiento* system. As private individuals
they could be sued by those whom they wronged; but as *regidores* they
elected, from among men of their own type and interests, the *alcaldes
ordinarios* — the municipal magistrates before whom, in first
instance, the suits would be heard. Their local authority — so long as
they agreed among themselves — could be lawfully challenged only by
the governor — who was often an interested party — or the Crown
itself.

Naturally the settlers, the missionaries and the governors failed to
agree among themselves: and the Crown was willing enough to
intervene. It was financially interested in the produce of the mines; it
was extremely sensitive to any suggestion of local independence,
whether quasi-feudal or municipal, and became more so after the
revolt of the *Comuneros* in Spain in the early fifteen-twenties; it was
responsible for defence and for the protection of trade, which
naturally called for the regulation of trade. Finally, the consciences of

succeeding rulers were troubled by the plight of the native peoples, and demanded closer supervision, with a view to the conversion and civilisation of the Indians and their protection against the rapacity of the settlers. Closer control was to be achieved partly by appointing salaried governors to replace the original self-appointed leaders and investors; and partly by creating judicial, administrative and financial machinery under more or less direct Crown control, to assist and also to check the work of the governors.

Ovando had been the first effective royal governor in the Indies, except for the brief interlude under Bobadilla. Ovando's administration, efficient though it was, had not given complete satisfaction; his native policy had been notoriously harsh and there had been talk of financial irregularities. After Ovando's retirement to Spain, full of riches and honours, the Crown once more recognised the claims of the Columbus family by sending Diego Colón out to Hispaniola as governor and viceroy. The new viceroy was a thoroughly Hispanicised Italian who had married into a great and ancient family. He brought with him a considerable retinue of both sexes and maintained a viceregal court whose elegance must have contrasted strangely with the squalid background of pioneering in the tropics. Despite this makeshift pomp, however, Diego Colón exercised much less personal power than Ovando. His authority was expressly confined to the islands; and during his government the foundations were laid of a whole system of courts and offices which was to limit the powers both of governors and of settlers in the future.

It was characteristic of Spanish ways of thought that the system of colonial government created in the second and third decades of the sixteenth century should be primarily judicial rather than administrative in character. Spain had carried over from the age of feudalism into the age of sovereignty the notion of jurisdiction as the essential function of authority. The king was still regarded primarily as a judge, an umpire. His authority was most directly and characteristically represented by the high courts of justice, and in the government of his dominions the school-trained lawyer was his most useful servant.

The professional lawyer was an admirable agent of centralised government. Though not always devoid of adventurous qualities, he had no excessive family pride, and as a rule no great ambition for military glory. His training gave him a deep respect for authority and a habit of careful attention to detail, while it discouraged any tendency towards rash or unauthorised action. A judge, moreover, representing the jurisdiction of the monarch, preserved a certain impersonality which helped him to control truculent *hidalgos*, who would have resented the authority of one of their own type. The *audiencias* of Valladolid, Galicia and Granada, courts of appeal representing the royal jurisdiction in their localities, had rendered valuable service in the unification of Spain under the Catholic monarchs. The conquest of the Indies represented to the legal mind an immense expansion of the area requiring unification. A direct branch of the royal jurisdiction was needed to control disorderly and avaricious colonial factions. The task was naturally entrusted to benches of professional judges.

The central Council of the Indies, established in 1511 as a permanent committee of the Council of Castile, and constituted as a separate organ of government in 1524, was a predominantly legal body. It combined, in the manner characteristic of Spanish institutions, the functions of a supreme court of appeal with those of an advisory council and a directive ministry for the supervision of colonial affairs. A corresponding institution on a smaller scale was established at the same time in the Indies. In 1511, after three successive governors had failed in the hopeless task of pleasing both missionaries and colonists, the Crown appointed an independent royal tribunal empowered to hear appeals from the decisions of the local magistrates, and in some cases of the governor himself. The court was modelled upon the *audiencias* of Spain, and may be regarded as the direct predecessor of the *audiencia* of Santo Domingo, formally established fifteen years later. Though the authority of Diego Colón did not extend to the mainland, the appellate jurisdiction of the *audiencia* did. In 1526 — the year of Diego Colón's death — the convention was established that the lawyer-president of the *audiencia* should also be governor and captain-general of Hispaniola. With him served — as judicial associates and as administrative advisers — the four judges (*oidores*) of the court, and the staff of lawyers — procurator-fiscal, advocates, notaries, clerks — which the cumbrous procedure of all Spanish courts made necessary. The services of such a tribunal, in checking the ill-treatment of natives by the colonists, in keeping watch upon the activities of colonial governors, and in sending home reasonably impartial reports and recommendations, proved so valuable that the institution was quickly extended as more provinces were conquered. Ten *audiencias* were created in the sixteenth century representing royal authority in the more important and populous centres throughout the Americas. The settlers, accustomed in the early years of conquest to a life of independent idleness, intrigue and rapine, found themselves confronted by active bodies of professionally trained judges, the colonial counterparts of the conscientious, scholarly, unbending men who were administering Castile. No doubt most *oidores* adapted themselves to colonial life, developed local contacts, demanded local (and illicit) perquisites; but they always represented peninsular ideas and interests, and their appointment created a tension which lasted throughout the colonial period and burst into open rebellion in the nineteenth century.

One of the most urgent tasks of the young administration was to regulate the relations between the conquering Spaniards and the conquered Indians. In this, account had to be taken of an interested third party — the Church. The Spanish settlement was a spiritual as well as a military conquest, and the principal local opposition to the rule of swordsmen came from the soldiers of the Church — the friars of the missionary orders. The conversion which the missionaries sought to achieve was more than a mere outward conformity. It was necessarily associated with social organisation, and the policy of the orders necessarily interfered with the control of Indian labour upon which Spanish economic activity depended. The campaign against the reckless exploitation of the natives began with a Christmas sermon preached by Fray Antonio de Montesinos at Santo Domingo in 1511, which gave great offence to Spaniards in the island and caused a great stir in Spain. Montesinos was sent home by his fellow Dominicans to plead the cause of the Indians at Court and after much deliberation the king's advisers produced the Laws of Burgos of 1512, the first European colonial code, which among a mass of detailed regulation enunciated three clear principles: the Indians were free men, not slaves; they were to be converted to Christianity by peaceful means, not by force; and they were to be made to work. The *repartimiento* or *encomienda* system introduced by Columbus and regularised by Ovando was to be continued, but the demands for labour and tribute made upon Indians by Spaniards were to be limited, and the *encomenderos* were to carry out their side of the bargain — protection and religious instruction — and to observe a whole series of rules designed to prevent ill-treatment. This definition of native rights was, for the Dominican agitators, unsatisfactory, and inadequate; but at least the Crown had admitted, by a formal enactment, that the Indians had rights. The enslavement of Indians was forbidden by law from then onwards, and the royal conscience was not allowed to slumber. Montesinos, having made his protest, relapsed into silence, so far as is known, but other religious took up his work, urging better treatment and greater liberty for Indians and closer control over the Spaniards. Most prominent among these followers of Montesinos was the great Dominican missionary and polemist Bartolomé de las Casas, whose

Brief Relation of the Destruction of the Indies is a horrifying catalogue of atrocities perpetrated during his time in Hispaniola. Las
Casas devoted the rest of his long life to the cause of Indian liberty,
continually urging the Crown, in his sermons and writings and by
personal agitation at Court, to enact more humane legislation and to
make the *audiencias* enforce it. He was himself appointed Protector of
the Indians in 1516, and over the next ten years sponsored a whole
series of social experiments designed to show that free Indians could
be induced, by preaching and force of example, to form civilised
Christian communities, without compulsion or enslavement. The
experiments merely demonstrated, in fact, that the Spanish settlers
could not live without Indian labour, or some substitute for it; and
that Indians would not work without coercion. The change of policy
inspired by Las Cases — though it bore striking fruit on the mainland
later — came too late to save the Indians of the Greater Antilles.

Widening the perspective, we see the process repeated in the
prolonged still-continuing agony of the indigenous people of the
mainland; and we see that throughout the Americas as well as in the
islands it began with two invasions that started with the first voyage of
discovery. One was the importation from Europe and Africa of
diseases such as small pox, measles, dysentery, influenza, leprosy,
yellow fever, typhoid, elephantiasis, against which the American
Indian had no immunity. The other, the importation and imposition
of systems of production and trade geared to the rise of capitalism in
Europe, involved men of many races and cultures. Fernan Braudel
summarized the consequences in his Perspective of the World: 'Indian
servitude could only survive where the population density and
coherence of the pre-existing society were sufficient to create
obedience and docility and to guarantee steady supplies of labor...
Elsewhere the indigenous population collapsed on the first impact of
the white conquests, whether in Brazil, where the natives fled from the
coasts to the interior, or in the United States (the thirteen orginal
colonies)... in the pupulated zones the Indian population proved easy
to regiment. Miraculously it survived the hardships of conquests and
civilization... Central Mexico which had once some 25 million
inhabitants was reduced, it is estimated, to a residual population of
one million. The same 'abysmae' collapse occurred in the island of
Hispaniola, in the Yucatan, in Central America and later in
Colombia... This demographic collapse was quite unprecedented,
out of all proportion even to the horrors of the Black Death in
fourtheenth century Europe. And yet the native population did not
entirely disappear... the exploitation of the Indians continued with

the semi-serfdom of the encomiendas, domestic service in the towns, and compulsory labor in the mines...'

Las Casas is sometimes accused of having suggested the substitution of African slaves for the dwindling Tainos. There is no evidence for the accusation; but it is true that even those Spaniards who insisted most strongly on the personal freedom of the Indians saw nothing inconsistent in negro slavery. The African, of course, made a better slave than the island Indian because he was stronger, less primitive, and more adaptable; but to the sixteenth-century mind the two cases were in all respects widely different. The objections to the enslavement of Indians were primarily on legal grounds. The Indians were the subjects of the King of Castile and were entitled to protection. Africans, on the other hand, were the subjects of independent kings. Europeans visited West Africa as traders, not as overlords. If the local rulers made war among themselves and sold their prisoners to slave dealers, that was not the fault of the King of Spain. The enslavement of prisoners of war was a normal proceeding in most parts of the world. In the Moorish wars and the constant fighting against the corsair towns on the Barbary coast prisoners were regularly enslaved on both sides, and all the naval powers of the Mediterranean employed slaves to row their galleys. The incidental suffering made little impression upon people accustomed to sudden death by violence or disease. The slave trade was carried on under Crown licence, and although some Dominicans had misgivings about it there was no serious opposition from the missionaries in general, or from government. The sixteenth century was not a tender-hearted age. In the West Indies the voices raised on behalf of the Indian, though loud, were largely ineffective. For the negro, no one spoke at all.

Consideration of the slave trade, and the official attitude towards it, leads naturally to the question of the regulation of trade in general. The Crown of Castile assumed as axiomatic its subjects' monopoly of trade and navigation in the Atlantic west of the 'line of demarcation', and its own right to draw a direct tribute from its American possessions. Both for the defence of monopoly and for the efficient collection of taxes and customs a tight regulation of transatlantic shipping was necessary. A subsidiary, but important, motive for regulation was the desire to prevent persons with Jewish or Muslim connections from going to the Indies, where they might cause considerable trouble both to the civil and ecclesiastical authorities. Muslim slaves from North Africa were particularly suspect. For these reasons trade to the Indies, almost from the beginning, was forced through a narrow bottle-neck — the harbour of Seville, seventy miles up the winding, muddy Guadalquivir. As early as 1503 a royal 'house of trade' — the *Casa de Contratación* — was established at Seville. It never actually traded, but developed as a government bureau for inspecting and licensing ships, cargoes, merchants, passengers and crews passing to and from the Indies. The *Casa* collected duties and licence fees and enforced regulations for the conduct of trade. It also contained within itself a count for the settlement of maritime disputes and a hydrographical department for the construction of charts and the training of navigators.

In the Indies there was no separate organisation for the regulation of trade, and in the early days none was needed. The royal treasury officials in the colonial capitals collected duty on incoming commodities, such as salt, which were the subject of Crown monopolies, and collected and despatched the Crown royalty on precious metals. There were no other receipts of importance; tithes were mostly devoted to ecclesiastical purposes in the islands, sales tax was a much later introduction, and such tribute as the island Indians could pay was not worth collecting. Santo Domingo was the western terminus of transatlantic trade; goods and passengers for the other islands made their way from there by means of local shipping.

So long as Spanish settlements in the New World were chiefly concentrated in the West Indian islands their trade could be concentrated in the port of Seville without hardship, since its total volume was small. The preservation of the Castilian monopoly presented no great problem. Occasional cargoes of hides and sugar were not sufficiently valuable to tempt interlopers to cross the Atlantic; the only danger lay in sporadic acts of piracy in European waters. The islands themselves were protected from foreign attack by their remoteness. The conquests of Mexico and, later, Peru, however, created a different situation. An insistent market soon grew up in the mainland provinces for flour, oil, wine, manufactured goods, and slaves. The volume of shipping increased rapidly, and the port of Seville could neither adequately supply the demand nor conveniently handle the shipping. The value of shipments also increased; after the discovery of the great silver-mines, east-bound cargoes contained a large and ever-growing proportion of specie. All this shipping, with its precious cargoes, had to pass through the West Indies. The legal bottle-neck at Seville was matched by a geographical bottle-neck in the West Indies, for the Florida Channel was the only convenient exit from the Gulf of Mexico. Ports such as Santo Domingo, on the south coast of the island chain, lost in commercial importance, while Havana, commanding the western approach to the Florida Channel, began to take its place as the chief port of call. Santo Domingo remained an important administrative centre — it had over a thousand householders in 1540 — and ships from the Isthmus continued to call there until the fifteen-sixties, when they shifted to Havana; but shipping from Mexico had used Havana from the beginning.

The danger in this change of commercial routes lay in the fact that the north coast had never been effectively settled. Havana, in the first half of the sixteenth century, was a small and squalid settlement, with an almost unpeopled hinterland. Its *vecinos* produced beef and bacon for sale to passing ships, and for export to the mainland. It had a good natural harbour, and sprang into activity whenever a ship put in; but it was undefended, and when defences began to be built in 1540 there were not enough people in the district to man them. Havana could offer little protection to the increasing volume of shipping which called on passage to Spain.

Spanish shipping to and from America in the middle decades of the sixteenth century was thus both valuable and vulnerable. It offered great temptations to interlopers and pirates in time of peace, and to all enemies of Spain in time of war. Its concentration in narrow but largely undefended channels made it easy to intercept. An early indication of what Spaniards could expect was given in 1523, when part of the loot sent by Cortés from Mexico to Charles V was captured off the Azores by the French privateer Jean Fleury. The value of this capture astonished Europe and concentrated envious attention upon the Spanish monopoly. The West Indian islands, relatively poor in themselves, soon began to attract the interest of foreigners, either as possible entrepôts for a smuggling trade with the Spanish empire, or as vantage points for attacks on Spanish shipping. To the Spanish government, on the other hand, they became bastions to be fortified and held at all cost.

CHAPTER III

The Challenge to Spain

For the first forty years of their existence the Spanish settlements in the West Indies remained unmolested by other Europeans, chiefly because of their remoteness and their poverty. From the 'thirties of the sixteenth century, however, as their harbours began to handle an increasing volume of Spanish shipping en route to the mainland, and to supply goods and services which earned mainland silver, they began to attract foreign attention and to suffer increasingly from foreign interference. This interference took two distinct forms. One form was smuggling — illicit but peaceful trading in slaves and European goods in exchange for sugar, hides and silver. The other consisted in armed raids on harbours and shipping, carried out by enemy ships in time of war, but also to some extent in peace-time, either by professional pirates or by vessels which were neither warships nor pirates, but unauthorised, unavowed privateers whom the Spaniards called *corsarios*.

To the Spanish government these distinctions were unimportant. Foreign ships, whether pirates, smugglers or men-of-war, in war or in peace, were all unwelcome in the Indies and were all to be treated as enemies and seized whenever possible. To the settlers, on the other hand, the distinctions were vitally important. Throughout most of the sixteenth century the inhabitants of the West Indian ports lived in constant anxiety, never knowing, when a strange sail appeared, whether it was to be welcomed officially as a Spaniard, received discreetly as a foreign trader, or fired upon as a raider. On the whole the West Indians welcomed smugglers, and the cheap goods which smugglers brought; while they resented the high prices charged by the Seville monopolists. They both feared and resented the constant outbreaks of war in Europe, which loosed fleets of privateers upon the West Indies. They deplored a naval policy which was largely ineffective against raiders, but which treated peaceful smugglers as if they were raiders, and so encouraged them to go armed and take to raiding. Even at this early date, therefore, there appeared a conflict of commercial interests between settlers and home government which was to remain characteristic of the West Indies throughout their history as European colonies.

Down to 1580 the principal smugglers were Portuguese and the most important contraband trade was in African slaves. From 1532 (when the four-year contract given by Charles V to the firm of Ehinger expired) down to 1580 the supply of slaves to the West Indies was officially managed by Spanish dealers who held licences from the Crown, each licence permitting the import of a stated number of slaves. The dealers were not, in fact, all Spaniards. Some were Flemish or Portuguese sub-contractors; but the essential thing was the possession of a Spanish licence. The dealers usually bought their slaves from Portuguese middle-men, who got them from the Portuguese-owned 'factories' and barracoons on the Guinea coast. Individual settlements in the West Indies habitually entered into contracts with licensed dealers for the supply of cargoes of slaves at a flat rate per head, the slaves being retailed on arrival to planters by the local officials. So many licences were issued that checking was difficult and fraud comparatively easy, especially as most local officials in the Indies connived at it. Slaves on passage, in those days of rudimentary medical and hygienic knowledge, formed a highly perishable cargo, and common sense as well as desire for profit recommended a direct voyage, without the delays imposed by Spanish commercial regulation. Despite the severe penalties imposed for such evasions, many Portuguese slavers carried shipments from Guinea to the West Indies without bothering to secure licences. These unlicensed slaves were unloaded in the smaller harbours of the islands, and naturally sold cheaper than the licensed imports. Isabela, Columbus's early foundation on the north coast of Hispaniola, was a favourite and characteristic haunt of smugglers. The place had dwindled to a mere hamlet, but behind it lay a fertile region of ranches and sugar plantations known then as La Vega, where slaves were in high demand and where return cargoes of sugar and hides could be obtained. The area was separated from Santo Domingo by a wide stretch of rough country, and the danger of official interference was very small. The activities of smugglers, by their nature, are not officially recorded so long as they are successful, so that evidence is scanty; but there is little doubt that considerable numbers of slaves entered the West Indies by such channels; and with the slaves came cargoes of European goods — wine, oil, tools, cloth, paper, and so on — from Teneriffe, Las Palmas, or Lisbon itself.

These activities were of benefit to the West Indian settlers, and the people engaged in them were mostly Portuguese, who, though they might break the law, would not resort to arms against their best customers; or else Germans or Flemings, who, though not Castilians, were still subjects of the emperor and unlikely to engage in piracy against his colonies. The settlers could deal with them without running any danger other than the wrath of their own government. A very different situation arose, however, when, in the fifteen-thirties, French ships began to make voyages to the Caribbean. Some of them were traders and smugglers like the Portuguese; but France and Spain were intermittently at war throughout Charles V's reign, and many French privateers cruised the Caribbean in search of plunder rather than of trading profit. Their first appearance in serious numbers was in 1536, and was caused by two European events — a fresh outbreak of France-Spanish hostilities, and a defensive alliance between France and Portugal. This was the Treaty of Lyon, whereby the French government undertook to forbid its subjects to attack Portuguese shipping or to poach upon Portuguese trade preserves in Africa. Accordingly, instead of cruising off the Azores to intercept Portuguese Indiamen, the more enterprising French privateers removed to the Bahamas to cruise against Spanish shipping. The myriad cays of the Bahamas were well suited to the purposes of piracy; for two hundred years they were to harbour fast, predatory craft, lying in wait for heavily laden ships beating out through the Florida Channel. The French took a number of prizes in the winter of 1536, enough to encourage Jean Ango, the great shipping magnate of Dieppe, to organise and finance a much bigger enterprise: an attack on an armed fleet which was known to be returning to Spain from the Isthmus carrying the spoils of the conquest of Peru. The Spanish fleet was commanded by the redoubtable Blasco Núñez Vela, later viceroy and captain-general of Peru. Ango had been the backer, fourteen years before, of Jean Fleury, who had captured part of Cortés' loot from Mexico. Ango's people were successful again. They captured nine Spanish ships out of a total sailing of twenty-odd, and sacked or held to ransom a number of the smaller ports of Hispaniola, including Yaguana, modern Port-au-Prince. They did not venture to attack Santo Domingo; and their attempt against Santiago, the capital of Cuba, was beaten off.

The truce of Nice in 1538 brought a respite from organised fighting; and when in 1542 war broke out again, the Spanish government was ready with a plan, the same plan that every beleaguered maritime power has used to protect its shipping against attack. All shipping to the Indies was to be sent by pre-arranged routes under convoy, and the principal harbours were to be fortified. From 1543 the long conflict between Spain and the interlopers in the West Indies took on its characteristic form: on the one side a defensive policy relying upon weight and strength, on the other a policy of attack relying upon manoeuvrability and speed. The conflict revealed yet another divergence of interest between the settlers and the home government; the authorities in Spain were chiefly concerned with the safe passage of the silver fleets, the settlers with the protection of their homes and harbours and with the safety of the local shipping among the islands and to the mainland. The generals of the fleets demanded heavier escorts and the support of cruiser squadrons; the colonial governors and *cabildos* begged the Crown for stronger fortifications and soldiers to man them. In the event, the fleets were better protected than the port towns, and the West Indians suffered most in the long series of Caribbean encounters. In the war of 1542–44 the convoys were well supported by frigates, which in the spring of 1543 succeeded temporarily in clearing the route of the silver ships through the islands; but the privateers merely transferred their activities to the coast of Venezuela, and later, when the fleets had passed and the warships were withdrawn, they returned to cruise for prizes in the Florida Channel and Mona and Windward Passages, so that Santo Domingo, Santiago and Havana were again put in constant fear of attack until the Treaty of Crespy in 1544 again gave some relief. By that treaty Francis I formally recognised the Spanish monopoly of Caribbean settlement and trade; but again, in 1552, a fresh war gave occasion for Caribbean raiding, and this time the privateers deliberately aimed their attacks at the principal harbours of the West Indies.

Havana was the pivot of the Spanish convoy system, at least for the homeward passage which chiefly interested the enemy. The system was not worked out in all its details until the fifteen-sixties, but the general idea remained the same from 1543. The fleet from the Isthmus started early in the year. It first put into Cartagena, where it remained for a week or so and then steered north-west — usually a comfortable reach with the wind on the starboard beam — until it could round Cape San Antonio and put into Havana. Meanwhile the Mexico *flota*, having waited until the 'norther' season was over, in April or May made its tedious three-week beat against the trade wind from Vera Cruz. From Havana the two fleets sailed in company for Spain in the course of the summer. Annual sailings out and home were intended, but not always achieved. While assembling in Havana harbour the ships refitted and provisioned for their Atlantic passage. During their stay the town was naturally crowded and full of activity, and considerable sums of money were spent — or lost in gaming — in a place which then had very little to offer in return. There was no regular water supply; fresh water was lightered from the Almendares river, just west of the town. There was little accommodation, and only a handful of the houses were built of stone. There was little government — only a *cabildo* of two magistrates and four *regidores*, until in 1550 the governor, Angulo, removed to Havana because — so they said in Santiago — he had private business interests there. Probably he had; one of his first acts was to build the first public slaughter-house in Havana — a matter of some importance for a town which lived largely by selling salt or dried meat to ships — and presumably the governor's cattle were to be slaughtered there, in the normal way of public life in the Indies. The change of capital was obviously sensible from a strategic point of view, and the Crown eventually approved it, despite bitter protests from the older and larger settlement. It was one more victory for general imperial considerations over local West Indian interests.

The facilities and attractions of Havana, then, in the early years of the convoy system were quite inadequate for the functions which trade and geography thrust upon the place. Its defences were equally inadequate, as events were soon to demonstrate. In 1553 François Le Clerc, whom the Spaniards called *Pie de Palo* — Timberleg — crossed the Atlantic with a fleet of ten French warships and began systematically to pillage and burn the port towns of the West Indies. In 1554 he took Santiago — the strongest settlement so far attempted by the French — and drove its inhabitants inland to comparative safety at Bayamo. In the following summer his lieutenant Jacques Sores, with two ships, captured Havana and razed it to the ground.

Sores' exploit naturally caused a great stir in Spain, and panic throughout the Indies. In France it gave rise to the first of a long series of comprehensive but abortive schemes for a large-scale naval expedition, which was to sack Santo Domingo, sail on to the Isthmus, seize Panama and capture the South Sea fleet, then intercept the Mexican *flota*, and return home by the Florida Channel. Probably Coligny was the author of this plan to ruin the war potential of Spain; Drake, Piet Heyn and Cromwell were all to entertain the same idea in later years, but none of them ever succeeded in carrying the whole programme into effect. For Spaniards, the sack of Havana pointed a more immediate and practical lesson. No one reading the records, then or now, could fail to be struck by the contrast between the importance of the event and the scale of the operation. Sores had anchored in the San Lázaro inlet, and landed his assault party in boats for an overland attack, thus outflanking the defences, such as they were. We do not know how many men were with him; but they cannot have been more than a hundred or so, and the Spaniards could only muster thirty-five, of whom nine were mounted. There were no Spanish ships in the area. The land defences consisted of a look-out post on the headland where the Morro now stands, and a small square fort on gently rising ground on the edge of the settlement, probably near the site of the present Foreign Office. This fort had been built on contract, with Crown money, by Juan de Lobera, who was a local rancher and *a regidor*. When the fort was complete Lobera had got himself appointed *alcaide* — commandant — at an annual salary, and had taken up rent-free residence inside. Those who disliked him insinuated that the place was designed for comfort rather than defence. It mounted six small guns, chiefly for the defence of the harbour. The guns, incidentally, were bronze pieces cast in Seville, using samples of Cuban copper sent from the Cobre mines near Santiago, in which Lobera had an interest. The only other weapons in the fort, apart from the defenders' own swords, were four crossbows. To do him justice, Lobera resisted for some hours, until the French set fire to the doors of the fort and smoked him out. He then surrendered, and soon reached agreement with Sores on the amount of his personal ransom. After his surrender the governor, who had withdrawn inland with most of the population, returned with such fighting men as he could muster to make a counter-attack which failed. Negotiations for ransom of the town ensued; but Sores refused the thousand *pesos* or so which were all the towns-people could offer, set fire to the buildings, and withdrew after a stay of nearly three weeks.

The capture of Havana, then, was a trifling operation in itself; but its details are of interest because they are typical of hundreds of similar episodes through a century and a half of West Indian history. Even the governor's march inland, an act not of cowardice but of common sense, was part of the normal pattern. Often the best defence of more or less unfortified settlements was an orderly withdrawal of the settlers, with their families, their cattle and their movable valuables, to hiding-places in the bush, from which ransom negotiations could be undertaken. The enemy, anxious to be gone, would usually accept a reasonable cash offer. Havana, however, had become too important a place to be 'defended' in this passive way; and Santo Domingo, Cartagena or Vera Cruz might any day suffer the fate which had befallen Havana. It is true that the Treaty of Câteau-Cambrésis in 1559 settled, mostly in favour of Spain, the questions

over which the two powers had officially been fighting; but the
Spaniards could not be sure that peace would endure for long, or that
the French government would be able, or even willing, to control such
of its privateer captains as chose to take to piracy on their own
account. Imperial safety, therefore, demanded not only powerful escorts for the fleets but also powerful defences for the chief harbours and towns of the West Indies, and mobile cruiser squadrons,
permanently based there, which could keep the sea-lanes clear
throughout the year. Co-ordination of the land and sea defences was
urgently necessary, and could be achieved only by unification of
command in the West Indies. The establishment of such a unified
command was entrusted, in the fifteen-sixties, to Pedro Menéndez de
Avilés, one of the ablest sea commanders of his time.

Before Menéndez took up his task in the West Indies, however,
matters took a new turn, due to the arrival on the scene of a new group
of interlopers, the English, led initially by the versatile and ingenious John Hawkins. Hawkins organised four trading voyages to the
Caribbean between 1562 and 1568, and commanded three of them
himself. He carried cloth and general merchandise from England, and
slaves, whom he purchased directly from dealers on the West African
coast. He proposed to sell his goods and slaves to Spanish settlers
in the Caribbean, and to secure cargoes of sugar, hides and silver for
the return voyage to England. Hawkins's plan thus anticipated the
triangular voyage of later times, and defied the monopolistic regulations both of Portugal and of Spain. He did not, however, intend
mere tip-and-run smuggling; still less, open piracy. He seems to have
entertained serious hopes of securing licences from Spain which would
legitimise his activities. England and Spain were at peace, and
traditionally friendly. Hawkins was known in Seville and had friends
and business correspondents there. He was prepared to pay all lawful
dues; and in return for a licence to trade he offered his services to the
Spanish Crown as a privateer, to assist in clearing pirates and foreign
smugglers from West Indian waters. In particular, he appreciated the
strategic importance of the Florida Channel and knew that the French
were trying to establish a settlement on the coast of Florida, under
René de Laudonnière, which could become very dangerous to Spanish
shipping. Hawkins hoped to demonstrate the value of his services by
destroying this colony at the beginning of its career.

Hawkins's plan failed completely in its larger aspect, though as
business ventures his first two voyages were highly successful. He was
right in assuming that Spanish planters and minor government
officials would be glad to do business with him. On the first voyage —

the only one to the islands — he passed along the north coast of Hispaniola, sold his slaves at Isabela, Puerto Plata and Monte Christi, paid the duty on them, and secured certificates of good conduct from the local officials. Prudently he kept well away from Santo Domingo. The other voyages were to mainland ports where the officials proved less amenable and had to be threatened before they would trade. On the last homeward trip Hawkins was driven by continued bad weather into the Gulf of Mexico and obliged to seek shelter at San Juan de Ulúa, the port of Vera Cruz. Here he was caught by the *flota* arriving from Spain. Most of his fleet was destroyed in the ensuing battle, and he himself eventually reached England in January 1569 after great hardships, with only fifteen surviving companions. The whole episode made clear that the Spanish government would tolerate no interlopers of any kind in American waters; any foreigner was a pirate and would be treated as such if caught. Foreign traders in the West Indies, therefore, must go secretly or go well armed. Meanwhile — and this may have been one of the reasons for Hawkins's failure — Admiral Menéndez's dispositions in the West Indies showed that the Spaniards could do for themselves what they refused to allow Hawkins to do for them.

Pedro Menéndez de Avilés served his king in high naval commands for nearly twenty years. For the greater part of that period Spain was nominally at peace with other European powers; though by that time what passed for peace in the West Indies demanded the services of a great admiral. No fair estimate can be formed of his skill as a naval tactician because he was never called on to command a fleet in any large-scale action against an adversary worthy of his steel. His dispositions in the West Indies, however, reveal him as a strategist of the first order, with a rare gift for appreciating a situation as a whole and for reconciling immediate necessities with the demands of long-term planning. He was remarkably successful in explaining naval needs to landsmen in high office, so that he enjoyed — and deserved — the confidence and support of Philip II throughout his career of command. He was a good, though exacting, disciplinarian; and as a naval administrator he was unsurpassed in the sixteenth century. His views on strategy and logistics had, curiously, something in common with those of Hawkins — who, at one stage in his career, was a very capable director of the queen's dockyards. Menéndez's appreciation of the West Indian situation resembled Hawkins's, though his ideas on remedial action were more comprehensive in their naval aspects, and naturally less flexible on their political side. To complete a sketch of a forceful and somewhat sombre character, Menéndez was honest, fearless, entirely loyal, and ruthlessly impatient of lesser men.

Menéndez's first important appointment was the command of the escort of the homeward-bound fleet of 1555–56. In 1561 he was appointed captain-general of the *Armada de la Carrera de Indias*, and in that capacity he took out and back, in 1562, the largest fleet which up till then had left Spain — forty-nine sail, of which six were men-of-war. During the next two years he was engaged in advising the Crown upon the regulations for the Indies trade, which were promulgated between 1564 and 1566. His proposals fell under three main heads: all sailings between Spain and the Indies were to be in convoy, except for urgent sailings of fast and well-armed ships which might be made licensed exceptions; *armadillas* — cruiser squadrons — were to be permanently based in the West Indies to seek out and attack corsairs upon their arrival in the area and to patrol the main trade routes all the year round; the principal harbours were to be strongly fortified and provided with regular garrisons. The most important harbours were Cartagena, guarding the eastern approach to the Isthmus; Santo Domingo, the administrative centre of the islands; Santiago; San Juan del Puerto Rico; and, most important of all, Havana. Havana was to be made, as nearly as possible, an impregnable fortress, to provide a safe place of assembly for all homeward-bound convoys. To complete the defence and control of the Florida Channel, another fortified base was to be constructed opposite Havana, on the coast of Florida itself. Menéndez made this suggestion early in the discussions, in anticipation of French attempts at occupation of that area; the actual settlement under Laudonnière naturally gave added force to his arguments. Philip II and the Council of the Indies accepted his comprehensive and very expensive plans in their entirety; and to establish the unity of command needed to carry them out Menéndez was made *adelantado* of Florida in 1565, and governor of Cuba in 1567.

The years which Menéndez spent in the West Indies were years of intense activity and, on the whole, conspicuous successes; for to achieve any co-ordinated defence at all at that time was a success. Although internecine religious war had removed France temporarily from the international arena, French corsairs were still active on their own account; and the revolt of the Netherlands and war with England were soon to bring the warships and privateers of the two strongest North Atlantic maritime powers to the West Indies in formidable strength. Menéndez shared with Drake and Nelson the strategic genius that treats all seas as one. His West Indian dispositions were only part of an over-all plan, in which the long-term remedy for the menace of

Caribbean privateering was a Spanish base in the Scilly Isles — a bold and brilliant anticipation of eighteenth-century strategic ideas. He was not allowed time to create the admiralty organisation which these plans required, for he died in 1574, in one of those swift epidemics that often ravaged the fleets of his time. Nevertheless, his work, in fortifying bases and drilling and organising the transatlantic convoys, was carried on by a series of able and energetic successors, and enabled the Spanish colonies to survive intact, their communications with Spain unbroken, through a long and wasting naval war. For sixty years the treasure fleets reached Spain safely and regularly, losing a few stragglers now and then, but never — until Piet Heyn's great exploit in 1627 — losing the major part of a shipment. From the point of view of peninsular Spain, Admiral Menéndez did all that could be expected of a master of his trade.

From a strictly West Indian point of view Menéndez was less obviously successful, because the islands were, in his mind, of secondary importance. He made of Havana an almost impregnable fortress, safe against enemy attack for over two hundred years, with a dockyard capable of building efficient light warships from local timber and of refitting any class of ship. He destroyed the French settlement in Florida and built a Spanish fort in its place. Santo Domingo and Santiago, on the other hand, though much more important as local centres of population, received relatively slight additions to their fortifications, sufficient to stand off casual raids, but not to face attack by organised fleets. Similarly, in operating against corsairs in the Caribbean, Menéndez and his successors were compelled by war and financial shortage to concentrate on the immediate problem of getting the *flotas* through, and to postpone the secondary task of protecting local shipping throughout the year. The 'Windward Squadrons', based on Cartagena and Santo Domingo, whose establishment Menéndez had advocated almost from the beginning, were not commissioned until 1582, eight years after his death. Light oared vessels were employed in this service, and proved very effective; but the expense of keeping the squadrons permanently in commission was very great, and their effectiveness was frequently impaired by shortage of funds for their maintenance.

Menéndez's whole policy, the very nature of his appointment, emphasised the decline of the island settlements in relation to the mainland, and their relegation to the position of mere ports of call. In Cuba Menéndez was heartily disliked. He sternly refused to allow settlers in Cuba to leave for the mainland: yet — so they complained — he did nothing for them in Cuba. His fortifications at Havana, his dockyard developments and ship-building activities, meant little or nothing to planters whose estates were mostly at the other end of the island. His troops — the few hundred men who formed the garrison at Havana — were a constant source of dispute: for the local people wanted them under local command and stationed at Santiago. Menéndez's appointment as governor and *adelantado* was a high-handed remedy for his bad relations with local governors and *cabildos*, who neither liked nor understood his policy, and obstructed him whenever they could. It was idle, of course, for small and relatively poor island settlements to urge their own local interests against the interests of Old and New Spain represented by a commander-in-chief of Menéndez's ability and vigour; especially since the works which he initiated were not paid for by the islanders. Cuba at this time contributed practically nothing to the royal treasury, and Hispaniola relatively little. The great works at Havana were paid for by *situados* from New Spain — subsidies sent by royal order from one provincial treasury to another. The West Indians had no control over the spending of this money, which was intended chiefly to protect the fleets. Despite Menéndez's vigour and success, therefore, despite the fifty-odd corsair ships which he captured during his career, the minor harbours of the West Indies were never safe from raiding. Even the principal cities, though safe enough against mere pirates, were still vulnerable to attack by organised fleets in time of war. Their situation grew worse as relations with England worsened, as religious bitterness came to reinforce the rapacity of the corsairs, and as that other naval genius, Francis Drake, was loosed upon the Indies in independent command of voyages of reprisal.

The place of Drake in the history of the West Indies is hard to assess in precise terms. He became the central figure in the attack upon the Spanish Indies, as Menéndez was the central figure of their defence. He personified in his day, and afterwards, the maritime genius and the Protestant religion of his countrymen. He created the legend of the bold corsair and the rich, defenceless Spaniard, which was to affect English policy in the Caribbean for many generations. He was the hero and the model of a host of poor gentlemen in England, small landlords who had been driven by inflation and social change to take to privateering, to 'get a ship and judiciously manage her'. For Spaniards, 'El Draque' was a name to frighten children. In sober fact, Drake evolved a coherent strategic West Indian plan in place of a series of small and uncoordinated raids; he carried his plan into effect with great, though not complete, success; he did great damage, acquired great booty and seriously weakened the fighting power of

Spain, without, however, breaking the Spanish monopoly of territorial possession in the Caribbean.

Drake began his acquaintance with the West Indies as an illicit trader; he was with Hawkins at San Juan de Ulúa, and in 1570 he went out again with two small ships taking cargoes of slaves to the islands and returning with hides and silver. On this voyage, and on a subsequent one in 1571, Drake also carried out a reconnaissance of the shores of the Isthmus and established contact with local wild Indians and with groups of *cimarrones* — 'maroon' or runaway slaves. The illicit trader was becoming perforce a more or less authorised privateer, and the savage alliances he made were to become a traditional part of English policy. In 1572, the year of the expulsion of the Spanish ambassador from England, Drake sailed on his first privateering raid, the famous voyage on which, with two small ships and seventy-odd men, he took Nombre de Dios by surprise and captured three mule-trains crossing the Isthmus loaded with treasure from Peru. The booty was enough to make every man in Drake's company rich for life. It arrived in Plymouth in 1573, the same year that Menéndez laid his plan for a Scilly Island base before Philip II.

In 1574 — the year of Menéndez's death — the English and Spanish governments patched up a grudging reconciliation. English captains continued to visit the Caribbean, trading with the smaller settlements and with the maroons, cruising with letters of reprisal, or making minor raids. None of them achieved successes comparable with Drake's. Their government left them of fend for themselves as pirates, and a number of them — notably Drake's friend John Oxenham — were caught and hanged by the Spaniards. Menéndez had succeeded, if not in making the Caribbean a Spanish lake, at least in making it a dangerous cruising-ground for mere raiders. Drake, who never regarded himself — nor was regarded, even by his enemies — as a pirate, kept away from the West Indies in those years. His great voyage of circumnavigation of 1577–80 had only an indirect bearing on West Indian affairs. He did not appear again in the Caribbean until 1585, when war between England and Spain was already certain.

Drake's 'Indies voyage' of 1585 was no mere raid, but a fullscale naval operation carried out by a fleet of more than twenty sail. The plan was similar to that which the French had projected thirty years before, but never put into effect. It included, first, an attack on Santo Domingo and on the port towns of Tierra Firme, in particular Cartagena; then a land attack on Nombre de Dios and Panama in conjunction with the maroons, in order to control both ends of the

land route across the Isthmus; and finally the capture of Havana.
Drake hoped to hold both Havana and Cartagena with permanent
English garrisons. Success would break up the whole communication
and supply system of the Spanish Indies. It would deny to Spain, for
years, perhaps permanently, the means of making war in Europe, and
would throw the Indies open to English exploitation. The conception
of such a plan is evidence, already by the end of the sixteenth century,
of the importance of the West Indies in the international rivalries of
Europe. Over and over again, for more than two hundred years,
English, Dutch and French admirals and statesmen mounted plans
similar, in whole or in part, to that of Drake. Some achieved partial
and temporary success, as Drake did; but the Caribbean proved too
big, the islands too scattered and too wild to be mastered in a single
campaign. The commander of a large-scale amphibious operation,
moreover, faced more serious health difficulties than the tip-and-run
raiders of earlier times, for his men had to live and fight ashore in
large numbers for a considerable length of time. Armies and navies,
coming fresh from Europe, wasted away in the fearful mortality of
tropical campaigning. The Spaniards, the mosquitoes and the climate
worked together to defeat every attempt.

Santo Domingo, the administrative capital for the West Indies and
Tierra Firme, was one of the largest cities in the Spanish empire,
impressively laid out with stone buildings and spacious streets and
plazas. It was fortified, and had a small garrison of trained soldiers.
Its capture was by far the most ambitious feat yet undertaken by
an English commander in the West Indies. Drake employed tactics
similar to those used earlier by Sores at Havana, but with a force more
than ten times the size of that of Sores. A successful surprise attack by
a party landed some miles down the coast synchronised with the
frontal assault upon the harbour by the main body of the fleet. Parties
of maroons from the mountains helped the attackers. Once inside the
walls Drake's people entrenched themselves in the main plaza and
opened negotiations for the ransom of the city. The bargaining lasted
over a month, during which time the invaders carried out a systematic
programme of looting and destruction in order to hasten the governor's decision. The plunder and ransom were both disappointing;
but the damage to the prosperity of the city was heavy and permanent. All the principal buildings were gutted, the guns and stores of
the fort taken away, and the ships of the island guard squadron
burned in the harbour.

Drake's next major objective, Cartagena, was a much smaller town
than Santo Domingo, but strategically much more important, and

likely to be a richer prize, for it was a collecting depot for goods and treasure to be loaded for Spain. It was well defended, and Drake's attack, in the teeth of brave and well-organised resistance, was perhaps the most brilliant of all his amphibious operations, involving intricate and dangerous pilotage and synchronised landings through heavy surf. As at Santo Domingo, he forced a way to the centre of the town, occupied the plaza, and systematically destroyed buildings while awaiting the result of ransom negotiations. Again the loot, though considerable, was disappointing, because most of the valuables in the city had been sent inland before the fighting began. The negotiations lasted for six weeks, and at the end of that time the English forces were reduced by casualties and sickness from their original number of 2300 to about 800 fit men. There could now be no question of holding Cartagena with an English garrison. Drake decided to abandon his attempt on the Isthmus, and to make for the Cayman Islands and thence for Cape San Antonio, where, with his ships refitted and his men refreshed, he hoped to intercept the *flota* from New Spain. The weather in May was bad, however, and the *flota* slipped through unmolested. Judging Havana too strong to be attacked, Drake sailed for home in June 1586, only pausing to destroy the fortifications which were being built at St. Augustine, on the site of the ill-fated French settlement in Florida.

The 'Indies voyage', though it failed in its larger aims, did great material damage to Spanish possessions and even greater damage to Spanish prestige. The Spanish authorities did not fail to note the lessons of their defeats. They concluded that Menéndez's appreciation of the West Indian position had been accurate, but that his policy had not been pursued vigorously enough. They set to work to remedy the weaknesses of his system; and in spite of the defeats which they suffered in their operations against England in Europe, they achieved remarkable success in the Caribbean. In the fifteen-nineties the defence forces of the Indies were all greatly strengthened by both land and by sea, despite the urgent need for ships and troops in Europe. A beginning was made by Antoneli, the best military engineer of his day, on the immense fortifications of Puerto Rico, the windward bastion of Caribbean defence — not so much because of the direct importance of the place to the Spaniards as because of the vital necessity of denying its use to Spain's enemies. At the same time, communications between the Caribbean bases were greatly improved by the provision of fast despatch boats. When in 1595 another great fleet left England, under the joint command of Drake and Hawkins, on what was to be for both their last Indies campaign, they found the Spaniards ready and able to resist. The English were defeated at San Juan del Puerto Rico (though, curiously enough, a less able leader, Cumberland, succeeded in taking the place — but not in holding it — three years later). They abandoned their project for a second attack on Cartagena. On the Isthmus — where the Spaniards had abandoned Nombre de Dios for the more defensible harbour of Puerto Bello — a picked party of 750 men set out overland for Panama, but were driven back to their boats by a combination of heavy rains and Spanish ambushes. After Drake's death off the coast of Veragua, Sir Thomas Baskerville, his successor in the command, was intercepted in the Florida Channel by a powerful fleet under Pedro Menéndez Márquez and had to fight his way out in a running battle, the first naval action between regular fleets to be fought in the West Indies. The action was inconclusive; but it cleared the Caribbean of the invaders at a time when Spain was suffering heavy defeats in Europe and could not have spared ships or men to reinforce the West Indies.

The attempts made by the French and the English in the sixteenth century to break the Spanish monopoly of trade and territorial power in the West Indies were thus, on the whole, failures; or, at least, their successes were only temporary. Sporadic raiding continued, and an extensive but still risky smuggling trade had developed; but Spain, exhausted as she was, lacking the men, the ships and the money to back her vast responsibilities and claims, still would not consider the open admission of foreign traders to her Caribbean preserves. In 1596, at the Treaty of The Hague, France under Henry of Navarre, England and the Netherlands formed an alliance against Spain which seemed strong enough to dismember the Spanish empire; and a joint English and Dutch fleet promptly destroyed a whole American convoy lying in Cadiz harbour, thus stopping communication between Spain and the Indies for nearly two years. The alliance failed to fulfil its promise, however; the French backed out and made their peace separately in the Treaty of Vervins in 1598. According to later accounts, Henry IV tried to secure a share of the American trade in this treaty. There is no contemporary evidence of these attempts; if made at all, they were unsuccessful, for the treaty is silent on the subject. The English and Dutch fought on; but in 1604, the pacific James I having succeeded Elizabeth, England also made a separate peace — the Treaty of London. In the negotiations for this treaty, however, a new and important principle was put forward. James announced that he was prepared to respect Spanish monopolistic claims in all territories effectively occupied by Spain, but that he recognised no Spanish rights in unoccupied parts of America. This contravened the basic assumption of Spanish imperialism in the Indies, and it was only after considerable haggling that the Spaniards agreed to a silence which their enemies might interpret as consent. In the Truce of Antwerp of 1609, which ended for twelve years the war between the Netherlands and Spain, and which recognised the Dutch as an independent nation, the same principle was embodied in a formal, if ambiguous, clause. So at the outset of their independent existence the Dutch gave notice of the role they were to play in West Indian history. Their West India Company was to be the foster-parent of the French and British empires in their West Indian aspect.

The Settlement of the
Outer Islands

At the end of the sixteenth century, as at the beginning, the only settled colonies in the West Indies were those of Spain. No other European nation had achieved anything, or indeed seriously contemplated anything worth achieving, in the way of permanent settlement. In all successful colonisation two sets of factors are necessary for success: the private, spontaneous, largely economic urges; and the directing, protecting, sometimes limiting policy of government. The two are equally essential; without the one the other can accomplish nothing. Neither was present in sufficient strength, either in France or in England, in the sixteenth century. Patrons, prospectors, merchants, emigrants, alike failed to see their interest in colonial ventures overseas. It is true that in England a land-labour problem existed and was growing more acute; but homestead emigrants found an outlet in Ireland rather than in the Americas. The West Indies certainly attracted adventurers; but they found scope for their activity in smuggling and raiding rather than in settling, and individual adventures lapsed easily and naturally into something closely akin to piracy. The hope of booty was high enough to cause a lack of capital for more constructive ventures, and the outcome was further to handicap the settler and the merchant by making them liable for the raids of the privateers. At the same time a long-term constructive policy of settlement appeared unattractive to governments when compared with the quicker returns and greater dividends to be gained by raids on Spain and the Spanish colonies. Governmental support and organisation, therefore, never advanced in the sixteenth century beyond the primitive urge to oppose Spain wherever she claimed to rule. Colonies and settlements were merely flanking movements in the attack on Spain, of secondary interest. In addition, settlement anywhere in the Caribbean was still at the end of the sixteenth century, a dangerous proposition, in which investors might lose their capital, and settlers their lives or liberty, in one stroke of Spanish retaliation.

Quebec, Plymouth, Jamestown, Virginia, Basseterre, Bridgetown

— these names began to appear on maps of the Americas in the first quarter of the seventeenth century, indicators that Britain and France had turned from raiding and plundering Spanish towns in the Caribbean to establishing settlements beyond Spain's reach in the outer islands and along the North American seaboard. Keeping pace with each other, the French settled Acadia in 1604 and founded Quebec in 1608 while, to the south, the English were in Virginia in 1607, began planting tobacco there in 1612 and in 1619 traded 'victualle' for a party of 20 African slaves held on a fugitive ship that had put into Jamestown. With this transaction the history of the African in North America begins. A year later the Pilgrim Fathers landed at Cape Cod and founded Plymouth; and in rapid succession came the settlement of New Hampshire (1622), St. Kitts and Barbados (1624), Nevis (1628), Massachusetts Bay (1629) Antigua, Montserrat and Maryland in 1632.

The rise to prominence of a third group of interlopers, the Dutch, materially altered the Caribbean picture, for their navy provided the screen behind which the English and French established their settlements. Their long war against Spain had ended in 1609 with their independence, but they remained more deeply committed than either the English or French to a commercial livelihood and to hostility against Spain. Their courage, determination and innovative use of technology had enabled them to transform the ever-threatening sea into an ally whose waters linked their cities by canals which served also as defensive moats. The North Sea and stormy Icelandic waters, a nursery for their seamen, served as the 'Dutch Gold Mine', providing the herrings that made the Dutch Europe's prosperous fishmonger. They maintained a profitable Mediteranean trade and gradually secured the lion's share of the Baltic trade, obtaining from it supplies of timber, pitch and tar that enabled them to build the world's largest merchant fleet. From that trade they obtained also rye and wheat which they traded with Portugal and Spain for salt, wine, oil, silver and sugar. In the course of time they further strengthened their economy by developing a trade in spices and pepper with the Far East; and, experts in shipbuilding, they met the challenge of longer voyages and larger cargoes by building a new type of vessel, the Dutch fly-boat, that required a smaller crew but had more storage capacity. Wealth flowed into Amsterdam, drawing to the city the great financiers of Europe. The United Provinces, about the size of Jamaica, became in Fernan Braudel's words, 'a high-voltage urban economy'.

The contraction of their trade with Spain and Portugal which resulted from the war caused them serious loss and drove them to seek supplies and markets farther afield. In particular it deprived them of salt, a vital commodity required in great quantities by the Dutch themselves for their fishing industry, and all over Europe for the preservation of meat. Most of the salt used in northern Europe in the late sixteenth century came from the south coast of Portugal and was carried in Dutch ships. Their normal supply reduced, the Dutch salt merchants turned first to the Cape Verde Islands and then to the Caribbean, where they discovered and began to exploit the great salt deposits of Araya, near Cumaná in Venezuela. The Araya salt-pan is an enclosed lagoon, about eight miles long, separated from the sea by a narrow strip of beach, and surrounded by a vast encrustation of salt left by evaporation. It is one of the hottest and most desolate places in the world; but Dutch skippers anchored there for weeks at a time, and employed their own crews in the work of breaking out and loading great lumps of the rock-hard salt. This point was noted, in the arguments used by William Usselinx, the famous proponent of West Indian settlement, to prove that white men could do hard manual work in tropical conditions. The salt ships were large, anything from 200 to 600 tons, and numerous; according to the governor of Cumaná they appeared off the coast of his province regularly at the rate of about ten a month between 1600 and 1605. Naturally, these ships did not come out in ballast, but brought European goods, which they sold along the Main and in the islands; and in addition to salt the Dutch took back tobacco from Guiana and Venezuela and hides from Hispaniola. Araya became the centre of a system of illicit trade, enlivened by occasional raiding, more serious than anything the Spanish Caribbean had yet known. The pearl fishery of Cumana was virtually closed by Dutch interference; and the islands became almost a Dutch commercial preserve. In 1605 seventeen foreign ships, mostly Dutch, were reported in the Bay of Gonaïves. The Dutch themselves admitted that their hide trade to Hispaniola employed twenty ships annually. The Spaniards could still retaliate; the armada sent out under Luis Fajardo in 1605, with orders to surprise the Dutch at Araya, achieved a notable success, captured twelve ships, and for several years closed the trade. The governors of Venezuela achieved a number of successes, also, in catching and hanging smugglers. But the measures taken by Spanish authorities to curb smuggling were destructive rather than creative, and damaged the interests of the colonists as much as those of the Dutch. Typical of such measures were the prohibition of tobacco-growing in Venezuela, to prevent sales to the Dutch; the proposal, made by the engineer Antoneli, to let in the sea and inundate the Araya lagoon; and the desperate decision, taken in 1605, to depopulate the north-west coast of Hispaniola. This last decision was enforced. The Spanish settlers of Puerto Plata, Monte Christi and Yaguana were ordered to leave their homes and move to the south coast, nearer to Santo Domingo and governmental control. Military force was needed to move them. Many fled to Cuba or turned pirate. Their cattle ran wild; and the vacuum so caused was filled by the buccaneers and later by the French.

The importance and the vulnerability of the West Indies, as emphasised by these events, naturally tempted the Dutch, as they tempted the English, to put forward open claims to navigate, trade and settle. The English claim that 'prescription without possession availeth nothing' was a reiteration of the doctrine of Grotius, and the persistent English approach to the West Indies as the 'apple of the eye' of the King of Spain, whence he derived his revenue which was his 'nervus belli', found an echo in the original plans for the Dutch West India Company. The proposals put forward by William Usselinx, the Calvinist refugee from Antwerp, at intervals from 1592 to 1621, had precisely the same objects as those of the English: the setting up of Protestant colonies which should be at once bases for raiding and smuggling, and sources of supply of ships' provisions and tropical 'staples'. In addition to the always valuable dyestuffs — indigo, fustic, logwood — there was a new and rapidly growing demand throughout Europe for tobacco. It was more satisfactory to buy such things by regular agreement from groups of European settlers than to rely upon getting supplies, uncertain in quantity and quality, from the Indians; and from the point of view of government, settlements might serve a double purpose, by providing a 'vent' for the unemployed, for paupers, vagrants, felons, and all manner of unwanted folk.

The first experiments in colonisation were made after the Treaty of London and in areas where they could be regarded, by a slight stretch, as compatible with peace with Spain — Virginia, Bermuda (by the accident of shipwreck) and Guiana — the 'wild coast' running between the Spanish possessions on the Orinoco and the Portuguese possessions on the Amazon. Such matters as fertile soil and healthy climate were largely guesswork in the seventeenth century. The Guiana coast — swampy, hot and fever-ridden — was to prove a singularly unsuitable place for inexperienced settlers, despite the legend of 'golden Manoa'; but Raleigh, the propagator of the legend, had been there in 1595, Keymis in 1596, the Dutch in 1598, and all had reported hopefully. In 1604 Charles Leigh attempted to plant a colony on the Wiapoco. The survivors were taken off, with Dutch help, two years later. Other equally unsuccessful ventures followed: Harcourt's attempt (1609–13), Raleigh's (1617–18), Roger North's (1619–21). In these enterprises English, Dutch and sometimes French adventurers worked in fairly close co-operation against the common enemy, Spain. Only the Dutch succeeded in making permanent settlements, on the Essequibo in 1616 and on the Berbice in 1624; but the English failures had important indirect results, for they led to the first establishments in the Lesser Antilles. In 1605 emigrants intended for Leigh's Wiapoco colony were landed on St. Lucia, where they were killed by the Caribs. In 1609 a similar group made an abortive attempt to settle in Grenada. Finally, in 1622, Thomas Warner, who had taken part in North's Guiana venture, but despaired of its success, on his return passage to England landed on St. Christopher, in what came to be called the Leeward group. Liking the look of the island, he went on to obtain patronage and capital in England, and returned in 1624 to begin the first permanent English settlement in the West Indies.

About this time a series of events occurred in Europe which was to alter the whole aspect of affairs in the Caribbean. In the United Provinces, Maurice of Nassau and the Orange party triumphed politically over the republicans. The Grand Pensionary, Oldenbarnevelt, champion of republican oligarchy and the East India interest, was executed in 1619. The Twelve Years' Truce expired in 1621. The Dutch girded themselves for renewed war with Spain, and the West India Company, which Usselinx had urged upon his countrymen for years, received its formal charter. Here at last was an organisation capable of challenging Spain in the West Indies — no mere temporary association of partners in smuggling or raiding, but a great permanent joint-stock corporation with at least a nominal capital of over seven million guilders. The company was not, however, the colonising concern originally proposed by Usselinx; it was to make its profits by war against Spain and Portugal. Plunder, conquest and commerce were its aims. It was to maintain its own fleet of warships, to be supplemented by the Estates General when formal war should be declared. It was to have the right to settle, build, administer and defend; and to hold a monopoly of trade on the coasts of West Africa and the Americas. This early recognition of the essential and complementary relation between Africa and the West Indies was highly significant for the future. Dutch slavers already possessed a 'factory' at Gorée and there is reason to believe that slave merchants were prominent in urging the foundation of the company. Certainly, throughout the company's history the purveying of slaves to Spanish, Portuguese, and, later, French and English settlements was a prominent and lucrative part of its sphere of interest.

The attack which the West India Company delivered against Spanish shipping — even though much of its energy was diverted to Brazil — was heavier and more sustained than anything which had gone before. It strained the overtaxed resources of Spain almost to breaking point, and enabled other groups of foreigners to settle unoccupied Caribbean islands without serious danger of Spanish interference. Behind the organised fleets of the Dutch company, moreover, there still operated a swarm of private Dutch merchants, more or less tolerated interlopers in the company's official preserve, picking up cargoes wherever they could find them, often in places too insignificant to be worth the company's attention. These enterprising poachers were ready to help settlers of any nationality with capital and with technical skill, to supply them with slaves and manufactured goods on long credit, and to buy their crops as soon as they had crops to sell. Every new colony in the West Indies meant more cargoes for Dutch shipping, as well as a blow against Spain. Dutch naval and economic strength sheltered and encouraged the infant Antillean settlements of France and England. From envy of the Dutch, and eventual rivalry with them, English and French governments learned a theory of mercantile imperialism which was to influence their colonial policies for two hundred years.

The directors of the West India Company — against Usselinx's advice — chose as the first object of their aggression the Portuguese sugar-planting area on the north-east coast of Brazil. They proposed also to capture the Portuguese slaving stations of São Jorge de Mina and São Paulo de Luanda in West Africa, without which the Brazil plantations were unworkable. We are not here directly concerned with the story of how the Dutch between 1624 and 1654 won and lost a great empire in the 'bulge' of Brazil, except in so far as that story affected the West Indies. Bahia, the principal city, in Usselinx's words, was 'not a cat to be taken without gloves'. The company's forces took the place in 1624, but lost it again in the following year. They did not renew the offensive in Brazil until 1630, and then against Recife, not Bahia. It was in the intervening five years that their naval commanders sought to recoup their losses in Brazil by raiding in the West Indies. In this they were overwhelmingly successful. Successive Dutch fleets carried out sweeps in the Caribbean which practically drove the local Spanish shipping from the sea; and in 1628 Piet Heyn, ablest and most celebrated of the company's admirals, in command of a fleet of thirty-one sail, surprised and intercepted the homeward-bound *flota* off Mantazas Bay, and captured the whole sailing almost without firing a shot. This triumph, achieved for the first time and not to be repeated for thirty years, yielded booty worth fifteen million guilders; enough to pay a dividend of 50 per cent to the company's shareholders, and to finance the renewed offensive in Brazil. It ruined Spanish credit in Europe. In the West Indies it paralysed for a time both communications and defence. It was followed by several years of systematic pillaging by smaller fleets. By 1630, except for the armed *flotas* — which by a miracle of determination continued their sailings — and for insignificant small craft, there was no Spanish shipping worth mention in the area. The trade of the islands and Tierra Firme was almost all in the hands of the Dutch and their allies. Spain still possessed the power to make occasional effective counter-attacks, as the story of Old Providence was to show, and she could still hold her settled colonies; but she could no longer dispossess other powers or prevent their acquisition of the islands which she had neglected to occupy.

The Dutch, though they were well aware that raiding would not pay indefinitely, did not avail themselves to any great extent of the opportunities for settlement in the West Indies. They seized between 1630 and 1640 Curaçao, Saba, St. Martin and St. Eustatius, all of which were confirmed to them by the Treaty of Münster in 1648. These small crumbs of land were of value chiefly as trading and smuggling depots, though Curaçao had valuable salt-pans, a matter of importance to the Dutch, since the Spaniards had succeeded in making Araya uncomfortable for the salt shippers. The island had only a handful of Spanish residents and was taken by a surprise attack with hardly a shot fired. It became the centre of Dutch power in the West Indies ever since, and in the first half of this century prospered as a free port and as a refinery centre for Venzuelan oil. The main efforts of the Dutch, however, were concentrated once again after 1630 upon Brazil. Meanwhile the accession of Charles I to the English throne, and of Richelieu to power in France, released a direct hostility to Spain which had recently been restrained. This hostility now took the form of colonisation as well as that of illicit trade. It was the English and the French who followed up the Dutch successes by establishing themselves permanently in the outer islands.

The opening of opportunities for settlement in the West Indies coincided with the great movement of emigration which was beginning to people the Atlantic coast of North America with Englishmen. Many reasons have been adduced for this seventeenth-century migration of Englishmen overseas, ranging from the growth of enclosure to the ecclesiastical policy of Laud; but the essential element in the situation was the conviction that in England there were more men than jobs or land, while in the New World there were more jobs and land than men. The organisers of new colonies at that time could always find men ready to try their luck. Government approved, or did not oppose, the growth of settlements which could serve as dumping-grounds for felons, paupers or schismatics, and which might produce 'naval stores' or other useful commodities. England, in short, undertook colonies of settlement rather than of trade or exploration; and this was as true of the West Indies, in the early days, as of Massachusetts or Virginia.

Thomas Warner, having secured the necessary financial backing in London, returned to St. Kitts in 1624 with forty or fifty companions to begin effective settlement. Shortly after his arrival a French party under d'Esnambuc also landed with the same design. The two groups, very sensibly in view of the danger of Carib raids, agreed to settle side by side, the French taking the northern and southern extremities, the English the centre — or rather the middle coastal strips, for the centre of the island is steep and uncultivable mountain. The English had much the better of this bargain, and there was frequent bickering over boundaries. Both groups of colonists were dispersed by a savage Spanish attack in 1629, but soon returned. Very shortly after the settlement of St. Kitts, in 1624, John Powell, returning home from Brazil, landed in Barbados, which was then quite uninhabited and forested to the water's edge. Struck by the beauty and apparent fertility of the place, he took possession in the name of King James. On arrival in England he persuaded Sir William Courteen, a London merchant with Dutch connections, to back the settlement of the island. All these settlements took root and led to further expansion. St. Croix in the Virgin Islands was jointly occupied by English and Dutch in 1625; Nevis was settled from St. Kitts in 1628, Antigua and Montserrat in 1632. There was an attempt to settle Tobago in 1625, and a settlement in St. Lucia from 1638 to 1641, when the Caribs again drove the settlers away. The French were behind the English in all this activity, for their urge to colonise was less spontaneous and depended more upon governmental encouragement. It was not until 1635 that Richelieu's hands were sufficiently free to allow him to intervene effectively in the West Indies. The establishment of the Compagnie des Isles d'Amérique and the settlement of Martinique and Guadeloupe date from that year. Both these islands, unlike Barbados, were inhabited by warlike Caribs. Their development in the early days was much slower than that of Barbados and St. Kitts.

The organisers of all these settlements quickly took steps to secure royal authority for their ventures, both in order to have clear titles to land, and to exercise official discipline over the settlers. For the French at St. Kitts the problem was relatively simple, because they had as yet no competitors among their own countrymen. Even so, d'Esnambuc procured from Richelieu a formal privilege, which, incidentally, included Barbados in its terms, though he never tried to put it into effect there. The English settlements were planted by a number of competing groups of investors, and in an atmosphere of bad geography and bad faith they all scrambled for patents and patronage in London. Warner and his friends secured the support of the Earl of Carlisle, an influential and able peer whose extravagance, excessive even in that extravagant age, led him to clutch at any opportunity of keeping his creditors quiet. Courteen's patron was the Earl of Pembroke. Both noblemen secured patents which included Barbados. The reckless ease with which such irreconcilable patents were granted bedevilled the early history of English colonisation, and is in itself an indication of the slight importance then attached by government to the whole affair. To quote Macpherson in *The Trade's Increase*, 'The West Indian islands, before they fell into the planting of sugar canes, were in those early times thought of little worth, otherwise the grants would not have been so readily made.' Eventually Carlisle, after a series of complex intrigues, got himself made Lord Proprietor of the Caribbee Islands, including St. Kitts, Nevis and Barbados. He confirmed Warner as his governor of St. Kitts, but imposed his own nominee, the ruffian Hawley, upon Barbados. Pembroke's patent was set aside; Courteen lost the large sums which he had invested, and many of his adherents lost their plantations in the disorders which followed.

The patent to Carlisle was the application to America of a form of grant long obsolete in England — a quasi-feudal grant of territory and jurisdiction to a prominent nobleman. The proprietor nominated the governor and other officials, and drew his revenue from rents and customs. Obviously a peer could obtain grants of this kind from the Stuart kings more easily than a group of merchants; and it was perhaps thought more appropriate that settlements in exposed positions should be made by feudal grant in the old tradition of knight-service rather than by trading companies. In fact the management of the concern was in the hands of a syndicate of London merchants, who were Carlisle's creditors and who sought to exploit his influence at Court in this way in the hope of securing something by way of repayment. Carlisle himself, having obtained the patent, took little interest in anything except his dues; and, as in most English colonies, the settlers exercised a considerable degree of self-government from the start. The grant, however, led to constant quarrelling among the heirs of the earl and the lessees of his rights, and their disputes were reflected in the bitter factions within the islands: Courteens against Carlisles, and, later, Royalists against Roundheads. St. Kitts, under the able and energetic Warner, held aloof from these squabbles, but Barbados was not brought to order until the arrival there, in 1650, of Francis, Lord Willoughby of Parham, as lessee of the Carlisle grant and also as governor-in-chief of the Caribbee Islands by virtue of a commission from the exiled Charles II. Willoughby was a moderate Royalist of great ability and deep conviction. 'I have never served my King', he wrote, on hearing of the battle of Worcester, 'in Expectation so much of his Prosperous Condicion as of my Dutye'; and his duty he conceived to be to keep Barbados for the time being out of English politics, especially as the Commonwealth government seemed determined to quarrel with the Dutch and to exclude Dutch ships from the islands. From the point of view of the islanders, whatever their politics, Willoughby's policy was obvious commonsense, and even at that early date the members of the Barbados Assembly were prepared to cavil at the orders of a parliament in which, as they said, they were not represented. The Commonwealth government, however, could not allow Royalist colonies to exist in virtual independence, and perhaps to serve as bases for Prince Rupert's fleet; so in 1652 a fleet under Sir George Ayscue appeared off Barbados and compelled Willoughby to submit to superior force. When Prince Rupert arrived in the area he could get no help from anyone except the French. Throughout the Commonwealth and Protectorate the proprietary patent was in abeyance. Governors, and a few other officials, came out from England; but they could not carry out their instructions and exclude all Royalists from office, because there were not enough Commonwealth men to run the government. Willoughby went to the Wild Coast and there founded a new colony in Surinam, which was ceded to the Dutch at the Treaty of Breda in 1667. He returned to Barbados after the Restoration, first as successor to the Carlisle rights, and subsequently (with due compensation for loss of the Propriety) as governor of the Caribbee Islands by Crown appointment. He spent the rest of his life consolidating and seeking to extend British occupation of the islands. He died in 1666 in an expedition against Martinique. He was one of the greatest and most devoted of early West Indians, holding it 'better...I and as many of our name as ever was borne should be suncke and perish, than those islands lost'.

Economically and socially Barbados — and indeed all the recently settled islands — must have presented difficult problems to a conscientious governor. The first record of a visit to the island is that of Sir Henry Colt in 1631, who described the slovenly management of the plantations, the rough and inefficient method of clearing by firing the bush — 'Your ground and plantation shows what you are, they lye like ye ruines of some village lately burned' — and the incessant quarrelling of the planters. At that time there were about 4000 people in the island. They were engaged partly in producing crops for their own subsistence, chiefly maize, and partly in growing tobacco for sale in Europe. Cotton was the only other crop of importance. At the time of the first settlements, tobacco was in great demand in Europe. The expansion of production in Virginia and Carolina had not yet forced down the price. It was grown mostly by small free-holders, farming from five to thirty acres, and employing the labour of indented servants, men who bound themselves to serve for a period of from three to seven years in return for having their passages paid, and in expectation of a grant of land at the expiry of their indenture. The situation of these men during their indentures was an unenviable one. They received no wage, but were supposed to be housed, fed and clothed by their masters. The quality of housing, in an island newly settled and only partly cleared, may be imagined. Food was mostly maize meal and the lowest grade of salt fish imported from North America. The master's rights to his servants' 'time' was absolute. If, for example, a free man married an indented woman, he was obliged to compensate her master by serving out the unexpired portion of her indenture. Indentures were transferable, so that indented servants could, in effect, be bought and sold. In a society where the magistrates were almost all planters, servants were naturally much at the mercy of their masters. There was no lack of emigrants, however. The miserable condition of a landless labourer in England, and the lure of free land in the West Indies, combined to supply a powerful incentive. By 1640 the population of Barbados was well over 30 000, which meant about 200 to the square mile — heavy overcrowding, by seventeenth-century standards. That of St. Kitts and Nevis at the same time was about 20 000. White population in all these islands reached its peak in the middle of the sixteen-forties. Thereafter it declined rapidly.

Both French and English islands from their beginning fell into the sphere of Dutch commercial activity. Only the Dutch possessed the necessary shipping to serve the needs of the area. In commerce, especially in seaborne commerce, the Dutch in the seventeenth century were the masters and teachers of Europe, not unnaturally, since trade was the whole life and livelihood of their state. Their capital was more fluid than the English or French, their business methods more up-to-date, their ships better designed for cheap and easy handling. They were the first Europeans to experiment with methods of sheathing ships' hulls against marine borers — a matter of vital importance in the tropics. Even when a choice offered — which was seldom — the planters preferred to ship their crops in Dutch ships, because the Dutchmen offered European goods at lower prices, longer credit and cheaper freight rates. It was said, too, that they understood the problems of stowage better and took greater care of their cargoes. They were directly interested in the prosperity of the islands with which they traded; and when tobacco became a drug upon the European market it was the Dutch who put the West Indians in the way of growing sugar instead. Amsterdam was a great city of warehouses from which all Europe was supplied with tropical and colonial products; and much of the profit to be derived from the colonial settlements of all European nations found its way into Dutch pockets.

Up to the middle of the seventeenth century governments, proprietors and planting companies accepted this situation philosophically, having neither the shipping nor the experience to compete with the Dutch. The first government to react against the Dutch monopoly was the Commonwealth government in England, and that partly for immediate political reasons. Barbados and Antigua, by their adherence to Charles II, gave the London merchants a pretext for attacking Dutch trade with those islands, under colour of a kind of disciplinary blockade. Pressure from the City secured in 1650 an act prohibiting all trade with the recalcitrant colonies 'because of their rebellion against the Commonwealth and Government of England'. The Barbadians under Willoughby refused obedience and maintained their Dutch commercial contacts. It was this, as much as West Indian royalism, which moved government to send Ayscue and his fleet to drive Willoughby out; but meanwhile it became clear that the real purpose of government was not merely to starve rebellious colonists into submission, but to replace Dutch shipping by English throughout the English colonies as a permanent policy. The Navigation Ordinance of 1651 prohibited the import of colonial products into England, except in English ships; and confined the import of European goods into English colonies to English ships or ships of the country where the goods originated. When the representatives of the Dutch government tried, by negotiation, to get the ordinance suspended, they were reminded that English traders had 'been always

strictly forbidden trade in all plantations . . . belonging to the people of
the United Provinces'; and were told that 'as for their trading to any
of the English plantations, it is forbidden by the late increase of the
navigation of this nation, from which we think not fit to recede'.

The boast was premature. English shipping to the West Indies had
not in fact developed sufficiently to supplant the Dutch, and the
islanders continued to trade in defiance of their government. Nevertheless, the intention of government was plain. The ordinance of
1651 was an act of economic war against the Dutch and in 1652 it
led to real war. The Protestant alliance of eighty years' standing had
broken up and a new Caribbean rivalry had emerged. The English government, and its mercantile advisers, now openly sought to
weaken the Dutch and to supplant them by imitating their methods.
In peace and in war, Dutch competition, Dutch influence and Dutch
example largely determined the nature of English colonial policy, as it
came to be formulated in the second half of the seventeenth century.
In this policy there were four main elements: the assertion of the
sovereignty of the metropolitan government; the fostering of staple
crops for shipment to the United Kingdom and subsequent sale in the
markets of Europe; the direction of trade into English ships bound for
English ports; and the concentration of this system on the West
Indies. The old colonies of settlement, based upon a balanced subsistence economy, nonconformist for both economic and constitutional
reasons, lost favour. A plantation system based upon some kind of
cheap forced labour came to be preferred. The production of tobacco,
cotton, dyestuffs, and later, sugar; the need for shipping; the demand
for food and timber from the mainland, for food, manufactured
goods, and, later, slaves from England — all made the West Indies the
colonies *par excellence* of the old colonial system.

In the minds of Cromwell and the restless, rancorous Protestant
gentry who supported him, the new rivalry with Holland did not
efface the old rivalry with Spain. It remains to notice two English
operations against actual Spanish territory in the Caribbean. One, the
settlement of Providence, was a failure. The other, the capture of
Jamaica, was a lasting success. Both owed something to Dutch inspiration. Both were intended to establish bases for trade and privateering as well as — perhaps rather than — colonies of settlement.

The Puritans, who were the chief Spaniard-haters in England,
for both religious and commercial reasons, were also conspicuous
colonisers. A company formed by prominent Puritans, including the
Earl of Warwick and John Pym, was incorporated in 1629 to settle
Santa Catalina, or Providence Island, off the coast of Nicaragua. The

island was peopled by settlers from England and from Bermuda, and in the early years both its planting and its seafaring activities showed some promise. By 1632 local agreements had been made with Dutch traders, who undertook to buy the first year's crop. The directors in England complained, but were gradually persuaded — since there was no alternative — to accept the Dutch as their dealers. In 1638 they sought and obtained formal permission for the arrangement. The settlers soon discovered, however, that it was easier to pay for Dutch goods with Spanish loot, and came to prefer raiding to planting as a source of profit, especially after 1631, when the company extended operations to Tortuga, off the north coast of Hispaniola. Tortuga was frankly a base for commerce raiding and little else. In settling colonies of this kind so near the Spanish coasts the company had attempted more than it could perform. The party at Tortuga was massacred by the Spaniards in 1635. In 1639 a Dutch offer to purchase Providence from the company was unwisely turned down. In 1641 a Spanish fleet recaptured the island and expelled the settlers; and the Providence Company came to an end. Tortuga became again, as it had been before the company's day, a rendezvous for wandering buccaneers. It fell eventually into the hands of the French, and later became the base for the French conquest of Saint-Domingue.

The capture of Jamaica differed from all previous English acquistions, in that it was a formal naval and military operation, organised and paid for by government. The accession of Cromwell to supreme power in 1653 permitted the return to a policy, almost traditional among the conservative-radical gentry of England, of open aggression against Spain in America. The famous 'Western design' in many ways resembled Drake's plan of 1585 for gaining control of the sea-ways of the West Indies. It displayed the same combination of cupidity, religious fervour, and national vanity. It was more ambitious, in that it contemplated permanent acquisitions of territory, to be settled as colonies by English planters, whereas Drake had only proposed to garrison one or two strategic harbours. It was more foolhardy. Drake had possessed accurate local knowledge and had commanded an efficient, well-disciplined force; but Cromwell's project was entrusted to an ill-led, ill-armed mob, and its planning was largely based on inaccurate and prejudiced intelligence. Thomas Gage, the renegade Dominican and author of *The English-American*, was a popular advocate and a violent partisan. The contempt for the enemy which marked all stages of the operation was due largely to his information and advice. Finally, neither Admiral Penn nor General Venables was a Drake.

About 2500 men, drafted from different units, were hurried on board at Portsmouth at the end of 1654. Five weeks later the expedition reached Barbados, where it assured its own unpopularity by seizing eleven Dutch ships in Carlisle Bay. For weeks it lay at Barbados, 'eating up the island'. The commanders requisitioned food and arms which the colony could ill spare; they seized money from the excise revenue; they recruited 4000 men — not only freemen volunteers, but (quite illegally) indented servants. Venables assumed temporary command of the island militia, and used the opportunity to oust Royalist officers. The Barbadians protested in vain. They were being punished by Cromwell for their earlier contumacy. They saw 4000 of their labourers taken from the island, and the safety of the island itself endangered, to help an English government which most of the planters disliked, in an endeavour to establish a colony which might eventually prove to be the ruin of Barbados. Nor were the commanding officers much better satisfied. Their recruits, according to Venables, were the scum of the colony, men 'so loose as not to be kept under discipline, and so cowardly as not to be made to fight'. It was a sad commentary upon the quality of indented servants, and the effect of indented labour in the tropics upon the character and physique of English emigrants. About 1200 men of slightly better quality were recruited in the Leeward Islands; but it was a mutinous, unwarlike mob which disembarked in Hispaniola in April 1655 in order to launch an overland attack on Santo Domingo. A serious tactical blunder was made, in landing too far from the town — over thirty miles — without giving any thought to the question of water supply for the march. The result of the attempt was a total rout at the hands of a much smaller force of Spanish regular cavalry, assisted by bands of local cattle-hunters. The attackers were saved from massacre only by the landing of a party of sailors to cover their flight back to the ships.

The capture of Jamaica was an afterthought, an attempt to retrieve the expedition from total disgrace; it was, however, a brilliant inspiration. Carew Reynell described Jamaica, with shrewd foresight, as the key of the Indies, equally apt for trade or for an attack on the Main, 'lying in the very belly of all commerce'. Jamaica, moreover, was a relatively easy prize. Since 1536 the 'marquisate' of Jamaica had been an appanage of the descendants of Columbus, as hereditary Admirals of the Indies, but they had done nothing to develop the island. Its Spanish population numbered only about 1500, and they were poor and ill-armed, living mostly by keeping or hunting cattle. The island had been held to ransom, only twelve years before, by the privateer William Jackson with but a few hundred men. When Venables' men landed in Hunt's Bay and marched on Spanish Town, they met with little resistance and soon both Penn and Venables were able to return to England, to face an angry Cromwell, leaving their juniors to conduct 'mopping-up' operations and to begin the work of settlement. The Spanish governor. Cristóbal Isasi, held out in the hills on the north side with a small band of Spaniards and loyal slaves, harassing the English in the south by frequent raids, and receiving occasional reinforcements and supplies from Cuba. The Cubans could do very little, however; a serious epidemic had recently decimated their population, and made it difficult for them to man their own defences. There was no hope of help from Spain; Blake's victory over the Spanish fleet at Santa Cruz in 1657 had made the despatch of a relief expedition impossible. Even so, it was not until 1660 that Isasi gave up the struggle and left the island, and not until 1670 that his government acquiesced in its loss. To this day Don Christopher's Cove, the little inlet in St. Ann where Isasi received his few supplies from Cuba, preserves the name of that brave and resourceful *guerrillero*. The few hundred slaves who had fled to the hills with their Spanish masters remained in the fastnesses of the Cockpit country and formed the nucleus of the redoubtable maroons.

Cromwell, though disappointed, resolved from the first to keep Jamaica, and went to war with Spain rather than give it up. A very important position had been gained, and no time was lost in drawing English attention to the fact. At first, settlement was slow and difficult. Officers and men of the conquering army received grants of land to plant and settle, chiefly in the fertile, well-watered bottom lands of the Rio Minho valley; but many of them died and few succeeded. Despite government propaganda, despite low taxation and the promise of virgin land, there was no such wave of migration towards Jamaica as there had been towards Barbados and the Leewards in the 'thirties. Jamaica never became a true colony of settlement. Its eventual prosperity — for it was to become immensely prosperous — was based from its beginnings on buccaneering, trade, and slave-grown sugar. At the same time sugar and slavery were invading the other English and French islands; and the profound social revolution which attended their introduction must next be considered.

CHAPTER V

The Sugar Revolution

The Dutch, without realizing it, started the sugar revolution. Intending a wholly commercial transaction, they set in motion forces that profoundly affected the history of the Caribbean and the Americas. Evidence of their all pervasive influence is written large in the physical landscape of North East Brazil, the Caribbean region and the deep south of the United States; in the ethnic composition of the various societies; in the diverse cultures, social mores and way of life; the evidence is less obvious but no less real in attitudes and modes of thought that have their origins deep in the sub-conscious. To review the beginning of the sugar revolution in the Caribbean is to review also the birth of today's West Indian society.

'Revolution' would be too strong a term if we were considering no more than a shift in the mode of production. The new world plantation was a powerful engine of economic and social change. Richard Sheridan describes it as 'a combination of African labor, European technology and management, Asiatic and American plants, European animal husbandry and American soil and climate... It established new trade routes and shipping lanes, shifted millions of hoe cultivators from one side of the Atlantic to the other, determined the movement and direction of capital, induced the growth of temperate zone colonies to supply intermediate products, produced a class of noveau riche planters and merchants and became a prize in the contest for power and plenty among the mercantile nations of Europe.'

In some respects the Plantation was versatile. The staple in the Caribbean was sugar; in the northern colonies it might be tobacco, cotton, indigo, rice. Its labour force might consist of African slaves, indentured East Indians or free peasants. It was organized for maximum profit, and this involved the exploitation of labour and land. The extent to which it retained its exploitative character in the Caribbean through the colonial period and after is indicated by Clive Thomas, in *Plantations, Peasants and State*, an analysis of the mode of sugar production in Guyana.

Such is the background to the sugar revolution in the Caribbean, where the first twenty years of West Indian settlement had been, for the French and the English, a period of greater activity than achievement, especially by comparison with the much larger and more solid development of the mainland colonies. Tobacco and indented labour were unsound bases for an island economy, as the West Indians discovered when tobacco prices dropped. All contemporary witnesses agreed that Barbados and Leeward Island tobacco was of poor quality and could not compete with Virginian. Nor did anatto or ginger provide adequate substitutes, since the demand for them was relatively small. Attempts to grow indigo in St. Kitts were failures, though some was grown in Barbados. Cotton — as de Poincy explained, writing from Saint-Christophe in 1639 to the directors of his company — required too much land. In islands where the area of usable land was limited, and where the initial cost of clearing bush was high, the only economic crops were those which gave both a high yield per acre and a high price. Sugar was the obvious choice; unlike tobacco, it could be grown only in the tropics. It could be grown by unskilled labour, for long periods on the same ground, without exhausting the soil. The demand for sugar in Europe was growing steadily and seemed insatiable. Sugar-cane, however, by reason of its perishable nature, must be milled and made into sugar almost immediately upon cutting. The planter must be a manufacturer too; or must at least have easy access to a factory. The manufacture of sugar demanded skill, technical knowledge, and equipment which nobody in England or France possessed. It could not be established in the English or French West Indies without help from outside; and such help could come only from Dutch sources. The Spaniards, who had been growing sugar in Hispaniola and on the mainland coast in relatively small quantities for a hundred and twenty years, had never officially recognised the existence of foreign colonies in the Caribbean. The Portuguese, with their much more extensive plantations in Brazil, were fully occupied after 1640 in the struggle to evict the Dutch from Pernambuco, and certainly had no motive for selling the secrets of the trade to foreign West Indians. The Dutch, however, had a powerful motive for doing so. As the universal dealers and carriers of the West Indies, it was to their advantage to encourage the production of any West Indian crop which could be sold in Europe. They had acquired in Brazil the necessary knowledge and experience. They could supply the equipment from Europe, and were prepared to lend the necessary capital. Dutchmen were the first founders of the sugar industry of the French and Bristish West Indies.

The first canes to be planted in Barbados, according to most contemporary accounts, were brought from Brazil by one Pieter Brower in 1637. For several years the only use of the cane was to make a sweet drink for immediate use. Attempts at sugar manufacture began in 1642, backed by Dutch merchants who supplied rollers, coppers and other equipment on credit against the first crop. Ligon's *History of Barbados* gives the following almost contemporary account — the earliest account we have:

'At the time we landed on this Island, which was in the beginning of *September, 1647*, we were informed, partly by those Planters we found there, and partly by our own observations, that the great work of Sugar-making, was but newly practised by the inhabitants there. Some of the most industrious men, having gotten Plants from *Fernambock*, a place in Brasil, the made tryall of them at the *Barbadoes*; and finding them to grow, they planted more and more, as they grew and multiplyed on the place, till they had such a considerable number, as they were worth the while to set up a very small *Ingenio*, and so make tryall what Sugar could be made upon that soyl. But, the secrets of the work being not well understood, the Sugars they made were very inconsiderable, and little worth, for two or three years. But...by new directions from *Brasill*, sometimes by strangers, and now and then by their own people, who...were content sometimes to make a voyage thither... And so returning with more Plants, and better Knowledge, they went on upon fresh hopes, but still short, of what they should be more skilful in: for, at our arrivall there, we found them ignorant in three main points, that much conduced to the work; *viz*. The manner of Planting, the time of Gathering, and the right placing of their Coppers in their Furnaces; [i.e. to conserve fuel and to prevent the flames reaching and setting fire to the boiling syrup] as also, the true way of covering their Rollers, with plates or bars of Iron: All which being rightly done, advance much in the performance of the main work. At the time of our arrivall there, we found many Sugar-works set up, and at work; but yet the Sugars they made, were but bare Muscavadoes, and few of them Merchantable commodities; so moist, and full of molosses, and so ill cur'd, as they were hardly worth the bringing home or *England*. But about the time I left the Island, which was in 1650, they were much better'd; for then they had the skill to know when the Canes were ripe, which was not, till they were fifteen months old; and before they gathered them at twelve, which was a main disadvantage to the making good Sugar;

for, the liquor wanting of the sweetnesse it ought to have, caused the Sugars to be lean, and unfit to keep. Besides, they were grown greater proficients, both in boyling and curing them, and had learnt the knowledge of making them white, . . . but not so excellent as those they make in *Brasill*, nor is theyr any likelyhood they can ever make such: . . . '

A more optimistic anonymous account describes the situation in its political context:

'. . . the Dutch beginning to lose their footing in Brazil [they were finally expelled in 1654] many came also from those parts, who taught the English the Art of making sugar, and having at that time [i.e. before 1650] free trade with all people at amity with England. . . their sugar yielded a good price, and they were plentifully supplied with all necessities of life and planting at very cheap rates, and had long credit given them by the Dutch, which together with their being governed by themselves, was the beginning and main cause of their prosperity, and grew and increased very much year by year in the production of their manufacture. . . '

In the French islands the story was similar except that there the industry was started by Dutch immigrants from Brazil who actually settled in the islands. The Company of the Isles of America made a contract as early as 1639 with one Trezel, who was to establish and manage a plantation of 3 000 acres and a mill in Martinique. Trezel failed, and so did several successors. The first successful factory was started — still with Dutch help — in Guadeloupe by the governor, Houel, in 1647. The following year the company became bankrupt, and the various islands were sold to individual proprietors. Saint-Christophe was acquired, presumably as an investment, by the Knights of Malta, who appointed de Poincy as their governor. Guadeloupe was purchased by Houel. Sugar production spread more slowly than in the English islands, largely owing to lack of labour. It is indicative of the greater prosperity of France at this time that in order to attract indented servants (*engagés*) the French planters had to offer better terms than the English. *Engagés* were rarely bound for more than three years, and often less. On the other hand, French manufacturing methods were more ambitious; for the proprietors, with the help of Dutch immigrants from Brazil, embarked in the 'sixties upon the operation of sugar refineries. The English islands produced chiefly muscavado — wet brown sugar — and only a little 'clayed' or 'plantation white'. The hold of Dutch merchants was even closer in the French islands than in the English. No attempt was made to break it until Colbert, from 1665 onwards, abolished the Proprieties and reorganised the French colonies in America on strictly mercantilist principles — which involved, at least temporarily, the closing of the refineries.

In the Spanish West Indies sugar was one product among several, and not the most important. In the French and English islands it became after about 1650 the only product of importance. The growth of this monoculture was much more than the spread of a profitable crop and a new industry. It was a revolution which changed the whole racial composition and social structure of the islands. Sugar was a rich man's crop. Considerable capital was needed to set up a factory; and a plantation, to run economically, had to be big enough to keep the factory supplied constantly with canes throughout the crop season. Once established, however, sugar plantations and factories soon became immensely profitable — far more so than, for instance, tobacco plantations. Successful sugar planters bought up the holdings of failing tobacco farmers. Barbados, which had supported a large population of small proprietors, became in a decade or so a land of relatively large estates; and the profits to be made from sugar encouraged clearing, so that by 1660 almost the whole usable area of the island was cleared and in use. A pitiful emigration of dispossessed small-holders left Barbados to try their luck in the mainland colonies, in Jamaica, in Surinam, Martinique, Guadeloupe, or (for the wilder sort) among the buccaneers. Many of these wanderers failed to find a resting place, and died in the search. As early as 1652 Colonel Modyford (later Sir Thomas, and governor of Jamaica) had written: 'This island of Barbados cannot last in a height of trade three years longer, the wood being almost already all spent, and therefore in prudence a place must presently be thought upon, where this great people may find sustenance and employment.' Fifteen years later a report from Barbados stated that the island contained 'not above 700 considerable proprietors, ... 12 000 good men formerly proprietors have gone off, wormed out of their small settlements by their more suttle and greedy neighbours.'

The size and complexity of the estates acquired in Barbados by 'suttle and greedy' planters, even in the early days of the industry, is indicated by Ligon, whose detailed *History* was published in 1657. He described a plantation, in which Modyford bought a half-interest in 1648, as containing '500 acres of land, with a faire Dwelling-House and *Ingenio* [presumably turned by cattle] in a room 400 feet square, a boyling house, filling house, cisternes and still house, with a curing house 100 feet long and 40 feet broad, with stables and smith's forge and room to lay provisions of Corne and Bonavist. Houses for Negroes and Indian Slaves, with 96 Negroes and 3 Indian women with their children, 28 Christians, 45 cattle for work, 8 milch cows, a dozen horses and mares and 11 *Assinigoes....* In this plantation of 500 acres, there was employed for sugar something more than 200 acres, about 80 acres for pasture, 120 for wood, 20 for Tobacco, 5 for Ginger, as many for Cotton Wool, 70 acres for provisions, viz. corne, potatoes, Plantaines, Cassavie and Bonavist; some few acres of which were for fruit, viz. Pines, Plantaines, Millions, Bonanas, Goaves, Water Millions, Oranges and Limons'. Modyford paid £7000 for his halfshare. Eight years earlier the whole estate had been worth only £400.

The revolution spread to Virginia and Maryland where the staple was tobacco. A catastrophic fall in the price of tobacco on the London market virtually wiped out the small holdings. Only those with capital to invest in large holdings survived. Gradually, as prices improved, large tobacco holdings manned by African slaves became the dominant force in the economy. The eight proprietors to whom Charles II granted Carolina quickly learned the lesson and opted for large estates, two of the major crops being cotton and indigo. Some Barbadians with expertise in these crops and some knowledge of estate management were prominent in establishing plantations in the Carolinas, and six of the first ten governors of North Carolina were Barbadians. The planters of Virginia, Maryland and the Carolinas echoed the statement by John Pinney, founder of the fortune of the Pinneys of Nevis, that 'negroes are the sinews of the plantation' and 'to make sugar without the assistance of negroes' was to attempt to make bricks without straw. The American economic historian, Gray, in his *History of Agriculture* quotes a Carolina colonist (1682): 'When I have land and what shall I do with it? What commodities shall I be able to produce that will yield me money in other countries, that I may be enabled to buy Negro-slaves, without which a planter can never do any great matter'.

Establishments of this type required a large and well-disciplined labour force, which the old practice of indenture could not adequately supply. Free land had been the essence of the indenture system. The landless labourer left England in the hope of becoming — if he lived long enough — a small proprietor. It was in that expectation that he signed his contract, went overseas, endured the years of hard work, the tropical climate, the poor food and housing, the arbitrary whims of a strange master. But when no land remained to grant; when small proprietors could not make ends meet, and sold or deserted their holdings; and when there was no ready sale for any crop but sugar, then no incentive remained, and the supply of volunteer indented labour dwindled and ceased. Only compulsion in one form or another could meet the need. Every conceivable method of propaganda was employed to recruit labour in Europe, especially in North Germany, where the Thirty Years War had left thousands homeless, ready with the credulity of utter misery to go to the West Indies or anywhere that offered a ray of hope. Crimping became a regular trade, in England and in continental ports. More legally, but no less brutally, the English penal system was adapted to West Indian needs. The Civil War produced a crop of Royalist prisoners who were shipped out, seething with bitterness, to Barbados. Irish rapparees spared in the massacre of Drogheda went the same way, to be 'derided by the negroes as white slaves'. Transportation became a regular punishment for vagrants, for political prisoners, and for many convicted felons. Magistrates in Bristol with West Indian connections were bribed — so it was said — to give transportation sentences. Jeffreys as Lord Chief Justice had hard things to say about magistrates who 'for a pint of sack...will bind people servants to the Indies'; but Jeffreys himself sent to a like fate hundreds of the Somerset yokels who followed Monmouth. The effect of all this was to create a class of poor white labourers, miserable, desperate and despised; men — to quote Josiah Child — 'such as, had there been no English Foreign Plantation in the World, could probably never have lived at home to do service for their country but must have come to be hanged or starved, or dyed untimely of some of those miserable Diseases, that proceed from Want and Vice'. They were treated accordingly, often enough. Transported — 'barbadoed' — persons were, in effect, slaves; but as their enslavement was limited to the term of their sentence they were less valuable than true slaves, and often, therefore, worse cared for. 'I have seen such cruelty there done to servants', says Ligon, 'as I do not think one Christian could have done to another.'

None of the methods of persuasion or compulsion employed in Europe produced labourers in sufficient numbers to meet West Indian demands, and eventually, as the Spaniards and Portuguese had done before them, the French and English planters found a solution of their labour problem in the purchase of slaves from outside Europe, mostly from that apparently inexhaustible reservoir of humanity, West Africa. The Dutch, in the late sixteen-thirties, had seized most of the Portuguese slave barracoons in West Africa, as the necessary complement of their Brazilian empire. They had slaves to sell and were anxious to extend the trade in the West Indies. As sugar-planting spread, so the number of white labourers declined and the number of blacks increased. Barbados had a few hundred blacks in 1640; by 1645 there were over 6000 blacks and about 40 000 whites; in 1685, 46 000 blacks and 20 000 whites, bond and free; twenty years later the number of Africans was about the same but the European population was down to 12 000. In the Leeward Islands the change began a decade or so later, but, once begun, was more rapid and more nearly complete than in Barbados. The systematic settlement of Jamaica began in 1664, upon the arrival of Sir Thomas Modyford as governor. Emigrants from Barbados formed a substantial proportion of the settlers, sugar was the main crop, and estates were large almost from the very beginning, some over 5000 acres and very few under 150. In 1673 the population was 7700 white and 9500 black. The white population remained almost constant for fifty years, but the number of black slaves in the same period rose to 74 000. In the French islands the process of change, in the early years, was slower. The white population of proprietors and *engagés*, though small, proved very tenacious. Even at the end of the seventeenth century, except in Saint-Domingue, most properties were still small, employing an average of less than a dozen slaves each. An official count in 1687 gave a total for all the islands of 18 000 whites and 27 000 slaves. Of the slaves, 16 000 were in Martinique and 7000 in Saint-Domingue. By 1701 the total number of slaves had increased to 44 000, while the white population remained stationary, or increased very slightly, in most islands; Martinique was not robbed of whites to settle Saint-Domingue as Barbados and Nevis were to settle Jamaica. After the turn of the century properties increased rapidly in size and the number of slaves went up by leaps and bounds. Martinique alone had 21 000 by 1710, and in Saint-Domingue the increase was more dramatic still. By the early eighteenth century, then, Africans formed in most of the British and French islands the great majority of the population. The Europeans had become a small garrison among the slaves.

For long it was difficult to form, from comtemporary accounts, any clear idea of the nature of this great body of people brought against their will from Africa. That difficulty has been removed by the historical and sociological research of African, European and New World scholars. The rationalizations used as a basis for justifying the European exploitation of Africa and the denial of civil rights to blacks in the Americas have been shown for what they were, the products of ignorance and prejudice. There are few more dramatic examples of the illuminating power of scholarship than the way in which this New body of knowledge enabled American blacks and whites to liberate themselves from myths about the African past and to recognize the intrinsic value of the African heritage.

The markets which chiefly supplied the West Indies lay on the great middle stretches of the coast — Sierra Leone, the Grain Coast (Liberia), the Ivory, Gold and Slave Coasts, the Oil Rivers of the Niger Delta, Cameroon, Gabon and Loango. Naturally people from this great area spoke many languages and exhibited many variations of culture and custom; but they also shared many traits in common. Their languages belonged to one or the other of two great families — Sudanic and Bantu. The principal tribes in the heart of the slaving area were the Fanti-Ashanti peoples of the Gold Coast, the Dahomeans, the Yoruba of western Nigeria and the Bini of southern Nigeria. All these peoples were composites of many groups, welded through a long process of conquest into kingdoms such as those of Songhay, Mali, Ghana in the Western Sudan; and at a later date Dahomey and the Akan-Asante empire which Osei Tutu and Anokye founded. Seeing the need for some unifying force that would hold together the diverse peoples of his empire, Anokye, in a great ceremony at Kumasi, established the Golden Stool of the Asante. The incident, and the ways in which Africans recognized and exercised authority, show a remarkable capacity for political organization; a quality that was displayed later in the Americas in the organisation of the Palmares Republic, settlements of Bush Negroes in the Guianas, the Maroon communities of Jamaica and the palenques of Colombia, as well as in the founding of the independent republic of Haiti.

Close knit families and kinship groups formed the basic units of a hierarchic social structure of which the chief or king was head. He exercised great, but not absolute power, for tradition decreed that he should rule with the advice of a Council of Elders, and that he should heed precedents enshrined in tribal history and passed on by word of mouth from generation to generation. In consequence, each man was in varying degree a custodian of his people's history, had a keen appreciation of family and tribal obligations and was guided by traditional values such as respect for the elders, the laws, the dignity of an individual and the requirements of social justice. This passion for justice impressed the fourteenth century Arab scholar and traveller, Ibn Batuta, who noted that 'of all peoples the blacks are those who most detest injustice. Their Sultan never forgives anyone who has been guilty of it'.

Religion and art forms reflected the African's vision of man and his world; they were part of everyday life, part of a community of ancestral spirits, living family and kinsfolk; the vibrant dance-forms, the rhythms of the drums, the vitality of the sculpture expressed the collective experience of the society. The quality may vary but the great works of African art speak the same language as the artifacts of the folk; both belong to the same tradition.

Slavery had long existed throughout the region and there were plantations in Dahomey and the Niger Delta that were worked by slaves. These were exceptional. In general, slavery was a form of domestic servitude involving two groups; debtors who pawned themselves and went to live with the creditor group, their labour going to the repayment of their debts; and prisoners taken in inter-tribal wars or, as the demand increased, taken in raids. They were valued as commodities that would be used to buy guns, gunpowder, hardware and European cloth.

But this commodity was human, and perishable. Subjected to the trauma of capture, sale, a long yoked march to the coast and confinement in festering barracoons, many died. Many others perished during the ocean voyage in the slave ships, 'floating tombs' the Brazilians called them. In the course of three centuries more than 10 million Africans were landed alive in the Americas. No one can tell how many died. Each westbound ship severed the life-giving ties with homeland, family, community, the past. To visit the old fortresses on the coast of Ghana, to see the subterranean dungeons in which the slaves were packed before being herded through narrow doors into boats and ferried to waiting ships is to be torn apart by the horror and brutality of the slave trade.

The Africans who came to the Americas were pitchforked into a slave society whose existence depended on their degradation and perpetual subjugation. The planter-historian Bryan Edward stated this frankly: 'in countries where slavery is established, the leading principle on which the government is supported is fear: or a sense of that absolute coercive necessity which...supersedes all questions of right'. Subjection was enforced by savage penalties that included dismemberment, mutilation and torture.

Slaves in the Dutch, English and French colonies endured a harsher fate, for by law they were 'pieces of property', not men and women. They were excluded from the sacraments of the Church, denied the right to marry, tethered to a particular place or plantation. Their bondage was perpetual, extending to the offspring. The slave owner usurped the role of the natural father by functioning as provider, protector, source of authority.

The arriving slaves were from different tribes and cultures —
Senegalese, Coromantees, Whydahs, Nagoes, Pawpaws, Eboes,
Mocoes, Congoes, Angolas, Mandingoes and so on. The names are
imprecise and misleading: some certainly refer to ports of shipment.
Beneath the variety of origin and language the newcomers showed
underlying similarities of behaviour. As might be expected of fighting
peoples, they reacted against their enslavement and exile with bitter
and active resentment. Their rejection of slavery took many forms:
calculated idleness, wilful carelessness and destructiveness in handling
the owner's property and feigned stupidity. More significant were
endemic marronage, risings, rebellions. What happened in Jamaica
was typical; nine uprisings and two Maroon wars between 1673 and
1798. In 1733, during the first Maroon war, a planter wrote 'no man
at North Side can be said to be master of a slave'. Between 1823 and
1832 there were a series of outbreaks, culminating in a great slave
rebellion. The warning given by Linton, one of the leaders of the 1832
rebellion, held true for the full period of Caribbean slavery, that if the
gentlemen do not keep a good look out 'the blacks will try the business
again, in two or three years'.

In later chapters we will consider the Haitian War of Independence
and other rebellions. It is important to see these and Maroonage as
part of a continuing region-wide struggle against slavery. As Richard
Price points out in *Maroon Societies*, for more than four centuries
'the communities formed by such runaways dotted the fringes of
plantation America from Brazil to the Southeastern United States,
from Peru to the American Southwest. Known variously as palenques,
quilombos, mocambos, cumbes, ladeiras of mambises these new
societies ranged from tiny bands that survived less than a year to
powerful states encompassing thousands of members and surviving
for generations or even centuries'.

The natural resilience, physical strength and creative adaptability of
the Africans enabled them to meet the challenges of enslavement and
exile by an unceasing struggle for freedom, justice and a place of their
own. Slowly they worked out a way of living which was not that of
any single African group nor a composite of African folkways but a
characteristically Caribbean amalgam. It is this process which gives
Caribbean history its continuity and significance.

CHAPTER VI

The Buccaneers

The Treaty of Breda, which ended the Second Dutch War in 1667, laid down a territorial division in the eastern Caribbean which was to endure without major change for half a century. The Dutch kept Willoughby's old settlement of Surinam; the French kept Tobago; St. Christopher was divided as before; and all other conquests were restored. The lines of future Anglo-French rivalry were clearly laid. Wars in plenty, it is true, lay ahead. In the Third Dutch War (1672–78), in which England joined with France in an attack on the commercial ascendancy of the Dutch, and in King William's War (1689–97), in which the alliances were reversed, war in Europe was reflected by fighting in the West Indies. The governors of settled islands, in particular Barbados and Martinique, led armed expeditions against neighbouring islands and made many temporary annexations. St. Eustatius — that scrub-covered rock in the Leeward Islands which Dutch genius made the richest free port in the Americas — was bandied about like a shuttle-cock; it changed hands ten times between 1664 and 1674. But usually the peace treaties restored the *status quo ante bellum*; and at least the wars were official wars, formally declared. The peace between wars was real peace, not a mere exchange of piracy for privateering. Intelligent and public-spirited governors like Willoughby, Stapleton, and Codrington, realising that the uncertain support of gangs of desperadoes could give no lasting assurances of safety in peace or war, gave no countenance to pirates within their governments.

Farther west, in the Greater Antilles and the sea surrounding them, no such convention yet existed. The long privateering war against Spain had sown dragons' teeth among the islands. For generations this continuous, irregular warfare had been a source of wealth to the bold or the lucky. In Jamaica, in western Hispaniola, in Tortuga, in the Bay Islands, there were whole communities of the men, commonly called buccaneers, with whom raiding was a habit, not easily or willingly discarded. To the buccaneers a treaty of peace meant merely a change from public employment to private enterprise; for the 'sweet trade' was their livelihood.

The word *boucan* means the process of curing strips of meat by smoking over a slow fire; and the *boucaniers* were originally men who lived by hunting and by selling hides and smoked meat to passing ships. All the islands of the Greater Antilles supported great herds of wild — or rather feral — pigs and horned cattle, the descendants of animals that escaped from Spanish ranches and multiplied and throve upon the virgin savannahs. The pursuit of these ownerless beasts offered a rough but not unattractive living to masterless men — marooned or shipwrecked sailors, deserters, escaped felons, runaway indented servants, and all such as disliked organised society; and many of them varied hunting with robbery by land or by sea. Spanish settlements and shipping, being nearest to hand, naturally suffered most. The Spanish governors did their best to round up these wild people living in the unsettled areas of the islands. In Hispaniola mobile lancer squadrons — 'cinquantaines' — were employed against them from about 1640, and attempts were made to starve them into surrender by killing out or driving away the herds on which they depended. The only result was to drive the buccaneers to further piracy, and to turn their antipathy to government in general into a vindictive hatred of Spanish government. By the middle of the century they had come to form dangerous outlaw bands, accustomed to hardship, well armed and (for so long as they chose to obey) well led. Like most wild and lawless communities; they possessed conventions of their own and were rigid in their adherence to the 'custom of the coast'. The best description of their ways is that of the indulgent du Tertre, who had dealings with them, and knew them well enough to say Mass occasionally on board their ships; for many of them retained vestiges of their religious allegiance. Political allegiance they had none, except on occasion as bloodthirsty and unreliable mercenaries. The presence of such bands in the heart of the Spanish Caribbean was a perpetual temptation to aggressive colonial governors, French or English, and a perpetual menace to trade and peaceful settlement.

The buccaneers included in their ranks desperadoes of many nations, or of none; but most of them were either English or French. The idea of employing them as auxiliaries for commerce raiding in time of war seems to have occurred first to a Frenchman, de Poincy, governor of Saint-Christophe on behalf of the Knights of Malta. De Poincy had had difficulty in controlling quarrels between his Catholic and Protestant settlers, and solved the problem in 1639 by sending the leading Huguenots away on an expedition to settle the island of

Tortuga as a French outpost. Tortuga had become an international haunt of buccaneers since the massacre of the Providence Company's settlers in 1635; but there had been quarrels there between French and English freebooters. The Huguenot leader, Le Vasseur, managed to get himself accepted as governor by the French among the buccaneers, and soon elbowed out the English. Le Vasseur was a competent military engineer, trained in the hard school of the siege of La Rochelle. He made himself virtually independent of de Poincy, systematically fortified Tortuga, and established himself there as a semi-official governor and robber leader. The island became the most notorious of the pirate strongholds from which attacks were launched against the Spaniards, and to which the resulting booty was carried for division.

Le Vasseur was a leader of unusual skill. After his death — he was assassinated in 1653 — the Spaniards defeated his successor and captured the island, driving the buccaneers back into the forests of northern Hispaniola; but the Spanish garrison, stationed at Tortuga in 1654, was withdrawn in 1655 to help in the defence of Santo Domingo against Penn and Venables, and the buccaneers came drifting back. D'Oyley, when governor of Jamaica, tried to attach the island stronghold to his government, but the French element was too strong, and he gave up the attempt. Instead, the English buccaneers, outnumbered in Tortuga, began more and more to make their headquarters at Port Royal.

To leave Tortuga and the Hispaniola forest camps and establish themselves openly in an English Crown colony the buccaneers needed at least the tacit approval of the governor. The attitude of the government of Jamaica depended, at any moment, upon its relations with Spain and with the surrounding colonies. There were two alternative policies. One was the old Commonwealth (and late Elizabethan) policy of continuous informal war against the Spanish colonies, encouraging the buccaneers to raid where they could and to bring their spoils to Jamaica. The other policy was to make Jamaica a commercial centre, selling slaves and manufactured goods to the Spaniards, by agreement if possible, or, failing agreement, by smuggling. Obviously the two policies could not be combined, because the second required the establishment of an understanding with the neighbouring Spaniards, and so necessarily involved calling off the buccaneers. Both the home government and the government of Jamaica wavered between these two policies for twenty years or more. During the initial fighting in Jamaica the buccaneers were welcomed and encouraged. Charles II, however, on his accession, attempted (while retaining Jamaica) to secure a trade with the Spanish Indies by agreement. In accordance with this policy Sir Thomas Modyford, an old Barbadian, was appointed in 1664 governor of Jamaica, bringing with him about a thousand Barbadian farmers who decided to settle in Jamaica. He did his best, at first, to convince his Spanish colleagues of his will and his ability to suppress the buccaneers, but without much success; for it he succeeded in driving them from Port Royal they merely transferred to Tortuga. By the end of 1664 Charles had become persuaded that his hopes of accommodation with Spain were unlikely to be fulfilled. At the same time he was confronted with war against the Dutch, and the possibility, which in 1666 became a fact, of having to fight Dutch and French together. The buccaneers were almost the only fighting men available in the West Indies. In order to enlist their help Modyford, in 1665, was authorised to grant commissions of 'reprisal' to buccaneer captains. The plunder they might secure from the Spaniards was to be their payment for their services in the war. Once again there was to be 'no peace beyond the Line'. Since the home government could not easily afford the expense of regular naval and military forces, it hoped to defend Jamaica, Barbados, and the other West Indian colonies by means of planter militias, using the buccaneers as a striking force by sea.

The main drawback to this plan of using the buccaneers as mercenaries, paid by plunder, was that they would only willingly serve where plunder was to be had — against the Spaniards, with whom England was technically at peace. The events of the Dutch wars showed how unreliable they were against Dutch or French. They proved useless against Saint-Christophe; they flatly refused to attack Curaçao; and although they took St. Eustatius in 1666, that island was seized by the French very shortly afterwards, and restored to the Dutch at the Treaty of Breda. It was not the efforts of the buccaneers, but the belated arrival of a small naval squadron under Berry, which enabled the Barbadians to take the offensive in 1667 and recapture Antigua and Montserrat. Against the Spaniards, on the other hand, under colour of 'reprisals' for real or fancied injuries, the Port Royal buccaneers maintained a campaign as brilliant as it was brutal. The success of their first big raid in Central America, where they penetrated far up the San Juan river and sacked the undefended town of Granada, upset the balance of Modyford's plans; but he, having no other force at his disposal, was obliged to truckle to success and welcome them back to Port Royal. Probably his disapproval was half-hearted; and from most of the inhabitants of Jamaica the buccaneers could count on an enthusiastic welcome. In 1665–66 under Mansfield (himself a Hollander) they raided the coasts of Cuba, temporarily recaptured Old Providence, and raked over the ruins of Granada for whatever might be left.

After this first Cuba raid Mansfield disappeared, and the leadership at Port Royal fell upon a greater and luckier ruffian, Henry Morgan, whose career provides an epitome of this period of West Indian history. He had come out as an indented servant to Barbados, but ran away to join the buccaneers and became prominent among them while still in his twenties; he exploited his position as a leader of mercenaries, acquired wealth and land, was knighted, became lieutenant-governor or Jamaica, and was found by Hans Sloane living there in 1668 in dropsical middleage, surrounded by doctors (including Sloane), peevishly disregarding their advice and drinking himself to death. He was at the height of his fame in the 'sixties and early 'seventies. In 1668 Modyford commissioned him, first to carry out a reconnaissance in Cuba, where he suspected that an expedition against Jamaica was fitting out, and then to make a diversionary attack on Puerto Bello, with a force of 400 English buccaneers. Puerto Bello was fortified and had a garrison of some 300 men: but Morgan took the place by the kind of surprise attack at which he excelled, advancing up creeks and through swamp and forest by night. The garrison, after surrender, were locked up in the fort, which was then blown up by firing the magazine. It was at Puerto Bello that Morgan first acquired his unexampled reputation for pillage and torture of prisoners. His men brought back 250000 pieces of eight, besides goods and munitions, to Port Royal, where — according to the unctuous Esquemeling, who probably sailed with them — 'they passed here some time in all sorts of vices and debauchery, according to their common manner of doing, spending with huge prodigality what others had gained with no small labour and toil'.

The raid on Puerto Bello established Morgan's reputation as a bold, skilful and lucky leader, and in the following year, 1669, he openly fitted out in Port Royal a fleet of ten sail with nearly a thousand men, for an attack on Cartagena, the centre of Spanish naval power in the southern Caribbean. At the last moment, however, Morgan decided that Cartagena was too strong for him — the buccaneers in general were not at their best in attacking formal fortifications — and sailed for Maracaibo instead. Maracaibo had been thoroughly sacked and looted the year before, by a force from Tortuga under the savage L'Ollonais, and the familiar routine of burning and torture produced only a small ransom; but on his way out from the lagoon Morgan encountered three Spanish men-of-war, carrying silver from Puerto

Bello, which had been ordered to intercept him. All three were captured, and burned or beached, so that Morgan returned to Port Royal with enough loot to satisfy his men, to keep the governor quiet, and to fit out yet another expedition in 1670. This was Morgan's last and biggest enterprise. Commissioned by Modyford in reprisal for a small Spanish raid on Jamaica, he sailed for the Main, with some 1500 men, including about 500 Frenchmen from Tortuga, sacked Santa Marta and Rio de la Hacha, paid Puerto Bello another devastating visit, and then, in December 1670, marched his men across the Isthmus, to attack Panama. The march took nine days. The citizen militia of Panama resisted to the best of their strength, which was not large; it was on this occasion that the Spaniards attempted the curious, but hopeless, expedient of stampeding herds of wild cattle in the hope of breaking the enemy's ranks. But Panama was doomed. Most of the inhabitants — those who failed to escape in the forest — were killed or tortured to death; the city was utterly destroyed by fire, and was never rebuilt upon its old site.

Panama was the climax of Morgan's bloodthirsty career, and the events of this last raid naturally invite comparison between his achievements and those of Drake a hundred years before. There was little enough similarity between the two men — the chivalrous, narrowly pious and patriotic naval officer, leading a sternly disciplined force against an empire at the height of its vigour and defended by admirals of genius; and the elected leader of bands of cut-throats, organising the pillage of almost undefended towns of the same empire in a period of hesitation and decline. Drake, moreover, brought his fleets from England, four thousand miles away; Morgan had a convenient base for his operations, in the midst of the enemy's possessions. Nevertheless, in his boldness, in his brilliant tactical skill, especially in combined operations, and in his leadership, Morgan was in the tradition of Drake. He covered most of Drake's ground, and the forces which he led were of the same order of size. The buccaneers of the seventeenth century were the debased and brutalised successors of the Protestant corsairs of the sixteenth.

Morgan got a formal vote of thanks from the Council of Jamaica in May 1671; but during his year of absence events had taken place in Europe which put an end to the use of buccaneers as an important instrument of English policy. The long negotiations between England and Spain, for a formal treaty of peace which should include America, concluded in 1670 with the Treaty of Madrid, which bound both parties to abstain from pillage and to revoke all letters of marque and reprisal. More significant still, by this treaty Spain for the first time acknowledged officially the presence of the English in the Caribbean: 'The Most Serene King of Great Britain, his heirs and successors, shall have, hold and possess for ever, with full right of sovereignty, ownership and possession, all the lands, regions, islands, colonies and dominions, situated in the West Indies or in any part of America, that the said King of Great Britain and his subjects at present hold and possess....'

The logical outcome of all this was the recall of Modyford, and his replacement by a governor who could be trusted at least to try to enforce the new policy; but for years Jamaica remained an open haunt of the ruffians whom he had protected. Modyford himself went to England and was lodged in the Tower, for appearance' sake, though he was soon released, and never brought to trial or deprived of his share of the buccaneers' loot. He died in Jamaica. His monument in Spanish Town Cathedral describes him as 'the best and longest Governor, the most considerable planter, the ablest and most upright judge, the island ever engaged'. His successor, Sir Thomas Lynch, made strenuous attempts to carry out the new policy, as lieutenant-governor, though with no armed force at his disposal he could not move very effectively against the buccaneers. Morgan was still swaggering about Port Royal, in possession of the gains of ten years of rapine; and under two of Lynch's successors, Vaughan and Carlisle, he was employed as lieutenant-governor, on the dubious principle of setting a thief to catch a thief. In 1677 six English buccaneering ships sacked Santa Marta, and neither Vaughan nor Morgan could lay them by the heels. Coxon, an old associate of Morgan, in 1678 raided the ports of the Gulf of Honduras, and loaded up his ships with cochineal, indigo and cacao. When he put into Port Royal, Morgan allowed him to refit there before sailing to Rhode Island to sell his loot — for the New England ports were the best market then for stolen cargoes. This same Coxon, in association with another pirate named Sawkins, actually crossed the Isthmus in 1680, seized some Spanish ships, and plundered a series of small harbours all down the Pacific coast, returning home by way of Cape Horn. This outrage occurred during the negotiations for the Treaty of Windsor between Spain and England. Every West Indian governor was alert to punish the perpetrators of it, and some of Coxon's men were caught and hanged. Even Morgan turned policemen in earnest; but it was not until 1685 that a small frigate squadron was sent to Jamaica for the purpose of hunting down pirates, and that buccaneers in considerable numbers came to 'swing and sun-dry' at Port Royal or Execution Dock. By time that Lynch had returned to the West Indies for his second period of office, and even in Jamaica public opinion had turned against the buccaneers. Both the West Indian interest in England and the merchants in the West Indies were determined to 'force a trade' with the Spanish colonies, by smuggling if need be, using Jamaica as a base and *entrepôt*. For this they needed real and not merely formal peace. As if to mark the end of an age, both Morgan himself and Albemarle, the last governor who countenanced the old ruffian, died in 1688; and old Port Royal, wicked, opulent and shabby, paid the price of its sins — so the pious believed — and disappeared beneath the sea in the great earthquake of 1692.

All this time Tortuga had remained wide open; for the French were not greatly interested in the prospects of local trade with the Spanish colonies, and still saw advantages to be gained from backing the buccaneers. The activities of the Tortuga *flibustiers* had one important indirect result, the establishment of Saint-Domingue, the western part of the great island of Hispaniola, as a French plantation. After the evacuation of the small Spanish settlements in 1605, the area for many years was inhabited chiefly by cattle-hunting buccaneers. The fortification of Tortuga in French hands gave them a supporting base to which they could retire by sea whenever the Spanish authorities tried to hunt them out; and similarly when French discipline at Tortuga became irksome they could disappear into the Hispaniola forests to resume their butcher's business. Not only in Tortuga, but in Hispaniola also, buccaneer harbours grew up, at Petit-Goave, Léogane and Port-de-Paix. The organisation of these nests of pirates into a colony began with the appointment of d'Ogéron as governor of Tortuga for the Compagnie des Indes in 1665. D'Ogéron already knew the West Indies well; he had been a planter in Martinique and Jamaica, a salt trader in the Caicos, and at times a buccaneer. The orders which the company gave him, to use Tortuga as a base to cover settlement in Hispaniola, probably originated in his own suggestions, and he carried them out with conviction and great ability, settling families on the land, often at his own expense; encouraging the cultivation of maize, tobacco and cacao, and organising their sale, often to the buccaneers; and even arranging for prostitutes to be rounded up in France and transported, in order to encourage the buccaneers to settle in domestic surroundings. With the buccaneers themselves he maintained friendly relations; he succeeded in making himself indispensable to them, both as the official approver of their raids and as an efficient, though grasping, middleman. Any successful West Indian governor at that time had to become a receiver of stolen goods if he wished, as both

Modyford and d'Ogéron did, to keep on good terms with the buccaneers and employ them as mercenaries. With great skill d'Ogéron separated his government by gradual degrees into two distinct communities: a comparatively respectable settlement in Saint-Domingue, where the spread of planting drove away the wild cattle and the development of trade discouraged piracy; and a strongly held base in Tortuga under his own control, where he hoped to discipline and militarise the 1500 or 2000 buccaneers who frequented the place.

The Tortuga buccaneers took a prominent part in the Caribbean fighting during the Third Dutch War from 1672 to 1678, which brought the Dutch West India Company to bankruptcy and ruin in 1674, and enabled the French to enforce a commercial monopoly in their own West Indian colonies. Like the English buccaneers, however, the French preferred raiding the Spanish Main to fighting the Dutch; and like the English, they balked at the task of attacking Curaçao. The major French successes of the war were in Europe. At the Treaties of Nijmegen in 1678 Louis XIV hoped, on the basis of European victories, to secure from Spain a recognition of his possession of Saint-Domingue. Had he succeeded in this he might well have decided to follow England's example and suppress the buccaneers. The Spanish government, however, refused to compromise on Saint-Domingue. At the same time Louis XIV was advised by D'Estrées that Spain was so weak that with a little additional pressure she would be compelled to grant France a share of the supposed 'riches of the Indies'. Accordingly the *flibustiers* were reprieved, maintained as a striking force, and backed by a strong fleet under D'Estrées. The years from 1678 to 1685 were the years of their greatest success and most savage reputation. During those years many of Morgan's old associates, preferring a pirate's life with a chance of the gallows to planting or standing up to their knees in water hauling logwood, left Jamaica for Tortuga and Saint Domingue to sail with van Horn, de Graaf, de Grammont or the Marquis de Maintenon. The Jamaica Assembly found it necessary to pass an Act forbidding British subjects to serve in foreign ships; but Morgan, in Jamaica, privately invested in some of the *flibustiers'* enterprises, many of which, for daring and cruelty, equalled his own. De Grammont established himself for six months in 1678 at a base near Maracaibo, whence he systematically raided the coastal settlements of Venezuela. The wretched settlers, indeed, had grown so accustomed to raiding that a hasty retirement to the woods, followed by ransom negotiations, was the automatic reaction to the appearance of a strange sail. De Maintenon robbed and almost destroyed the

Margarita pearl fishery and pillaged the small Spanish settlements which were then the only habitations of white men in Trinidad. He invested the proceeds of these raids in sugar, and became the owner of the biggest plantation and factory in Martinique. The most successful and daring of all the French enterprises, however, was led by the two Hollanders, van Horn and de Graaf, with de Grammont as van Horn's lieutenant. This party in 1683 took and sacked the hitherto untouched port of San Juan de Ulúa, Vera Cruz. Their fleet was surprised in harbour, just as Hawkins had been a hundred years before, by the arrival of the *flota* from Spain; but times had changed. The *flota* was now a small fleet, only fourteen sail, and the captain-general dared not attack, but stood off and on outside the harbour while the buccaneers loaded their ships with money, goods and slaves, and sailed away to a nearby cay to divide the spoil. There the leaders fell to fighting over the division, and van Horn died of his wounds; but de Graaf and de Grammont survived to make another large-scale raid, against Yucatán in 1685, in which the city of Campeche was reduced to ashes.

These seven years, 1678 to 1685, were, ironically but characteristically, years of official peace, except for the brief war between Spain and France from December 1683 to July 1684, begun partly as the result of the Vera Cruz episode and terminated by the Truce of Ratisbon. Throughout the period the depredations of the buccaneers, though chiefly aimed against Spanish settlements, spared no ship which looked a likely prize. They were costly and embarrassing auxiliaries; and eventually the French government, like the English ten years before, was compelled by repeated protests to take measures against what had become a major international plague. Political circumstances pointed the same way. Common fear of France had begun to range England and the United Provinces on the side of Spain, both in Europe and in the Caribbean; and although neither did anything to help Spain in 1683, both were vigorous in their protests against the buccaneers. Moreover the possibility now lay before Louis XIV of acquiring the whole of the Spanish Indies by inheritance from the sickly idiot king Charles II; or else of imposing a successor who would grant the French a privileged position in the American trade. This was a more attractive prospect than mere casual plunder or piecemeal conquest. Already the Dutch, at the Treaty of The Hague in 1673, and the English, at the Treaty of Windsor in 1680, had made with Spain mutual and permanent promises to cease raiding. Only France still stuck to the convention of 'no peace beyond the Line'. At the Truce of Ratisbon France, too, abandoned the old convention, with its savage implications, and agreed that 'All hostilities shall cease on both sides, both by land and by sea and other waters, in all Kingdoms, countries, provinces, territories and dominions...within Europe and without, both on this side of and beyond the Line....' As a guarantee of peace the truce was no more effective than any other of the numerous treaties of the period; but it marked the official end of buccaneering.

The actual end naturally took some time to achieve. The first governor with definite orders to put down buccaneering was de Cussy, appointed to Saint-Domingue in 1684. He could think of no better way of doing it than buying the leaders. De Grammont died at sea before his new royal commission could take effect, but de Graaf was successfully bribed into the royal service, as Morgan had been, and like Morgan played a part in the suppression of his former comrades. He lived to be one of the founders of the new French colony of Louisiana in the early eighteenth century. The final disbandment of the *flibustiers*, however, and the creation of lasting order the prosperity in Saint-Domingue was the work of an abler governor than de Cussy and a better sea commander than de Graaf. Jean-Baptiste du Casse began his seafaring career in the employment of the Compagnie de Sénégal, following up D'Estrées' capture of Gorée in 1677 by establishing his company's factory there. He first went to the West Indies, as a slaver, in 1680. From slaving he took to privateering, achieved a great local reputation, and in 1691 was appointed governor of Saint-Domingue. By that time William III was firmly established on the throne of England and most of Europe was allied against France in the war which bears his name. Du Casse's part in the war, besides the defence of Saint-Domingue, included two considerable offensive operations. The first was an invasion of Jamaica in 1694, which did great damage to crops, mills and dwellings and which was called off, apparently in the full tide of success, for reasons which have never been fully explained. The second was the successful and immensely lucrative capture of Cartagena, in 1697, in which du Casse and a force of buccaneers served alongside a formal naval squadron under de Pointis. In this engagement the buccaneers, for the first time, were paid the same exiguous share of the prize-money as naval seamen. They protested, and thanks to du Casse their protests were upheld; but once paid off they were disbanded and never employed again. Some became planters and some pirates, but under the rule of du Casse and his successors, with naval force in the area, they ceased to influence policy and were never again a serious menace.

As for du Casse, his ability found recognition in France; he became an admiral, served with great distinction the Kings of France and

Spain in the war of the Spanish Succession, and ended his days as a Knight of the Orders of St. Louis and of the Golden Fleece — the last a distinction usually reserved for princes. His most enduring memorial, however, was Saint-Domingue, which by the Treaty of Ryswyck in 1697 was at last formally ceded to France. Du Casse gave it a firm and efficient administration, replaced piracy by peaceful trade, cattle-hunting by planting. He compelled the remaining buccaneers in Tortuga to evacuate the island and settle in Saint-Domingue. Saint-Domingue became for France a bigger and richer Jamaica. Like Jamaica, it developed as a land of large sugar plantations worked by slaves. In the eighteenth century it came to be regarded as the most valuable tropical possession of its size in the world.

With the Peace of Ryswyck, then, the age of the buccaneers came to an end. At no other time in Western history can a few thousand desperadoes have created a reign of terror over so vast an area, or have exercised so great and so continuous an influence upon the policy of civilised states. Their toll had been a terrible one. During the six years of Morgan's ascendancy, from 1655 to 1661, they had sacked eighteen cities, four towns, and nearly forty villages: Cumaná once, Cumanagote twice, Maracaibo and Gibraltar in Venezuela twice, Rio de la Hacha five times, Santa Marta three times, Tolú eight times, Puerto Bello once, Chagre twice, Panama once, Santa Catalina twice, Granada in Nicaragua twice, Campeche three times, Santiago de Cuba once, and other towns and villages in Cuba and Hispaniola for thirty leagues inland innumerable times; and this fearful tale of outrage does not include the English expeditions made after 1670, nor the still more wholesale depredations of the French. The development of the Greater Antilles as productive settlements was impossible while the buccaneers continued to receive support. Their suppression, delayed by political and strategic needs, was economically essential to merchant and planter alike. It did not, of course, mean an end to fighting; for in the eighteenth century the Caribbean was one of the principal theatres of a maritime war that lasted, with comparatively brief intervals, from the days of du Casse to those of Nelson. But eighteenth-century wars were fought by disciplined forces under responsible leaders, not by gangs of ruffians for private profit, at the expense of individuals. It was a sign of the growing importance of the West Indies in the economy and in the estimation of the Western world, that the age of the buccaneers should be followed by the age of the admirals.

CHAPTER VII

The Atlantic Slave Trade

The Spanish American Silver Trade and the Atlantic Slave Trade provided the means of exchange and the labour force that lifted Western Europe to prosperity and power in the eighteenth century, and accelerated the development of a global economy. Silver from Peru and Mexico went first to Cadiz and Seville, whence it found its way to the Baltic, India and China to pay for Europe's imports of tea, silk, cotton and spices. The Atlantic Slave Trade was the vital link in a dynamic trading system that moved European manufactured goods to expanding markets in Africa, African slaves to the Americas and American sugar and tobacco to Britian and France. It was, in the eighteenth century, regarded as the indispensable handmaid of the sugar industry. If supply lessened or was interrupted the industry failed. The problem of organizing a regular and reliable supply of slaves became a major preoccupation of governments.

Naturally, in a mercantilist world which regarded monopoly as an essential measure of defence, and commercial competition as a mild form of war, the slave trade gave rise to incessant international dispute; and in the West Indies dispute was sharpened and complicated by the disproportion between territorial possessions and maritime strength. Of the five peoples most prominent in Caribbean trade, four — Portuguese, Dutch, English, French — acquired slaving bases in West Africa and engaged actively in the trade; but the Spaniards, while possessing by far the biggest and most populous colonial empire, never secured a firm foothold on the slave coasts and never (at least until the nineteenth century) appeared as serious competitors in the trade. They were always customers, never, or very rarely, suppliers. The policy of each of the other four powers, therefore, was to establish a monopoly of the supply of slaves to their own colonies; to sell a surplus to foreign colonies wherever possible; and above all to secure a share — or, better still, a monopoly if possible — in the supply of slaves to the Spanish colonies. In fact the Spaniards in the West Indies did not need, and could not afford to buy, very large numbers of slaves in the seventeenth century; the great days of Cuban sugar were still to come; but an exaggerated notion of the importance of the Spanish empire as a source of wealth and as a market for goods and slaves was prevalent throughout northern Europe, and persisted until the nineteenth century. It was the mercantilised version of the legend of Eldorado — a coveted prize, equally elusive, and no less a cause of misunderstanding and war.

In the sixteenth century Spanish America had depended chiefly upon the Portuguese for its supply of slaves. By means of fictions before 1580, openly thereafter, Portuguese slavers had shipped cargoes under individual licence from Seville, or else had smuggled slaves into the Indies. In 1595 the Spanish government, accepting the inevitable, had consented to the first of a long series of slave *Asientos*. This was an agreement for farming out the slave trade, or the greater part of it, to a contractor who was to organise the whole business, maintaining his own stations in Spain, in Africa, and in the Indies. He was to take over from the government the task of selling licences to sub-contractors, remitting the licence fees to the Crown. He and his sub-contractors might ship slaves directly from Africa to America, making their own arrangements for convoy and escort if necessary. From 1595 to 1640 Spanish America got most of its slaves from Lisbon slavers under agreements of this kind. From the sixteen-twenties, however, the effects of Dutch competition and hostility began to make themselves felt, both in West Africa and in the Caribbean; Portuguese contractors found it increasingly difficult to obtain and deliver cargoes, and were compelled to raise their prices. Finally in 1640 Portugal revolted successfully against Spanish rule and the *Asiento* broke down. From 1640 to the end of the seventeenth century the slave trade to the Spanish Indies was mainly contraband in Dutch hands. With the slave trade went an equally lucrative illicit trade in the main products, of Spanish America — sugar, tobacco, cacao, cochineal, hides and silver. The Spanish trade monopoly, never very complete in practice, broke down almost entirely during this period.

In the sixteen-forties, when Dutch commercial ascendancy was at its height, sugar was introduced into Barbados and the Leeward Islands, and the English planters also began to buy slaves from Dutch traders; but this practice soon attracted adverse comment in England. It was contrary to mercantile policy to buy so valuable a commodity from foreigners, and the Navigation Acts made it illegal for Dutch ships to trade to English colonies. An alternative method of supply had to be found. An open trade would be dangerous in face of the inevitable hostility of the Dutch, firmly entrenched on the African coast. The English Crown had not the resources to undertake the building of forts and the provision of armed ships, so a company had to be formed for the purpose, and in 1663 Charles II granted a charter to the Company of Royal Adventurers of England trading into Africa. This group was the immediate successor of a company formed three years before for trading in ivory, dyewoods and gold. The 1663 charter changed it into a slaving concern. It was the direct predecessor of the larger and more powerful association incorporated in 1672 as the Royal Africa Company. Several members of the royal family were shareholders in this enterprise, which was to supply the English sugar colonies with 3000 slaves a year at an average price of £17, or one ton of sugar, per slave. The purchase price in Africa at that time was about £3.

The Company drove a thriving trade but was perpetually on the verge of bankruptcy because frequent wars interrupted its trade and caused losses of shipping and forts, with the result that it had to put up the price of its slaves to £25 or £30. Interlopers constantly invaded its monopoly and undercut its prices and its agents defrauded it by buying slaves at their own account, shipping them with the company's slaves, and selling them privately at lower prices. The colonists pressed for a free trade in slaves and attacked the Company's monopoly so persistently that in 1698 Parliament passed an Act opening the whole African trade to all British subjects, the Company receiving a duty on imports into Africa and on certain exports to enable it to maintain its forts for the protection of traders.

The French, during the second half of the seventeenth century, had begun to take a close interest in the West African coast, particularly in Senegal, where French slavers, sailing mostly from Nantes, had almost ousted the Dutch by the end of the century. The French had a trade plan very similar to that of the English: a monopoly, operated by chartered companies, of the supply of slaves both to their own islands and to the Spanish possessions in the Caribbean. Political circumstances favoured their design. A union between the French and Spanish crowns, or at least a Bourbon prince on the Spanish throne, seemed at the end of the century to be a likely development; and no more suitable contractor for the *Asiento* could be found. An *Asiento*, was accordingly concluded with the French Guinea Company in 1702. Naturally this arrangement did not suit the English or the Dutch; and while, no doubt, the principal concern of the English in the war of the Spanish Succession was to keep Louis XIV and his relatives off the throne of Spain, the Netherlands and the Indies, at least a subsidiary motive was to prevent the French Guinea Company from keeping the slave *Asiento*.

The war was fought in Europe. Operations in the Caribbean were of a defensive kind, and English settlements and shipping suffered heavily. Victories in Europe enabled Britain, at the Treaty of Utrecht in 1713, to gain her objectives — that the Netherlands and Spanish America should not fall under French domination and that the *Asiento* be transferred from the French Company to the South Sea Company which was floated expressly for the purpose.

Gradually signs of conflict appeared. The peace settlement had assigned the *Asiento* for the supply of slaves to the Company for thirty years and had granted to it the novel privilege of sending a shipload of general merchandise to Spanish America every year. The Spanish were convinced that the Company was engaged in smuggling. The Company's slaving monopoly was breached by illicit traders of other nations who supplied slaves of inferior quality at lower prices. The West Indian planters hated the Company because it raised the price of slaves and exported the best to the Spanish colonies. The private traders of Jamaica hated it because of its obvious intention of superseding them in a trade which was an essential part of their economy. They imported great quantities of food and timber, largely from North America and since the North Americans preferred to buy their sugar and molasses from the French, who sold it cheaper, the imports of the English islands had to be paid for in money. To obtain the necessary bullion the English islands were especially obliged to develop their smuggling trade with Spanish America. The illicit cutting of logwood in Campechee and the Bay of Honduras was in part an answer — quite an inadequate answer — to the problem of the drain of money from the West Indies. But the Company carried goods from England direct to Puerto Bello and sought to supply the local irregular trade. Spain for her part, determined to distinguish between smugglers and traders, claimed and exercised the right to stop and search foreign ships anywhere in the Western hemisphere. Claims and counterclaims multiplied, public indignation against Spain piled up in England and, in 1738, Captain Jenkins supplied the spark that set the tinder ablaze — an emotional account of Spanish *guarda costas* boarding his ship and cutting off one of his ears in the ensuing dispute. He produced the carefully preserved ear as evidence. 'It was the undoubted right of British subjects to sail their ships in any part of the seas of America,' the House of Commons thundered. In 1739 war was declared between Britain and Spain.

We need not trace the events in the war of Captain Jenkin's ear. It is enough for our purposes that the primary cause was the Slave Trade, over which Britain intended to keep control. Few in England at the time questioned the value of the trade or doubted for a moment that it was worth fighting for. The point of view of the man in the street may be summed up in the words of an anonymous and typical English pamphlet of 1749:

'The most approved Judges of the Commercial Interests of these Kingdoms have ever been of the opinion that our West-India and African Trades are the most nationally beneficial of any we carry on. It is also allowed on all Hands, that the trade to Africa is the Branch which renders our American Colonies and Plantations so advantageous to Great Britain: that Traffic only affording our Planters a constant supply of Negro Servants for the Culture of their Lands in the Produce of Sugars, Tobacco, Rice, Rum, Cotton, Fustick, Pimento, and all other our Plantation Produce: so that the extensive Employment of our Shipping in, to, and from America, the great Brood of Seamen consequent thereupon, and the daily Bread of the most considerable Part of our British Manufactures, are owing primarily to the Labour of Negroes; who, as they were the first happy instruments of raising our Plantations: so their Labour only can support and preserve them, and render them still more and more profitable to their Mother-Kingdom. The Negroe-Trade therefore, and the natural consequences resulting from it, may be justly esteemed an inexhaustible Fund of Wealth and Naval Power to this Nation.'

The Mediteranean Basin slave trade, which involved some 70 000 African slaves in the period 1415 to 1525, was large by 15th Century standards but it shrinks to pygmy proportions when compared with the Atlantic Slave Trade of the 18th Century, which expanded rapidly to meet the European and North American demand for sugar and sugar products. What had been regarded as a luxury became a daily necessity for the rapidly growing population of Europe and North America. Not only were there more people but they had more money to spend. The population of England climbed from 5.8 million in 1700 to 6.5 million in 1760, 8.25 million in 1790 and 12 million in 1820. With this increase went urban growth and the rise of a proletariat. The story was the same in France, other European countries and in the North American colonies where the population increased sixfold between 1700 and 1760. As the market expanded so the demand for sugar grew, spurred not only by population growth but also by new imports such as tea from India.

Sugar planters clamoured for African slaves, without whom they could not expand production. As John Gee wrote in 1729, 'all this great treasure proceeds chiefly from the labour of negroes in the plantation.' Elsa Govia saw the same picture in terms of man rather than money: 'The slave with his hoe and his basket of dung symbolized the prosperity or ruin of sugar cultivation in those islands.'

The number of slaves imported rose sharply. Between 1791 and 1801 the British Caribbean, smaller in area than the smallest country in Spanish America, imported 1 401 000 slaves, twice as many as all Spanish America. Jamaica alone took 662 000 between 1701 and 1810; the Leewards 301 900; Barbados 252 000. French traders were as active as the British. Philip Curtin estimates that in the years 1711–1720 French slavers carried 46 000 slaves to the French colonies, most of them to the Antilles. Recent studies enable us to form a fairly accurate idea of the number of Africans brought to the Americas between 1518 and 1870, when the trade came to an end. Estimates range between 10 and 15 million. This long continued, forced population transfer depopulated large areas of Africa and transformed the ethnic structure of the population of the Caribbean, the United States and Brazil. As Curtin observes, 'both North and South Americans who came by way of the slave trade were the most numerous of Old World immigrants before the late 18th Century.' In the West Indies the change was dramatic. Bryan Edwards, writing in the 1780's, estimated the total population of the West Indies at about 520 000 made up of 455 664 blacks and 65 300 whites, with about 20 000 of mixed race.

There is a grim side to this account of population growth in Europe, the Caribbean and North America. In the sugar islands the demand for more slaves was due to an excessively high mortality rate as well as to greater demand for sugar. The product was precious but not the slave. Planter doctrine ran that it was cheaper to buy than to breed. John Newton, at one time captain of a slaver and later an Anglican priest, said Antigua planters had assured him that it was more economical to work the slaves out and replace them, and that a slave rarely lived more than 9 years after importation. Henry Coor, who with a small gang of slaves serviced some Jamaican sugar estates for about 15 years, testified in 1791 before a British Parliamentary Inquiry that 'I have heard many overseers say "I have made my employer 20, 30 or 40 more hogsheads of sugar than any of my predecessors. . . and though I have killed 30 or 40 Negroes per year or more, yet the produce has been more than adequate to that loss".' The statistics indicate a very high death rate. In Barbados, for example, between 1712 and 1768 about 200 000 slaves were imported but the population increased by only 26000. The exploiters rationalized their savagery in the way the Nazis did with the Jews, or the South African Government with apartheid, treating blacks as sub-human, inferior beings. Elkins, in his *Analysis of Slavery as a Problem in American Institutional Life*, quotes a statement by a Barbados planter in Carolina 'that Negroes were beasts and had no more souls than beasts. . . that they (his fellow Barbadians) went not to those parts to save souls or propagate religion but to get money'.

Slavers made long passages. The triangular voyage was usually at least twelve months. A ship would sail from its home port in England or France with a cargo of 'trade goods' — woollen or cotton cloth in bright colours, firearms and other weapons, tools, pots and pans, and trinkets. The run down to the Coast might take two, three, even four months. Arrived off the Coast, negotiations began, usually through resident middlemen, most of whom were Portuguese, for slaving the ship. Slaves might be picked up in small lots here and there; or more commonly assembled in hulks, or in barracoons ashore. All this trading might take many weeks. Meanwhile, 'trade goods' were landed in payment, water barricoes filled ashore, and temporary decks constructed by the ship's carpenters. On these extra decks the slaves were to travel, lying prone all night and most of the day, for there was no room to stand upright, except during periods of exercise on deck. As soon as a cargo was assembled the slaves were hurried on board, and the ship set sail without delay, carronades trained inboard and gunner's mates standing by with lighted matches until the Coast was out of sight. Once at sea, the danger of mutiny was less, and slaves could be allowed on deck for exercise, though always under strict guard. Arrived in the islands, after a middle passage in which speed was the best safeguard against mortality, the process was reversed; the slaves might be sold on board, if the demand for them was urgent, but usually they were landed, 'refreshed' for a short period ashore on fresh provisions, doctored in various ways to improve their health and appearance, and then sold at auction, usually in small lots, by the agent of the slaving firm, to factors or local planters. Planters were bad payers, and many of the transactions involved credit. Unless there was a great shortage of slaves, the planter usually had the advantage in these transactions, because the slaver was in a hurry to dispose of his perishable cargo and get under way again. Payment might be in local currency — sometimes at an arbitrary rate of exchange fixed to the purchaser's advantage — or in bills if the purchaser's credit was good; but more commonly it was in produce, and there again prices were a fruitful source of disagreement.

The process of sale or barter might take many weeks. For the ship's company this was a period of rest and release from strain, for once a slave was sold his new owner was responsible for him. Ship's discipline relaxed; many seamen deserted in the West Indies, and others had to be signed on, usually at rates of pay far higher than those ruling in Europe — a frequent cause of dispute. Some worn-out ships also remained in the islands, being adjudged unequal to the homeward passage. The French, but not usually the English, enforced a system of inspection to determine seaworthiness at this stage. Eventually, sales made, crew rounded up and formalities done, the ship's people dismantled the slave decks and loaded in the return cargo, usually sugar, for the last lap — and usually quickest and least eventful part — of the voyage: passage back to Europe.

The pattern of the 'triangular voyage' was never neat and consistent, and in the later eighteenth century it changed considerably. The commitments of planters to their factors increasingly obliged them to ship their sugars in the factors' ships. For this reason, and also because they could not time their sailings to coincide with harvests, slavers found increasing difficulty in getting return cargoes, and often returned to Europe in ballast. This in turn encouraged differentiation of design between slavers, built for speed, with high 'tween-decks, and sugar freighters, built for capacity, with deep holds. In the period we are considering, however — the first half of the eighteenth century — this specialisation had hardly begun and slavers still usually carried sugar back to Europe. The ships then engaged in the trade were of all sizes from fifty to over five hundred tons, and of all designs and rigs. Seaworthiness and stout construction were more important than speed, for the triangular voyage was as exacting for the ships as for the men. Relatively few ships survived more than about ten years in the trade, which meant perhaps half a dozen voyages. The chief home ports were London, Bristol and Liverpool in England — London declining relatively in importance and Liverpool gaining rapidly in the course of the eighteenth century — and in France Bayonne, Bordeaux, La Rochelle, Dunkerque, and above all Nantes. In all these ports slaving firms were prominent in the local merchant communities, for the trade created markets for half a dozen connected trades. Slaving required good capital backing. A firm normally operated at least three ships: one outward, one homeward, and one refitting; the cost of fitting out a ship and freighting it for the trade was high, the wage bill was heavy, and heavy dues had to be paid to the old monopolist companies — the Royal Africa Company in England (down to 1730 when its dues were replaced by a parliamentary subsidy charged upon the duties), and in France the Compagnie des Indes, as reorganised after the fall of Law. These bodies no longer traded extensively, but performed services of defence on the Coast and exacted licence fees from other traders. Reserve capital was needed, also, to meet the possibilities of total loss of ship or cargo through the hazards of the sea, or mutiny, or epidemic. But for the merchant with adequate capital, given capable captains and reasonable luck, the trade was enormously profitable; for each voyage brought three distinct profits, and a ship very rarely needed to make a passage in ballast. Investors, economic pamphleteers, and politicians in France and England thought nothing of the miseries of the trade because they never saw them. Only the factors on the Coast, and the slaving ships' companies, saw the brutalities of the round-up at the barracoons and the close-packed horror of the middle passage; and they were men hardened to such sights, and paid to ply their trade. The ordinary man in Europe saw only the returns.

Nobody of importance — except Walpole, worldly-wise and weary — seemed to think it strange that England should enter enthusiastically upon a major war to retain and increase its share in so rich an enterprise.

The trade touches present day life closely at many points. Its most obvious consequence, written in black and white, is the presence of some 60 million people of African descent in that part of the Atlantic Basin which extends from Brazil through Surinam, the Guianas, the Caribbean, the southern and eastern seaboard of the United States to the Great Lakes. People of African descent form a preponderant majority in the older plantation islands of the Caribbean, Barbados, Tobago, the Leewards and Windwards, Jamaica and Haiti; they form a large proportion of the population of Guyana, Surinam and Trinidad; they constitute a large proportion of the population of Brazil and of the United States. Further, the importation of Africans into the islands of the Caribbean, many of them small and limited in resources, led in time to over-population, so that emigration became a major feature of Caribbean history. Blacks from the Caribbean moved to the coastland of Central America, to Panama, Cuba and the United States, and when most of these exits were closed they made their way to Britain, to London, Bristol, the industrial midlands. It is one of the ironies of history that eighteenth century Britain moved Africa to the Caribbean and in the decade of the 1950's the Caribbean moved Africa to Britain.

Another major consequence had its origins in the inner life of the African, his concept of himself and his world, of past and future, of the spirit world and his relationship to it, and combined with this his response to the circumstances in which he was placed. History reveals the deep need of all men for roots and self-expression, for belonging to, and indentifying with a community that has a memory of its past. In contrast with the Jews who throughout their long exile were held together by a Book which kept alive their sense of history and of a divine purpose, the African was separated from his past and subjected to a perpetual exile.

The need for self-expression remained, and with it certain inherited modes of thought, gifts of insight, a quick eye for colour and pattern, a quick respose to the harmony and rhythms of shape, form, sound, and a sense of the dynamism in all things, material as well as human. In satisfying his need for self-expression by using these gifts the African opened up new perceptions and insights in the cultures of the Americas. To travel through North-Eastern Brazil, the Caribbean and the United States is to become aware of the rich diversity of the African contribution, of the range and vitality of cultural modes of expression at all levels, from the village to the sophistication of theatre, concert hall and museum; in folk art, folk medicine, in cults and ritual and cuisine, in language, craft work, in music, painting, sculpture, literature and drama.

Finally, the trade in man as a piece of property, and the plantation which owned man as a chattel and not a human being, raised questions of conscience in the minds of some; of a few to begin with, such as Judge Sam Sewall, whose *Selling of Joseph* was the first American protest against slavery, and the Quakers who in 1727 demanded that slavery be abolished. The number grew as diverse forces affected the climate of opinion in the Western world: the French encyclopedists, Montesquieu, Wesley and the evangelicals, the spread of radical ideas about liberty, fraternity and equality, and the emergence of new economic interests that challenged mercantilism, these created an intellectual ferment out of which came some of the most powerful contemporary Western concepts and notions.

The slave trade and slavery stood out as examples of the denial of freedom and human dignity. Public debate intensified. Passionate partisans produced a flood of pamphlets, but the issues of freedom and human rights remained central. The story of the British abolition movement and emancipation is told in later chapters, but it is appropriate to emphasise the centrality of these two issues in the public debate which the slave trade provoked. They remain central issues in our own time.

CHAPTER VIII

Commerce and War
1739–1763

The North Atlantic Basin, by 1740, had expanded into a great trading area across which the merchant fleets of Britain, France and New England moved ceaselessly, each in a closed circuit that bound mother country and colonies together. Ships, westward bound, carried foodstuffs, manufactured goods, building materials and, from West Africa, slaves. Eastward bound ships from the British and French West Indies carried sugar and molasses, indigo and cotton.

The cargoes shipped from British North American ports reflected the greater economic diversity of the mainland colonies. Virginia and Maryland exported tobacco from their slave plantations; Carolina, cotton, indigo and rice from its tidewater plantations. The middle colonies, self-sufficient in agricultural products, exported cereals, especially wheat, flour and bread, cattle, sheep, hogs, horses, all in great demand in the islands. Farther north, New England exported cod, the best quality for the Catholic countries of Europe and 'refuse fish' for the slave plantations of the West Indies. Next in importance to cod was rum, processed from molasses imported from the French and British West Indies. In the 1660's there were more than 60 distilleries in Massachusetts alone, producing in excess of 2.5 million gallons. North of New England, the French were active in the valley of the St. Lawrence, fanning out from Quebec which Champlain had founded in 1608, and thrusting south down the Ohio.

Spain had passed the peak of her power. Holland's attempt to dominate world trade had been defeated. The contest lay between Britain and France. Each aimed at securing more territory in order to increase the production of staples, secure a larger market for manufactured goods, control the sources that supplied slaves and naval supplies required for enlarging the merchant fleets and navies.

By 1739 the stage was set for war between Britain and France to decide which would gain the ascendancy. 76 years — including 45 years of actual warfare — passed before that question was settled.

As we trace the earlier phases of this conflict we will take note of the attitude of West Indians and of North Americans, particularly their irritation over trading restrictions and the support given to the British forces by their militia, whose officers included George Washington.

The war of Captain Jenkin's ear between England and Spain hung fire up to 1744, when France, Spain's ally, declared war on Britain and on Russia. The immediate cause was the bitter rivalry between two existing sets of sugar colonies. The French Caribbean islands — larger in area and with soil less exhausted — were competing more and more successfully with the English islands in the production of cheap sugar and in trade with Europe and English North America. Since England could not control the supply of sugar, none of the peaceful methods known to mercantilist economists could avail against this growing competition. The Molasses Act, which had been passed in 1733 at the instigation of the West India interest in England to stop French West Indian trade with English North America, proved difficult to enforce, and naturally irritated the North Americans, whose interests it attacked. Fiscal concessions, such as the removal of sugar from the 'enumerated' list in 1739 to permit direct export to Europe, were of little help to the English planters, because they did not remove the basic cause of difficulty — high production costs. Depression in the English West Indies affected too many English interests to be tolerated; and in that time of truculent trade rivalry, if peaceful measures would not serve, war was welcomed as a possible solution of commercial problems.

War offered the English an opportunity to cripple French sugar production, since they could not defeat it in open competition. Planters on both sides disliked the acquisition of fresh sugar-producing territory; they feared that increased production would lower prices within their protected markets. Each side hoped not to acquire and exploit the enemy's colonies but to destroy and depopulate them; to burn the canes, to wreck the machinery, and, above all, to carry off the slaves, who were the most necessary, most valuable, and most mobile part of the planters' capital. Failing the destruction of the enemy's colonies, the next-best thing was to cut off their trade, starve them of provisions and slaves, and prevent them from selling their sugar. In this war naval activity was, in practice, almost confined to this second type of operation. By 1744 the energies of both combatants were taxed elsewhere, in Europe and North America. Forces were not available for major operations in the West Indies, and the fighting there was little more than a rehearsal for the much sterner struggle which was to break out in 1756.

As a rehearsal, the war had lessons to offer. It revealed the disadvantage which the French suffered through having no naval bases in the West Indies. Fleets for particular operations were sent out direct from France. This policy ensured that ships arrived in the West Indies fresh from dockyard and in good repair, and sometimes gave them the advantage of surprise; but it had also serious disadvantages. Having no repair facilities, fleets had to time their sailings so as to arrive after the hurricane season, and leave to go back to France before the hurricane season of the following year. This meant that their time away from France was at most about ten months. Usually it was less, because wooden warships could only carry stores and provisions for about six months. A fleet could not easily be victualled on the station, for the West Indian islands did not then — and do not now — produce any considerable surplus of food. Warships were sometimes sent out *en flûte*; that is, with the lower tier of guns struck down and the space on the gun deck filled with provisions. Some extra stores could be brought out in this way; but it was dangerous for a ship to throw away half of its fire-power if there was any likelihood of its having to fight on the way out. Also, when the fleet arrived it had to put in to harbour to land the extra stores and remount the guns. This was a long and heavy job and had to be done with the help of slaves requisitioned from unwilling planters. Apart from this question of stores, some time might have to be spent in harbour on arrival, in order to establish contact with the military governors and obtain up-to-date intelligence; and a very few days in a West Indian harbour sufficed for men fresh from France to fall ill of yellow fever or malaria, sometimes in such numbers that the fleet could not put to sea. It became axiomatic in French naval circles, therefore, that a force sent to the West Indies must engage the enemy at once or not at all. Over and over again French fleets came out, and returned having accomplished little or nothing.

The English system, first worked out and applied in the seventeen-forties, was quite different. The West India interest in England was already powerful politically; it insisted on squadrons of warships permanently stationed in the West Indies. There were two naval dockyards: one at Port Royal in Jamaica, the other at English Harbour in Antigua. Today, the Port Royal yard has disappeared and that at English Harbour has become a yacht marina and tourist attraction; but in many tricks of speech and manner people in Antigua and Jamaica to this day show the influence of these naval bases, of close contact with ships and sailors through several generations in the hey-day of wooden warships. The West Indian dockyards were not very large or very efficient, but they could effect ordinary repairs; and during the hurricane season ships could either go into dock for refit or could be sent off cruising for prizes in the southern Caribbean, out of harm's way. Food and other stores could be kept in bulk at the dockyards and replenished by convoys from North America. The crews, being on the station for two or three years, had time to fall ill and get well again, though of course a certain proportion always died on first arrival. The station system was expensive and wasteful because it entailed keeping ships hanging about the West Indies for long periods doing nothing, and also because the ships deteriorated and became foul under tropical conditions much faster than at home. The system did not remove the need for major expeditions, because the squadrons were necessarily small; and whenever a fleet of any size broke out from France reinforcements from England had to be sent hurrying after it. Sometimes the reinforcements arrived too late; but in general, for protecting trade and for attacking or defending small and ill-armed islands, small squadrons all the time were better than big fleets occasionally. The English could count on retaining the initiative at sea in the Caribbean for the greater part of every year. The superiority of the English system was eventually recognised by the French themselves, who, somewhat belatedly, established a naval base for the Windward Islands at Martinique in 1784.

The main weakness of the English position was colonial indiscipline. The dependence of the French islands upon North America for grain and timber and upon Ireland for beef should have given the English an important tactical advantage; but in war as in peace the shippers of New England continued to trade with the enemy, either directly or through the neutral Dutch harbours in Curaçao or St. Eustatius. The privateers which sailed from Martinique to prey upon English shipping were often stored with North American provisions; meanwhile the English islands went short, and sometimes had to be supplied with food from England. It was largely the profit-seeking of the New Englanders which prevented the British navy from achieving its object: the commercial isolation of France in the Caribbean. The British imperial structure, like the Spanish, though for different reasons, creaked ominously under the stress of war.

The Treaty of Aix-la-Chapelle, which ended the war in 1748, settled no important question between France and England in the West Indies. No territories changed hands. Four disputed islands in the Windward group — Dominica, St. Lucia, St. Vincent and Tobago — were declared 'neutral', and both parties agreed to evacuate them; but even had the colonial governments honestly wished to carry out this agreement, it would have been difficult to round up the unorganised groups of squatters, mostly French, who drifted in from the older colonies. The islands remained an English grievance and a bone of contention for the next war; in this respect, as in others, the treaty between England and France was only a truce. The commercial treaty of 1750, which supplemented the general European settlement and wound up the maritime quarrel between England and Spain, was similarly inconclusive. It contained no reference to the freedom of navigation in whose name the war had begun. The irritating problem of the Honduras log-wood camps, which had expanded considerably during the war, with the encouragement of Trelawny, the governor of Jamaica, remained unsolved. The South Sea Company had almost ceased to present a problem; it no longer traded; its last 'annual ship' had sailed in 1733, and its slave trade ended in 1739. Under the treaty it received £100 000 in return for the surrender of all claims under the *Asiento*. Thus the English gave up the long attempt to force or persuade the Spaniards to allow direct trade to their colonies, while the Spaniards took a leaf out of the English (and French) book and themselves organised new joint-stock companies to handle certain colonial trades. The trade of Cuba, for instance, was from 1740 to 1760 officially a monopoly in the hands of the Compañia de Comercio de la Habana, which undertook in exchange to build warships and suppress smuggling. Illicit local trade between the English and Spanish islands went on, but it remained as illicit as ever, and could no longer be hidden by the *Asiento*. During the second half of the century the Spanish government proved increasingly willing to reorganise its trade system, and increasingly able to protect its monopoly. What the English lost by the process, the French gained. They had stuck steadily to the lawful channel of trade, consigning goods for Spanish America through Spanish merchants at Cadiz; and the greater part of this trade was in their hands by 1750. Meanwhile their commercial competition in the West Indies and their strategic pressure in North America steadily increased.

Slaving and smuggling to Spanish America, however, were for most West Indians profitable side-lines. The sugar trade was what mattered most, and for British sugar planters the war seemed to have served its purpose. The years from 1748 to 1756 were their golden age. Prices remained reasonably steady and fairly high — the average was *33s. 8d.*, which was 50 per cent higher than that for the decade before the war, and high enough to allow efficient planters a net return of 7 to 10 per cent. Production was increasing steadily — it trebled between 1700 and 1760 — but so was the capacity of the English market, which now absorbed the whole product of the British West Indies, and demanded more. Grocers and refiners in England, indeed, were beginning to murmur at the high prices of British West Indian sugar, and to ask for leave, failing an increase in British production, to import foreign sugar; but no-one in authority in mercantilist England paid much attention to such unorthodox proposals. Jamaica, with its large area of virgin land, was the chief beneficiary of this steady expansion of a protected market; the economy of Barbados and the Leeward Islands was propped up rather than expanded; but for all the British islands, war was the guarantee of prosperity. War had incidental disadvantages — privateering losses, high freight and insurance rates, and so forth, which offset war-time rises in the price of sugar. But war crippled the commerce of the productive French islands; it raised national anti-French feeling; it caused people in England to shelve the economic question of the merits of British dependence on British-grown sugar. War, or the constant possibility of war, in the middle eighteenth century was to the advantage of the British West Indies; and no one in England doubted that the West Indies were worth fighting for.

The Seven Years War began, not in the West Indies, but in Europe and North America, and in the mind of one leading statesman at least — Pitt — there was no doubt that the major purpose of war in the Americas was to safeguard English North America by seizing Canada. Nevertheless, the West Indies were again a centre of heavy fighting, and the forces employed there were far larger than in the previous war; far larger, incidentally, than those used in the simultaneous struggle in India. Great expeditions were sent out on both sides, and their commanders now had orders to annex the enemy's sugar colonies, not merely to pillage them. This change of policy, though supported by the West India interest in London, had its origin in European events. At the outset of the war England had lost Minorca to the French. The capture of this important naval base affected the West Indies directly, by releasing units of the French Mediterranean fleet for service in the Caribbean. Subsequently the English took from the French Cape Breton Island with its great fortress, Louisbourg. Each side considered the possession of both places essential, and each hoped to recover its loss without surrendering its gain. Both therefore set about making other conquests to serve as ransoms at the peace. For this purpose they naturally picked on the valuable and very vulnerable islands of the West Indies. It was to secure a bargaining counter, to avoid surrendering Cape Breton Island for Minorca, that Pitt was moved to attack Martinique; though later in the war, when victory exceeded even his expectation, he began to favour the retention of some at least of England's West Indian gains for their own sake.

The change of policy was favoured even by the West Indians. The presence of full-scale naval war in the Caribbean reminded them of their small numbers and of their weakness against an enemy fleet or a slave mutiny, and forced upon them a more strategic, a less purely commercial appreciation of their position. The planters of Barbados and Antigua, weary of constant alarms, began to realise that their properties would be safer if Martinique, Guadeloupe and the neutral islands were in English hands, at least for the duration of the war. If it were decided at the peace to keep any islands captured from the French, then the dangers of the admission of their sugars to the English market would have to be faced; but even that danger might be avoided by evicting the French inhabitants and by forbidding their English successors to plant sugar. By such arguments as these even the sluggish island militias were stirred to a military activity less purely defensive than usual; and local hostilities ranging from slave raids to plans for outright conquest were endlessly discussed in the first two years of the war.

Ultimately, however, most of the serious fighting was done not by militia-men or by privateers but by the line-of-battle fleets of the contending powers. In 1757 the French launched an ingenious plan of co-ordination by three naval squadrons off North Africa, the West Indies and North America, which damaged English trade considerably and put Jamaica in fear of invasion for some weeks; but the necessity of going to the relief of Louisbourg prevented any of the French admirals from achieving much in the Caribbean. After 1757 the French gave up the attempt to maintain a constant relief of squadrons in West Indian waters. Theoretically the best English naval defence of the West Indies was therefore a thorough blockade of the Channel and Atlantic ports. The English West Indians, however, would never accept this reasoning. They liked to have warships in sight, in their harbours or cruising off-shore. The Jamaicans would not even agree that a squadron off Antigua, up to windward and near the route from Europe, was an adequate defence of their island. They clung to their station squadrons, and clamoured for battle fleets to be sent to the Caribbean.

Late in 1758 Pitt, now possessing in Louisbourg the key to Canada and confident of success in Europe, launched two attacks, one direct and one indirect, against the French West Indies. The indirect attack was against the French stations in West Africa, and culminated in the capture of Gorée by Keppel. This comparatively minor operation achieved economic results out of all proportion to the cost of the force employed. It crippled the French slave trade and seriously hampered the working of the sugar plantations in the French West Indies. Meanwhile a series of English naval victories in the Mediterranean and the Bay of Biscay destroyed or delayed the French fleets intended for America, and created favourable opportunities for England in the Caribbean. The combined naval and military force under Moore and Barrington sent to attack the French West Indies found Martinique too strong for it, but seized, in the spring of 1759, the wealthy island of Guadeloupe. A French fleet under Admiral Bompar arriving just too late to raise the siege. The planters of Guadeloupe were allowed to capitulate on very favourable terms. They were to be neutral between France and England while the war lasted; their goods were to be admitted to English markets; their slaves exempted from *corvée*; they retained French law under English military occupation and were fully protected in possession of their property. English planters, indeed, were forbidden to settle, and nothing was done to alter the French character of the colony. After the initial damage of the fighting had been repaired, the island began to enjoy a new prosperity, for English and American merchants rushed in to supply the food, the timber and the slaves for which it starved. Feckless planters escaped from their debts to French *commissionaires* and were allowed to run up new debts to English factors from Antigua. Best of all, they found at last a safe European and North American market for their sugar. The planters of Guadeloupe were envied alike by their compatriots in Martinique and by their English rivals. This was precisely the kind of conquest most disliked by the English planters; it struck directly at their profits without giving them any permanent promise of security. The flooding of the London market with Guadeloupe sugars was one reason for the drop in sugar prices in 1760, and explains the bitter complaints of the West India interest against the terms of the capitulation.

During the second half of 1759 and through 1760 no major operations were undertaken in the Caribbean, chiefly because the attention of both belligerents was concentrated on events in Europe and North America. In 1761 there followed a period of abortive and insincere haggling over peace, in which Choiseul played for time by demanding terms which England would not accept, in the expectation that Spain would be brought in on the side of France. Apart from its dynastic connection with France, Spain had a number of serious grievances against England. Some of these concerned the West Indies directly; in particular, the question of the logwood camps. The Treaty of Aix-la-

Chapelle had provided for a mutual restoration of conquests; but the English government did not regard the camps as a conquest, and had taken no steps to evacuate them. The governors of Jamaica, indeed, had continued to support the logwood cutters after the end of the war, and the Belize settlement now numbered some five hundred people, with a rudimentary system of government of their own. Further south, on the Mosquito Shore of Nicaragua, English agents continued to intrigue with the Indians against Spanish government, and in 1749 Trelawny even appointed a resident superintendent there. The local Spaniards tried every method, from peaceful penetration by missionaries to armed expeditions, to win over the Indians and to evict the Baymen from their settlements. The Spanish government was prepared to offer supplies of logwood on reasonable terms in return for the evacuation of the camps; but this the English would not accept, being naturally unwilling to depend upon a Spanish monopoly. In 1753 an armed attack, believed to have been ordered by Ensenada in Madrid, was launched against Belize, and the Baymen were temporarily driven away to Black River. They soon returned, and rebuilt their settlement with the help of soldiers from Jamaica; and English indignation over the attack helped to bring about Ensenada's fall from office. The dispute continued to disturb Anglo-Spanish relations, even after the appointment of the anglophile Wall as Foreign Minister.

After the outbreak of the Seven Years War other disputes emerged. The Treaty of Commerce of 1750 had never been executed to Spanish satisfaction. In peace the English had done little to restrain their smugglers; in war they showed the arrogant disregard of the rights of neutral shipping which belligerent naval powers commonly display. The Admiralty either could not or would not control the activities of privateers. Spanish merchant shipping was repeatedly molested, even in Spanish territorial waters. The situation grew worse when the hardpressed French threw open the trade of their starving Caribbean colonies to neutrals, for under the 'rule of the war of 1756' any Spanish ship suspected of having touched at a French colonial port was liable to seizure. Worse still, as the tide of war turned in favour of England and against France, it seemed clear that Pitt intended, if he could, to seize all the French possessions in North America and the Caribbean, including the neutral islands in the Windward group, to which Spain made some shadowy claim. If England and France made peace upon such conditions, Spain would be left to negotiate alone with an England all-powerful in the West Indies. It was in these circumstances that the Spanish government agreed to the Family

Compact of 1761, which bound Spain to declare war before May 1762 if peace had not been made between France and England. Peace was not made, and the English government anticipated events by declaring war on Spain in January.

The entry of Spain into the war brought no relief to France in the Caribbean. In the same month that war was declared Rodney, fresh from England with a powerful fleet, took Martinique. Again a strong French squadron, this time under Blénac, was hurried out from France. Its departure was delayed, however, by repeated interceptions of necessary stores on their way coastwise to Brest, and it reached the West Indies too late to save Martinique. Blénac's arrival off Saint-Domingue in March 1762 caused the usual panic in Jamaica; but Rodney, with his great fleet up to windward, was able to detach a squadron large enough to deter Blénac from attacking Jamaica, and Blénac's expedition soon found itself blockaded harmlessly at Cap Français. It might indeed have been destroyed before it got there, but for the short-sighted cowardice of the governor and council of Jamaica, who insisted on most of the available naval strength remaining in Kingston harbour to protect them.

To the annoyance of the English planting interest, the inhabitants of Martinique were granted a capitulation similar to that of Guadeloupe; though since nobody expected Martinique to be kept at the peace, its capitulation was less likely to be of permanent importance. The neutral islands were less fortunate, no doubt because Rodney thought that his government might wish to retain them. Dominica had surrendered to a North American force in June 1761; Tobago was for all practical purposes British already; and Rodney reduced St. Lucia, St. Vincent and Grenada to submission shortly after the capture of Martinique. Of all the French possessions in the West Indies only Saint-Domingue remained.

Meanwhile Spain, far from helping to save the French colonies, began to lose her own. The English government at once prepared an attack on Havana; and profiting by former experience, the Admiralty planned the operation in detail and avoided the uncertainties and delays which had beset Cathcart's expedition in 1740. The chief difficulty was the presence in the West Indies of Blénac's fleet, which, having failed either to save Martinique or to join with the Spaniards to attack Jamaica, might at least have been expected to go to the help of Havana; especially since Rodney, always ready to subordinate considerations of strategy to those of prize-money, had sent many of his ships away cruising off the Main, and now had none to spare. But Blénac, short of victuals and with half his men sick, allowed himself to be bottled up at Cap Français while the force commanded by Pocock and Albemarle sailed through the islands, picked up more ships and men from Jamaica, and proceeded undisturbed to reduce Havana. Havana had been thought by the Spaniards to be impregnable. Its fall in August 1762 made a great stir; the captors destroyed a considerable Spanish naval force and collected great sums in prize-money, while the English politicians, when they heard of it, were encouraged to raise their peace terms still higher. Two other misfortunes befell Spain in the same year. An English fleet sailing from the East Indies captured Manila; and an invasion of Portugal, intended by Charles III as a diversion, proved an unexpected failure. Lisbon was never in serious danger, and the English, though they abandoned the war in Germany, did not allow themselves to be diverted from Havana. In October 1762 Charles III capitulated. The French had been pressing him for some months to make peace. After the fall of Havana Choiseul had to admit that France and Spain together were no match for England at sea. France could no longer face the strain of unsuccessful war, and in Europe her ally Austria was also at last ready for peace.

The English ministers were almost as eager for peace as Choiseul, though for somewhat different reasons. George III was anxious to be rid of responsibility in Germany. Pitt, who would have fought till he deprived the Bourbons of every colony they possessed, had given place to the timorous and inexperienced Bute. Many English politicians felt nervous about the tremendous ascendancy achieved in the colonial field, and feared a future combination of all the other colonial powers against England. The North American colonists were becoming restive; with Canada subdued, they saw no need of further fighting, and such enthusiasm as they had shown for West Indian conquests had evaporated. They intended, after all, to go on trading to the French West Indian islands, whether those islands became British or remained French. For all these reasons, the Treaty of Paris was concluded in haste and embodied the concessions and compromises which haste entailed.

The numerous and valuable conquests made in the late stages of the war proved an embarrassment to English ministers in their attempts to hasten the peace settlement. Something must be sacrificed to have peace; but something beyond the original objects of the war must be kept to satisfy popular clamour. The principal object of the war had been to safeguard the North American colonies, and to achieve this end there was little doubt that Canada, or part of it at least, would have to be retained; on the other hand, the trade and revenue of Canada were small, and the public reasonably expected the acquisitions at the peace to pay part of the cost of the war. The French West Indian islands would bring in an immediate revenue. They could more easily be settled with Englishmen than the vast spaces of Canada; and West Indian planters habitually returned to England to spend their money, while most settlers in North America stuck to their farms and business and kept their money, if they had any, in the colonies. These were plausible reasons for preferring West Indian to North American acquisitions. Guadeloupe in particular was a tempting prize. The slave traders naturally pressed for its retention. Exporting merchants in England pointed out the need for developing more sugar land, since the British islands were not producing enough sugar to allow for re-export to the Continent. Even the English West India interest was partly converted to a policy of annexation, for the planters and their advocates had learned what dangerous neighbours Martinique and Guadeloupe could be, particularly as privateering bases. Many people in England thought that Guadeloupe should be kept, even in preference to Canada, and the question of Guadeloupe against Canada was made the subject of much acrimonious debate.

It is unlikely that the British government paid much serious attention to this debate so long as Guadeloupe alone was in question; but the conquest of Martinique in 1762 raised the problem of choosing between Canada on the one hand and all the French West Indies except Saint-Domingue on the other. Rodney attached great strategic importance to Martinique. If, as seemed likely, the French would not make peace without Martinique, then England might keep Guadeloupe in payment. Bute, however, apparently thought that France would not yield any settled colony, and decided in the end on a compromise. He agreed to restore both Martinique and Guadeloupe, and, as a necessary adjunct, the French slaving stations in West Africa; but he demanded the cession of Grenada, all the neutral islands and the whole continent of North America east of the Mississippi. These were all almost empty territories, open to English enterprise, and containing few Frenchmen to make trouble for government. With the cession of territory was to be included the right of navigating the Mississippi itself. In the final peace terms all these demands were agreed, except that France insisted on retaining St. Lucia, on the ground that the island was essential to the defence of Martinique — a very good reason, as Pitt complained, for England to keep it; but the French had their way.

Bute's very moderate proposals were as good as the French could hope for, but they ignored the claim of Spain to be considered. Spain had been dragged into war in the interests of France, had suffered serious losses, and was now being urged to make a hasty peace, also in the interests of France. Charles III resented the prospect of Englishmen in the Gulf of Mexico, firmly established in Florida, running their smuggling trade under cover of the Mississippi navigation, intercepting the Mexican *flotas* with greater ease than before. Choiseul was obliged to recognise the force of the Spanish arguments, and decided eventually to buy Spanish acquiescence by ceding Louisiana to Spain.

The old disputes between Spain and England were settled without much difficulty. The logwood settlements in Honduras received for the first time a precarious recognition. Spain agreed to tolerate the presence of the cutters and to respect their property; England agreed not to fortify the camps. Neither the boundaries of the settlements nor the rights of the cutters were defined, and the exact position of the English in Honduras continued to be disputed for the next twenty years. Finally, England restored Cuba to Spain and obtained Florida in exchange; and Spain renewed the treaties of commerce with England which were in force when the war began.

From the English point of view Bute's willingness to make colonial concessions in order — as he thought — to hasten a lasting peace was wasted, for a lasting peace with France was scarcely possible at that time. The long conflict of England, France and Spain in the Americas was by no means ended. Choiseul, far from being contented with England's moderation, began planning and organising for revenge almost as soon as the treaty was signed. Bute's desire for peace merely led him to accept terms less favourable than those he might have obtained; and Pitt, for all his factious ill-temper, was right in saying so. In the West Indies the concessions made were remarkable. Cuba commanded much of the American trade of Spain, Martinique much of the West Indian trade of France, and all these islands were also in close though illicit commercial contact with British North America — a contact which might have flourished the more if it had become open and lawful. There were good reasons, both strategic and economic, for England to retain some of these West Indian conquests; yet all were cheerfully restored, with little to show for their capture. No doubt the risk of prolonging a 'bloody and expensive war' had to be considered, and probably the English peace-makers assumed that English predominance at sea would always assure the mastery of the Caribbean, without the retention of the French and Spanish bases. Yet Pitt's forebodings were to be realised in his own lifetime. The English naval command of the Caribbean, so glibly postulated in the seventeen-sixties, was to prove insufficient in the seventeen-seventies and -eighties to prevent the French from capturing many islands in the Leeward and Windward groups and threatening the safety of the whole of the British West Indies. The great superiority achieved by England in the Caribbean during the Seven Years War — and the last opportunity to unite the greater part of the West Indies under one flag — was thrown away at the peace, in return for continental gains, which, though immense, were some of them very short-lived.

CHAPTER IX

The First American War of Independence 1763-1783

The final rounds in the British-French conflict had yet to be fought. Forty-five years of uneasy peace and global warfare lay ahead. Up to this point four European powers, Britain, France, Portugal and Spain controlled the Americas and the Caribbean, made the critical decisions, regulated trade and commerce. In King William's War and the Seven Year War British and French colonists supported their respective mother countries. Washington commanded American militiamen under bumbling General Braddock, and later they fought alongside British regulars in a successful attack on Louisburg in Nova Scotia and in campaigns in the Ohio Valley. There were no signs then that within ten years Washington would be leading American militiamen against the British.

The clash at Lexington in 1775, between British troops and North American colonists, marked the beginning of the first in a series of American wars of independence that ended in 1823. The Haitian struggle for freedom under Toussaint L'Ouverture ended in 1805 with the independence of Haiti. Bolivar led Gran Colombia to independence in 1819 after routing Spanish troops at Boyaca. Under Jose de San Martin Argentina gained her independence in 1816, Chile followed in 1819 and in 1823 Costa Rica, Guatemala, Honduras, Nicaragua and San Salvador established the Confederation of United Provinces of Central America.

The battle cry was liberty; not abstract liberty which, said Edmund Burke, 'like other mere abstractions is not to be found...the great contests for freedom in this country were from the earliest struggle against despotism and now it moved the people of the Americas to times chiefly upon the question of taxing the people must, in effect themselves, mediately or immediately, possess the power of granting their own money, or no shadow of liberty could subsist'. In 1774 he prophesied that the lovers of freedom would be free. Washington, in general orders from his headquarters in 1776 confirmed that prophecy: 'Let us therefore...show the whole world that a Freeman, contending for liberty on his own ground, is superior to any slavish mercenary on earth.' Toussaint L'Ouverture said this when the French took him captive by treachery: 'In overthrowing me you have cut down in St. Domingue only the trunk of the tree of liberty. It will spring up again by the roots, for they are numerous and deep.' Bolivar repeated the theme on Monte Sacro in Rome: 'Here civilization . . . has shown itself in all its aspects — but as for solving the great problem of man's liberty, it would seem that the matter was unknown and that the solution of that mysterious problem must take place in the New World.' James Monroe enshrined the guardianship of American liberty in United States policy in his message to Congress in December 1823: 'that the American continents, by the free and independent condition which they have assumed and maintained, are henceforth not to be considered as subjects for future colonization by any European power.' Rebellious colonists and rebellious slaves with a passion for liberty put Americans in charge of their affairs in these fifty years.

While these things were being done Britain, and in time other European nations, began to move from a largely agrarian economy to one based on industry. The transition began in Britain in the 1760's, made her the workshop of the world in less than a century, transformed the structure of British society and established her economic ascendancy throughout the Americas.

These events were in the future, but already, in the 1760's, the pace of change was quickening. France, goaded on by the energetic Choiseul, was rapidly rebuilding her navy. She awaited only financial recovery and a suitable opportunity.

The Spaniards had gained a great stretch of the coast of the Gulf of Mexico and had recovered Cuba — with interest, for many of the officers of the British and colonial forces who occupied the island acquired a taste for Cuban cigars, the best in the world, and even more for Cuban snuff; their return home was the beginning of the spread of that taste through Northern Europe and North America. The occupation was important in another direction also: in fostering the development of a young but growing sugar industry. Tobacco, the principal Cuban crop, was grown on small properties; the large slave-worked sugar plantation was comparatively rare; but during the British occupation optimistic traders, who thought that England might keep the island, had introduced some 10 000 slaves, all or almost all destined to work on sugar plantations. The influx of slaves continued after the peace, under an *Asiento* granted in 1763 to the Marqués de Casa Enrile and his associates; and many were also introduced by smugglers, English and Spanish. In general the events of 1762 accelerated — if they did not originate — a striking development and a significant change of direction in the economic activity of Cuba. At the same time, however, a more ambitious and flexible strategy of defence, together with the abandonment of the old convoy system, caused a decline in the purely military importance of Havana and a great increase in that of Puerto Rico, far out to windward. In the post-war years the great forts of San Cristóbal and San Felipe del Morro were developed, on plans derived from Vauban, into the most powerful stronghold in all the Americas. Like the Morro at Havana, these works were paid for by *situados* from Mexico.

The French had lost immense tracts of mainland territory and had ceded a few undeveloped islands; but their position in the West Indies remained strong. Martinique, it is true, had suffered heavily both from English maritime pressure during the war and from the commercial speculations of the Jesuits before, but its good harbours, its fertile soil, and its windward position made it a valuable asset, well worth recovering. It remained the seat of government, and the chief market and shipping station, of the French Windward Islands. Guadeloupe, less important strategically, exceeded Martinique in productivity, and had prospered under four years of British occupation; for during that period it had sold its sugars openly on the London market and had imported some 40 000 slaves through British merchants. Saint-Domingue, relatively untroubled by the war, was now economically much more important than either, and was by a considerable margin the biggest producer of sugar in the West Indies. Finally, the restoration of Gorée assured to the French the all-important supply of slaves, without which the production of sugar under eighteenth-century conditions could not be maintained.

For the French West Indies the Peace of Paris ushered in a golden age. All the energy and trade which had been absorbed by Canada and Louisiana were now directed to the West Indian islands. Their sugar production already exceeded that of the British islands. In 1767, the first year for which sets of comparable figures are available, the French islands exported about 77 000 tons, the British (including the newly ceded islands) about 72 000. The French exports, moreover, included a high proportion — nearly 30 000 tons — of 'clayed' or semi-refined sugar, while the English product was nearly all raw muscavado, the commonest and cheapest form of exportable sugar. In the next three decades both French and English production increased steadily, but the French maintained their lead. On the eve of the Revolution the French islands were exporting about 100 000 tons of sugar annually, the British islands from 85 000 to 90 000. The possibilities of expansion of wealth seemed to some contemporaries to have no limit. 'The labours of the people settled in these islands', wrote the Abbé Raynal, 'are the sole bases of the African trade; they extend the fisheries and culture of North America, afford a good market for the manufactures of Asia, and double, perhaps treble, the activity of all Europe. They may be considered as the principal cause of the rapid motion which now agitates the universe. This ferment must increase, in proportion as cultures, that are so capable of being extended, shall approach nearer to their higher degree of perfection.'

The prosperity of the French islands was due in some measure to their close commercial contact with the British North American colonies; a contact which, even in war-time, proved extremely difficult to break. French sugar was cheaper than English, partly because the French planters still had access to virgin land and were not put to the heavy expense of manuring; partly because the export duties on sugar were lower in the French islands — only 1 per cent and no 'enumeration' duty. Molasses and rum were very much cheaper, because the French preference for brandy, and the heavy protection given to brandy in France, made rum almost unsaleable there, so that French West Indian sugar manufacturers would almost give molasses away to anyone who would come and fetch it. The New Englanders found a ready market in both French and English islands for provisions, chiefly grain and salt fish; for timber, chiefly barrel staves; and for horses. They tended more and more to sell these commodities in the English islands for cash, or bills on London, and to buy sugar and molasses — in defiance of the Molasses Act — chiefly from the French. Some of the vessels engaged in the slave trade followed the same line, turning their triangular trade into a quadrangular one; and undoubtedly some of the French sugar carried to New England in this way was re-exported to England as British grown.

The British islands had had their golden age in the years between the wars, and most British West Indians in 1763 hoped for a return to what they regarded as normal. Those who had fulminated against the capitulations in Guadeloupe and Martinique could congratulate themselves that those islands had been handed back to France, though not in as devastated a condition as the British planters would have liked. Nevertheless, the more far-sighted planters were justifiably uneasy. The older islands were in in bad shape. They still carried a serious economic handicap, in the old $4\frac{1}{2}$ per cent export duty on their produce, which government had never levied in Jamaica and now failed to extract from the ceded islands. Their exhausted land was giving poorer and poorer yields and demanding frequent replanting and generous manuring. These heavy hand-operations in turn necessitated a larger labour force; but indented servants were almost unobtainable and the price of slaves went up and up. For this, the ceded islands were to some extent responsible; they attracted the poorer class of white settler who wished to acquire small holdings, thereby reducing the white population of older colonies; but at the same time they were turning to sugar and demanding slaves for plantation work. The steady expansion of sugar production both in Jamaica and in the ceded islands prevented the price on the London market from rising to cover the increasing cost of production. In the ceded islands, and to some extent in Jamaica, relief could be found by the cultivation of other export crops — coffee (then in high demand in Europe), cacao, cotton; the ceded islands in particular avoided the worst evils of monoculture and absentee ownership. But Barbados and the Leeward Islands were almost entirely, Jamaica largely, dependent upon the export of sugar for their livelihood and all suffered from price fluctuations and high taxation in the years following the war. As an aggravation of misfortune, Jamaica experienced in 1764 a prolonged drought which destroyed both crops and cattle in the northern half of the island.

In these circumstances the British West Indians, as they have always done throughout their history, turned to government for relief. They wanted lower duties on their sugar, cheaper slaves, the prohibition of North American trade with the French islands, and easier facilities for borrowing upon West Indian security; but they found government less automatically willing than formerly to legislate in their interests. The Seven Years War had drawn the attention of English mercantilists to wider economic horizons. Other groups were beginning to make their voices heard. Grocers, refiners and distillers wanted cheap sugar and molasses and did not greatly care whether or not these products were British grown. Slavers wanted a plantation market for their slaves, British or foreign, island or continental, wherever demand was brisk and prices high. Manufacturers of textiles and hardware, in the first enthusiasm of industrial revolution, wanted large, populous and wealthy provinces as markets for their wares, rather than small islands which produced nothing but sugar and bought nothing in large quantity but slaves. Interest was beginning to shift from the West Indies to continental America, North and South; from the Caribbean to the Atlantic as a whole. Ominous things had been said about the West Indies during the debates on the Peace of Paris. Shelburne, defending the restoration of Guadeloupe, had remarked that 'wherever sugar grows population decreases' and that 'our sugar isles weaken and depopulate our Mother Country'. It was the discovery that they were no longer the pampered favourites of government which made the English West Indian planters, factors and merchants band together for the defence of a privileged position which they felt to be threatened. The years following the Peace of Paris saw the rise of the Society of West Indian Merchants and the Society of West Indian Planters and Merchants in London, and a number of similar bodies in the out-ports. The West Indians used all available means, public and private, commercial and political, to urge their views upon government, and organised one of the most compact and powerful parliamentary lobbies England has ever known.

Wealthy, persuasive and determined though they were, the West Indians were not by any means uniformly successful in their political approaches. They lost nothing, it is true. The protection which their sugar enjoyed in the English market was not yet assailed. On the other hand, they failed to gain much. Government in those years was endeavouring to reorganise and tighten imperial administration as a whole, to formulate an imperial policy, and to make the empire pay its share of the cost of the war. Reduction of duties was out of the question. Colonial provincialism, suggestions for the benefit of one group of colonies at the expense of others, or at the expense of Great Britain, were out of favour. In dealing with the question of French West Indian trade, for example, government acceded neither to the North American argument for no duty, or only a negligible duty, on foreign molasses; nor to the West Indian plea for the total prohibition of the trade, or a prohibitive duty. More concerned with financial and administrative reorganisation than with strict adherence to mercantile principles, the Sugar Act of 1764 lowered the duty from sixpence to threepence a gallon; and for the first time effective measures were taken to collect the duty.

In some directions, on the other hand, the West India interest won small but useful victories. One minor but significant achievement was the order given to the victualling office in 1775 to contract for West Indian rum instead of French brandy for use in the Navy. Other victories concerned borrowing facilities in the West Indies. An Act of 1773 — passed against strenuous opposition — permitted foreigners to make loans at 5 per cent interest, with the same rights in recovering debts in peace and war as if they had been British subjects. A further Act, designed to induce wealthy Englishmen to invest in the colonies, authorised the lending of money against West Indian real estate at whatever interest charge might prevail where the property lay, even though the charge exceeded the legal English rate (5 per cent at that time). These measures made borrowing a great deal easier, and West Indians were all too ready to avail themselves of such facilities.

One familiar source of British West Indian profit had formerly been the illicit trade between the British islands and Spanish America. This trade had much declined since the war. Choiseul had persuaded the Spanish government to reduce drastically the duties on the direct trade between Cadiz and the Spanish-American ports, a reduction which favoured France indirectly, since most of the goods carried were French. At the same time, easing of internal restrictions had stimulated Spanish colonial trade, and the colonies were more prosperous than they had ever been. Foreign smuggling had been rendered more difficult by a general tightening up of Spanish administration. The rapacious and venal irregulars who had formerly manned the *guarda costa* service were being replaced by paid men recruited in Spain. The time was not very propitious, therefore, for an attempt to revive the British West Indian trade; but the attempt was made, not indeed by running goods in British ships, but by offering inducements to Spanish ships to trade, within fixed limits, in British West Indian ports.

Free ports already existed in the West Indies. The Dutch islands of St. Eustatius and Curaçao, producing nothing themselves, were prosperous clearing houses for manufactured goods and tropical products, and were used by the shipping of many nations. The French also began, immediately after the war, to develop a free port system, designed in their case to provide sugar estates with plantation supplies. Ports were opened at Martinique and Guadeloupe in 1763, in St. Lucia and at Mole St. Nicholas in Saint-Domingue in 1767. These ports were much frequented by foreign traders, chiefly North American, who exchanged timber, livestock and provisions for molasses, rum and European merchandise; and the trade in general seems to have been a success. The English were not primarily concerned to secure plantation supplies, which they could get readily from their own North American colonies; their object was to earn money to pay for such supplies, by means of an export trade to the Spanish and French colonies. With this end in view they adopted in 1766 a modified form of the free port system already used by the Dutch and the French.

The British Free Ports Act of 1766 was not a departure from mercantilist principles, but in most respects a logical development of them. It opened four ports in Jamaica — Kingston, Lucea, Montego Bay and Savannah-la-Mar, and two in Dominica — Roseau and

Prince Rupert's Bay — to foreign shipping. Foreigners might purchase and export slaves, or any British goods legally imported, except naval stores and tobacco. They might pay for these purchases either in coin or in their own colonial produce, subject to certain exceptions. At the Jamaican free ports it was forbiddean to import goods which Jamaica itself produced — sugar, coffee, pimento, ginger, molasses and tobacco — and manufactured goods. In Dominica, where trade with the French islands was the object of the measure, sugar, coffee, and the rest, were allowed to be imported. Precautions — which proved ineffective — were taken to prevent the re-export of such commodities to North America. They were to be sold in England as foreign produce, the small quantity of sugar produced in Dominica itself being warehoused separately and sold as British grown. These cumbersome regulations in Dominica proved unworkable. It was absurd, in any case, to try to restrict a fertile island to the rôle of a mere entrepôt. The act had little effect in drawing French sugar into British warehouses — except smuggled French sugar which the Dominica planters marketed as their own. In Jamaica a considerable amount of export business was done with Cuba, chiefly in slaves, which were sold to the Spanish Asiento Company, and with Puerto Rico; but the arrangement threw upon Spanish traders the risk of seizure by their own *guarda costas*, and provoked the Spanish authorities to counter-measures, such as procuring copies of the Jamaican customs-house register and prosecuting such of their people as were caught trading. Naturally the Spaniards were wary of such risks. The act revealed that Great Britain would no longer go to war to protect her own subjects in illicit trade; it came too late to arrest the decline in trade with the Spanish colonies and its consequence, the acute shortage of currency. Sugar prices remained low. The coffee market — chiefly in Germany — crashed disastrously in 1773, largely because of duties and restrictions imposed by the German princes. Nature added to the list of disasters in 1772, when a hurricane devastated the Leeward Islands. All in all, the British West Indies were in poor condition. The great days of the slave plantation were passing, leaving behind, as in Virginia and Maryland, a heavy burden of debt, an unfavourable balance of trade with Britain and impoverished land.

The British West Indians, concerned about their depressed economy, watched with dismay the intensifying conflict between the mainland colonies and Britain. At times when self-interest demanded it, as in the case of the Molasses Act, they had used their political power to lobby against the mainland colonies, but there were many close connections, cultural and sentimental as well as commercial between the two groups of colonies. The West Indian colonies had constitutions similar to those of the rebellious thirteen; they had representative government but not responsible government. They had largely the same grievances — taxation without representation, interference with their legislative freedom, an adverse trade balance, the incoveniences and restrictions of the Acts of Trade, though in some respects these last were not as burdensome as in the northern colonies where the economy was more diversified and industrial development was possible. Paliament ensured the under-development of the North American colonies by laws such as the Hat Act of 1732 which prohibited the manufacture of hats and the Iron Act of 1750 which forbad the establishment of iron working establishments and removed the duty on colonial pig iron and iron bar shipped to England.

Reference to events in the northern colonies and Britian in 1767–78 reveal, however, fundamental differences between the two groups. In 1767, Townshend, greatly gifted yet with few accomplishments, persuaded Parliament to impose duties on lead, paint, paper and tea imported into the colonies. The bill irritated the colonists but it might have been accepted by the colonial legislatives if it had not said that part of the proceeds would go toward meeting the cost of the civil list and the salaries of judges. In December of that year John Dickinson, a Philadelphia lawyer, started publishing the Farmers Letter, which almost immediately began to exercise a powerful influence on public opinion; and he stirred opposition to the duties on the ground that Britain hoped it would pass because the amount involved was small, and she could then use it as a precedent for future taxation.

Incensed by this, and by the movement of British troops to Boston, the Massachusetts Assembly refused to quarter the troops. Thereupon the royal governor dissolved the Assembly. The central issue was no longer a dispute over trade regulations but rather the Crown's encroachment on the freedom of the colonial legislature.

In that year (1768) John Wilkes, an English politician who had founded the anti-Lord North paper, the north Briton, and who had been expelled from Parliament for denigrating the King, was elected to Parliament by Middlesex. The government expelled him, Middlesex re-elected him and the process was repeated a third time. The city of London was in an uproar. Middlesex and a large section of the British public, like Massachusetts and the other northern colonies, had a common cause, that of resisting the invasion of their civil liberties. One of the leading advocates of Wilkes was a West Indian planter, William Beckford, Lord Mayor of London. The Council and

Aldermen of the City of London condemned the government's attack on British liberty and on the liberty of the American colonies. This unanimity is not surprising, for, as Edmund Burke emphasized in his speech on Conciliation with America, 'the people of the colonies are Englishmen... They are therefore devoted not only to liberty, but to liberty according to English ideas and on English principles... We cannot, I fear, falsify the pedigree of this fierce people... An Englishman is the unfittest person on earth to argue another Englishman into slavery.'

The American colonists made their protest in their own country. The sense of identity as an American had begun to take hold. Years later de Tocqueville observed that the revolution had already been accomplished in their minds: 'The great advantage of the Americans is that they have arrived at a state of democracy without having to endure a democratic revolution.'

For Beckford and West Indian planter society England was homeland. Defence against the French and a monopoly of the sugar market were essential. Like North America, the West Indies were taxed to pay part of the cost of imperial defence; but there lay the difference.

The North American colonies believed that they did not need the defence for which they were asked to pay. The West Indies needed it and knew they needed it. The islands were rich and vulnerable; their free population was small and many of their leading landowners lived in England. The Royal Navy was their only sure defence. For all these reasons, as well as from loyalty, the British West Indians refused to join the American rebels; the only colony, other than the thirteen, to send representatives to Congress was Bermuda, where a few enterprising people made a business of stealing munitions from the royal arsenals and selling them to the Americans. In the West Indies proper, people smuggled and grumbled, and hoped that the war would be short.

The West Indians could not stay out of the war, however; France in 1778, Spain in 1779, joined in the fighting with the intention not only of assisting the Revolution in North America but also of seizing or plundering the British possessions in the Caribbean. The West Indians suffered all the dangers and hardships of a major international war. Apart from actual fighting, they were heavily taxed, their trade was interrupted and they were cut off from their main source of food. The price of flour in Barbados rose, in the first year of the war, from between *15s.* and *25s.* to between *30s.* and *37s. 6d.* and at times, as in 1780–81, there was a danger of actual starvation. Two major hurricanes and a tidal wave increased the islanders' misery. The slave population of Barbados fell from 68 500 in 1773 to 57 400 In 1783, as a result largely of malnutrition and physical disaster. Jamaica, which grew a larger proportion of its own food and could be more easily supplied from the areas under British control in Georgia and South Carolina, was less hardly hit, but even so the island suffered severe distress.

The planters had difficulty not only in obtaining supplies but in getting their sugars away. In the first year of the war the quantity shipped to London fell by nearly half, insurance rates reached 23 per cent and freights rose similarly. Prices rose too, but with such violent fluctuations that planters could have no certainty of covering their costs at any given moment; and in any case there were limits to what grocers and refiners in England would pay. The refineries, indeed, raised again their old demand that when the price of sugar on the London market reached a certain figure importations of foreign prize sugar at a low rate of duty should be allowed. The West India interest in the House of Commons was again strong enough to block this proposal, but it could not prevent the importation, at British rates, of sugar from Dutch Guiana during its occupation by British forces; nor, more serious still, could it prevent doubling of the British rates of duty in the course of the war.

While Jamaica and Barbados thus experienced the commercial strangulation which in former wars had been the lot of Martinique and Guadeloupe, most of the other British islands suffered actual capture. For the first time in a hundred years the French and Spanish navies were able to establish a superiority of forces in the Caribbean for long periods continuously. The French fleet, thanks to Choiseul, was at the peak of its fighting strength; the Spanish fleet, though less efficiently manned, included many new ships of excellent design, built under French influence. The British, with many ships tied down in support of the armies in America, were hard put to it to provide a defence for their own coasts and had no force to spare for a blockade of the French ports. French and Spanish fleets could cross the Atlantic at will and deliver their attacks in North America or the West Indies, as opportunity, the time of year and the state of the weather suggested; operating in the Caribbean, as a rule, in the spring and early summer, on the continental seaboard in the late summer and autumn, returning to the West Indies with the end of the hurricane season and the onset of the North American winter.

The defences of the outer islands went down like ninepins before these repeated blows. The French began with the capture of Dominica in September 1778. To this the British fleet under Byron replied in kind by taking St. Lucia three months later — a considerable victory, won against d'Estaing's fleet as well as the land garrison. St. Lucia became — as Rodney had always predicted — the base from which the British could watch the movements of the French at their centre, Martinique; but even from this point of vantage the British forces were inadequate to prevent the French capturing St. Vincent and Grenada in the early summer of 1779. Spain declared war in June of that year, but the initial operations of the Spanish fleet were directed against England itself, not against the British West Indies. The combined Bourbon fleets were prevented, as usual, from striking a decisive blow in the Caribbean — against Jamaica, for example — by the shortness of the operating season for fleets sent out from Europe each year. The great armament which de Guichen brought out in 1780 achieved little but an indecisive battle against Rodney's fleet off Martinique.

During all this time the comparative weakness of the British at sea had greatly favoured neutral trade; but the habitual high-handedness of the British Navy in dealing with such neutral ships as it caught trading with the enemy as usual exasperated neutral governments. The Dutch were the people most concerned. Their Leeward Island colony of St. Eustatius was a free port, and a vast depot for the supply of munitions to America. In 1780 John Adams visited The Hague and persuaded the Dutch government to recognise North American independence; and the British, in what was almost the only firm and well-judged stroke to the credit of Lord North's cabinet, declared war. Holland was much less dangerous as an open than as a secret enemy, and St. Eustatius was almost undefended. Rodney, in spite of the damage which his ships sustained in the 1780 hurricane, took the place, with hardly a short fired, early in 1781, and found there over a hundred and fifty sail of contraband traders and a vast stock of goods of all kinds — a greater haul even than Havana twenty years before. The island never recovered from the thorough plunder and devastation to which Rodney subjected it. The three Guianese colonies, Demerara, Essequibo and Berbice, soon followed, and Curaçao might have fallen too, but that Rodney characteristically preferred to lie at St. Eustatius supervising the sale of prizes. He had some justification for making hay while the sun shone; St. Eustatius was recaptured by de Bouillé in November 1781, but by that time most of the loot had been sold or carried away, and Rodney himself was back in England.

Meanwhile Cornwallis had surrendered at Yorktown and the

French fleet was thus released for West Indian operations under its ablest commander, de Grasse. Not only St. Eustatius, but Demerara, Essequibo, Berbice and Tobago were recaptured by the French in the course of 1781. The Spaniards, operating from New Orleans, took Pensacola and reconquered Florida, which they had ceded to Great Britain in 1763; and shortly afterwards captured New Providence, the capital of the Bahamas. The Caribbean obviously was to be the final battle-ground of the fleets, with the British islands, so long coveted, the objects of the triumphant Bourbon combination.

St. Kitts fell early in 1782. Its small British garrison was shut up in the fortress of Brimstone Hill by an army of 8000 men landed by de Bouillé, and Hood's bold and successful action against de Bouillé's ships in Basse-Terre road came too late to affect the issue ashore. The inhabitants did nothing to help the garrison. Their capitulation to the French was unheroic, but it was prudent common sense; and by it they secured terms very like those granted by the British to Guadeloupe in the previous war. The terms were so favourable, indeed, that men of property, whose plantations had been saved from plunder by the surrender, chiefly feared that their good relations with the French commanders might be endangered by the patriotic indiscretions of the blacks and the poor whites. In Nevis and Montserrat, which surrendered shortly afterwards, events followed much the same course.

It was at this critical juncture that Rodney returned from England with a fleet which, joined to Hood's squadron, made him approximately equal to de Grasse in strength. He brought de Grasse to action in April 1782 near the Saintes, the small rocky islets between Guadeloupe and Dominica, and in the battle which followed his genius as a tactician more than redeemed the negligences of which — in pursuit of prize-money — he had been guilty in the past. De Grasse himself and seven of his ships were taken, and his fleet scattered. The attack on Jamaica was put off, and eventually abandoned, for towards the end of the same year the combatants, compelled by their financial exhaustion and their enormous commercial and maritime losses, began to treat for peace. In the Treaty of Versailles Great Britain recovered Grenada, St. Vincent, St. Kitts, Montserrat, Nevis and Dominica. The right to fell logwood in Central America was restored on the former ambiguous and precarious terms. New Providence had already been recaptured. France recovered St. Lucia. The only changes in Caribbean territory were the cession of Florida to Spain and Tobago to France. These were trivial results indeed for years of bitter and destructive fighting; but nobody in France, Spain or England yet appeared to question whether the West Indies were worth the enormous cost of war.

The British West Indies had been the scene of the fiercest and most destructive of the Caribbean land fighting during the war; and the British West Indies were the worst sufferers by the terms of the peace, which recognised the United States as an independent country. The immediate reaction of the West Indians, who had resented the war from the first, was an attempt to ignore its results. Their representatives in London petitioned for a resumption of trade on the old terms. The petition — not unnaturally in the circumstances — was refused. The logical but rigid views expressed in Lord Sheffield's *Observations on the Commerce of the American States* (1783) found favour with Parliament; the more liberal views of Pitt were rejected. The United States were now a foreign power, outside the system of imperial preferential trade. An Act of 1783, subsequent Orders in Counil, and a consolidating Act in 1788, together laid down the new policy. They provided that sugar, rum, molasses, coffee and pimento could be exported to the United States on the same terms as to a British colony; timber, livestock, grain, flour and bread could be imported from the United States, but only in British ships; United States meat and fish could not be imported at all. Supplies formerly obtained from the thirteen colonies must now be sought in Canada, Nova Scotia, and Newfoundland, in limited quantity and at a higher price.

Attempts were made from 1784 to persuade government to extend the Free Ports Act to allow American ships to trade to British West Indian ports on the same terms as Spanish and French colonial ships. The French had taken action on these lines immediately after the war; *arrêts* of 1783 and 1784 had opened still more ports in Saint-Domingue and the French Windward Islands to foreign shipping, and slaves and great quantities of provisions were being brought in by American ships. The British Board of Trade, however, though it studied the French regulations in some detail, refused to entertain so glaring a departure from the principles of the Acts of Trade, and the British West Indians, failing to twist the Free Ports Act to their own purposes, lost interest in the Act. The Free Port trade before the war had been largely in the hands of North Americans settled in the West Indies. After the war it languished despite all the efforts of the British Government to revive it.

The obvious recourse of the British West Indians was smuggling; and once again the Navy made itself unpopular, as Nelson did at Nevis, by attempts to enforce the law. But the price of supplies still went up. White oak staves for hogsheads in 1784 cost four or five times their pre-war price. Rice, formerly imported from the Carolinas, more than doubled in price as a result of the war. Meat and fish from Canada cost 30 to 40 per cent more than pre-war imports from the thirteen colonies. Local food crops in Jamaica were devastated by hurricanes in three successive years, in 1784, 1785 and 1786, and the lieutenant-governor reported the loss of 15 000 slaves as a result of famine. At the same time the duty on sugar, increased to meet the cost of the war, was raised again to *12s. 4d.* in 1787, to *15s.* per hundredweight in 1791. No wonder that reports were all of distress, of the burden of mortgages, of estates sold for debt. It is true that the quantity and value of the sugar sent to England was still increasing — it increased by about 30 per cent from 1772 to 1788; but most of the profit was absorbed by the London factors and did not reach the planters. West Indians were becoming acutely aware of the twin dangers of over-dependence on sugar as a cash crop for export and on imported meat and grain for food, and were eagerly seeking ways of escape. In 1791 the Jamaica Assembly resolved that 'Every encouragement is to be given to the cultivation of Yams, Cocos, Maize, Plantains and such products as the Breadfruit, Nutmeg, Cloves, Cinnamon. . . and Coffee: it being believed that the cultivation of such exotics would, without doubt, in the course of a few years, lessen the dependence of the sugar islands on North America for food and necessaries; and not only supply subsistence for future generations, but, probably, furnish fresh incitements to Industry, new improvements in the Arts, and new subjects of Commerce'. Coconuts, coffee and nutmeg did indeed become valuable crops, taking their places beside the native cacao and pimento; and Barbados and the Leeward Islands, towards the end of the century, achieved an extraordinary expansion of their production and export of cotton, which a newly mechanised industry in England was demanding in vast quantity. At the same time, the British government was sufficiently impressed by the urgency of the food problem to send warships cruising in the East Indies and Pacific to collect plants for introduction into the West Indies. Nevertheless, sugar remained the chief crop and the determining factor of West Indian life. The British sugar islands were to enjoy one more reprieve, a brief Indian summer of prosperity and public consideration, before the long bleak neglect of the nineteenth century. This reprieve resulted not from efforts to diversify their economy — useful though such efforts were — but from the destruction of the rival French sugar trade by the disasters of revolution and resulting war.

CHAPTER X

A House Divided Against Itself

While the North Americans, guided by Montesquieu's Doctrine of the Separation of Powers, were drafting a constitution that would protect them from future tyranny, the West Indian colonists were striving to perpetuate their brand of tyranny in the sugar islands. Self-interest, idealism and an emerging national consciousness held the mainland states together but in the islands division and coercion were the key words. Elsa Goveia, in her *Study of the Slave Society of the Leeward Islands at the end of the Eighteenth Century*, describes how racial discrimination was woven into the fabric of social life: 'West Indian whites in the plantation colonies had come to regard their racial identity and exclusiveness as the bulwork of their power and privileges and they used their control of the colonial society to ensure that no Negro, slave or free, should be able to regard himself as the equal of a white, however poor or humble his origins or status might be...racial inequality and subordination had become the fundamental principles of economic, political and social organisation. The slave societies of the islands was integrated on the basis of a hierarchy of racial groupings linked to differences of civil and political status and of economic and social opportunity.'

Elsa Goveia's analysis leads us to a theme which, like the black struggle for freedom, gives continuity to Caribbean history and provides the people of the United States and the Caribbean with a base of shared historical experience. It is the struggle for civil rights which began in the islands with free non-white people and, in the nineteenth century, included East Indian indentured labourers. The two themes, though closely intertwined, are separate. Political independence and acts of emancipation made possible the creation of a free society but they did not signify the end of racial discrimination or the establishment of a just society. In Haiti, for example, after the declaration of independence and the expulsion of the whites, a brown élite seized power, consolidated its hold on positions of privilege and used skin colour to separate themselves from black patois-speaking Haitians. In

Grenada, free mulattoes obtained most of their demands for full citizenship in 1823, and in Jamaica the legislature passed an act abolishing civil disabilities in 1834, but in both countries the ethnic factor continued to determine social standing up to and beyond the 1970's.

Alongside these dominant themes there runs a process which, up to recently, was disregarded or considered of no importance, the adjustment of the blacks to their new world environment. It was, indeed, much more than an adjustment or an effort to survive; it was a putting down of roots by the Africans, the only group of immigrants to come to the Americas against their will. The motivation to settle was not there, nor commitment to a principle such as that which sustained the Puritans when, as William Bradford said 'what could sustain them but the spirit of God and His Grace?'. The blacks were sustained by an almost unreal resilience of spirit, an ability to do what had to be done though it was not of their choosing, by a creative pragmatism. Gradually, throughout plantation America, they fashioned folk cultures that, whether in Brazil or Surinam, the Guianas, the islands or the Deep South, all had certain unique features that sprang out of the African heritage and the African experience of the slave plantation.

Let us turn, now, to the condition of the sugar islands on the eve of revolution and war. In the three centuries following their discovery they had produced for export a series of major crops — tobacco, cacao, indigo, sugar, cotton. Sugar was incomparably the most important, yielding greater return to the acre and driving out most of the other crops from the smaller islands. Coffee was important in Jamaica and Saint Domingue, where it could be grown in different places, in different soils and at different altitudes. Most of the islands depended on the cultivation, manufacture and export of sugar and to that extent their economy can be called a monoculture.

There was an inexorable tenacity about sugar. Once a mill and boiling house had been established, land bought and planted to cane, slaves purchased and trained, there was no breaking its grip on the place. The preparation was too costly and too specialised to allow change; the alternatives were to produce sugar or ruinate. During the eighteenth century the scale of manufacture tended to increase, and with it the intensity and completeness of monoculture. The slow and primitive cattle mills gave place to windmills, which ground much faster; their ruined towers can be seen on every side in the Leeward Islands. Windmills in their turn were replaced, wherever the supply of water allowed, by more powerful and reliable water-mills. In the latter half of the century great ingenuity was exercised in Saint-Domingue and in Jamaica, in designing and fitting huge over-shot wheels which could be turned by comparatively small streams, the water being carried by aqueducts to the point where power was required, and then channelled away to irrigate low-lying fields. The ruins of many fine aqueducts and mills solidly built of cut stone still stand as monuments to the prosperity and energy of the industry at this time. All this improvement in machinery demanded a quicker flow of canes to feed the iron maws of the mills. More land had to be taken in, more slaves bought and trained; more and more capital was needed and was obtained by mortgages and other forms of borrowing. Patrick Browne, in his *Civil and Natural History of Jamaica* (1756), writing of Jamaica in its most prosperous days, remarked that the planters, 'though rich and in easy circumstances, are seldom out of debt, for the charges attending a sugar settlement are very considerable and their natural propensity to increase their possessions constantly engaging them in new disbursements and contracts'. This was all very well while prices were high and steady; but every monoculture is vulnerable to fluctuations in price. A monoculture which exports the greater part of its product and which operates under a heavy load of capital debt is trebly vulnerable.

The largest part of a planter's capital was sunk in his slaves. The peculiarities of sugar cultivation demanded a large and disciplined force of unskilled labour, available at short notice, capable of being concentrated and driven hard during the seasonal crises of the plantation year. Of these crises, the most important was 'crop' — the period of several months in the spring of every year when the cane was cut and milled and the sugar made. All careful planters agreed on the importance of getting crop over as quickly as possible. During crop all the ordinary work of cultivation ceased; the mill ground incessantly day and night; and there was little rest for man or beast. The work was not particularly skilled: the only manual jobs which called for skill and judgement were those of boiling and of 'striking' — the damping of the fire under the 'tache' or final copper when the syrup was sufficiently evaporated to allow the sugar crystals to form. But the work of cutting and carting the cane, ladling the syrup from one boiler to another in the boiling house and manhandling the heavy casks to the curing house, where they stood for weeks while the molasses dripped away — these were laborious tasks on which every available hand was needed, by shifts, day and night while crop lasted.

The exigencies of crop fixed the size of the labour force, without which an estate could not be worked; and this fact helps to explain the laborious and primitive nature of field operations during the rest of the year. The slaves were there all the time; they could not be paid off, as casual cane-cutting labour is paid off today; they might as well be used. There was very little incentive, therefore, for planters to introduce labour-saving devices or even to conduct their field work by ordinary European standards of efficiency. The biggest operation of the planter's year, next to crop, was the replanting of cane. Cane roots could be left in the ground after cutting, to send up ratoons which could be cut and milled the following year; but ratoons yielded less sugar each year, and after a period of three or four years the roots had to be grubbed up. About a third to a quarter of the land in cane, therefore, must be replanted each year, in rotation. The ground was prepared by the process known as 'holing'; slaves armed with heavy digging hoes dug out holes some four feet square and nine inches deep, into which manure was forked, and cane cuttings planted. As the cane grew it was banked up by hoeing the soil back into the hole. The planting process was extremely and unnecessarily laborious, and could have been done far more quickly and efficiently by the use of ploughs; but a planter had little incentive to buy ploughs and to train ploughmen and plough cattle when he could dispose, out of crop, of the labour of a large gang of slaves. The plough was only beginning to make headway in most islands at the end of the eighteenth century.

The rest of the slaves' year was occupied in harrowing, trashing, weeding (this last a job for children) and in the odd jobs of any estate — cutting wood, cleaning drains, patching roads and so on. Some field hands naturally became specialised as carters or as penners in charge of cattle. Most plantations had also a certain number of trades-men among their slaves — carpenters, coopers, masons, and so on; on large properties it was not uncommon to employ a few European workmen, paying them a high wage and requiring them to train slaves in their trades. These European artisans were troublesome employees, difficult to fit into the social structure of an estate; but the quality of the masonry and joinery in eighteenth-century mills and estate houses shows that the training they gave was not wasted; that the African slave was perfectly capable of becoming a skilled craftsman, and was willing to learn if some small incentive could be provided. Money and greater freedom of movement were both in-centives towards this end. A skilled slave was a valuable piece of property; the practice of hiring out such slaves by the day or by the job was common, and the slaves had considerable opportunities of earning money for themselves, over what their owners received for their hire. Finally, in addition to field hands and tradesmen, a number of slaves — often an unnecessarily large number — were occupied in the domestic service of great house and overseer; to take a slave off domestic or specialised work and send him (or her) to field labour was usually regarded as a punishment; the reverse process, a promotion.

The lodging, clothing and feeding of these armies of slaves was one of the major problems of the West Indian economy. Slaves usually built their huts themselves, of timber, wattle-and-daub and thatch, mostly grown on the estate. Two suits a year was the usual allowance in both French and British islands — and various types of coarse linen cloth — osnaburg, Dutch stripes, Guinée bleue — were manufactured expressly for this market in England and France. As for food, the proprietor of a plantation could import it, or grow it on part of his land, or allow land and time to his slaves to grow it for themselves. In Saint-Domingue and Jamaica, which were the chief sugar-planting areas in the eighteenth century, it was the custom to set aside marginal land, usually in the foothills, as provision grounds. Slaves were able to grow there all their own vegetable requirements — yams, plantains and the like — and to have a surplus for sale at the Sunday markets which were the main social gatherings of the slaves' week. This habit was of great importance for the future, for it prepared the development of the independent peasantry who inhabit the hills of Haiti and Jamaica to this day. In the outer islands mountain land was not usually available in sufficient quantity for provision grounds; planters used part of their land for growing maize and plantains — planting corn was traditionally the task of the 'second gang' composed of old men, nursing women and older children; but even in Martinique and Guadeloupe considerable amounts of corn, rice and the like had to be imported; and islands such as Antigua, where nearly all the land was either in cane, or cotton, or pasture, imported nearly all their food. Throughout the sugar islands such animal food as the slaves got — chiefly salt fish and an occasional treat of salt beef — came from outside (as of course did the wine, the wheaten flour and other delicacies which European taste demanded). Most plantations throughout the area had to devote at least half or two-thirds of their land to the production of food for slaves, pasture for draught animals, and woodland for fuel and timber; but nevertheless all the islands were dependent to some extent — some almost entirely — on imports of food for their slaves. Interruptions of supply, such as occurred in time of war, always caused distress and sometimes widespread disaster.

Governments in France and England, and in the several islands, were very keenly aware of the danger of starvation in time of war. Both during and after the War of American Independence, strenuous attempts were made to introduce new food plants. Two plants of very great economic importance were introduced in the course of the war. The ackee tree came to Jamaica from West Africa in 1778. The famous gastronomic marriage which gives Jamaica its most characteristic dish dates from that time. As had often happened in the past, the ships which brought slaves to the West Indies brought also the plants with which they were to be fed. The first ackee slips were bought by Dr. Clarke, the first island botanist of Jamaica, from the captain of a slaver. More important still was the mango, an Asiatic tree which now grows all round the world within the tropics. The mango has had a long assoication with the slave trade. To this day in some parts of Central Africa lines of mango trees planted by Arab slavers mark the routes down which slave caravans were driven to the coast. The first plants to reach the West Indies were part of a collection despatched to the French islands from Mauritius at the command of the French government, in 1782. The ship carrying the collection was taken in prize by an English frigate, H.M.S. *Flora*, Captain Marshall. The admiral commanding on the station — the great Rodney himself — recognising the potential value of the capture, sent the plants to Jamaica, where they were propagated in Mr. East's garden at Gordon Town. Like the ackee, the mango flourished spontaneously and has spread throughout the West Indies. Many improved varieties have since been introduced, and possibly no single plant is now more important in feeding the very poor during the summer months.

Not only West Africa, but the Far East and the Pacific were laid under contribution. Cook's voyage had revealed a wealth of plant life hitherto unknown to Europeans. The breadfruit tree, found and described by Cook at Tahiti, especially caught the public imagination, and in 1787 H.M.S. *Bounty* was ordered to Tahiti to collect breadfruit and other plants. She was commanded by William Bligh, who had been Cook's lieutenant. The mutiny of part of the ship's company prevented Bligh from accomplishing his task; but in 1793 he was despatched upon a similar errand in the even more appropriately named *Providence* brig, and this time returned with a cargo of manna which included several hundred young breadfruit trees. The trees were planted in the government botanical gardens at Bath in St. Thomas, and from there distributed all over the island. Incidentally the foundation of a number of botanical gardens in various parts of the West Indies at this time was evidence of the importance attached to the problem of introducing new forms of cheap starch for feeding field labourers, as well as of a general interest in botany for its own sake. Bligh received handsome recognition of his services from the

Jamaica Assembly; but the slaves perversely refused to eat the breadfruit, preferring the more familiar yams and plantains. Breadfruit was fed to pigs for fifty years. It was not until after Emancipation, in the middle of the nineteenth century, that it came to be widely adopted for human food.

From the food of slaves one passes naturally to their discipline and management. The age was a barbarous one. So were its penalties. The amount of sheer evil in Europe was high. In Britain, for example, where the peasantry were better off than in Europe, apprentices were beaten and murdered, children taught to rob and a favourite national festival was a hanging day at Tyburn. Keith Feiling, in his History of England, writes, 'In London the existence of the poor could hardly be considered life. Until 1750 burials stood to baptisms as 3 to 2; the same year St. Margaret's, Westminster, found that 83 of 106 individuals in its workhouse had died; from 1730 to 1749 London infantile mortality averaged 74 per cent.' Sailors and soldiers were flogged without mercy and subjected to other barbarous forms of punishment.

The penalties were even more severe in the sugar islands, where there were no restraints against arbitrary punishment and fear of rebellion killed any natural feeling of sympathy or pity in the white minority. In 1748, for example, the Jamaica Assembly rejected a bill that would have prohibited the mutilation or dismembering of slaves by their owners without the consent of a magistrate. The slaves were viewed as property and the owner would tolerate no interference with his property rights. In the last half century or so of West Indian slavery the treatment of slaves undoubtedly grew milder, partly because of the steady increase of the proportion of creole slaves — people who knew 'the ropes' and the language and were less likely to fall foul of the authorities than slaves fresh from Africa; partly because accumulated experience of slave management taught less savage and more effective ways of making them work; partly because anti-slavery agitation compelled colonial assemblies to make laws protecting slaves against cruel and irresponsible masters. By then the barbarities described by Sloane were unknown, or at least very rare. A slave's expectation of decent treatment depended upon his owner, who was likely to act in conformity with current opinion and custom if he were resident; but many owners were not resident; and, resident or not, an owner's wishes were interpreted, again arbitarily, by the overseer, by the book keeper and by the driver with his cart whip in the field, who was himself a promoted slave with all the promoted slave's temptations to exercise a petty tyranny.

Mutiny or the fear of mutiny was a constant feature of plantation life in most West Indian islands. Most risings were quickly put down, but a few were successful, and nearly all were bloody and indiscriminate. The Danish island of Saint John, for instance, was the scene of a rising in 1733 in which *all* the resident Europeans were murdered, with the exception of a handful who fled to St. Thomas. In due course troops were sent from Martinique, who methodically hunted down and shot the rebels, so that the island was deserted except for a handful of fishermen, until recent times, when it has become an expensive and exclusive resort for wealthy North Americans. Both Jamaica and Saint-Domingue had bad reputations as the scene of frequent mutinies. This may have been due partly to the presence in the mountain forests of villages of 'maroons' — the descendants of many generations of runaways — whose jungle freedom might inspire slaves with the desire to imitate, and who sometimes harboured fugitives; though in Jamaica the two maroon 'wars' of 1734 and 1795 had terminated in treaties whereby the maroons were to be available as mercenaries to track down runaway slaves; and very savage auxiliaries they were. Considering the slovenly and haphazard discipline of many plantations, and the small number of white inhabitants, it is surprising that revolts were not more frequent still; conversely, considering the dark undercurrents of resentment, the lurking danger of revolt lying beneath the smiling scene that casual visitors so often described, it is astonishing that the resident whites were not more vigilant. Habit and long familiarity no doubt supplied the chief explanation, on both sides; plantation slavery also, impersonal and wholesale though it was, did not entirely preclude the growth of affectionate loyalties, particularly where household slaves and stable hands were concerned. But the chief source of hope and friendship lay in the teaching of missionaries.

The eighteenth century was not a conspicuously religious age. Neither French nor English colonial governments — unlike the Spanish in earlier times — made serious provision for the religious instruction of slaves. The *Code Noir* did indeed proclaim its chief end to be 'maintenir la discipline de l'Eglise catholique'; but the chief methods of giving effect to this aim consisted in negative measures such as the expulsion of Jews, the prohibition of Protestant worship in public, the confinement of public office to Catholics, and so forth. In the British islands the eighteenth-century torpor of the Established Church was more pronounced than in England itself. The West Indies — absurdly — were part of the diocese of London. The clergy were often indolent or absent; few of them paid much attention to catechising slaves. Nor did private piety provide much stimulus to effort. The bequest of the Codrington estates in Barbados — complete with their labour force of slaves — to the Society for the Propagation of the Gospel, was very exceptional. Codrington had no imitators on a comparable scale, and his benefaction was rendered almost ineffective in the eighteenth century by mismanagement of its funds. The Christian instruction of slaves in the British islands was left largely to sectarian missionaries, who achieved their biggest eighteenth-century successes in Jamaica.

As early as 1754 four Moravian missionaries had arrived in the island, the first of a devoted and successful band. The American blacks who introduced the Baptist creed about the end of the War of Independence were not people whom the most humane planters could regard with much confidence, and the first English Baptists did not arrive until 1814. Before that the Methodist mission made its beginning in 1789 and the Scottish Missionary Society in 1800. The missions provoked intermittent opposition, which became more obstructive and violent as planters began to associate missionaries, rightly or wrongly, with the spread of anti-slavery ideas; but opposition could not prevent the alteration in the tone of society which the missions in Jamaica and Antigua slowly brought about. The missionaries might not be able — and some of them certainly were not willing — to teach slaves to rest content in their slavery; but they could, and did, teach slaves ways of life which discouraged murderous mutiny.

Making all allowance for these various palliatives, legal, economic, religious and humane, it is clear that the slave society of the sugar islands was, at best, vaguely restless, inarticulately unhappy; at worst savagely and explosively resentful. Slave labour was unwilling, wasteful, inefficient. It was expensive, both because of the high capital cost of buying slaves, and of the high recurrent cost of feeding, clothing, supervising, and coercing them. It was employed because there seemed to be no alternative way of making sugar. What, then, of the people who ran the system, and — in a financial sense at least — profited by it? How did dependence on slaves affect the slave-owners? For one thing, it drove them away. Next to slavery itself, the most striking characteristic of West Indian society was absentee ownership. This was especially true in the largest and most prosperous of the sugar colonies — Saint-Domingue and Jamaica; but it was true to a greater or less extent wherever sugar was grown. There were considerable numbers of European smallholders in some islands; but the economic and social state of the *petits blancs* in Martinique and

Guadeloupe, of the 'redlegs' in Barbados, was not such as to tempt other Europeans to imitate them. Except among merchants, shop-keepers, and a handful of professional men, the ambition of most white West Indians not born to property was to manage an estate, then to own one, and ultimately to retire to Europe on the proceeds. The general disinclination to reside continuously in the West Indies was attributed to many causes: the unhealthy climate (a much exaggerated cause); the lack of cultured society and entertainment (though this was as much a consequence as a cause of absenteeism); the lack of educational facilities for children. To these should probably be added the insecurity and — to any moderately sensitive person — the unpleasantness of living at close quarters with a slave society based on coercion; the large number of West Indian properties which fell into the hands of residents in England through the foreclosure of mortgages; and the discovery that growing sugar was less lucrative than dealing in it. A considerable number of successful planters — the Pinneys of Nevis, the Lascelles of Barbados, to quote only two examples — returned to Europe not immediately as country gentlemen but as factors, selling sugar on commission, and advancing credit to their planter correspondents. Some of them did very well at it, thus increasing four- and five-fold the fortunes which originated in the cane-fields of the West Indies, and made possible — for the skilful or the lucky — landed opulence, public office, and political influence in England.

The absentee proprietor has long been the scapegoat of the West Indian economic scene; and before examining the economic inefficiencies of absentee ownership it is only fair to recall that without it the West Indies would have been unable to present their difficulties and needs to their home governments with force and success, as they did, in fact, for many years. The absentee was not only a powerful advocate at home; he was also a link with European culture. To him the West Indies largely owe their lovely heritage of eighteenth-century buildings — now, alas, fast crumbling into ruins — and a considerable body of historical, scientific, and literary work. Absenteeism, it should be remembered, is a relative term. Estates — especially slave-worked sugar estates — do not run themselves. Absentee proprietors often found it necessary to visit their West Indian properties, to see conditions for themselves, to check the dishonesty or incompetence of their representatives and employees, to take their place in local society and be entertained with the lavishness and deference due to their possessions. More sensitive than resident planters, many of them (like 'Monk' Lewis in Jamaica) used their visits to effect improvements in the conditions and treatment of their slaves; and their visits were usually periods of festivity on their estates. Usually the visits were short, however — a year or two at most. Having set matters to rights, the owners returned to Europe, and plantation life slipped back into its old slovenly routine. Many of the elegant 'great houses' stood empty most of the time, or were occupied by overseers, often with their slave concubines and a troop of mulatto children. The resident planters and the handful of resident professional or business men stood attorneys for the absentees. A single attorney might be responsible for a dozen estates, exercising a cursory supervision over the overseers. Every overseer wanted to become an attorney. Overseers were paid annual salaries — not very generous as a rule, considering their responsibilities, and the hard and lonely life they had to lead, in the fields all day, and half the night in the boiling house in crop time. It is not surprising that many of them made ends meet by means of illicit perquisites, using their employers' slaves for their own undertakings, feeding their own animals upon their employers' produce, and so on. Attorneys moved in a different social class and had opportunities for peculation on a larger scale, especially if they happened to be merchants as well as planters. Sometimes a planter would act as attorney for an absent friend without remuneration, but most attorneys received a commission for their trouble, calculated upon the gross shipments of sugar; a system of payment which constantly tempted them to sacrifice the long-term interests of the estate to considerations of immediate profit. Thus, not only was estate labour expensive and unreliable; estate management also, being inadequately supervised, was often inefficient and dishonest. Owners, attorneys, and overseers often drew more income between them than the estates could bear. The more prudent invested their profits, but in Europe, not in the West Indies. The more feckless squandered in good times, borrowed in bad, and carried on their business under an increasing load of debt.

The resident planter-attorneys, little groups of local Pooh-Bahs, were the real rulers of island society; they filled the public bodies — not only the nominated councils, but also the elected but no less oligarchic assemblies, which had existed from the beginning in the British islands, and were introduced into the French by decree in 1787. Through these bodies they were able, as a rule, to impose their views upon the royal representatives, and especially to prevent any serious modifications of slavery. They supplied the officers for the local militias in the British islands, and for the *maréchaussées* created in the French islands after the Seven Years War. In the British islands, planters also filled, in effect, most of the public offices; for though the more important officials — colonial secretaries, attorney-generals, provost-marshals, and the like — were appointed by letters-patent in England, the actual work was commonly done by deputies resident in the islands, who were remunerated by fees and who paid a rent for their deputations to the principals. The principals tended to be friends of ministers, persons politically prominent or useful in England. Their appointment was a kind of pension. Office, like land, was thus a form of property, often owned by absentees; a circumstance which helps to explain the venality and incompetence of eighteenth-century colonial administration, and the sense of frustration which afflicted all energetic and conscientious governors.

West Indian society was elaborately stratified. Naturally a clear legal and social line divided free men, participants in society, from slaves, the instruments of wealth. Another line, less sharp but still important, divided white from black or brown among those who were free (white men had almost disappeared from the ranks of those who were not free). Among the free and white there were still further subdivisions based upon wealth and social standing. In the French islands a recognisably sharp division separated the *grands blancs*, who were considerable proprietors, from the *petits blancs*, who were smallholders, small shopkeepers, artisans, or beachcombers. In the British islands the attorney did not, as a rule, sit with the overseer nor the overseer with his poor devils of book-keepers. In both sets of colonies full participation in local political life was naturally confined to those who were both free and white and who owned property. There were distinctions among slaves too — brown from black, creole from African, skilled from unskilled, household from praedial, to say nothing of the differences between tribes among those recently arrived from Africa. It is impossible to say how much these distinctions meant to plantation slaves, especially since some of them arose from the economic needs of the estate rather than from social differences; but many risings were organised and led by creoles, often trusted household slaves with some smattering of education. Toussaint, as we shall see, was such a person. A favoured place in the slave hierarchy did not necessarily make a man more contented with slavery.

A slave could buy his freedom under certain conditions — the rules varied from place to place — or he could be manumitted by the act of his owner. Some planters freed their slaves and turned them adrift when they became too old to work, in order to be rid of the expense of feeding them. Some inserted clauses in their wills granting freedom to favourite slaves; though this was held by some to be a dangerous practice, because it tempted slaves to hasten their freedom by poisoning their masters. Owners often liberated their slave concubines or their mulatto children; and *petits blancs*, especially in the French islands, quite often married slave women, who thus became free. By one way or another, a large class of free coloured people grew up in the course of the eighteenth century. Some of them acquired property and became prosperous. They developed a characteristic dislike and contempt for slaves and for black people generally; but at the same time they attracted the envy and hatred of the poor whites without acquiring *entrée* into the society of white planters. Thus, whereas in the early part of the century society had been stratified almost entirely according to wealth and status, in the latter part colour in itself became a more and more important element in stratification. The dislike and suspicion with which white people regarded the *gens de couleur* was partly due to social prejudice or economic envy, but still more it arose from fear; the coloured minority might one day make common cause with the black majority, perhaps even lead a slave insurrection against the whites. This powerful mixture of motives found expression in legislation, designed both to preserve social differences between white and coloured and to keep the *affranchis* disarmed and politically impotent. Legislation based frankly on colour was something of a novelty in the West Indies, especially in the French islands. The *Code Noir* had granted to *affranchis* all the rights of free men, irrespective of colour; but in 1766 the Minister of Marine declared: 'Tous les nègres ont été transportés aux colonies comme esclaves; l'esclavage a imprimé une tache ineffeçable sur leur postérité; et par conséquent ceux qui en descendent ne peuvent jamais entrer dans la classe des blancs. S'il était un temps où ils pouvaient être réputés blancs, ils pourraient prétendre comme eux à toutes les places ou dignités, ce qui serait absolument contraire aux constitutions des colonies.' Accordingly, *gens de couleur* in Saint-Domingue were debarred from office in courts or militia, and from certain lucrative professions; they were forbidden to use fire-arms without special licence, or to wear side-arms — the badge of gentility — at all; the cut and material of their clothes were prescribed, to distinguish them from white persons; and from 1779 they were subjected to extremely irksome curfew regulations. These successive abrogations of rights conferred by the *Code Noir* were enacted on the insistence of the white colonists in the *Conseils souverains*; it was one field of legislation in which *grands blancs* and *petits blancs* found themselves in agreement. The assemblies in most of the British islands legislated in the same spirit, though usually with less attention to sumptuary detail.

Naturally such attacks provoked the most bitter resentment among a class of people who were beginning to approximate, in wealth and numbers, to the position of the resident white planters in many islands. The injured pride of free persons of colour was potentially as explosive as the resentment of slaves against their enslavement.

This brief and general description of the state of the West Indian colonies in the later eighteenth century admits, naturally, of many exceptions, and applies fully only to those places where sugar was the major crop. A small but interesting exception was the territory of the logwood camps — Belize or British Honduras. The Baymen owned slaves, but in small numbers, and masters and slaves worked side by side, cutting the logwood in the dry weather and floating it in bundles down the creeks in the rains — hard, exacting work, but productive of a comradeship quite different from the master-slave relation of the sugar islands. Other exceptions to the general rule were the ceded islands of the Windward group, which had become the refuge of smallholders squeezed out from the sugar colonies. They produced a considerable variety of crops, including spices such as nutmeg (still a major crop in Grenada), and grew most of their own food. It is true that in the last decades of the eighteenth century sugar — and with it, plantation slavery — was gaining ground in the ceded islands, and continued to do so throughout the French wars; but it never dominated their economy, and in the nineteenth century it almost disappeared. More significant, and on a far larger scale, were the differences between the Spanish islands and the rest of the West Indies. Cuba, Santo Domingo and Puerto Rico never commanded the close attention of their home government in the eighteenth century, as Saint-Domingue and Jamaica constantly did. Economically and politically (though not strategically) they were unimportant fragments of a great land empire. They were relatively poor, Puerto Rico especially. They had a predominantly white population, including many small proprietors, who had occupied themselves since the sixteenth century in tobacco growing and cattle ranching. Fine tobacco was the principal export of Cuba. Santo Domingo grew and exported sugar, as it had done for three centuries, but not in very large quantities. The social pattern of these colonies, therefore, was quite different from that of Jamaica and Saint-Domingue. Since 1762, however, the pattern had begun to change, especially in Cuba. Sugar and coffee were gaining ground, slaves were being imported (many through Jamaica), *latifundia* of the characteristic West Indian type were being established, the virgin lands of Camagüey and Oriente were beginning to be colonised. In the nineteenth century Cuba was to outstrip all other West Indian islands producing slave-grown sugar.

All the West Indies, but especially the French and English sugar islands, depended heavily upon the outside world, both for their livelihood and for their defence. They imported much of their food and almost all their manufactured goods. They lived by selling a small number of tropical products in European markets, and depended on the protection of those markets by preferential duties and other means to maintain the price of their exports. Trade with their home countries was their lifeline; if it should be cut off they starved, and its maintenance demanded constant heavy expenditure of naval force. Rich and vulnerable as they were, they could not even defend their own coasts. Their free population was too small to provide an adequate militia. Planter-militiamen made reluctant volunteers, understandably unwilling to serve away from their homes, and to leave their wives and children at the mercy of their slaves. The islands could not, in fact, simultaneously defend themselves against foreign attack and against the possibilities of servile mutiny; and so they needed professional troops for their defence. This was true of all the islands — even of the Spanish islands with their much larger European populations; and while the French and British planters supplied slaves to construct forts, and paid — albeit tardily, stingily, reluctantly — for the maintenance of their garrisons, the Spanish islands relied on subventions from Mexico to pay for the vast fortifications which their defence required.

The question was, how long would home governments go on granting special privileges to colonies whose economic system was being denounced as inefficient, whose social structure was an anachronism, but whose leading landowners were by-words for ostentatious wealth? Sugar, it is true, was still a very valuable product, but less valuable, relatively, than it had been; and other parts of the world were beginning to produce it for export. How long could the West Indians hope to maintain absentee ownership and estate slavery by means of preferential duties and costly naval and military defence? By a curious irony of history, the French Revolution and the resulting wars brought a reprieve to the West Indies, except to Saint-Domingue; but the reprieve could only be brief. Bryan Edwards rightly expressed the apprehensions of his class and time when he proclaimed in the House of Commons in 1798 that 'The time in which we live will constitute an awful period in the history of the world; for a spirit of subversion is gone forth, which sets at nought the wisdom of our ancestors and the lessons of experience.'

CHAPTER XI

The Second American War
of Independence

Three Americans tower over these tempestuous years of revolution and war: George Washington, white farmer and soldier, Toussaint L'Ouverture, black slave from plantation America 'where nothing heroic was allowed', and Simon Bolivar, brown aristocratic intellectual; all three creoles, native-born; each united to the other by an unshakeable commitment to liberty. George Washington, in his inaugural address of 1789 spoke of 'The preservation of the sacred fire of liberty and the destiny of the republican model of government...as deeply, perhaps as finally staked on the experiment entrusted to the hands of the American people'. Toussaint, in the moment of his betrayal, warned his French captors that the roots of the tree of liberty were numerous and deep. Bolivar vowed that he would give 'neither respite to my arm nor rest to my soul till we have broken the chains which oppress us by the will of the Spanish power.'

Washington, leader of the first war of American Independence, and Bolivar, leader of the third war, continue to inspire their countrymen. In time the Caribbean will claim as its own the leader of the second war of American Independence, which was a part of the African resistance to slavery. In Edward Brathwaite's words 'slave revolt/resistance...was resistance against totemic authority, against law and custom, against the loss of Africa, against the loss of an imaginary Africa, against a set of people who had been inured into thinking and believing and reacting in a certain way and who had systems of defending themselves against and controlling 'others' who often outnumbered them by ten to one. It was also the more difficult resistance against persons they had often come to know, or to hate, or to care about; against walls that had to be scaled under fire, with a resolve that somehow had to be kept intact.' The movement of ideas from France and the United States influenced planters and slaves throughout plantation America and the Haitian revolution translated the battle-cries of white revolution into black action. To quote Brathwaite again, 'the second round of Caribbean revolts begins, not after 1807 in the "creole" period, but coincidentally with the Haitian revolution intself: unrest throughout the archipelago and into the Guianas after 1795 was directly sparked by news of Haiti; the Second Maroon War in Jamaica 1795–96; slave revolts in Surinam (1798) in conjunction with Maroons; Fedon's rebellion in Grenada (1795–97); the Second Black Carib (Maroon) War in St. Vincent (1795–96); the so-called Brigand's War in St. Lucia (1796–97), not to mention the state of mind in Martinique and Guadeloupe; the black regimental soldiers' mutinies in Dominica (1802) and Jamaica (1808); trouble in Belize and Tobago, plots and unrest in Trinidad; the Second Maroon War in Dominica (1809); and Barbados (1816). These uprisings were most of them as heavily or significantly 'African' as the revolt in Haiti itself had been, which we begin to focus on more clearly when we begin to use Haiti as exemplar; the role of Maroons, the role of black soldiers; the role of Afro-Caribbean religion as both motivation and weapon. All these were present in full measure in Haiti'. The Haitian revolution was an explosion of internal forces generated by black reaction to the slave and sugar plantation. It demonstrated to blacks everywhere how cries of liberty, fraternity and equality could be used to destroy slavery.

The planters of Jamaica and Saint-Domingue were well aware of the dangers of a 'spirit of subversion'; though it is curious that on the very eve of the French Revolution many people in Saint-Domingue thought that the Jamaicans were in greater danger than they were themselves. There was not much to choose, however. De Rouvray, the officer commanding the troops in Saint-Domingue, and also a big proprietor, wrote to a friend in 1783, 'Une colonie à esclaves est une ville menacée d'assaut; on y marche sur des barils de pourdre.' It was a trite metaphor, one much used at the time. History is full of examples of the extraordinary carelessness with which people who live in powder magazines handle naked lights. If ever a body of responsible people played recklessly with fire, it was the planters of Saint-Domingue — or at least a vociferous group among them — between 1788 and 1791. These were the people who insisted on sending delegates to the 1789 meeting of the Estates General, and who in 1791 openly defied the French government, upon whose support they depended, in the long run, for both livelihood and safety.

There was nothing inherently surprising in the spectacle of a land-owning, slave-owning aristocracy raising the cry of 'liberty', in the sense of liberty to run their colony in their own way. Something of the sort had already happened in some of the English North American colonies, and was to happen soon in Spanish America. The Saint-Domingue planters, however, were very vulnerable to attack. The 'liberty' which they sought from the Estates General was obviously liberty to proceed even more drastically than before against slaves and free persons of colour; but the institution of slavery was under fire in France, particularly from the *Amis des Noirs*, a body recently formed in imitation of Clarkson's abolition society in England, but more radical and more vociferous. The 'Rights of Man' were fashionable table talk; there was every possibility that the Estates General, if asked for 'liberty', might interpret the term in a sense very different from that desired by the *grands blancs* of Saint-Domingue. The situation in the colony was full of danger. At any moment the planters might need regular troops to deal with servile outbreaks. Their best policy was to lie low (as Isle-de-France and Bourbon successfully did), to say nothing which might bring colonial affairs into the public eye in France, to rally all respectable owners of property behind the existing government of their own colony. The more prudent among them understood this; but to the more hot-headed the meeting of the Estates General seemed too good an opportunity to be missed. The matter was openly and endlessly discussed. 'Even at table,' wrote Baron de Wimpffen in high alarm in 1790, 'surrounded by mulattoes and negroes, they indulge themselves in the most imprudent discussions on liberty etc. To discuss the "Rights of Man" before such people — what is it but to teach them that power dwells with strength, and strength with numbers?'

The extremists won their point, as extremists are apt to do in times of trouble. Irregular, and probably illegal, meetings of landowners in Saint-Domingue and in France prepared lists of nominations, and the Colonial Assembly allowed itself to be goaded into electing representatives, some of whom were resident in the colony, some in France. The assemblies of Martinique and Guadeloupe did the same; and eventually six of these colonial deputies, after much argument, were admitted to the Estates General in their tennis-court days — the first occasion in European history on which colonial representatives had sat in a metropolitan legislative assembly. They at once became involved in a long oratorical duel with the *Amis des Noirs*. Their demands for colonial autonomy were met by counter-demands that the National Assembly (as it now styled itself) should legislate on the rights of free persons of colour. The dangers of such a course were ably set out by Moreau de Saint-Méry, who represented Martinique in the assembly, and who published his *Considérations* — the ablest of the many expositions of the colonial point of view — in March 1791. 'If the National Assembly,' he wrote, 'has the misfortune to legislate on the mulatto status, all is over. The colonists will believe themselves betrayed; the mulattoes, instigated by their friends, will go to the last extremity. And then the slaves, who possess the same friends and the same means of action, will seek to attain the same results. The colonies will soon be only a vast shambles: and France — ? Yes! The mulattoes themselves are but pawns in a larger game. For if once our slaves suspect that there is a power other than their masters which holds the final disposition of their fate; if they once see that the mulattoes have successfully invoked this power and by its aid have become our equals — then France must renounce all hope of preserving her colonies.'

Moreau's forebodings worked themselves out in Saint-Domingue with the grim inevitability of classical tragedy. The National Assembly at first promised not to legislate on colonial matters unless invited to do so by the colonists, but it wavered under rhetorical bombardment and finally came down, albeit timidly, on the side of the *Amis des Noirs*. Its decree of 15 May 1791 provided that persons of colour born of free parents, if qualified in other respects, should be entitled to vote for the provincial and colonial assemblies, which had been established by royal decree only four years earlier. The white inhabitants of Saint-Domingue perceived in this decree the thin end of the egalitarian wedge, and their reaction was frankly mutinous. The colonists refused to obey the decree; the governor refused to enforce it; and there was much wild talk of secession from France. The mulattoes in some parishes were already in arms, demanding what they regarded as their rights; indeed the execution upon the wheel of one of their leaders, a young Parisian-educated zealot named Ogé, had greatly influenced French opinion against the colonists. The dispute over the May decree apparently absorbed the attention of both whites and mulattoes so completely that most of them ignored the premonitory rumblings of slave unrest. They were taken by surprise when, in August 1791, in answer to signals conveyed by drumbeats or through nocturnal ritual gatherings, the slave population of the northern plain rose in revolt, systematically setting fire to cane fields and houses and murdering the white inhabitants. Within a few weeks the whole plain was a smoking ruin, given over to bands of rebels.

The northern rising was the first concerted slave revolt on a large scale in the history of the West Indies. It was a terrifying revelation of the explosive force of stifled savage hatred. Once it had begun, it clearly could not be suppressed by the few thousand white inhabitants and the handful of regular troops available, without help. The mulattoes feared the slaves as much as the whites did; but suspicion and prejudice amounting to hatred prevented any effective alliance. The almost incredible savagery with which the fighting was conducted on both sides was described by Bryan Edwards, who was in Cap Français at the time. Edwards estimated that in the first two months 2000 whites were killed, 180 sugar plantations and 900 coffee and indigo settlements were destroyed; and 10 000 slaves died, either fighting, or by famine, or at the executioner's hands. The total white population of the province cannot have been more than 10 000 as against at least twenty times that number of slaves. Cap Français and a string of fortified camps in the western mountains were soon the only places under white control in the north province. In the west there was as yet no slave revolt, but whites and mulattoes were at war with one another, and the mulattoes under their leader Rigaud were gaining the upper hand, except in Port-au-Prince, which was terrorised by a poor-white mob under criminal leaders. In the south the white planters had armed their slaves — who had remained obedient — against the mulattoes. Everywhere, *grands blancs* and *petits blancs*, royalists and revolutionaries, mulattoes and blacks, *affranchis* and slaves, fought and plundered in shifting alliances and bloody confusion. The only hope of restoring order lay in the despatch of troops from France. The Jacobin party in the National Assembly, however, resolutely opposed any move in support of slave-owning colonists and a royal governor; they found chaos in Saint-Domingue (with the consequent rise in the price of sugar and coffee) a useful stick to beat the government with: they made resounding speeches about the sufferings of the slaves and the oppressions practised by the colonists, and effectually blocked all attempts to send troops to the colony. It was only in September 1792, after the Jacobins had gained control of the Assembly, that an army reached Saint-Domingue, and then it was a revolutionary army, under the orders of Jacobin 'commissioners' sent out to enforce the rule of liberty, equality and fraternity. In this they were fanatically sincere; but the practical results of their efforts were immense bloodshed and complete disorganisation. Their leader, Sonthonax, faced with royalist resistance, had no choice but to associate himself with the revolted slaves, who in June 1793; at his instigation, entered and sacked the town of Cap Français. In August he proclaimed a conditional emancipation. This decree, when subsequently confirmed by the republican government in France, had momentous consequences; but its immediate effect was small. It alienated the mulattoes, many of whom were, or had been, slave-owners; it did not affect the slaves who

— in the north at least — had already thrown off all civil authority. Of the surviving whites in the north, those who could get away fled either to the United States or to other West Indian islands — to Cuba, to Jamaica, and particularly to Puerto Rico, where the west-coast town of Mayagüez retains its French peculiarities to this day.

These events in Saint-Domingue naturally caused grave alarm to the Spanish government in Santo Domingo and the British government in Jamaica. The miseries and resentments of slavery were international. Among the slave leaders in Saint-Domingue, Boukman came from Jamaica, Christophe from St. Kitts. Colonial governments might well fear the contagious spread of rebellion. When in 1793 both Spain and England became involved in war with revolutionary France, both governments sent expeditions to invade Saint-Domingue. The immediate purpose of these invasions was to rescue the white colonists and help them to suppress the slave rising; incidentally to embarrass the French government; and ultimately — for the English at least — to annex all or part of the colony. A small British army, backed by a naval squadron, entered the country through the port of Jérémie in the south; a district which had long been in close contact, commercial and cultural, with Jamaica. Everywhere the British were welcomed as deliverers by the French colonists. In March 1794 they took Port-au-Prince; but the question whether, under British rule, the slave-worked sugar estates and coffee walks of Saint-Domingue could recover their old productivity was never answered. The outbreak of the second maroon war in Jamaica in 1795 — inspired by the example of the French islands and, it was believed, by actual French agents — thoroughly alarmed the government of Jamaica and prevented adequate reinforcements being sent from that island; and though considerable forces eventually arrived from England, they were all fresh 'unseasoned' troops. After four years of wasting war, the invasion petered out, defeated by yellow fever, by force of numbers, and by the military skill of François-Dominique Toussaint.

Toussaint 'L'Ouverture', the first of a remarkable series of Haitian black leaders, had been a slave on a north-plain estate. He took little or no part in the 1791 rising, but in the subsequent confusion became the leader of one of the many marauding bands which roamed the plain. On the outbreak of war between Spain and the republic he entered the Spanish service as a royalist mercenary, and built up a force of some four thousand irregular but very effective black troops. In 1794, however, alarmed by the progress of the English and the restoration of slavery which an English victory might entail, and moved also, no doubt, by personal ambition, he deserted with his troops from the Spanish army, murdered the Spanish officers who opposed his defection, and offered his services to the battered and discredited army of republican France. His defection in itself was enough to disorganise the Spanish forces in Saint-Domingue. In 1795 the Spanish and French governments in Europe made peace at the Treaty of Bâle. The Spaniards rid themselves of responsibility by ceding Santo Domingo to France; but no action was taken by the French to occupy the colony, and after Napoleon's accession to power the Spaniards were left in possession. Toussaint's energies, meanwhile, were directed against the English invaders and their allies, the French planters in Saint-Domingue. He quickly became the dominant figure on the republican side. By 1798 he had so worn down the invaders that the English commanding officer, Maitland, was glad to withdraw his depleted forces in return for an amnesty to his partisans and — significant clause — a commercial treaty. In signing such an agreement Toussaint acted like an independent ruler; and so, in fact, he was. His ascendancy among the black population was unrivalled. He commanded an army devoted to his person and enjoyed the respect, indeed the friendship, of powerful people abroad. It was his friendship with John Adams that enabled him to secure from the United States the ships and supplies he needed to fight the English.

The English expelled, Toussaint turned upon the mulatto faction of the west and south, defeated its leader Rigaud, himself a soldier of considerable ability, and sacked the town of Les Cayes which had been its headquarters. There followed a systematic round-up, mutilation, and murder of some ten thousand mulattoes, men, women, and children. As if to complete the tragedy of that year, torrential rain fell all through the autumn of 1800. The irrigation dams of the Artibonite and Cul-de-Sac, weakened by ten years of neglect, were broken. The whole prosperity of west and south depended on these irrigation works; but they were never repaired, and the area they served became the eroded wilderness it is today.

Politically, by 1800 Toussaint was supreme within the colony. He was able to secure either the compliance or the removal of all officials sent out to the colony from France. He had, already in 1799, been formally appointed governor-general by the Directorate — a face-saving gesture, for his real power was military and personal. In Saint-Domingue, as in France, the fashion for liberty, equality and fraternity was, by that time, outmoded. After 1800 Toussaint put a stop to indiscriminate massacres, respected his contracts (such as the commercial treaty with England) and ordered his mobs of ex-slaves back to work. With the docility of men weary of war, idleness and famine, they obeyed him; he even induced some of the white *émigrés* to return to their estates, and between 1800 and 1802 the shattered economy of the colony began slowly to revive. In 1801 he drew up a constitution, some clauses of which have a remarkably modern ring. Saint-Domingue was declared to be 'une seule colonie qui fait partie de l'Empire française, mais qui est soumise à des lois particulières'. This document was submitted to the French government for confirmation, but promulgated in anticipation of approval. In it Toussaint proclaimed that his own tenure of office was to be for life; a step which Napoleon himself had not yet ventured to take.

There was no room within the French empire for two dictators; and Napoleon's irritation at the prestige and pretensions of 'gilded Africans' was partly responsible for Toussaint's fall. Napoleon had other motives, however, more practical than mere irritation. His political plans called for alliance with Spain; but Toussaint in 1801, in defiance of Napoleon's orders, had carried out a rapid and successful invasion of Spanish Santo Domingo, and showed no disposition to relinquish his conquest. Napoleon, moreover, shared with Pitt, and most other statesmen of the day, an exaggerated — because out-of-date — estimate of the value and importance of West Indian possessions. Saint-Domingue had been in the past a source of great wealth to some Frenchmen, and indirectly to France; it could be so again. Geographically and strategically Saint-Domingue was the centre from which measures for rebuilding the French colonial system in the Americas could best be taken. France had once more recovered Louisiana from Spain. Napoleon — as later became evident — intended to restore the old system, slavery and all, in Saint-Domingue and Guadeloupe. None of these plans could be executed while Toussaint ruled Saint-Domingue, and his removal could be achieved only through a military reconquest of the island.

The formidable army which General le Clerc, Napoleon's brother-in-law, brought to this task in 1802 was considerably larger than the force which the English had employed eight years before, and le Clerc, in a series of capable but very costly jungle campaigns, achieved his first task, that of reducing Toussaint to obedience and taking over his office as governor-general. Most of Toussaint's supporters — Dessalines, Christophe, Maurepas, and the rest, came over into French service, each with his band of followers, and Toussaint himself was arrested, or rather kidnapped, and shipped to France, where he died in prison. But le Clerc soon found that campaigning in the mountains and forests of Saint-Domingue was very different from fighting in Europe. His army could not live off the country, for the country had little or no food. Everything had to be bought at famine prices, in uncertain quantities, from Yankee traders. Then, the same enemy which had wasted Maitland's army — yellow fever — took its daily toll of le Clerc's men; and his hard-won prestige with the leaders of the black bands was presently destroyed by the news which came from Guadeloupe. Napoleon's General Richepanse had regained control of that island, and had re-introduced slavery and the slave trade. Thousands of excited, resentful blacks in Saint-Domingue sprang to arms once more, believing (correctly) that le Clerc's instructions contemplated similar action there. At this critical moment le Clerc himself died of fever. Napoleon in 1803 broke the Peace of Amiens, resumed the war in Europe, and washed his hands of the Saint-Domingue affair — indeed, of the whole scheme of American empire, for Louisiana was sold in the same year. Le Clerc's successor never got the reinforcements he had been promised; at the end of 1803, with his starved, ragged, fever-stricken remnant of an army, he surrendered to the British in Jamaica. Meanwhile Dessalines, ablest, most savage and most ruthless of Toussaint's former vassals, embarked on a campaign of literal extermination against the surviving whites, in a country ravaged from end to end by war.

Dessalines, unlike Toussaint, was African born. At the out-break of the revolt he was a slave on the plantation of a free black, whose name he assumed and whose property he seized as soon as the insurrection gave him the opportunity of murdering his master. He quickly rose to power in the *entourage* of Toussaint, and was Toussaint's enthusiastic agent in the massacre of mulattoes in the south in 1800. He was the obvious successor to Toussaint; and in 1804 he proclaimed himself an independent ruler — Emperor of Haiti, choosing the Taino word for 'mountainous' to replace the name of Saint-Domingue. He ruled until 1806. After his death, and for the rest of the war period and beyond, the country was divided between his rival successors, the black Christophe and the mulatto Pétion. Christophe's régime in the north was an astonishing *tour-de-force*, of which his great citadel stands as a grim witness to this day. Without administrative machinery to his hand, he held his kingdom together by sheer force of will, ruling through a kind of military feudalism based on forced labour, without the name of slavery. While he lived (till 1820) he kept the great estates going and delayed the running-down of the economic machine. Pétion, more easy-going, permitted in the south the popular but economically disastrous subdivision of the land into small peasant plots, which became in time the pattern all over Haiti. As a result, sugar production dwindled almost to nothing. Coffee — largely a peasant crop in the mountains — diminished too, though less seriously and with more hope of revival. After 1810 it was the principal crop. The export figures for Haiti as a whole are eloquent witnesses of all these changes.

	Sugar	*Coffee*
1791	163 405 220 lb.	68 151 180 lb.
1802	53 400 000 lb.	34 370 000 lb.
1804	47 600 000 lb.	31 000 000 lb.
1818	1 896 449 lb.	20 280 589 lb.
1825	2020 lb.	36 034 300 lb.

These two men, then — Christophe, the illiterate black warrior, and Pétion, the cultivated, unpractical mulatto — between them presaged the whole indigent, disorderly history of independent Haiti.

In the early years of the revolution events in the smaller French islands appeared to be taking the same course as in Saint-Domingue; but Martinique and Guadeloupe were older, more unified, socially stronger. They had a much higher proportion of resident planters and did not suffer in the same degree as Saint-Domingue from the ferocious hatreds of race and class. On the other hand, they were important commercial centres as well as plantation colonies. There was a sharp divergence of interests between the merchants of Saint-Pierre and Basse-Terre and the white planters who were often their debtors. The free mulattoes (who here as elsewhere were agitating for a recognition of equality) were a third element in the conflict, tending, however, to follow the white planters, because some of them were planters themselves, and all of them feared slave insurrection. Left to themselves, the planter assemblies, with mulatto support, could probably have controlled the situation; but in 1792 Jacobin commissioners arrived from France, rallied commercial and poor-white support for the republic and compelled the governors to submit. Their activities drove the royalist planters into the arms of the English.

Both French and British governments assumed that without their sugar islands they could not pay for the war, and neither dared leave the other a free hand in the Caribbean. The West Indies were inevitably once again the scene of heavy fighting. Both sides made serious miscalculations. The French, during the revolutionary years, underestimated the destructive forces let loose by premature declarations of emancipation and equality. The English overestimated the effective support they would get from predominantly royalist French planters. The French had the advantage of a revolutionary battle-cry which rallied the forces of social and economic discontent; the English had the superior force at sea. The French could make revolutions, but not always control them; the English could capture islands, but not always hold them. Both sides sent fleets to the West Indies in 1793. The British captured Tobago in that year, and Martinique, Guadeloupe and St. Lucia in 1794. In Martinique their alliance with the royalists was effective. Slavery and internal peace were both maintained, and with access to the British market the sugar industry of the island entered upon a period of notable prosperity. Guadeloupe and St. Lucia, it is true, were quickly recaptured through the efforts of the Jacobin commissioner Victor Hugues, who arrived with a fleet shortly afterwards. Hugues proclaimed immediate emancipation and engineered a concerted rising of slaves, not only against the English but against the local planters. He set on foot also those intrigues with the maroons of Jamaica and the Caribs of St. Vincent, which contributed in each island to a desperate outbreak in 1795. Abercromby's expedition recovered St. Lucia in that year, however, and the inclusion of the United Netherlands and Spain within the French system gave the British an excuse to seize Demerara and Essequibo in 1796, Trinidad in 1797. The year 1801 found Great Britain supreme in the Caribbean, with the French practically confined to Guadeloupe and the Spaniards to Cuba and Puerto Rico; the whole island of Hispaniola being then in the hands of Toussaint L'Ouverture.

All conquests except Trinidad were returned by the Peace of Amiens in 1801, and Napoleon used the respite for an attempt to re-establish metropolitan control of the French West Indies. In Guadeloupe General Richepanse overthrew the mulatto group who had seized power after Hugues' departure, and restored the old régime, slavery and all, with dire consequences, as we have seen, in Saint-Domingue. After the failure of le Clerc, however, Napoleon gave up the West Indian situation as hopeless, and on the renewal of hostilities in 1803 the British reoccupied all that they had held before the peace. After Trafalgar they had nothing to fear in that area from French or Spanish arms. The final settlement of 1815 added St. Lucia, Tobago, Trinidad, and (by purchase) Demerara, Essequibo and Berbice to the British Empire. Martinique and Guadeloupe were restored to France, partly because of the over-riding British desire for security on the Channel coasts, which made 'Antwerp and Flushing out of the hands of France' worth — as Harrowby put it — 'twenty Martiniques'. The restoration was a drastic one, for Louis XVIII re-introduced the administrative, constitutional and social structure not of 1788 but of 1763.

For the British islands the long war — despite the alarms of the revolutionary years — brought an economic reprieve. Before the slave rising of 1791 Saint-Domingue had been exporting nearly as much sugar as the whole of the British West Indies. Its removal from effective competition was exactly what the British planters had hoped for for half a century. The price of muscavado in London rose from *54s. 3d.* a hundredweight in 1792 to *69s. 2d.* in 1796. The price of coffee doubled in about the same period; and Jamaican exports of both commodities greatly increased, despite war-time rises in costs of production, freights and insurance, and despite the steady increase in duties on colonial produce. There were, as usual, violent fluctuations. Muscavado dropped to *25s. 6d.* at the end of 1802, but rose again with the resumption of hostilities and continued to rise until 1807. In that year there was another sharp drop, due partly to the conquest of foreign sugar colonies and partly to the carrying of foreign sugars directly to Europe in American ships, but the rise was resumed the following year; the embargo, the Non-Inter course Act, and eventually the Anglo-American war forced prices higher and higher, and in 1814 muscavado reached a peak of *100s*.

Not only sugar and coffee but cotton also reached record levels of production and price during the war. For most of the eighteenth century Great Britain had bought most of its raw cotton from the East. The rapidly increasing demand for cotton, noticeable in Lancashire and Lanarkshire by the end of the 'seventies could not be met from Eastern sources. The chief beneficiaries of it were the West Indian colonies, which by 1790 were supplying over 70 per cent of British needs. After that date the competition of the green seed cotton of the southern states of the Union, cleaned by Whitney's patent gin, steadily overcame the more expensive hand-cleaned sea island cotton of the West Indies; for West Indian cotton never enjoyed the degree of protection accorded to sugar. But at least until about 1810 cotton remained an important and profitable West Indian product, especially in captured Guiana, where the saline mud of the Courantyne coast was particularly suited to its cultivation.

Finally, the disturbed state of the Spanish colonies, and the English foothold in Spain after 1808, allowed an increase in trade with Latin America, sometimes legal, but more often not. The Anglo-American war and the blockade of American ports temporarily removed a dangerous competitor. British exports to Cuba, for instance, more than trebled during the two years of the war. Jamaica and Trinidad both profited greatly from this increase of Latin American trade between 1808 and 1815.

All in all, then, the war dealt kindly with the British West Indies; but their war-time prosperity could only be temporary. The hey-day of West Indian cotton was over before the end of thê war. The prices of sugar and coffee would inevitably drop with the coming of peace; but duties would remain, since the war must be paid for; and the East India interest in England might at any time succeed in reducing or abolishing the preferential which had hitherto favoured West Indian against East Indian sugar. Even if this danger could be avoided, it was fairly certain that British West Indian sugar would once again be confined to the British market. Beet sugar was already being produced on a small scale in France; and larger, newer plantation colonies were producing cane sugar more cheaply than Barbados or Jamaica. Saint-Domingue, it is true, was out of the running, apparently for ever, but Cuba had taken its place as the most dangerous West Indian competitor. Demerara and Trinidad, newly acquired and undeveloped, might compete with Cuba in producing cheap sugar, if they could get slaves; but the slave trade had been made illegal for British subjects by Act of Parliament in 1807, while the Cubans could still get all the slaves they wanted from Spanish and Yankee slavers. Moreover, the British West Indian planters had every reason to fear that, once the war ended, the attack on the institution of slavery itself in British territory would be resumed. In this respect also the war had allowed them a respite, for the excesses of revolution in France had brought all radical ideas into disrepute, and events in Haiti had shown what could happen when slaves were loosed suddenly from control. But these warnings would be forgotten with the peace; humanitarian, religious and economic objections to slavery would be voiced again with redoubled force and conviction. Very few West Indians believed that sugar could be produced without slaves. After their war-time Indian summer, therefore, the men who ran and lived by the plantation system of the British West Indies looked forward to a bleak economic future and a long rearguard action against the forces of change.

CHAPTER XII

Freedom Without National Identity

The Caribbean islands share a family likeness, a central mountain range with lateral ridges or a huddle of mountains cramped for space and a broken rim of coastal plain; and throughout the archipelago checker-board fields of sugar cane, reminders that the likeness extends across time as well as space, revealing itself in the social configuration, the traditional economic dependence, the recurring cycle of plantation prosperity and decline. The extraordinary range of differences in size, the sharp definition of territory, the lack of a physical centre which might exercise a centripetal force on the whole derives the family likeness of meaning; and the closed circles of imperial political and trading systems induced the islanders to see each island as a world. As a result Fort de France was nearer to Paris than to Barbados, Havana nearer to Madrid than to Kingston, Kingston nearer to London than to Port-au-Prince. Although aeroplanes and wireless waves now span the distance, the isolation still exists in West Indian consciousness and will continue to do so until national history is set in the context of Caribbean history. Once this is done the history of the whole illumines the history of each, revealing significant differences in the rhythm and pace of change and opening up new perceptions of climactic events such as the Second American War of Independence, the Abolition of Slavery, the Emancipation of Slaves and the growth of a black yeomanry.

Cuban history, for example, throws light on the events in the English speaking Caribbean in the nineteenth century, for as Sydney Mintz points out, 'the Hispanic Caribbean came to represent a final chapter and capstone in the plantation cycle. . . . They were the first to plant the sugar cane; the first to have slaves; the first to undertake the organisation of slave-operated plantations. And yet the infant Hispaniolan, Puerto Rican and Cuban sugar industries stagnated, and the epic of the slave plantation was left for the British, the Dutch, the French, the Danes and others to write much later. Only when those nations had already began to turn away from the plantation economy did the Hispanic islands stir once more.'

We will pursue this in a later chapter but it is necessary to emphasize here the relevance of Cuban history and to recognize that it raises such critical questions for West Indians as: how did Cuba escape the grip of the sugar plantation for so long?; how is it that the population of Cuba in 1800 was predominantly creolized European with a great measure of vertical mobility for free coloured as well as whites in marked contrast with the population of the English or French islands?; how is it that at an early period in his country's history, a Cuban could affirm with such intensity 'Soy Cubano'?; how is it that Puerto Rico moved from a free agrarian society of small holders and peasantry to plantations and a rural proletariat whereas the English-speaking Caribbean moved from plantations to a combination of large estates ánd small holdings?; and how is it that the slave-plantation flourished in Cuba and the Carolinas in the period of the abolition of the British slave trade and of the emancipation of slaves in the British empire?

Up to the late eighteenth century most people in England — or France, or Holland, or Portugal — accepted without question the necessity of slavery and of the slave trade. Overseas trade in general was held to be the chief source of national wealth and power. The slave trade, because it made large profits, supplied essential labour, and employed many ships, was necessary, just as child labour or the press-gang were necessary. Only a few cranks doubted the propriety of the trade. George Fox, as early as 1671, had urged the Quakers in Barbados to treat their slaves kindly and to free those who had served long and well. A few years later the first formal and public protest against slavery was made by the Quakers of Germantown in Pennsylvania, and slavery was forbidden in that state; but the attitude of these Quakers was exceptional. It was not shared even by all Quakers, and certainly did not reflect any general moral misgivings about slavery and the slave trade. If positive justification of the trade were needed, it could be found in the rationalisation that the victims were slaves before the traders bought them; their removal to the West Indies, it was argued, took them from barbarous owners and brought them into contact with civilised society and Christian belief.

In the later eighteenth century economists began to question the validity of the assumptions on which the regulations of the old colonial system had been based. Already when Adam Smith wrote, the economy of Britain was being transformed by the growth of large-scale industry. People were moving from the land into the towns, and from the craftsman's work-shop into the factory. Beside the old society of land-owners, farmers and labourers there was growing up a new urban society, divided no less sharply between industrial employers and factory hands. Mechanical inventions like the spinning-jenny, the water-frame and the power loom promised to English industrialists the power to clothe the whole world in factory-made textiles; and nothing less than the whole world must be their market. It might be true that 'five hundred thousand negroes are constantly clad by the clothiers of Yorkshire and Wiltshire.... London, Birmingham, Bristol and Carron supply alike the mill-work, the nails, the hoes, the tools, the utensils of domestic life and the implements of husbandry'; nevertheless, the market offered by a few thousand planters parsimoniously buying osnaburg to clothe their slaves was trifling compared with the expanding societies of North and South America and the vast populations of the East. Moreover, an industrialised society demanded, above all things, cheap food, and West Indian sugar was not cheap. The British West Indies could not possibly compete in open trade, in a world market, with the larger sugar-producing regions that were coming into production — with Cuba, with Mauritius, and with the East Indies. The West Indian monopoly was becoming an expensive anachronism.

While the economists and the industrialists were attacking West Indian monopoly, the reformers, humanitarians and intellectuals were attacking West Indian slavery. Rousseau and his successors had sentimentalised the savage and popularised the gospel of liberty, equality and fraternity. Their ideas had influenced American leaders in the War of Independence and had helped to prepare the way for revolution in France. The example, the theories and the slogans of the French Revolution had influenced the leaders in the Haitian revolt. The same ideas had affected England also; but in England radicalism was less political, less intellectual, and at the same time less violent. The ideas of liberty and equality there received force and religious sanction from the evangelical movement in which Wesley and Whitfield were the leaders. Their appeal was to conscience; slavery was wrong because all men were the sons of God. Out of this movement came the missionary societies; the Baptist Missionary Society in 1792, the London Missionary Society in 1795 and the British and Foreign Bible Society in 1803. Out of this movement also came the humanitarians like Howard, Elizabeth Fry and Shaftesbury with their campaigns against the abuses in prisons and against child-labour. There were others, men of strong religious convictions like the 'Saints' or the 'Clapham sect', who used their political power to attack slavery and who founded the first English colony in Africa by organising and financing a company in 1787 to establish Sierra Leone as a home for freed slaves. Closely associated with this group were many of the leaders in the campaign against slavery: Thomas Clarkson, Granville Sharp, James Ramsay, William Wilberforce.

The story of the long campaign for abolition shows how swiftly and how profoundly the new political and religious ideas were affecting Englishmen, and how powerful and far-reaching were the economic changes that were in progress. It also affords one of the earliest and best illustrations of the modern methods of influencing political decisions by organising and mobilising public opinion.

The first man to begin public agitation against the slave trade was Granville Sharp, who began life as a draper's assistant in London and later held a government post at the Ordinance Office. At this time there were some ten thousand black slaves in England, the property of West Indians who lived in England. Granville Sharp came into contact with one of these slaves, Joseph Strong, whose master was a lawyer from Barbados, David Lisle. The owner had turned Strong adrift because he was ill and useless. The slave would have died but for the help which Granville Sharp and his brother, a doctor, had given him. With care and treatment he recovered, and found employment. Then, one day, some two years later, Lisle came upon Strong, claimed him as his property and sold him for £30 to a Jamaican planter, who had him put in prison until he could be shipped to the West Indies. Sharp took up the case and managed to have Strong set free. He was a persistent man, and did not stop with this success; there might be other cases like that of Strong, and so he decided to press for a court decision on whether slavery was permitted in England. After several unsuccessful attempts to obtain a decision he took up the case of James Somerset, who, like Strong, had been turned adrift by his master. Somerset recovered with Sharp's help, and on recovery he was claimed by his master. Sharp resisted the claim and the case finally went before the Chief Justice, Lord Mansfield, who, on 22 June 1772, declared that in the absence of positive law on the subject the right of property in slaves could not be upheld before the courts in England. This celebrated judgement had the effect of immediately liberating, in law, all who had been held as slaves in England. It was the first major victory in the attrack on the slave trade, and the opponents of the trade now began to organise themselves. The Quakers formed an anti-slavery society, and they were joined, among others, by Sharp, Clarkson and by James Ramsay, a clergyman who had worked in the West Indies for nineteen years and who wrote and spoke with great effect of the abuses and cruelties of slavery. Clarkson soon became one of the leaders of the abolitionist cause, and he used every method of publicity to influence and rouse public opinion and to press for political action. In its political sphere the movement found a leader of conviction, in some respects a genius, William Wilberforce. Up to the time of his conversion in 1784 Wilberforce had shown no interest in the abolition movement. Witty, eloquent, and wealthy, he had lived an active political and social life but had not identified himself with any particular interest or cause. He was generally popular and was the close friend of Pitt. Now, having come under the influence of John Newton, once captain of a slave ship and now a clergyman, and having read Clarkson's book, he decided to devote his life to the campaign against slavery and the English slave-trade. The first step was taken in 1788 when Dolben, who had been horrified at conditions he had seen on board a slave ship in the Thames, introduced a Bill to limit the number of slaves ships might carry in proportion to their tonnage. Public interest was mounting and was maintained by a spate of pamphlets and by devices like Wedgewood's cameo which showed a negro kneeling in entreaty for freedom, the chains hanging from his wrists and fettered legs. Anti-slavery groups were organised, and sent hundreds of petitions to the House of Commons, the first occasion on which this form of political pressure had been tried on such a scale. With this support in the country, and with considerable sympathy in the House, Wilberforce, with the assistance of Fox and Pitt, won the agreement of the House to the proposal that the slave trade ought to be abolished, and that it should come to an end after four years.

Many different forces in England contributed to the campaign against the slave trade and helped to bring slavery itself into disrepute; but from the point of view of the West Indian planter, all abolitionists and emancipationists had two things in common, ignorance of West Indian conditions, and indifference to West Indian interests. The British islands had come to depend almost entirely on the sugar trade for their livelihood. The way in which the sugar was marketed, and the planter financed, tied the West Indian economy very closely to that of England. The crop grown on a West Indian estate was consigned to a factor in England who acted as the planter's agent, sold the goods on his behalf, deducted his commission, and credited the planter with the balance. In addition he bought such goods as the planter needed, shipped them to him, advanced money to him, and financed him as a bank would nowadays. Since sugar-planting was a hazardous business, subject to sudden losses by hurricane and drought and other natural or man-made disasters, and since planters often made matters worse by extravagance, estates were usually heavily encumbered, and often fell into the reluctant hands of factor or banker by way of foreclosure. In 1772, for example, there were 775 working sugar estates in Jamaica; twenty years later just over one half were still in the hands of their owners as going concerns. About two-fifths had been sold for debt or thrown up. While the sugar trade flourished, said Postlethwayt, 'both planters and merchants grew immensely rich and the trade and navigation of Great Britain was carried on to a much greater height than ever it was before'. When it languished, he might have added, merchants grew less rich, and many planters were ruined.

Any threat to this trade, therefore, united planter and merchant, and the combination had great political influence. The sugar business, after all, represented some £50 000 000 of capital invested in estates alone, to say nothing of the working capital of the factors. More than half of these investments were held by people resident in England. The wealth and social standing of the absentee proprietors enabled them to influence the colonial legislatures and gave them also a direct entry into the House of Commons as members and as lobbyists. The West India interest was powerful and well organised, experienced and skilful both in the control of production and in the use of political influence. Some of its members, it is true, adopted a comparatively liberal view and supported proposals, such as those of Ellis, for improving the social condition of the slaves and giving them full legal protection, in an effort to lift the birth-rate above the death-rate and so reduce the importation of new slaves. The majority, however, seeing themselves threatened with rising costs, falling prices, and eventual ruin, resisted bitterly the proposals for abolishing the slave trade. The legislature of the Leeward Islands, in resolving 'that no power shall endeavour to deprive us of obtaining slaves from Africa', expressed the dismay and indignation of the planting community in general.

It was not West Indian defiance, however, so much as international circumstances, which turned Wilberforce's estimate of four years into fifteen. The French Revolution and the Napoleonic Wars demanded the full attention of government and people. The slave trade was reprieved or forgotten, and abolition, thanks to the indiscretions of Clarkson, momentarily shared the disrepute of the radical political ideas current in France. It was in those years that Wilberforce became indispensable to the cause he had embraced, urgently moving his resolution against the trade year after year. In 1803 his Bill passed the House of Commons but was defeated in the Lords. Finally in 1807 a fortuitous circumstance, a turn of the political wheel, made victory possible. The Act for the abolition of the slave trade came into force on January 1, 1808.

The Abolition Act put Britain out of the slave trade at a time when more than one-half of the trade was in British hands. It did not put an end to the trade itself, for others moved in to take what the British gave up. The United States government declared the trade illegal in 1808, a measure which commanded widespread public support, for cotton was not yet king, and at that time there were many in the south who would have echoed Patrick Henry's declaration about slavery: 'I tremble for my country when I reflect that God is just.' Many Americans, however, continued to engage in the trade, evading the law by selling their ships nominally to Spain. English traders also, tempted by the profits, sometimes became slave smugglers, but they were subject to laws which became increasingly severe; in 1811 an Act of Parliament made slave trading a felony and in 1827 it was declared to be piracy and so punishable by death. Other nations also legislated against the trade. Denmark had done so even before Britain, in 1804; Sweden followed in 1813 and Holland in 1814. France declared the trade illegal in 1818 and Spain did the same in 1820, but both of these powers were half-hearted about the matter and slave dealing was for long an open business in ports like Nantes, which had some eighty slave ships and where the profits from the trade were said to have amounted to 90 000 000 francs in the year 1815. The total number of slaves taken from West Africa after the Abolition Act of 1808 may in fact have been greater than the total of those taken before that date; it is certain that both Cuba and Brazil imported greater numbers after 1808 than they did during the earlier period. Cuba was importing slaves up to 1865, Brazil even later.

In Cuba and in the United States the demand for slaves increased after 1808 because of the greatly expanded production of sugar, cotton and tobacco. Slave labour enabled Louisiana to become a sugar State which, by 1830, was able to supply one-half the sugar required in the United States. Slave labour, the cultivation of improved types of cotton, and Eli Whitney's invention of the saw-gin which cleaned short-fibred cotton well and cheaply, enabled the South to become the world's greatest supplier of cotton. The West Indies never had a chance to keep the British market. From 1796 to 1800 they had supplied Britain with 70 per cent of its cotton; in 1803 they supplied 57 000 lb. against 45 000 lb. from the United States; but between 1816–20 the United States was supplying 47 per cent of the cotton imported into Britain, while the West Indies supplied 7 per cent. Slave labour also enabled tobacco planters to spread the cultivation of the crop from Virginia into Kentucky and Tennessee, and slave labour transformed the fertile plains of Cuba into great sugar estates. In Cuba and in the southern States production was on a scale beyond that of which the British West Indies were capable, and the prosperity which flowed from the mass-production of one or two crops united the southern States in support of slavery in the same way that the West Indies and the British government had been united in favour of slavery throughout most of the eighteenth century. An illicit slave trade sprang up even in the British Caribbean and continued up to the time of the Emancipation Act. The Slave Trade Consolidated Act permitted an owner leaving one of the islands to take with him one or more domestic slaves to attend him on the voyage. This gave a chance for dishonest persons to sell slaves illegally from one island to another. A Barbados official complained in 1827 that many slaves had been taken from the island in that year alone, and that the trade was increasing.

Meanwhile in England public opinion, after a period of relative indifference, was beginning to show interest in the conditions of slavery itself. In the years immediately following the French war the British government sponsored a policy of amelioration and urged the West Indian governments to enact legislation in conformity with this end — to give slaves religious instruction, put a stop to Sunday markets and Sunday labour, permit and legalise the marriage of slaves, prohibit flogging, and limit the owner's power to punish. There were at this time about three-quarters of a million slaves in the British Caribbean territories, about one-half of these being in Jamaica and one-tenth in the newly acquired mainland territory of Guiana. Self-interest alone dictated greater care in conserving these numbers, when they could no longer be replaced by fresh imports; but planter-legislators, already in desperate financial straits, and exasperated by the unremitting attacks of people in England who knew little, and cared less, about their troubles, would not see their interest in this light. They were, moreover, difficult to coerce. Newly acquired places like Trinidad, British Guiana and St. Lucia, it is true, had no independent legislatures. They were governed by Order in Council and the members of their legislatures were nominated, not elected. The Crown, therefore, was able to introduce reforms in these 'Crown colonies' without much difficulty. In the older colonies, on the other hand, the assemblies resisted the amelioration policy as long as they were able; and even when they had been induced, with many grumbles, to pass Amelioration Acts, the problems, of enforcement were formidable. Planters were still very much the masters within the bounds of their own estates, as far as the slaves were concerned. The officials who were to carry out reforms were often in sympathy with the planters and sometimes were themselves slave owners. These two factors contributed to the relative failure of the policy of amelioration and the increasing demand in England for outright abolition of slavery itself.

An impoverished and increasingly discredited West India interest thus found itself engaged in a long defensive action against the forces of change. It had to face charges of inefficient estate management as well as of cruelty and general immorality where slaves were concerned. Abolitionists and economic theorists alike proclaimed that slavery was wasteful and inefficient, as well as inhumane. The supporters of slavery could only reply that, inefficient though the system might be, there was no other known way of growing sugar. Nothing reveals more clearly than this the intellectual as well as financial bankruptcy of West Indian society at the time. Nobody now dared attempt a philosophical defence of slavery as an absolute good, as a means of civilising the savage or evangelising the heathen. The best that the West Indians could claim for their most important social institution was that it was a necessary evil.

In England the government after 1823 was subjected to increasing pressure from the abolitionists, led by Wilberforce and Buxton but within the West Indies the pressure on the local legislatures came from the missionaries, the free mulattoes and the slaves. The missionaries brought the evangelical movement contacts with Quakers and Baptists were with the United States. In Jamaica, for example, the Baptist Church was founded by two negroes, George Lisle and Moses Baker, who were brought to the island in 1783 by loyalist families who left America after the Declaration of Independence. Lisle set up a chapel in Kingston, and persecution and imprisonment failed to prevent him from preaching. He converted Moses Baker, who came from the Bahamas, and in turn Baker began to instruct the slaves and to set up churches; but as their movement grew both Baker and Lisle appealed to the Baptist Missionary Society for help, and in 1814 the first Baptist missionary was sent out from England. The Methodist and Baptist missionaries were bitterly opposed by many of the planters on the ground that the 'Chapels and meeting houses were centres of subversive activity and that religious instruction was a pretence for stirring up the slaves to rebellion'.

The fear of mutiny can never be far from the thoughts of slave owners; and any gathering of slaves was suspect. Governor Bentinck writing from British Guiana in 1812 to Liverpool, expressed this general feeling in these words: 'In a country like this where on an extent of coast of near 150 miles there is a population of only 1746 white inhabitants and 847 people of colour that could in case of necessity be called on to repel an insurrection of 31 484 male slaves, if such a calamitous event should ever arise, too many precautions cannot be taken to prevent as far as possible the assemblage of negroes in considerable numbers under any pretence whatsoever.' Woodford, governor of Trinidad, said that his principal objection to the Methodist preacher is 'that he teaches and allows the slaves to preach'; later, having 'heard and seen nothing of the Methodizzies since the last took himself off, I hope I am quit of them, but let me entreat you to do what you can about a Bishop for us'.

In England, during the turbulent and troubled period of reform, the evangelical movement had generated forces of change while at the same time teaching and encouraging good order and respect for authority, and so it had been one of the most powerful influences for stability. Similarly, in the West Indies, there is evidence that the missionaries laboured to give religious instruction without inciting the slaves. They were, in fact, a restraining influence, and the slave risings of this period were remarkably free from excesses of cruelty and bloodshed. But as the emancipation movement in England grew more powerful and as the slaves began to grow more restive, the feeling against the missionaries became stronger and more hostile; not only planters, but the clergy of the established church and some officials made common cause against them.

In Barbados a riotous crowd pulled down a Methodist chapel, the missionary, Shrewsbury, escaping to St. Vincent. In Jamaica, in 1832, the Colonial Church Union was formed 'to resist by all constitutional means, the encroachments of their enemies', and they soon showed what they meant by 'constitutional means' by burning non-conformist chapels and attacking missionaries on the theory that 'to get rid of the rooks you must destroy their nests'. The issue was no longer whether or not religious instruction should be given but whether the system which prevented religious instruction being given should be destroyed. Seeing this, the Baptist missionaries sent William Knibb to England to discuss the problem with the Baptist Missionary Society. Knibb was a man of remarkable foresight and courage; he had been one of the first to be attacked by the Church Union, who destroyed 'that pestilential hole, Knibb's preaching shop'. On arrival in England he heard of the passing of the Bill for the reform of the House of Commons and cried, 'Thank God, now I'll have slavery down.' When his society tried to prevent him from campaigning for abolition he told them that he would go forward even if he had to take his wife and children by the hand and walk barefoot through the kingdom. So effective was Knibb's agitation that his biographer Hinton said the planters 'had flung the firebrand from their hearths but it had fallen on the powder magazine'.

The free mulattoes were comparatively few in number, and were for the most part more concerned to secure for themselves the privileges enjoyed by white people, than to advance the cause of the slaves. They included men of substance and culture, and so were bound by common interests with the planters. In Grenada in 1823 they obtained most of their demand for full citizenship, but in Jamaica the assembly obstinately withstood their claims. Rebuffed by the assemblies in Barbados and in Jamaica, they appealed to the British government. Finally, in Jamaica in 1832 most of them sided with the missionaries and negroes and advocated emancipation.

The slaves grew more and more restive. With the abolition of the slave trade the importation of new African slaves had ceased, but not slavery itself. The creole slaves knew of the words and acts of the British Parliament, of the work of Wilberforce and the abolitionists, and of the attempts at amelioration, and resentment exploded in a series of creole risings. At Le Resouvenir in Demerara in 1823 the slaves demanded immediate emancipation and killed two overseers who resisted them. Martial law was declared, a hundred rioters were killed, Smith, an 'independent' missionary at Bethel Chapel was arrested, tried, sentenced to death and thrown into prison where he soon died. The belief was widespread among the slaves that the planters were withholding their freedom from them. This, reported the Earl of Manchester, was the reason for a slave rising in Jamaica in 1823: 'all those executed were fully impressed that they were entitled to their freedom and that the cause they had embraced was just.'

On December 27, 1831 cane field fires on Kensington Estate in western Jamaica signalled the outbreak of the Baptist War, the largest best organised rebellion of creole slaves in the history of the English speaking Caribbean. The rebellion deserves fuller attention than can be given to it here, for it differed in many ways from earlier risings. The rebels, being creole, had a common language and could communicate easily with each other; they were for the most part of the Christian faith, converts of the evangelical missionaries, and they were led by men who shared the belief of their leader in the Bible teaching of the brotherhood of man and in the natural equality of man with regard to freedom; who were convinced that slavery was immoral and unjust, that the King had made them free and that the whites intended to withhold their freedom from them. They knew that many whites both despised and feared them and believed the rumour that they intended to kill all male blacks and keep the women and children in slavery; that, as their leader Sam Sharpe said 'if the black men did not stand up for themselves and take their freedom, the whites would put them out at the muzzles of their guns and shoot them like pigeons.' The rising was unique in the quality of its leadership and in the method of resistance, which included force of arms, destruction of property and also the planned withdrawal of labour: 'the whole party bound themselves by oath not to work after Christmas as slaves, but to assert their claim to freedom and to be faithful to each other'. It was unique in the method of instruction, planning and preparation for Sharpe used the religious structure of class-meetings and prayer meetings to instruct the slaves, and unique in the emphasis on non-violence. In this Sharpe who is honoured by Jamaicans as a national hero, anticipated Gandhi and Martin Luther King. The figures speak for themselves. The rebels killed 12 whites and destroyed property valued at 1.25 million pounds. The white authorities killed 207 rebel slaves in the field and executed 312. The rebellion was put down but the rebels won by making emancipation a matter of extreme urgency.

In England, also, there were riots and disorders, in the autumn of 1831, when the House of Lords threw out the Reform Bill. The various aspects of reform were linked together in the minds of English liberals. Opposition to the abolition of slavery was becoming as dangerous politically as opposition to parliamentary reform. The abolitionists had public opinion behind them, for a variety of religious, humane, and economic reasons, and they had convinced, tenacious and skilful leaders. Wilberforce, it is true, had relinquished his leadership to Buxton, and some of the older leaders were dead; but George Stephen and Zachary Macaulay were among the most vigorous minds in the public life of the time, and the policy of the Colonial Office itself was already strongly influenced by James Stephen, most upright and most conscientious of public servants, and devoted to the cause of emancipation. Agitation, mutiny, political pressure, and administrative skill all played their part in preparing the Emancipation Act which finally became law in 1833.

The analogous movement for the emancipation of slaves in the remaining fragments of the French American empire followed a similar course about fifteen years later. Slavery had been abolished in law by the Revolution, but — except in Saint-Domingue — the abolition had not been effective; the institution of slavery was re-established by Napoleon, and retained under the restored Bourbons.

The example of English legislation, and the warnings offered by a series of widespread conspiracies among the slaves (of which the most serious were those of Carbet in 1822, and again in 1824, and that of the Grande Anse in 1833, all in Martinique) forced upon the government a policy of amelioration similar to that pursued by the English government fifteen years earlier. Naturally the establishment of the July Monarchy in 1830 made the adoption of such a policy much easier politically. In 1832 the tax on manumission was abolished, and the procedure for manumission simplified. In 1833 the registration of slaves was made compulsory, and mutilation and branding of captured runaways prohibited. In 1836 it was enacted that all slaves brought into France became free immediately. All this legislation was enacted by the central assembly in France, and not, as in the British islands, passed by local legislatures under metropolitan pressure. Like the corresponding British legislation, however, it was inadequate to the situation, and could not be consistently enforced because of the opposition of colonial magnates and officials. In France, as in England earlier, the conviction grew among those who disliked slavery that only complete emancipation would suffice. The *Société pour l'abolition de l'esclavage* was formed in 1834, and the first serious draft of an emancipation law was proposed in the assembly in 1838. The West Indian slave owners, being represented in the assembly, were able to oppose this and subsequent proposals more directly than their English counterparts had done, and they did so with more conviction, defending slavery not only as economically necessary but as socially desirable, given the savagery and idleness of the slaves. 'Ce n'est pas l'esclavage qui a rendu les races nègres paresseuses,' one of them roundly declared, 'c'est leur paresse qui les a fait tomber dans l'esclavage.' The arguments used on both sides were rational and secular. French abolitionists, unlike the 'Saints' in England, had no particular religious bent. Schoelcher, their most eminent and zealous leader, shared to the full Wilberforce's humanity, and was better informed — he had travelled in the southern States — but he lacked Wilberforce's evangelical fervour. The debate, with all its acrimonies and cries of ruin, raged intermittently until 1848. In that year Schoelcher proposed the final and successful enactment, abolishing slavery forthwith throughout the French colonies and authorising the payment of compensation to the former owners. By the middle of the nineteenth century, then, West Indian slavery survived only in the Spanish islands. In the French and British colonies there were no more slaves; but the task of equipping men for freedom still lay ahead.

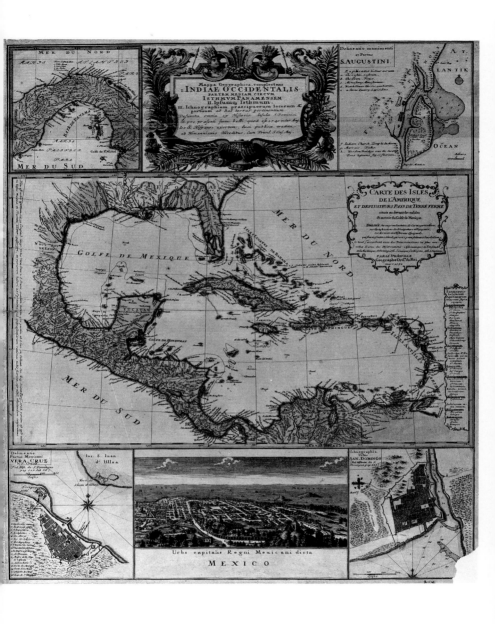

Carte d'Iles de l'Amerique (1731) by Jean Baptiste d'Aville

[Historical Association of Southern Florida]

Portrait of Columbus

Departure of Columbus from Patos

Twentieth century version of the triangular trade

Sugar: the buildings of an eighteenth-century mill
[Packer, Kingston]

Sugar: a modern mill
[Packer, Kingston]

Hoeing a cane-piece, c. 1830

A negroes' dance in the island of Dominica, by Brunias, published by Thomas Palser, Westminster Bridge, London, c. 1810

Religion, ceremony and music

Havana harbour *[British Museum]*

Coconuts: shelling copra
[Packer, Kingston]

Ground provisions in the market

[Packer, Kingston]

Ground provisions on a peasant holding

[Packer, Kingston]

Devon House, Jamaica, a fine example of an old plantation house
[*Bill Lennox*]

'He found the right spot'

Meeting of Caribbean Heads of Governments in Barbados, 1967.

Left to right: George Price (Belize), William Bramble (Montserrat), John Compton (St. Lucia), Dr. Eric Williams (Trinidad & Tobago), Hugh Shearer (Jamaica), Errol Barrow (Barbados), Forbes Burnham (Guyana), Vere Bird (Antigua), Milton Cato (St. Vincent), Unknown (probably Dominica). *[Ministry of Education, Barbados]*

Trinidad offshore oil operation
[*Anne Bolt*]

US intervention in Grenada
[*Associated Press*]

CHAPTER XIII

'The Best and Worst of Times'

The cassis tree, which grows throughout the West Indies, is a symbol of alternating despair and hope. Most West Indian trees are evergreen; but the cassia loses its leaves, and the bark peels from its grey-white trunk, as from a dead stick. Then suddenly, overnight, the tree becomes a cascade of golden flowers, as short-lived as it is lovely.

The period in West Indian history which followed emancipation was like the death and rebirth of the cassia tree. It was the best and worst of times. One disaster followed another; bankruptcy and financial chaos in the eighteen-forties, droughts and epidemics in the eighteen-fifties, rioting and bloodshed in the eighteen-sixties. Yet in these disastrous years the initiative and courage of newly emancipated people were creating an independent peasantry. Radical constitutional changes were made in some territories, while the abolition of imperial preferences completed the destruction of the old plantation system. A rigid slave society marked by division and dominated by fear disintegrated and conditions were created for the growth, however slowly, of a new and dynamic society. The transition from slavery to 'full free' by way of apprenticeship, the rise of the free villages, the collapse of the plantation system, the encouragement of immigration and the extension of Crown colony government make this period one of the most fruitful and significant in West Indian history.

On the eve of emancipation the population of the British Caribbean was made up of three main groups. One of these consisted of a comparatively small number of white persons, all of them free: officials, plantation owners, merchants, professional men, attorneys, overseers, book-keepers, master craftsmen. They controlled the economic and political life of the country, and in the long-established colonies were practically self-governing in local affairs. The second group consisted of free people of colour, whose rights as citizens were limited. They owned property, were permitted to carry arms and to give evidence in a court of law, but had not the right to vote or to offer themselves for election. Below them in standing were the slaves, who had no direct part whatever in the political life of the islands.

This description is generally accurate for those islands which had been British for some time and where the plantation system was well-established. Trinidad was a notable exception. In 1783 the island was largely undeveloped, and its population was very small: 126 white persons, 295 free persons of colour and 310 slaves. These were all subject to Spanish law, and this provided that free persons, white or coloured, should have full rights of citizenship after five years' residence. The population grew rapidly. Some white planters were attracted from other islands by the abundance of available land, and a number of free persons of colour took refuge there from Saint-Domingue. By 1809 the group of coloured persons who were free formed one-fifth of the total population of about 30 000, while the group or whites was less than one-twelfth. In 1829 there were 4326 white persons, 16 412 free coloured, and 22 436 slaves. The coloured group never suffered to the same extent from special political disabilities as did the group in Jamaica, for the British retained the system of administration which they found in Trinidad. In 1828, as a result of agitation in the West Indies and in England, all civil and military distinctions between free British subjects of any colour were abolished by Order in Council in all the Crown colonies. Jamaica legislated in the same sense in 1830, Barbados in 1831.

In the British Caribbean, as a whole, the third social group was by far the largest. It included about three-quarters of a million slaves. Some of these were occupied with domestic duties; others were the technicians of the plantations, the carpenters, masons, boiler-men for example; and about three-fourths of the full number were praedial or field workers, or belonged to 'jobbing gangs' which might be hired out. The slaves had certain rights which were theirs by custom, and other rights which were theirs by law; they were entitled to allowances of food and clothing; in Jamaica they had the use of land on which to grow food, and were supposed to have every Sunday and every other Saturday for their own work; and usually they were allowed to keep small stock.

With emancipation, through the Order in Council that removed civil disabilities, the newly freed blacks became, in most British Colonies, equal before the law with any other British subjects — on paper but not in fact, as the Morant Bay uprising and the riots of the 1930's were to reveal. The trouble was that the social structure based on slavery remained virtually intact. The system of government remained oligarchic, the masses were excluded from the political system, skin colour determined status and opportunities for social mobility.

There was no common base of ideas and shared values, no unifying national sentiment as there was in Cuba, though still a colony.

Emancipation confronted the British government with the task of reconciling two irreconcileables, setting free the labour force of black slaves and providing the plantations with a supply of coerced black labour. Liberal officials believed that the blacks should be free but had no trust in their ability to cope with freedom. Magistrates were to be sent out from England for 'The effectual superintendence of the said apprenticed labourers, and the execution of this Act', and they were given jurisdiction over every 'Question, matter, being or thing incident to or arising out of the relations subsisting between such apprenticed labourers and the persons respectively entitled to their services'.

When the Secretary of State sent the Emancipation Act to the legislative colonies he pointed out that no scheme of probation other than the apprenticeship system would be allowed, but that they were free to shorten the period of apprenticeship or to do away with it altogether. Antigua followed this latter course. The planters owned practically all the land and were in a position to enforce a minimum wage and to make sure that free labour would cost less than slave labour. Mathieson in *British Slave Emancipation* tells how on August 1, 1834 masters and slaves rejoiced together at religious services and how, on the Monday following, the freed slaves found that the planters had combined to set a fixed daily wage of one shilling for skilled workers and nine pence for others.

Apprenticeship was adopted in all the Crown colonies and in the other legislative colonies. The British government looked on this as a period of transition during which labourers would be prepared for full freedom by a series of social reforms and by the enjoyment of fuller rights. Many planters, however, regarded the system as 'a part of the compensation, a short and partial reprieve granted that they might squeeze the last juice out of compulsory labour before the great ruin of freedom set in.'

As Mathieson points out: 'the Act which abolished slavery did not emancipate the slaves. . . . As a social institution slavery disappeared . . . and it came back as a system of industry, the negroes. . . having to work as slaves for so many hours a week.' Yet there was from the start this fundamental difference, that those who had been owners of labour had become the buyers, and those who had been slaves were now the sellers of labour. It took time for the owners to recognise their loss of power, and there were difficulties and misunderstanding when at one and the same time freedom was proclaimed and forced labour demanded. In St. Christopher martial law had to be proclaimed and a number of ex-slaves punished before the apprentices would work. There was some unrest and dissatisfaction among the apprentices in Trinidad, Tobago, British Guiana and in Jamaica, but on the whole the system worked. The disputes were generally about wages and the continuance of rights, particularly with respect to the growing of food and the use of land. This problem was not acute in Barbados, where food was imported. The hope had been expressed in Nevis in 1782 that 'in a year or two this island will be able to raise much provision towards supporting its own slaves but hitherto it has been our invariable custom to depend almost entirely on America'. This was true of all the Leeward Islands, so that here and in Barbados scarcity of land compelled labour to work on the estates to get wages to buy food. Labour disputes were acute in Jamaica where it was customary to give the slaves 'grounds' on which to grow their food. This had been one way in which the estates kept their costs down and, at the same time, 'anchored' the slave to the estate. The custom had been a stabilising factor under slavery. Under apprenticeship, with labour and production costs rising, some planters saw a chance of keeping wages down by charging rent for the 'grounds' and they caused resentment and ill-will when they evicted those who would not or could not pay these rents.

The contrast is indicated by Gurney, who visited the West Indies in 1838. In St. Kitts a stipendiary magistrate reported that the negroes 'will do an infinity of work for wages', and in Antigua the late Speaker of the Assembly had declared that 'the free labour system is the cheapest', whereas in Jamaica 'the question of tenancy has been mixed up with that of labour' and evictions had caused bitter resentment.

One of the best accounts of the difficulties of this period of transition is given by Sir Charles Metcalfe, when governor of Jamaica, in a despatch to the Secretary of State in 1839. He wrote: 'When the freedom of slaves was established, the great question that agitated the island was, on what terms free labour could be obtained for the cultivation of the estates, from which the wealth of Jamaica has hitherto been derived. It naturally became the interest of the owners of properties to obtain labour on the cheapest, and that of the labouring population to sell it on the dearest terms; and a struggle with these opposite views commenced between the two parties.

'The practice which prevailed in slavery, of granting grounds to the labourers, from which they derived the means of subsistence in esculents for themselves and their families, and by the sale of surplus produce, gave a great advantage to the labourers when they acquired freedom, as it rendered them in a great degree independent of labour, and enabled them to hold out for terms. The proprietors could not hold out with the same safety, for the want of labour on their properties, at some, if not all, periods of the year, must have been ruinous. The wages of labour, therefore, have been hitherto settled more at the will of the labourer than at that of his employer, and this must continue to be the case until a great increase of the labouring population shall make labour cheaper, or until labourers shall be more dependent on labour, or until such a number of properties shall be thrown out of cultivation by the impossibility of meeting the expense as may produce the same effect as an increase in the labouring population. . . .

'As a counterpoise to the power of the labourers over wages, the proprietors have that of charging rent for the houses and grounds tenanted by the labourers, and this right is often exercised with a veiw to counterbalance, as much as possible, the payment of wages, and not with reference purely to the value of the house and grounds. Thus in many instances the rent of a house is charged, not as a rate fixed for the house, but at a rate fixed for each occupant of the house. These counter-claims for rent and wages keep up much irritation and litigation, but will, it is to be hoped, in time, be settled on the basis of mutual interest. . . .

'The conduct of the labouring population is represented by the stipendiary magistrates, whose reports are the most frequent channels of official information possessed by the government, as being orderly and irreproachable; and I see no reason to doubt the truth of their representations. . . . The stipendiary magistrates are a class, with individual exceptions, offensive to the proprietary interest. This is not surprising. The magistracy of the country consisted, formerly exclusively of proprietors, or their representatives, performing their duties gratuitously. . . . During the apprenticeship and since the recent granting of freedom it was scarcely possible to entrust the dispensation of justice entirely to those who were themselves so much interested in the questions likely to arise for discussion. Nevertheless, the establishment of stipendiary magistrates was extremely grating to the landed interests; and added to the abolition of slavery, became a second revolution in the island. The annoyance was aggravated in a great degree, partly by the inexperience and unfitness of some of the stipendiary magistrates, and partly from their receiving a bias from the purpose for which they were appointed, and by their regarding themselves rather as protectors of the labourers than as dispensers of equal justice to all parties. . . .'

The system of apprenticeship for field workers was terminated in 1838, two years earlier than had been intended. In islands where there was a higher proportion of resident owners and where labour relations were, therefore, generally better, and where there was very little land available for further cultivation, the system seems to have worked fairly well. It is indeed possible that islands like Barbados and St. Kitts did not need the system and might very well have followed the example of Antigua, since the plantations dominated the economy of the islands and the labourers had few other sources of livelihood. In other islands like Montserrat and Dominica there were only a handful of white planters with limited resources and the demand for labour was, therefore, small. In these, apprenticeship mattered little. It was in British Guiana and in Jamaica, where there was land and where the estates were powerful, that friction and dissatisfaction arose. This was inevitable, for the system was an attempt at a compromise between two irreconcilables: slavery and freedom. It set out to provide forced labour, to limit the mobility of labour, and to continue the system of allowances — rent-free gardens and supplies of fish and meat — all of which had been characteristic of slavery, while at the same time requiring payment for labour and causing competition between employers for such labour as there was. Wage agreements between masters and apprentices were made difficult because some indulgences were a legal right, and some were not; as a result, the apprentice often demanded as a right what the master withheld as a wage. Nor could disputes be terminated by out-right refusals to do any labour, because the apprentice was compelled to give his $40\frac{1}{2}$ hours per week; or by the threat of dismissal, for the apprentice was fixed to the estate. In short, the coercive power of the master, the essential force of slavery, had been removed; and the full freedom to bargain, the essential force of free labour, had not been substituted. The efforts of the stipendiary magistrates, the unskilled interpreters of a vague law, though often brave, could hardly have solved the difficulties inherent in the system.

In those places where the estates were powerful and where land was also available there developed a remarkable movement in the establishment of an independent peasantry. The movement began before emancipation, and sprang from a desire for land and liberty. During slavery negroes had broken away from the Surinam and Guiana plantations to establish settlements in the interior, and they had escaped from the sugar estates on the Jamaican lowlands to maroon villages in remote mountain valleys. These settlements were active and corporate units. Their success owed much to the efforts which had been made by governments in the late eighteenth century to introduce new food crops, particularly starchy ground provisions such as cocos and improved varieties of yam, and tree crops such as ackee and breadfruit, which produced over long periods with little effort, conserved water, and provided shade for the peasant cultivator. Yams, plantains, ackees and later breadfruit were the chief Jamaican peasant foods. Accounts from Guiana tell of the cultivation of rice, yams, tannias and tobacco by the bush negroes and of the 'encampments' of run-away negroes on the east coast of Demerara. The establishment of free villages was not begun as a result of emancipation, but with freedom it became possible for many people to do legally what a few hitherto had done illegally. So, along the banks of the Berbice and Demerara rivers in British Guiana there sprang up settlements of newly emancipated people who pooled their resources, bought land, 'parcelled it out, and so called a regular Negro Colony into existence'. The same process took place in Trinidad, where, in Montserrat Ward for instance, peons from the mainland and newly freed negroes squatted and established villages. In Guiana, the movement was on an impressive scale. In Berbice, in 1838, out of a population of 20 000 there were 15 000 who were newly emancipated, none of whom owned land. Four years later over 1000 of these families owned 7000 acres purchased at a cost of more than $10 000.

A vast land-settlement scheme was in fact put through in Guiana by people who acted very largely under their own leadership and by pooling their resources. The result was that up to the end of 1848, over 400 estates had been bought, and more than 10 000 houses had been built and occupied by 44 443 persons. By 1852 it was estimated that there were more than 70 000 persons of the labouring class in British Guiana and that these owned property in houses and lands for which they had paid £1 000 000.

There was a similar wave of settlement in Jamaica, where also land space exceeded the supply of labour. In Guiana the expansion was on to land that was fertile and rich. The choice was more restricted in Jamaica, and it seems likely that a large number of persons would have preferred to live in their old villages and to cultivate their grounds. Many estate owners, however, thought that they could compel labour to accept their terms if they could deprive them of the use of these 'grounds' and so they drove them from the estates by high rentals and by ejections. Missionaries like Knibb, Phillippo, Clark, Dendy and Burchell gave a lead in the establishment of free villages, and the general result of this process which transformed the emancipated slave into a peasant proprietor is described by Sir Charles Metcalfe in 1840 in a letter to Lord John Russell: 'The accompanying statement shows that a large increase has taken place from 1838 to 1840 in the number of proprietors of small freeholds in the several rural parishes of this island, the increase consisting almost entirely of emancipated negroes. It appears that the number of such freeholders assessed in 1838 was 2014; and in 1840, 7848. There was no assessment in the intermediate year, owing to the suspension of ordinary taxation.'

Five years later William Knibb described the progress of settlement in these words: 'By the census taken during last year, I find that there were full 19 000 persons, formerly slaves, who had purchased land on which they were erecting their own cottages. In St. James' parish there were 10 new villages, with 1020 houses; in Trelawny, the parish in which I live, there were 23 free villages, and 1590 houses; in St. Mary's, 15 free villages, with 632 houses; in St. Thomas, in the Vale, 10 free villages with 1780 houses.' By the middle of the century communities of peasant farmers had grown up throughout the islands. They were practically self-supporting, getting the cash they needed by the sale of the ground provisions which they cultivated.

While these settlements of smallholders were being established the plantation system was crumbling. The boom in sugar at the beginning of the century had been caused by the collapse of sugar production in Saint-Domingue and by the exceptional circumstances of war. After the war prices fell disastrously. The disturbed state of Europe lessened the demand and the interruption of trade with the United States made it difficult and costly to obtain timber and food. The American trade was re-opened in 1822, but by then competition from Cuba and the East Indies had increased and there was a rising demand for the removal of the preferential duty of *10s.* per cwt. which West Indian sugar enjoyed over East Indian sugar. In the boom years much marginal land had been planted in cane, and in addition the general cost of production was high. In the middle of the Napoleonic war it cost the planter from *35s.* to *36s.* to produce I cwt. of sugar. The result was that when prices fell to what had been the normal *30s.* to *35s.* and even below, only the most efficient estates could stay in business, and production steadily declined.

Production costs had been increased by the abolition of the slave trade in 1807, and the Emancipation Act of 1833 had the effect of increasing the shortage of labour and so sending up its cost. In Barbados and St. Kitts, where labour was in excess of land-space, production was fairly well maintained, but in the other territories there was a fall in production during the period of apprenticeship and a further fall after full emancipation. Apprenticeship seems to have put a brake on the downward trend which had begun early in the century. The introduction of the Bourbon cane helped planters to lift the production of sugar per acre, but this on the credit side was not enough to counterbalance the heavy debit items of labour shortage and low prices.

Full emancipation caused a radical change in the way in which the plantations were financed. Under slavery the planter had been able to operate with comparatively little working capital. He did not have to pay wages, and he could cut his expenditure on food supplies for the estate by letting the slaves grow as much food as possible. He sold his sugar through an agent in London, who purchased supplies for him and advanced money to carry him over bad years. This method of finance suited the West India merchants in London because they could collect the interest on money they had lent by insisting that their debtors' sugar should pass through their hands. It suited the planters because it gave them the credit which they needed.

'Full free' meant payment for labour. The estate had to find cash to pay wages, as well as to equip the estate with labour-saving devices like ploughs and harrows, and with steam engines for the mills. The labour bill for an estate in the eighteen-forties might be as much as two-thirds of the total cost of production and it was a bill that had to be paid on time, so that the planter needed two or three times more working capital than formerly. The West Indies had always been short of currency and coins of almost every variety had been in circulation before the abolition of slavery — Spanish dollars, doubloons, pistoles, escudos, and, latterly, United States dollars. Now planters had to find cash, much of it in small denominations. Most West Indian planters were already heavily in debt to their London agents, and could not expect much further accommodation from that source. They had been paid £20 000 000 in compensation for the loss of their slaves, it is true; but little of this went into the planters' pockets. Most of the money went to the merchants to pay off mortgages and sub-mortgages. There was little left for capital development or for working the estate and some planters could not even raise the cash to pay their labourers. The banks which were founded in the eighteen-thirties to meet the desperate need for capital — the Colonial Bank for the West Indies in London in 1836, the Planters' Bank in Jamaica in 1837 — were very shaky affairs. Under slavery a man's wealth had been reckoned by the number of slaves he owned. Now it was reckoned in terms of money, and money was even shorter than labour.

Prices continued to fall. Sewell says that 'between 1805 and 1825 the price... fell 25 per cent... between 1825 and 1835 it fell another 25 per cent... between 1835 and 1850 it fell away 25 per cent again.' The ruin was completed by the introduction of free trade and the removal of the preferential duty on West Indian sugar between 1846 and 1854. In 1847 also there occurred a commercial crisis in the United Kingdom which sent thirteen West India houses into bankruptcy within twelve months. The West India bank with its headquarters in Barbados failed, and so did the Planters' Bank in Jamaica. The West Indian planters were desperate. The figures for Jamaica, which produced one-half of the sugar sold in the British market at the time, show how catastrophic was the collapse of the industry in that island. From 71 000 tons in 1832 production fell to 25 000 tons in 1852. In 1840 the price had been £49 per ton in bond in England. It fell to £23 in 1846. Between 1846 and 1852, 474 sugar and coffee plantations and 132 grass pens valued in 1841 at £2 441 000, were wholly or partly abandoned. The value of property fell sharply. In 1777 Rose Hall Estate, consisting of 1095 acres with 260 slaves, had been sold for £18 000. In 1857 one-third of the same estate was sold for £300.

George Price, writing in 1866, described the collapse of the sugar estates in Jamaica in these words: 'In the district around, about 300 square miles, I found in 1842 nineteen sugar estates in full operation, having on them the usual white managers and people — other whites, attracted by the considerable amount of money in circulation, being also settled in the district. In 1864 all these estates had long ceased cultivation, except that with which I was connected; trees were growing out of the walls and roofs of nearly all the buildings; and all around was bush. With the exception of three or four, all the whites had vanished. There had in fact been two movements — the flight of labour from the estates and the flight of capital and of white owners. In 1844 there had been 15 775 white persons in the island and in 1861 the number had fallen to 13 815.

Britain at this time was putting its surplus capital into expanding industries, new developing overseas territories, and the railways and steamships that were revolutionising transport. The West Indies, grown shabby and threadbare, could not hope to attract new capital. Any industry would have been hard put to it to face a combination of increased labour costs and falling prices; add to these the lack of capital to cover day-to-day expenses and essential reorganisation and the reasons for the collapse of the sugar industry in the British West Indies became plain. Jamaica appeared to be following, by less violent stages, the same path as Saint-Domingue.

At this critical period of transition from slavery to freedom, owners usually were not present to initiate reforms or to supply leadership. The Marquess of Sligo complained that the Jamaica House of Assembly was made up almost entirely of attorneys and overseers. The drain on local resources is shown by the fact that the exports from Jamaica were normally nearly double the imports in value, the difference representing the profits drawn by absent owners. When prices fell and profits diminished owners began to sell out, but many estates went into chancery because, by law, the estates remained subject to any encumbrances or liens which had been put on them. The buyer purchased both the estate and any charges to which it ws subject. St. Lucia was the first island to change this by setting up a mortgage office in 1829 and by passing a law in 1833 which authorised the seizure of real estate property and the sale of this property without encumbrances. The benefits were immediate. Between 1833 and 1843 sixty-nine out of the eighty-one estates in the island were sold free of mortgages. Then in 1854 the first West Indies Encumbered Estates Act was passed, and the principle of encumbered estates being sold without encumbrances was adopted by St. Vincent in 1857 and by Jamaica in 1861. The estates were sold out or were broken up and sold to small-holders.

The position of the sugar industry was better in some British territories than in others. For all of them the critical years were from 1845 to 1854, the year of the complete equalisation of the sugar duties. In 1854 the price fell to *21s. 5d.* per cwt. in bond, but after that it began to rise again and in 1857 it reached *35s. 7d.* per cwt. Production rose, and by 1860 the islands and British Guiana had weathered the storm. Barbados was able to do this mainly because labour was available; Trinidad and British Guiana managed to achieve comparative prosperity because of Indian labour. Many owners and attorneys had seen that the labour shortages which began with the passing of the Abolition Act of 1807 would become more acute with the passing of the Emancipation Act of 1833. In Barbados, Antigua and St. Kitts the problem was not so much one of the scarcity of labour as of its irregularity, but in Trinidad the development of the island had been retarded by the acute shortage of labour. The shortage was also acute in British Guiana and in Jamaica. Many of the emancipated people disliked estate labour and preferred to grow food on their own 'ground', working only for such cash as was needed and nothing more. Moveover, the position was affected by the withdrawal of women and children from the estate labour force, the reduction in hours of labour, the increased mobility of the worker and his preference for other kinds of work. The planters believed that the answer to the problem was immigration — finding new sources of labour and bringing them into West Indies on contract.

Immigration was in keeping with the spirit of the age. The eighteenth century had seen the movement under compulsion of vast numbers of people from West Africa to the Americas. The nineteenth century saw an even greater free movement of people from Europe and Asia. In the sixty years after Waterloo some 7 000 000 people went from the United Kingdom alone to the colonies. In the ten years immediately after 1815 the population of Canada rose from 80 000 to 150 000. At the same time, in the East, the Chinese were making their way down through Indo-China to Java and the islands of the Pacific. The emigration of Indian labour on a large scale began in 1830 when a French merchant took 130 Indian artisans to Bourbon. By 1847 there were 7000 Indians in Mauritius and the movement of Indians into Africa had also begun.

In the West Indies the planters seeking cheap labour, pressed for immigration on a large scale. Jamaica desired European immigration so as to settle the highlands of the interior with white smallholders who would be a counterbalance to the blacks, but the effort failed. In 1834 and 1835 batches of labourers were taken from Madeira into British Guiana, while from Trinidad and from Guiana the planters sent agents into the British islands to recruit labour. This immigration has continued up to the present time in spite of legal barriers; in 1952 it was found that there were some 11 000 illegal West Indian immigrants in Trinidad alone. Efforts were also made, with some success, to bring free Africans to the West Indies. African immigration, insignificant in comparison with East Indian, lasted for thirty years and involved 36 000 people, one-third of whom returned to Africa. On the other hand, East Indian immigration involved more than ten times as many persons and covered a period of about eighty years.

The British government was suspicious of any scheme that might conceivably lead to a revival of slavery, and it did not grant any substantial concession until John Gladstone became interested in the recruitment of Indian labour and obtained permission to bring Indian labourers into Guiana on five-year contracts. Ill-treatment and sickness caused many deaths, and Lord John Russell informed the Governor of British Guiana in 1840 that he would be unwilling 'to adopt any measure to favour the transfer of labourers from British India to Guiana, after the failure of the former experiment'. Nevertheless, the planters persisted in their attempts to attract labour from overseas and by 1842 very nearly 5000 Madeirans had been brought in. The history of Trinidad and of Guiana is dominated by the labour question at this period and by the attempts to solve it by immigration. Under pressure from the West Indies and the Colonial Office, the embargo on immigration from India was lifted and a second attempt was made during the years 1845–46 to bring Indians to the West Indies. This attempt also failed.

Up to 1850, then, the results of these attempts to encourage immigration were disappointing. During the years 1841–47 British Guiana alone spent £360 655 on immigration, and in return obtained 12 237 labourers from India, 12 898 from the West Indian islands, 8645 from Africa, and some 16 000 from Madeira — a total of about 50 000 persons. The Africans showed a strong and understandable tendency to walk off into the bush and set up as peasant squatters. The Madeirans suffered from an appallingly high mortality rate, due largely to their own indifference to — or ignorance of — the most elementary rules of health in the tropics. Only the Indians worked steadily on the sugar estates and so contributed directly to the labour supply, and their numbers were inadequate to the need. Things went from bad to worse with sugar and finally the House of Commons lent £250 000 to help the industry, four-fifths of the amount to be spent on immigration. The mortality rate had been high among indented Indian labourers also — though less than among the Madeirans — because large numbers of uneducated people had been removed from the things they were used to, thrown on their own in a strange land, given inadequate medical attention and insufficient food. The local commission which was appointed to spend the loan money emphasised that immigration from India was the only way to save the sugar industry and arrangements were made to bring Indians into the country under improved conditions, with compulsory provision of housing and medical attention. Much of the 'barrack' housing in British Guiana dates from this time. Between 1884 and 1914 some 239 000 Indians were brought into British Guiana under indenture and only about one in every four of these were repatriated. Already in 1883 Indians formed more than one-quarter of the population of British Guiana — 65 000 out of 250 000. In Trinidad, similarly, by 1883 East Indians formed about one-third of a total population of 153 000.

In Trinidad and British Guiana the steady increase of the East Indian population was reflected directly in the figures of sugar production. In British Guiana production dropped steadily from 60 000 tons in 1830 to 23 000 tons in 1846. It was hard hit by the crisis of 1847 and by the equalisation of duties, but from 1848 it began to rise, and thereafter it increased steadily: 38 000 tons in 1851, 63 000 in 1861, 92 000 in 1871. The trends in Trinidad were similar, on a smaller scale, and both colonies showed a striking contrast with Jamaica, where production declined throughout the century from a high figure of nearly 100 000 tons in 1805 to a low figure of under 13 000 tons in 1888. In Jamaica, lack of labour was probably a less serious difficulty than lack of capital; there was considerable opposition to Indian immigration, or rather to the spending of money on immigration, and in 1883 there were only 13 000 Indians in a population of 580 000.

Slowly, separately, battling against neglect and poverty, despised and discriminated against, the descendants of African slaves and East Indian indentured labourers developed a system of agriculture based on small holdings, owned or rented. The contribution of the incoming East Indians will be discussed later. The contribution of the freed slaves was evident by 1860. By that time, Jamaica had more than 50 000 holdings of under 50 acres each; St. Lucia, St. Vincent, Grenada and Tobago had more than 10 000 freeholders. In Grenada and St. Vincent there were about 20 000 people living in cottages built in the years following emancipation. The provision grounds and Sunday markets of the plantation had enabled them to retain their traditional skills in agriculture and trading, and the importation of new food crops and fruit trees had augmented their food supply. Among them were grannies and nanas who served as midwives, counsellors, healers skilled in the use of herbs and plants for tisanes and baths. There were among them leaders who met the need for capital by organising partnerships for saving and for work, still called by their folknames, su-su, group work, day-for-day, morning work, gyap, combite. Some were skilled in the crafts and skills of the plantation, in the care of livestock, in masonry, carpentry, iron work, in burning charcoal and lime. From the new homesteads came the elementary school teachers, native clergy, church-elders, village shop-keepers who set new patterns of social mobility. They were aided by the non-conformist, Anglican and Roman Catholic Churches as well as by grants from the British government. In 1833, two years after its first grant for primary education in Britain, the British government provided £25 000 for education in the West Indies. Further grants were made up to 1846. The Mico Trust provided money for Mico Teacher training Colleges in Demerara, Trinidad and Jamaica and Mico Schools were started in St. Lucia and Trinidad. The various religious denominations added funds of their own and staff. But by 1850 hard times had set in, the enthusiasm of the first years slackened, public expenditure on education fell, poverty increased, and tensions built up among the folk, who were angered by continuing deprivation and injustice.

By 1860 the freed slaves and their descendants might very well have used the language the Chartists used in their petition to the British House of Commons in 1838 — the year in which West Indian apprenticeship ended: — 'our slavery has been exchanged for an apprenticeship of liberty, which has aggravated the painful feelings of our social degradation by adding to them the sickening of still deferred hope . . . The good of the many, as it is the only legitimate end, so it must be the sole study of the government'. The folk had, nevertheless, taken an important step toward changing the institutions and social values of plantation society by providing an alternative system of agriculture. A statement quoted by Guerra y Sanchez from a report by the Cuban commissioners to the Information Board of that country, which had an established peasantry is relevant: 'A country's agriculture . . . rests on the society which produced it, and it develops according to the institutions which govern that society. It will grow and flourish or stagnate and decay, together with those institutions. The agricultural process is intimately related to the other institutional forces which give shape to the character and government of a people.'

Patterns of Colonial Government

Columbus advised the King and Queen of Spain in the Journal of his first Voyage, 'that Your Highnesses ought not to consent that any foreigner does business or sets foot here, except Christian Catholics, since this was the end and the beginning of the enterprise, that it should be for the enhancement and glory of the Christian religion, nor should anyone who is not a good Christian come to these parts'.

We have seen how the Spanish barricades to the Caribbean were breached and how tobacco, sugar, and religion propelled European nations and peoples across the Atlantic to North America and the West Indies, and we have considered the various forces that brought into existence a world vastly different from that of which Columbus dreamed and for which Spain bled herself white. We have noted the many discontinuities in Caribbean history, and we have found a unifying theme in the struggle for freedom of the mass of the Caribbean people, most of them black. We find another theme emerging as we review the different patterns of colonial government and a gradual advance in local self-government in the mainland colonies.

In the early period, New England, Virginia, Cuba, Barbados and Jamaica provided a valuable range of insights into this process. Guerra y Sanchez, for example, points out that in 1536 the Cabildo of Sancti Spiritus trespassed on the royal prerogative by making a grant of land to a petitioner, and so established a precedent which cabildos in Havana and elsewhere followed. This encroachment by the oligarchic municipal councils on the Crown's prerogative took place during two centuries of neglect following on the colonization of Cuba; it strengthened the local institutions, encouraged a sense of Cuban identity and provided valuable experience in self-government.

New England and Virginia also benefitted from imperial neglect during the first century after settlement. William Bradford, in his account of Plymouth Plantation, emphasized that 'they knew they were Englishmen who came over this great ocean and were ready to perish in this wilderness', and both the North American and the older British West Indian colonies based on their heritage the claim to a representative system of government with elected Houses of Assembly and elected local government authorities. But not even the Pilgrim fathers went quite as far as did Colonel Rainborough and the Levellers in their debate with Cromwell's son-in-law General Ireton, at Putney in 1647: 'For really I think that the poorest he that is in England hath a life to live, as the greatest he, and therefore, sir, I think it's clear, that every man that is to live under a government ought first by his own consent to put himself under that government...I should doubt whether he was an Englishman or no, that should doubt of these things.' The Levellers were 125 years ahead of the United States, 150 years ahead of Great Britain and some 300 years ahead of the West Indies. The Putney debate highlights the difference between the rights of propertied man which were safeguarded by a franchise based on properly qualification, and the rights of man, which are more adequately protected by universal adult suffrage. Ireton replied that 'no person hath a right to an interest or share in the disposing of the affairs of the Kingdom...that hath not a permanent fixed interest in the Kingdom', a view that chimed with liberal thought in the 17th and 18th centuries.

A general consideration, then, is the movement from self-government and a restricted franchise to universal adult suffrage and independence. Interwoven with this is the active involvement of local communities in the administration of their affairs and a habit of voluntary public service, often as unpaid agents or officers of the local unit. In Frank Rossiter's words, 'the towns were self-governing in the most obvious sense — through the famous town meeting, the select-men, and a host of unpaid minor officials: constables, tithingmen, surveyors, fence viewers, field drivers... In 1720 and average Massachusetts town, Ipswich, had ninety-seven regular officials'. As for the Vestrymen, Jefferson said they were usually the most discreet farmers, 'well-acquainted with the details and economy of private life...and they find sufficient inducements to execute their charge well, in their philanthropy...the approbation of their neighbours, and the distinction which that gives them'. We have, then, two sets of institutions that have their origin in the English tradition, each similar to the other in structure, the North American functioning in a free society with the involvement and leadership of resident property owners, the West Indian functioning in a plantation system based on slavery or indentured labour, serving as an instrument of coercion and discrimination. When Britain acquired other colonies in the

Caribbean direct crown colony rule was introduced, and retained for a century without the introduction of any degree of elected representation. Eric Williams etched in acid the picture of the colony of Trinidad in 1911; 'This was a government unrepresentative of the people and not responsible to it; an economy almost exclusively in non-native hands, and a native population which were hewers of wood and drawers of water for its foreign overlords.'

The preservation of old variety was most evident, as might be expected, in the field of local government — the municipal and parochial structure, which everywhere in the West Indies had preceded the establishment of central administration. The people who went out from England in the early years to settle and plant in St. Kitts and Nevis, in Antigua, Barbados and Jamaica, transferred to these lands the pattern of local government to which they were accustomed. Within a few years of its settlement Barbados was divided into six parishes, each with its vestry. The freeholders met each year to elect the 'trustees' for the following twelve months; these had the power to levy rates for the poor, for the support of the clergy, and for the upkeep of the roads. In Jamaica and in the Cayman Islands also the parish vestry began to function at an early date. A characteristic extract from the vestry book of the parish of St. Elizabeth in Jamaica deals with the raising of revenue in 1695: 'At a meeting of the Justice and Vestry of the first Tuesday in February. . .ordered that Negroes young and old be valued at ten pounds a Head and Cattle of all sorts at Thirty Shillings a head and sheep and goats at five pounds a score and that the tax be leveyed at *12s. 6d.* for every hundred pounds and if that be not sufficient to defray the parish charge then the Vestry meet and levy the said tax to be at *15s.* for every hundred inhabitants.' The vestry minutes show low local government, the method by which a community learns to manage and direct its own business, had taken firm root in these early colonies. The vestry licensed teachers, maintained roads, paid the parson, punished vagrants and looked after the poor, and the freeholders of the parish were taxed for these and other purposes.

This development of local government in the older West Indian territories is in contrast with the highly centralised administrative system which the Spaniards established in Trinidad. The Spanish governors in Trinidad had autocratic powers that were limited in two ways: the necessity of having most of the sentences pronounced by the governor confirmed by the royal *audiencia* in Caracas, and secondly by the *residencia* — the special inquiry held at the end of a governor's term of office, either by his successor or by an official sent out from

Spain, who reviewed the governor's actions with a view to redressing grievances. The *cabildo* or municipal council of Port-of-Spain also exercised some influence on the government, and so there was a measure of local government through the municipality but none through the parish. The British retained the Spanish system for some years after they took Trinidad in 1797, without the administrative checks that have been mentioned, and so they helped to establish tradition of a strong central government without any effective system of local government.

British Guiana and British Honduras introduced yet other variations. At the beginning of the seventeenth century the main stream of English settlement had been towards Virginia, the Caribbee islands and the coast of Guiana, but the danger of Spanish and Portuguese attacks, and the decision of the Pilgrim Fathers to cross the North Atlantic to New England, had turned the main flow to North America and away from South America. The Dutch, on the other hand, had turned from New Amsterdam on the Hudson to enlarge their holdings in South America. In 1667, by the Treaty of Breda, they took over Surinam, which had been settled from Barbados under the leadership of Francis Lord Willoughby. Much earlier in the century they had pushed up the Guiana rivers, the Cayenne and the Essequibo, founding Fort Kijk-over-al at the place where the Mazaruni and Cuyuni meet the Essequibo.

> *There runs a dream of perished lost foundations*
> *Through these Guiana rivers to the sea,*

and there runs through the law of British Guiana today the influence of its former rulers. The Dutch system of administration was planned for controlling trade depots, and not for creating settlements of free planters. Trade was the main object. When settlements grew up the profits of the Dutch West India Company were the first concern, and the company ruled until 1792, when Guiana was put under the control of a council set up by the States General. At no time was local opinion allowed to have much influence on the government of the colony. The company had a Court of Policy, made up of its officials, for each of the provinces of Essequibo, Demerara and Berbice. The first opportunity for the settlers to participate was when, in 1738, a planter was appointed to the Essequibo Court of Policy. Later, one un-official member was also appointed to each of the Courts of Policy for Berbice and Demerara. Then, in 1743, Gravesande set up the College of Kiezers or Electors. The members of this were elected for life by resident planters who owned more than twenty-five slaves, and they only had to give a double nomination to the Director General of the Colony when the unofficial member died or left the colony. Rarely in a democracy can so little have been given to so many by so few. Agitation led to a reform in 1787, the Plan of Redress, by which Essequibo and Demerara were given one Court of Policy, and the planters were given more representation through the College of Kiezers. Later, in 1795, the governor accepted the proposal made by the planters for a 'Combined Court' made up of six 'Financial Representatives' elected for two years by resident planters and the members of the Court of Policy. The planters argued that the Court of Policy, as it stood, with its official majority, gave them no voice in the levying of colonial taxes. The Combined Courts, on which their representatives had a majority, was to vote on the raising of taxes and examination of accounts but was to have no other powers. The British, when they took over the government, were confronted with the task of making this intricate system work. It could hardly be expected to work well. Since the Combined Court had a majority of settlers, and the Dutch Crown had capitulated, the colonists claimed that legislative rights had passed to them and that no change could be made in the constitution without their consent. It was not until 1831, for instance, that local consent could be secured for so obvious a measure as the union of Demerara, Essequibo and Berbice in the single administration of British Guiana.

The fundamental weakness in the Dutch system of administration was the separation of powers; the official majority in the Court of Policy was responsible for governing while the unofficial majority in the Combined Court controlled the purse. This same weakness was the main defect also in the British islands with Houses of Assembly. Charles II declared that Englishmen who settled in Jamaica and their children 'shall from their respective births be reputed to be free denizens of England; and shall have the same privileges, to all intents and purposes, as our free born subjects of England'. Within a few years of this declaration the Crown took over from the proprietors the government of the Caribbee Islands also, but retained the consitution, with governor, council and assembly. When the administration of the Leeward Islands was separated from that of Barbados in 1672 one governor was appointed with a council and assembly in each island. The pattern of government in all these British West Indian islands was very much like that of England in miniature. There were, wrote Long, 'three estates of which the governor (as representing the King) is head. Having no order of nobility here, the place of a house of peers is supplied by a council of twelve gentlemen appointed by the King, which in the system of our legislature forms the upper house. The lower house is composed (as in Britain) of the representatives of the people, elected by the freeholders'. There was this essential difference, however, between the constitution of Britain and of the West Indian colonies — that the English system represented a stage in national development, a process in which full power finally passed into the hands of the House of Commons. The West Indian system remained fixed and rigid for very nearly two centuries. In England those with or without the franchise were free citizens, and public opinion could be used to compel constitutional change. In the West Indies the free citizens were a small section of the community and it was vital to them to preserve the situation which existed. They were cut off from an appeal to more than a very limited section of the public in a society with a rigid social and economic structure.

Another basic weakness of the West Indian constitution was that the power to govern lay with the assembly and the responsibility to govern lay with the governor. The instructions which were given to the Earl of Carlisle when he was appointed governor of Jamaica show how much was expected of him. He was captain-general and vice-admiral of the fleet; with the Legislative Council he was the supreme tribunal in civil matters; he had the final voice in the passing of legislation; he had to preserve good relations with the assembly and keep the machine of government working. If a Chinese philosopher were told of the many tasks that a governor had to perform, says Edward Long, he would point out that they were for a superman who had been specially trained to undertake them.

The Legislative Council was a pale reflection of the House of Lords. It advised the governor when sitting as an executive body, formed the upper house of the legislature, and with the governor was the highest court of appeal in civil matters. The really effective body was the House of Assembly. The independence of colonial assemblies sometimes provoked the governors to bitter outbursts like that of Sir Richard Dutton to the Barbados assembly in 1681: 'I have never heard that the King hath granted you a new Magna Charta, though you dispute all his commands as though he had.' They claimed privileges similar to those of the House of Commons; they controlled finance, and used the power of the purse to encroach on the prerogatives of the council and of the governor. In Jamaica the Assembly had been designed to play a minor role and its powers were limited in the governor's instructions, but by 1752 Governor Knowles reported that 'the Assembly of Jamaica had succeeded in making itself the predominant element in Government'. Lord Hamilton declared in 1760 that 'it is extreme vanity in them to assume all the privileges of the House of Commons' but, vanity or not, the claim was made good by the strangle-hold which they obtained on finance. He who pays the piper calls the tune, and the Assembly would not vote money if it objected to the governor's policy. It went further, and prevented him from using his power of dissolution to govern without it, by voting money for not more than six or twelve months at a time. Another method it used for getting its way was that of 'tacking' a measure it wanted on to a money bill; if the governor wanted the money he had to take the measure that was 'tacked' to the bill. In 1791, for example, the Jamaica House of Assembly 'married' a clause giving help to the Haitian planters during a rebellion to a money bill. The council objected and the Assembly branded the objection as 'officious, indecent, and irregular'.

The assemblies in their old shape could never have become the instruments of genuine self-government. They had power, but it was power to obstruct. The governors were entirely responsible for carrying on the government, and, as Wrong points out, the result was that 'In all the islands, large and small, the machinery of government groaned and grated and deadlock ensued deadlock. . . .' The local legislatures resented interference from the British Parliament, where the absentee proprietors and West India merchants had a powerful influence; though they were thrown into close alliance with the West India interest in England in the struggle over the abolition of the slave trade.

The number of these independent, factious and quarrelsome West Indian assemblies was multiplied after 1763 when, by treaty with France, the islands of Grenada, Dominica and St. Vincent were ceded to Britain. The government in them was modelled after that of the Leeward Islands. The original plan was for one governor-general and one legislature, but this was too much for the planters and merchants of each island. Chiefly because of their pressure the ceded islands, within twelve years, had three separate governments. The Board of Trade, mindful of the difficulties which had arisen in Barbados, the Leewards and Jamaica, tried at first to limit the powers of the assemblies in the ceded islands and for nearly five years after the first assembly met all the laws that were passed in the islands were disallowed by the Privy Council. The attempt at imposing restraints failed. In 1772 the governor was given authority to sign any bills that were based on the precedents of legislation in the Leeward Islands.

Though the assemblies in the ceded islands successfully enlarged their powers they never had the prestige and importance of the assemblies in the older islands because they represented smaller communities, each with a few hundred English residents. Small or large, however, the British Parliament did not generally interfere with the decisions of the colonial assemblies. The loss of the American colonies was a sharp reminder of the difficulties caused by interference. But during the first quarter of the nineteenth century a change took place. The Quebec Act of 1774 had provided that French Canadians should keep their own system of law and religion, but had placed all legislative power in the hands of the Crown, and the Crown delegated only very limited powers to the Legislative Assembly which it set up. This was a useful precedent for dealing with the West Indian territories that became British at the turn of the century — St. Lucia and Trinidad, Berbice and Demerara. In each of these conquered territories the laws and institutions to which the people were accustomed were retained, but in Trinidad and St. Lucia, and in British Guiana as far as possible, the Crown kept legislative power firmly in its own hands. Trinidad was allowed to retain most of the system of government which Spain had established there, though in fact there were about 1700 French and British settlers in the island in 1803 as compared with some 500 Spanish. The governor had autocratic powers such as the Spanish governor had possessed, but without checks imposed by the Spanish use of the royal *audiencia*. Then, in 1810, after some years of dissatisfaction and agitation Liverpool announced the decision to keep the power in the hands of the Crown, since the British Parliament would find it easier to protect the 'people of colour' and to enforce legislation in connection with the abolition of the slave trade. The despatch is explicit, stating that 'It is essential, for this purpose, that in a new Colony, the Crown should not divest itself of its Power of Legislation, and that neither the Crown nor Parliament should be subject to the embarrassments which, on such an occasion, might perhaps arise from the conflicting Views of the Imperial Parliament, and of a Subordinate Legislature'.

This was one of the reasons why the British government's policy of ameliorating the condition of the slaves was carried out more effectively in Trinidad than in Jamaica or Barbados, where the general stand taken by the assemblies was well expressed by a member, who remarked: 'It is impossible for any reflecting man to pursue, without dismay, a Despatch from the Secretary of States for colonies threatening, in most direct terms, to legislate for us in England, unless we adopt, in toto, and without hesitation, a certain plan of government for our slaves. . . .'

In the first half of the nineteenth century, then, there were two fundamentally different systems of government in the British West Indies, that of the legislative islands and that of the Crown colonies. During the latter half of the century the old representative system fell to pieces and disappeared, except in Barbados, and Crown colony government became general. Subsequently, in the twentieth century the change began from Crown colony to representative and responsible government.

During this first half of the nineteenth century, also, there began a reform in administration. In the eighteenth century there had been no professional civil service, and absenteeism was characteristic of government in the West Indies just as it was of industry. Society accepted political patronage or clientage as normal, and one way in which the government rewarded its supporters was by giving them sinecures and colonial patent offices. Long, in 1774, stated that 'the most executive offices in this island (the governor's excepted) are granted by the Crown to persons residing in England, and by these patentees are farmed or rented to deputies and sub-deputies acting in Jamaica, who remit annually several thousand pounds to their principals.' Even in the early Crown colonies the practice prevailed, for Rodway mentions a colonial secretary of British Guiana who, in 1824, had never been to the colony but was drawing £13 000 a year in fees. Out of this amount he paid two deputies.

Within the British West Indies the variations and contrasts in the pattern of government multiplied after emancipation. The old representative system was replaced by Crown colony government in many of the islands but was retained in Barbados; the system of Crown colony government which was introduced in British Guiana and Jamaica differed from that in Trinidad; yet other variations developed in British Honduras; a federal system managed to survive in the Leeward Islands but never developed in the Windward Islands; finally, a century after emancipation, responsible government became the deliberate aim of the political parties of the West Indies and of the government of the United Kingdom, and the federation of the British West Indies became a live political issue.

The old representative system decayed and perished in Jamaica and in the other parts of the West Indies for three main reasons. The first was absenteeism, which deprived the West Indies of the services of people of position and ability who might have identified themselves with the community. The West Indian assemblies recognised this, and tried unsuccessfully to check absenteeism by such proposals as putting higher taxes on the property of absentees. Emancipation was another and powerful reason. In the West Indian slave society of the eighteenth century, when slaves were property, they were technically represented by their owners. Emancipation wrought a vast social and political change; it set three-quarters of a million people free, without making any attempt to train them for the duties of citizenship. Its effect was to render the oligarchic rule of planter-attorneys more of an anachronism than ever. Henry Taylor at the Colonial Office advocated a policy of 'trusteeship' that involved abolishing the House of Assembly and introducing Crown colony government. He summed up the whole paradox of the situation in this way: 'To effect by force from without the greatest of all social changes and yet to leave the political framework of this totally different society the same as it was, would seem, even in a more theoretical view, to be in the nature of a political solecism.' The suggestion was then to sweep away the old representative system and in 1839 a Bill was in fact introduced into the British Parliament to suspend the House of Assembly for five years. Peel spoke against this Bill in parliament and Burge, Q. C., agent for Jamaica, appeared at the Bar of the House of Commons and of the House of Lords in defence of the ancient constitutional rights of Jamaica. Mutilated in the House of Lords, the Bill eventually merely empowered the governor, with the consent of the council, to enact measures for the government of Jamaica two months after the House of Assembly had thrown them out. The third factor was the Act (1846) of the British Parliament which provided for the progressive equalization of duties on British and foreign sugar. The wealth of Jamaica had been based on a monopoly propped up by differential duties; this final blow to the Jamaican economy went far to destroy the Assembly's power, for the Assembly had built up its power by control of the purse, and the purse was now empty.

The Jamaica Assembly at that time contained two recognisable parties; one was the Planters' Party, reinforced by the professional and mercantile elements, and it took the lead in a policy of retrenchment; the officials who received fixed salaries were the favourite targets for attacks by those gentlemen. The second was the 'coloured party' which also supported a policy of retrenchment, because it hoped by so doing to render offices less attractive to Europeans. The coloured politicians did not want the old assembly abolished, because they hoped that soon they would command a majority in the Assembly and they hoped to keep the greater part of the revenue dependent on annual grants. In 1853 when Sir Henry Barkly became governor he brought with him proposals from the Duke of Newcastle, then Secretary of State, that all public monies should be levied and disbursed, and all public accounts audited, by paid officials responsible to the Crown. These proposals implied that the Assembly was to abdicate its financial powers, since at that time 'It imposed the taxes, supervised their collection, voted their appropriation, expended the money voted and audited the accounts'. It was further suggested that annual estimates of revenue and expenditure should be framed on the responsibility of the governor and the initiation of money votes should be made under his authority and direction. The Duke of Newcastle made it clear that if the Assembly refused to consider those measures then they were not to assume that they would continue to enjoy the power and privilege of paralysing government. In 1853 a Bill was drafted providing for an executive committee, the component parts of which were three members of the House of Assembly, and one from the Legislative Council. They were to be the authoritative emissaries of the governor in disclosing the policy of the Crown and they had the duty of proposing money votes in the name of the Crown. The Act made it clear that the responsibility for the government of the colony was still the governor's, and the chairman of the West India Committee described this new form of government as an attempt to have responsible and representative government without party. Though it had certain advantages, the new constitutional experiment failed because it did not define with any precision the locus of responsibility. Of the executive committee Wrong says: '... when there was any fundamental disagreement between the Governor and Assembly the new Committee had either to act as the undignified messengers of the Governor to a hostile Assembly, or as the impotent spokesman of the Assembly to the Governor whom they could not control, and in each case they were equally powerless.' The first faltering steps taken in Jamaica in the direction of responsible government led to a blind alley. But despite the inadequacy of the machinery of government, it might have functioned, as it did in Barbados, where an executive committee was established in 1886.

Jamaica, however, lacked the first and essential attribute of responsible government — a real public opinion. The electoral figures for the year 1864 illustrate this. The population was roughly 450 000; the number of voters on the register was 1903, and those who voted numbered 1457. There was no foundation on which the structure of responsible government might be raised. In Jamaica, as in most of the other West Indian islands at this period, there was an almost complete lack of candidates able and willing to devote themselves to the task of government. Total apathy towards political matters and a supreme indifference pervaded the West Indian atmosphere. With the disappearance of this inertia, there was revealed a society completely lacking in balance and stability. Violent passions, bitter animosities and a complete absence of toleration overwhelmed the island in the outbreak of 1865. Only then was the political bankruptcy of the island revealed and the problem of government squarely faced.

The end came suddenly, as a result of the rising which took place in the parish of St. Thomas in October 1865. On the 12th of December, the assembly signed its own death warrant. The Speaker of the House of Commons remarked, cynically, 'The only good law the Assembly passed was that by which it abolished itself.' By the Jamaica Act which was passed on the 12th of December 1865, and an Imperial Act of the following year, the Queen was empowered to prescribe a new constitution in such a form and with such powers as Her Majesty saw fit. This Act of 1866 is an important statute, for it is the authority for all subsequent constitutional amendments in Jamaica. By an order in council under the act, Crown colony government was established in Jamaica and power and responsibility now passed into the hands of the governor.

The old representative system was soon discarded in the other legislative colonies, with the exception of Barbados. This island had never suffered to the same extent from absenteeism as had the other islands, nor had the economic consequences of emancipation been as severe as in Jamaica because the island was fully developed. There was no vacant land to tempt squatters into the bush. The Barbadians formed a compact community, whose members recognised their dependence upon one another in spite of racial and social divisions, and had worked out an accepted method of living together. The economic stability of the island was shown by the way in which it weathered the economic storms of the eighteen-forties and maintained its production of sugar. A constitutional crisis developed in 1876 but this was over the political issue of federation with the Windward Islands. In the riots which occurred eight people were killed, and at one time it looked as if the old constitution would be abolished and Crown colony government introduced. There was a bitter quarrel between governor and assembly, but after the governor had been transferred and the federation issue dropped tempers cooled. The device was adopted of setting up an executive committee rather after the fashion of the Jamaica pattern of 1853 and the old constitution was retained.

With the exception of Barbados the British colonies in the Caribbean were now Crown colonies — that is, in each the Crown retained control of the executive. Trinidad and St. Lucia were models of complete Crown colony government, with an executive council consisting of the chief officials and a few unofficial advisers, and a Legislative Council made up of the principal public officers and a number of unofficial representatives nominated by the governor, official members being in the majority. Jamaica, too, had pure Crown colony government from 1866 to 1885, and a modified form thereafter. In British Guiana elements of the old oligarchic system remained down to 1891, with an oligarchy based on a very limited franchise, using its control of the purse to protect the interests of its own section of the population. As in the older legislative colonies control was separated from executive responsibility. Executive power was exercised in Crown colony fashion.

Crown colony government performed useful tasks in the West Indies, particularly in the field of public works and services. It was paternal and impartial. It put an end to the bickering and frequent deadlocks which had been characteristic of the old representative system in its later years, and gave full scope to the constructive activities of vigorous governors such as Sir John Peter Grant and Sir Henry Blake in Jamaica. It prepared the way for social and economic development, for it introduced a policy of trusteeship for the whole community; its basic principle being 'the direct protection by the Crown of the unrepresented classes, which takes the place of representation'. This was not mere window-dressing. All in all, the system functioned reasonably well, considering the daunting economic situation with which it had to deal, and the social resentments which it inherited. It was, by its nature, however, a temporary and expensive makeshift, without roots in public support. Even before the end of the nineteenth century it underwent modifications of detail in several colonies. In Jamaica a 'moderate step in advance' was taken in 1884, in the formation of a Legislative Council consisting in the governor and an equal number of official and unofficial members. The latter were to be elected on a restricted franchise, and could only be outvoted by the official members if the governor certified that the passage of a particular Act or vote was a matter of paramount importance. A somewhat similar change took place in 1891 in British Guiana, where the unofficial members of the Court of Policy (the legislature in other than financial affairs) were thereafter to be chosen by direct election. In general, however, Crown colony government was not drastically modified, or even widely criticised, until after the First World War. The re-establishment of responsentative government, or the establishment of responsible governments, on the old narrow franchise, would have been politically difficult, if not impossible. It was not until after the First World War, however, that local nationalisms became clamant on a wider basis, and that people in the West Indies and in England began to consider the possibility of inexperienced, largely illiterate black electorates taking direct part in the political life of the islands.

The institution of Crown colony government in many British possessions was a somewhat exceptional episode, in an empire which had always possessed — and was later to recapture — a strong tradition of decentralisation. In the French empire, on the other hand, the dominant tradition was that of centralised government. The French West Indian islands, down to the very eve of the Revolution, possessed no legislatures of their own, for the *Conseils Souverains* were advisory bodies. Colonial assemblies were instituted in 1787; and in the early years of the Revolution the colonies also secured representation in the National Assembly — a device characteristic of French constitutional ideas and quite foreign to English. Under the restored Bourbons, colonial government had reverted to the system, not of 1789, but of 1763; the remaining remnants of the French-American empire — Martinique, Guadeloupe, Cayenne — lost both the power of legislating for themselves and the opportunity of influencing metropolitan legislation. Under the July monarchy a liberalising policy was resumed. Free persons of colour were granted full civil rights in 1831 (in Jamaica the corresponding data was 1830). In 1834 Colonial Councils were created in Martinique and Guadeloupe, whose members were to be elected on a restricted franchise. At the first election in Martinique, 750 persons were qualified to vote, and 650 voted; 25 free persons of colour were qualified to vote, and 6 voted; no coloured person was elected. The legislative powers of the councils were very limited, and they could at all times be overridden by the National Assembly. The revolution of 1848 in France, however, was followed by the grant to the colonies, once again, of direct representation in the National Assembly upon a greatly enlarged franchise. Each island elected three representatives, and the first group of deputies elected included Schoelcher and Pory-Papy, along with others who had been prominent in the movement for emancipation. The group comprised one white Frenchman (Schoelcher) and one white *Martiniquais*, Perrinon. The other representatives were all coloured West Indians, and one of them (Bissette), elected as a replacement in 1849, was an extreme left-wing member of the emancipation party, a rival of Schoelcher, who had served two terms of banishment for seditious propaganda. Since then, the West Indian senators and deputies in Paris have usually been coloured, though certainly no less French for that. The parliamentary representation of the West Indies was suspended in 1854, but restored in 1871, after a period of rioting in Martinique which reflected the troubles of the Commune in Paris. Schoelcher, now an old man, was one of the deputies elected in 1871.

The events. of 1848–49, which marked the end of slavery, fore-shadowed also the end of white political supremacy — though not economic power — in Martinique and Guadeloupe. They marked also the rejection of any attempt to develop decentralised autonomy, and the acceptance of the opposite policy of integrating the colonies more closely with the home country. The French West Indies were on the way to becoming departments of metropolitan France, as they are, in law, today.

CHAPTER XV

The United States and the Hispanic Caribbean 1800–1900

The Caribbean Basin Initiative, the massive movement of people from the islands to North America and the increasingly powerful impact of the Caribbean on the United States and Canada will be considered in the concluding chapters of this book, but it is proper to refer to them for they have their origins in the events narrated here. After giving an account of happenings in Santo Domingo we will refer in greater detail to Cuba.

The city of Santo Domingo, once the capital of the Indies, had become in the course of the eighteenth century a somnolent backwater. Its administrative importance had disappeared, for the authority of captain-general and *audiencia* was now confined to the island. Commerce had passed it by. Its countryside displayed none of the feverish activity and savage hatreds so characteristic of French Saint-Domingue. Its mountains were uninhabited; its fertile savannahs were divided among great estates, patriarchal, isolated, self-sufficing, lazily producing cattle and a little sugar on portions of their land, with the help of relatively small gangs of slaves. The colony had twice the area of Saint-Domingue, and less than half the population. It was an easy prey for the semi-militarised mobs which came swarming over the frontiers from Haiti in 1801. For four years, from 1801 to 1805, the territory was given over to plunder and sporadic massacres at the hands of the followers of Toussaint and Dessalines. From 1805 to 1808 a remnant of le Clerc's French army, under General Ferrand, supported by occasional French ships from Martinique, gained control and expelled the Haitians; but in 1808 the news of the Bonapartist *coup* in Spain brought about a local revolt, aided by British warships, against the French, in the name of Ferdinand VII. The leader of the revolt, Sánchez Ramírez, was confirmed by the Council of Regency in Spain as intendant and captain-general, but was replaced by a peninsular Spaniard as soon as Ferdinand, with the help of Wellington's army, had climbed back on to his throne; colonial administration, marked by irksome restriction in small matters and procrastinating incompetence in great, held sway until 1821, when a fresh revolution in Spain unseated Ferdinand once more. The mulatto president of Haiti, Boyer, who inherited Toussaint's policy and much of his ability, selected this moment for a fresh invasion, and in 1822, after a few more weeks of independence and a futile proposal for union with Bolívar's Gran Colombia, Santo Domingo fell once more under Haitian rule; a régime of extortion by illiterate officials and soldiers, hostile to everything Spanish and everything white, which lasted until 1844.

The two periods of Haitian domination, and a third, unsuccessful, invasion by the megalomaniac Soulouque in 1849, created a mutual hatred between the two neighbouring peoples which is still alive and in quite recent times has broken out in ugly incidents. They caused also the emigration of many of the Spanish inhabitants, so that Santo Domingo, which had possessed a fairly numerous white aristocracy, became largely mulatto, and so remained, though under later republican governments some of the white exiles returned to their abandoned lands. Santo Domingo came also to resemble Haiti in its poverty, its dis-organisation and the violence of its public life. After a successful national rising had expelled the Haitians, the new Dominican republic entered on a long period of faction fights in which the principal chieftains were the uncouth *caudillo* Santana — a tough and merciless fighter, both for independence and for his own hand — and Báez, his more cultivated but hardly more scrupulous rival. In 1861 Santana persuaded the Spanish government to reoccupy Santo Domingo, and became himself the new captain-general; but the occupation was a failure, unpopular with the Dominicans and burdensome to Spain, which had constantly to spend money on suppressing revolts, and on reinforcing a garrison depleted by yellow fever. These expenses, and rumbles of disapproval from the north at the end of the Civil War, caused the Spaniards to withdraw in 1865. The only result of the reoccupation was an increase in the white population.

Three years later Báez, despairing as Santana had done of respectable independence, persuaded President Grant's government to annex the Dominican republic to the United States; but the treaty drafted for the purpose was rejected by the United States Senate. Báez went into exile and the country slipped further into anarchy, in which the contending factions were distinguishable chiefly by the labels 'red', 'blue', and 'green'. Anarchy led naturally to dictatorship, in the person of Ulises Heureaux, who was the perfect type of tropical tyrant, astute, fearless, vindictive, corrupt. Heureaux governed with considerable success — in the sense of enforcing order and suppressing revolts — for eighteen years; but his private army, his spy system, and his many mistresses were more than the country could afford, and he himself was irreplaceable. His assassination in 1899 left the republic without organised government and burdened with a public debt on which it inevitably defaulted. Various European governments applied diplomatic pressure, in varying degrees, on behalf of creditors who were their nationals; and the upshot was gradually increasing American control, fiscal at first, then political, culminating in 1916 in American military government.

Cuba offers a remarkable contrast to other Caribbean islands. About as large as Pennsylvania and slightly larger than Scotland, Wales and Northern Ireland combined, it is in the archipelago a whale amongst the minnows, as large as all the other 50 inhabited islands put together, ten times as large as Jamaica, 340 times as large as Grenada. Its population density is of the order of 205 to the square mile, in contrast with Puerto Rico's 800 and Barbados' 1400.

The contrast extends into history. After Columbus discovered the Indies and claimed them for Spain, the Spanish Crown directed that houses, lots and lands should be distributed to all who went to settle in the Indies, and that those who remained for four years should become owners of their allotments. 'The first division and allotments of Cuban land', writes Guerra y Sanchez, 'were guided by a purpose radically different from that of the English Kings a century later when they disposed of Barbados and other Caribbean islands occupied by Britain. The English practice was designed to enrich an influential individual, the Spanish to promote their colonization of the Indies'. Further, although African slaves and the sugar cane were introduced into the Caribbean by Spain , cattle ranching remained the primary occupation for more than three centuries, so that the slave and sugar plantation did not determine the social structure as it did in the plantation islands. Land was available in abundance, the population was predominantly European, a Hispanic creole culture emerged and with it a sense of community, of wholeness, of identity. Haiti also developed a sense of identity as a people at an early date but remained fragmented by skin tone and hierarchic divisions taken over from slave plantation society. In Cuba early in the sixteenth century, in a period of benign neglect, the municipalities (*cabildos*) assumed the right to distribute land, some to large scale landholders for cattle ranching, (*hatos*), some to small holders for farming (*estancias*). The practice was legalized by Alonso Caceres, who was appointed magistrate of the royal court of appeal (*audiencia*) in 1574; he went further, by providing that land for *estancias* might be granted within a region already assigned as a *hato*. As a result, the *hato* could not block the development of *estancias* nor hinder the spread of farming. Caceres was moved to do this by his analysis of what had happened in Santo Domingo where 'land seizure resulted in scarcity and poverty for the majority of people, who were exploited by a small wealthy majority'. This community of free people, isolated in great measure from other trading systems by Spain's laws against trading with foreigners, had an intellectual centre of their own, the University of Havana, which was founded in 1721, some twenty years before Charles Leslie, on a visit to Jamaica, recorded that there, learning and the scholar were held in contempt. The University of Havana had gained strength by 1800, for that indefatigable and perceptive traveller Alexander Humboldt reported that he found in Havana a lively interest in the political relations and the state of the colonies with their mother countries, but that interest in the sciences was less advanced than in Mexico. By the 1840's the University was the centre of an active intellectual life and a valuable link with other centres of Hispanic culture such as Mexico City, Caracas and Bogota, as well as with those in Spain.

A distinguished Cuban scholar Fernando Ortiz, has described Cuban history as a counterpoint, in which sugar and tobacco are the contrasting, interwoven themes. The fine tobacco of Cuba is one of the most difficult crops in the world to cultivate. Martí wrote lovingly of the devotion of the tobacco-grower, caring for each individual plant 'with his protecting hands, against the excessive heat of the sun, the treacherous cricket, the rough pruner, the rotting damp'. The same patient manual skill is needed in the curing of the leaves and the manufacture of cigars. There is no place in the fine tobacco trade for slave labour, for mass production, for the heat and hurry of the great *central*. Tobacco — in Cuba at least — has always been traditionally a small man's crop. On the eve of the French Revolution there were more than 10 000 *vegueros*, each cultivating his small property with the help of his family, and perhaps one or two hired hands. They were concentrated in a few favoured districts: the famous Vuelta Abajo in Pinar del Río; Vuelta Arriba; and the neighbourhood of Santiago. Their number, and the total area of their holdings, was increasing, for tobacco fetched a good price in the twenty years from the end of the Seven Years War to the outbreak of the French Revolution.

The purchase and manufacture of tobacco, however, was a government monopoly. The royal *Factoría* fixed the amount purchased, and the price, in a completely arbitrary fashion, having regard only to increasing revenue. The *vegueros* were in a very weak bargaining position in dealing with the grasping and corrupt officials of the *Factoría*; and the vexations caused by the monopoly were among the causes of the sharp decline in production which coincided with the French war. There were other and greater causes, however, the most important being the war itself. The war cut off Cuban tobacco from its European market. At the same time, a great and expanding market, almost unaffected (at first) by the war, was opening up in North America; but North Americans did not want Cuban tobacco, which would compete with their own Virginia product. They wanted sugar and coffee; and Saint-Domingue, formerly their principal source of supply, was put out of effective competition by revolution. The war, therefore, produced a boom in sugar and a disastrous slump in tobacco. Cuban tobacco production by 1803 had fallen to one-sixth of what it had been in 1788. Sugar production more than doubled in the course of the war. It was still, in 1815, at 42 000 tons, not much more than half that of Jamaica; but Jamaican production stood still from 1815 to 1820, and then declined, while that of Cuba continued its astonishing increase. It was to reach 500 000 tons in the 'sixties and twice to exceed a million tons before the end of the century.

This remarkable growth of sugar production was made possible largely by the great extent of virgin land. Sugar planters purchased old cattle grants, which had existed since the sixteenth and seventeenth centuries and had never been fully used. It owed much, also, to official policy. The Spanish government, advised by the distinguished planter-economist Arango y Parreño, appreciated the possibility of Cuba becoming a source of wealth comparable with Mexico and had the wit to adjust its economic policy to that end. It declared an open trade in slaves in 1791, and greatly reduced the duties upon them; it allowed traders, of whatever nationality, who imported slaves to Cuba, to export rum and certain other trade commodities free of duty. It permitted the import of North American provisions to feed slaves. A little later, it abolished import duties on tools and equipment used in producing sugar and coffee, even if they were of foreign origin. Technical development in the Cuban sugar industry, fostered by this policy, was very rapid. French refugees from Haiti are said to have popularised overshot water mills and to have introduced enclosed furnaces in place of open hearths. The first steam-driven mills were installed in 1819, and the vacuum pan was generally adopted at an early date. Cuba was the first sugar-producing area to recognise the economic effect of large capacity, and from the establishment of

Alava, the first of the great *centrals*, was far in advance of any other country in this respect. Refineries also were established during the war, and the refined product might be exported to any part of the empire. No government, in a mercantilist age, could be expected to go much further.

Economic development, especially the development of a large-scale industry employing slave labour, must exact its social price. On a vastly increased scale, in mechanised nineteenth-century conditions, the old story of West Indian economic history was repeating itself once more — sugar driving out tobacco, big properties driving out small cultivators, slaves driving out free peasants, black labour driving out white labour. Like the other islands, Cuba was to run the risks of an exporting monoculture. Already at the beginning of the century there was formed the close connection with the North American market which was to make the island at once the greatest single sugar producer in the world, and an economic dependency of the United States. The consequences of dependence were to follow as the century progressed; dealer would dictate to producer, foreign capital would replace native capital, absentee control would replace local ownership.

The census of 1817 — the first held in Cuba — revealed a population of 630000, of whom 291000 were white, 224000 slaves, 115000 free persons of colour. Already the whites were a minority. The implications of this situation, to people with Haiti fresh in their minds, were clear, and the energetic intendant Ramírez, with the advice of Arango, set to work on mĕasures designed to redress the balance. The tobacco monopoly was at last abolished; legislation was enacted protecting the titles of smallholders; free passages, free land, and other privileges were offered to European immigrants. A decree of 1818 finally removed all prohibitions of trade with foreigners — a matter of great importance to the tobacco growers (though import duties still discriminated heavily in favour of Spanish shippers). More surprising, in 1817 the Spanish government agreed to a treaty with Great Britain providing for the suppressing of the slave trade. Some of this legislation, notably that which sought to encourage white immigration, had considerable effect. The growing demand in Europe for Cuban cigars, together with the freeing of trade, sufficed to rehabilitate the tobacco industry. On the other hand, those decrees which struck at powerful vested interests, as might be expected, proved very difficult to enforce. In particular a clandestine but barely concealed slave trade continued to flourish. Most Cubans regarded the treaty of 1817 as an attempt on the part of Great Britain to prevent the rise of a competitor in the sugar trade, and the Spanish government was lukewarm, if not insincere. The number of slaves brought annually to Cuba mounted steadily in the 'twenties and 'thirties, to reach a peak of 12 000-odd in 1837; and the trade was not effectively suppressed until 1865.

The steady increase in the numbers of slaves, and the fear of servile mutiny, were important factors in preventing the growth of a serious independence movement in Cuba in the early nineteenth century. Cuba, also, being an island and the principal base for Spanish naval and military operations against the mainland colonies, offered little opportunity for revolt; and the leaders of Cuban society were too fully occupied in making money to devote much attention to political agitations. The loyalty of the 'ever-faithful island' was not entirely proof, however, against the influence of the separatist movement in the rest of Latin America, and the political disorganisation of Spain itself, at that time. Events on the mainland, and divided counsels in Spain, were inevitably reflected in unrest and occasional conspiracy in Cuba. Most of the conspiracies sought, not separate independence, but annexation by Gran Colombia or by the United States. In 1823 the government discovered and suppressed several subversive organisations, including one known as the *Soles y Rayos de Bolívar*, of which the young poet Heredia was a member. The leaders, including Heredia, were exiled. The outcome of these commotions was a decree of 1825 conferring upon the captain-general 'todo el lleno de las facultades que por las reales ordenanzas se concedían a los gobernadores de plazas sitiadas'. This meant virtually absolute power; specifically, the power to deport, without trial, any person whose presence the governor thought undesirable. It was the colonial counterpart of the rigid absolutism of Ferdinand VII, who after the liberal revolutionary interlude of 1821–22 had been restored to full power with the help of a French army.

The decree of 1825 accentuated the already serious ill-feeling between the Cuban creoles and the peninsular Spaniards resident in Cuba. The *peninsulares*, whether officials or business men, resented the social exclusiveness of the wealthy creole families: the creoles disliked the rapacity and the petty tyrannies of peninsular officials and regarded themselves as entitled by their social standing to a greater part in the conduct of political affairs. Havana, like most Spanish-American cities, had its liberal periodicals, its reading-circles, its political discussion groups. The creoles naturally resented the absolutism of the 1825 decree; the *peninsulares* welcomed it, as a means both of putting the local people in their place and of enforcing discriminatory regulations and duties in favour of Spanish trade. The slave trade in particular was mostly in the hands of penīnsular Spaniards, and officials, mostly *peninsulares* also, connived at it, or were lukewarm in enforcing decrees against it. Many creoles, on the other hand — including even some proprietors of sugar estates — had serious misgivings about the steady increase of the black population and wanted the trade controlled or suppressed.

On its political side, the decree was not at once made a weapon of serious oppression. Under Vives, the easy-going captain-general of the time, and under his successor, Ricafort, government was inert and incompetent rather than repressive; and in 1833 public attention was taken off politics by a devastating epidemic of Asiatic cholera. The selection in 1834 of the inflexible, unpopular, but extremely able martinet Tacón as captain-general, brought an electric change. Tacón's appointment was the immediate consequence of the death of Ferdinand VII, the accession of the child Isabel II, and the reliance of the Regency upon a liberal, constitutional ministry to rally support against the Carlists. Spanish liberalism, then as on many subsequent occasions, stood for centralisation, for Benthamite efficiency; liberals in Spain had little sympathy with the wealthy, conservative, slave-owning creoles, who had so consistently shouted their loyalty to Ferdinand VII; and no Spanish government, liberal or otherwise, could contemplate even a suspicion of separatist intrigue in Cuba, the last remaining source of extensive colonial wealth and patronage. Most of the Spanish liberal politicians of 1834 believed, or professed to believe, that the concessions granted by the Cortes of 1812 had led directly to the loss of the Indies. So instead of repealing the decree of 1825, the liberal ministry reissued it, and appointed a captain-general who would make use of it — a soldier who valued discipline and firm administration as ends in themselves, who regarded the talk of liberal intellectuals with intense suspicion and who notoriously disliked the Cubans.

Tacón's four years of office were years of relentless activity in which he took from the Cubans all the political and social influence which they — or at least their leaders — desired, and showered upon them administrative reforms, many of which they did not want and would never have thought of. He effected great improvements in police administration, in the maintenance of order and the prevention of crime, in the organisation of markets, in street cleaning, sanitation and water supply. He was an indefatigable road builder, and encouraged the construction of the first Cuban railway, from Havana to Guines. His public buildings ranged from a national theatre to the vast, new, sanitary fish market, which still bears his name. At the same time he was ruthless in the suppression of disaffection and arbitrary in matters of justice. Newly constituted military courts, with summary jurisdiction, took over much of the criminal work of the *audiencia* and the municipal magistrates. He used his absolute powers to exclude creoles from places of responsibility and profit and to promote peninsular Spaniards. He antagonised the young liberals by condemning to exile their leader, the eminent writer and pamphleteer José Antonio Saco, author of the *History of Slavery*. He insulted the venerable Arango, whose loyalty and respectability were beyond question. He offended creole conservatism by his outspoken contempt for local social precedence, and undermined the colonial social structure traditionally centred in the captain-general's palace; for an outraged aristocracy refused to accept palace invitations. The hostility between creole and Spaniard, long latent in the social and political life of Cuba, became bitter and open in Tacón's day, especially after 1837, when the sole remaining constitutional right of the Cubans, that of representation in the Spanish Cortes, introduced in 1834, was finally withdrawn. Conspiracy was the inevitable answer, and in the cafés of New York and Madrid exiles from Cuba were beginning to hatch plots for the termination of Spanish rule.

Tacón had no successor of his own stamp; after him, colonial administration relapsed into venal and incompetent inertia. The fault lay not so much with the captains-general, some of whom — Valdés and Concha, notably — were able and energetic, and most of whom were conscientious, as with unreliable subordinates. There was still no serious independence movement, however. The Cubans were too afraid of their slaves, who increased in number year by year throughout the 'thirties and early 'forties as the sugar industry expanded. There was good reason for alarm. The treaty of 1817 with Great Britain had made the slave trade illegal in Cuba. A fresh and more explicit treaty in 1835 reaffirmed the determination of both governments to end the trade. By 1840 the majority of slaves were, in strict law, automatically entitled to their freedom if they could prove to the satisfaction of the Anglo-Spanish mixed commission at Havana that they had been brought to Cuba after 1820. Events in the British West Indies between 1833 and 1838 had made a considerable stir in Cuba, and were well known to the slaves. The proprietors thus faced two different, but related, dangers: if the Spanish government gave way to British insistence, and fulfilled its treaty obligations, there would be a serious attempt to stop the trade, probably backed by

British naval force and followed by a rush of manumissions; if it did not, there might be widespread servile revolts. The activities of British agents and the friendly relations between the governments of Espartero and that of Palmerston, seemed to point to the first possibility. In fact, however, the Spanish government stood firm, and the British, not wishing to intervene in a manner which would seriously offend the United States, retreated. Instead, in 1843, a series of revolts broke out among embittered and disappointed slaves, chiefly in the neighbourhood of Matanzas. The risings were suppressed with prompt and brutal severity, among those executed being a number of free coloured men suspected of complicity, including the mulatto poet Placido. The episode revealed to Cubans of property the dangerous instability of the internal situation of the island. It caused a strong revulsion of feeling against the further import of slaves; after 1845 the trade declined, though Spanish officials were still prepared to connive at it and a few thousand continued to enter the island annually down to 1865. The problem of slavery remained, however. Many white Cubans were ashamed of slavery, but almost all feared emancipation. With the example of Jamaica before them, they were convinced that sugar estates could not be worked without slavery. Much as they disliked Spanish officials, they preferred a Spanish colony to a black republic. The events of 1840–43, however, had shaken their confidence in the will and ability of Spain to protect them. They knew, or surmised, that British intervention for the purpose of abolishing slavery had been prevented largely by the attitude of the United States. They saw in the southern states a slave-owning society with problems similar to those of Cuba, but with vastly greater power. If independence was too bold an aspiration for the Cubans, and colonial rule was uncongenial, annexation to the United States seemed more and more to offer an attractive third alternative.

North American statesmen from Jefferson onwards had from time to time expressed interest in Cuba, but proposals for the acquisition of the island were not made in public by responsible people until the late eighteen-forties; a period remarkable for the territorial aggressiveness of United States' foreign policy in other directions also. The desire to annex Cuba was compounded of general and particular motives: a feeling that Cuba, like other territories adjacent to the United States, was 'destined' to become part of the Union; a desire, in the south, to acquire more slave territory; an understandable irritation with Spanish commercial discrimination and obstructiveness; and a characteristic itch to intervene wherever a colonial people was alleged to be struggling for liberty. To these positive motives was added a negative one: suspicion of Great Britain. The British government throughout this period was pressing Spain not only to co-operate in suppressing the slave trade but also to emancipate the Cuban slaves. British motives were partly moral and humanitarian, partly economic, because Cuban 'slave' sugar was underselling Jamaican 'free'. In urging emancipation on the Spaniards Palmerston in 1851 went so far as to say that it would 'create a most powerful element of resistance to any scheme for annexation to the United States'. It was partly to forestall the emergence of such black 'resistance', and the extension of British influence, that Polk in 1848 approached Spain with an offer to buy Cuba, which was promptly refused.

The Cuban struggle for liberty at this time — in so far as it existed at all — consisted chiefly of agitation by committees of exiles in New York, and occasional ineffectual filibustering expeditions. Three such raids were organised between 1849 and 1852 by General Narciso López, with American arms and a largely American following. López failed to arouse enthusiasm in Cuba, and eventually he was captured by the Spaniards and shot with some fifty of his followers. A diplomatic counterpart to filibustering was supplied by Soulé, the United States ambassador to Spain, who in 1854 induced his colleagues in England and France to join him in an open report to the Secretary of State, urging the acquisition of Cuba by purchase, or, failing that, by force. This document, the 'Ostend Manifesto', when its contents became public, provoked the celebrated European description of American diplomacy as 'a very singular profession, which combines with the utmost publicity the habitual pursuit of dishonourable objects by clandestine means'. The manifesto was repudiated by the United States government, as the López raids had been; but political agitation for the purchase of Cuba continued, until it was interrupted by the civil war.

Within Cuba itself the strongest support for annexation had come from slave-holding landowners. The civil war, by abolishing slavery in the United States, deprived them, and their counterparts in the southern States, of their principal reason for wanting annexation. Opposition to Spanish rule was not thereby silenced, however; it continued to grow throughout the 'sixties, and from being a movement for annexation led by landowners who sought chiefly to postpone emancipation, it became a movement for independence led by doctrinaire liberals — many of whom, in the coffee-growing areas at least, were also landowners — who were prepared to accept emancipation, and indeed to welcome and promote it. Its principal support was the *junta* of Cuban exiles in New York, which organised propaganda, gun-running and the collection of money; but the acknowledged political leader of the conspirators for independence in Cuba itself was Carlos Manuel de Céspedes, lawyer, landowner and liberal, who had already, in 1855, served a term of imprisonment for outspoken criticism of the government.

Céspedes' conduct of affairs was distinguished by courage and singleness of purpose rather than by the guile and the organising skill characteristic of successful conspirators. His declaration of Cuban independence, at Yara in 1868, preceded by the manumission of his own slaves and accompanied by the histrionics customary on such occasions, was premature. It was precipitated by heavy land taxation and by indignation at the manner in which government, in 1867, had evaded its promises of constitutional reform. No adequate preparations had been made, either to secure general support or to raise and equip an army. Consequently the Ten Years War which followed the declaration at Yara was not so much a popular uprising as a series of irregular guerrilla campaigns in the wild country at the eastern end of the island. In the east, the fighting was bitter and its results devastating; but it never seriously affected Havana and the west. The leader of the insurgents in the field, Máximo Gómez, was not even a Cuban, but a Santo Domingan. Céspedes, elected 'president' by his followers in 1868, was thrust aside in 1873, and killed in a Spanish raid soon afterwards. He left a name for disinterested patriotism which is revered in Cuba to this day.

The Ten Years War would probably have ended much sooner, but for the internecine struggles distracting Spain itself at the same time. The Carlist War ended in 1876, and the Spanish government then took vigorous steps to stamp out the insurrection, despatching to Cuba its most distinguished soldier, Martínez Campos, who also displayed a capacity for negotiation and compromise uncommon in Spanish civil wars. The war came to an end with the Treaty of Zanjón in 1878. The insurgents surrendered. Martínez Campos promised a variety of constitutional and fiscal reforms, including representation in the Cortes — a useless and almost unworkable concession. Provision was made for the gradual emancipation of slaves; a decree to that effect, without compensation, was issued in 1880, and the process finally completed in 1886; meanwhile a vigorous policy of encouragement for white immigration, sponsored by the newly formed liberal party, was set on foot. In general, the treaty combined liberal provisions of an academic kind — some of which were afterwards repudiated or evaded — with a series of severe blows at the creole landowning interest which — in the eastern provinces at least — had supported the rising. It was a treaty of exhaustion. It was followed by seventeen years of uneasy peace.

The Ten Years War inevitably aroused great interest and indignation in the United States. Public sympathy with the insurgents was outspoken and widespread and often took the form of filibustering and gun-running expeditions, against which the Spanish government protested vigorously but in vain. The war caused serious damage to North American property, and occasional interference with ships wearing the American flag. The most notorious case of this kind was that of the *Virginius*, which made a number of voyages under United States registry, carrying arms to the Cuban insurgents, until 1873, when it was intercepted by a Spanish cruiser and taken into Santiago. There, fifty-three of the ship's company — mostly American citizens — were shot, upon summary conviction by a drum-head court-martial. The remaining ninety-three were saved only by the intervention of the captain of a British warship which happened to be in the harbour. For a few weeks this ugly incident seemed serious enough for war; but the United States attorney-general decided that the *Virginius* was not entitled to wear the American flag. The Spanish government agreed to compensate the families of those who had been executed; and the matter dropped. The truth was that the United States government was not in a bellicose mood, its navy was in no condition to fight, and its attention was concentrated on internal troubles arising from the Civil War. It made no public pronouncements in favour of the insurgents. It never recognised them as belligerents, despite the efforts of Morales Lemus, the distinguished liberal who represented their interests at Washington. It would, indeed, have found great practical difficulty in conducting regular relations with the peripatetic administration of Céspedes and his successors.

The United States government could not escape the Cuban problem, however. After the Ten Years War four possible lines of political development presented themselves to the Cubans: colonial government as before; local autonomy under a loose allegiance to the Spanish Crown; complete independence; or annexation to the United States. Each of these possibilities had its supporters, either in the openly organised political parties which first took shape at this time or in conspiratorial groups; the choice between them must inevitably be influenced, perhaps decided, by the attitude of the United States. At the same time, American economic interests and influence in Cuba increased steadily in the last two decades of the nineteenth century, and with it American resentment of disturbance and of fiscal discrimination. It was a period of great economic difficulty for the

Cubans. The war itself had caused widespread devastation, especially in the east. The coffee industry was permanently ruined, and Cuba began to import coffee. The cost of suppressing the rising was made a charge upon the finances of the island, which was thus saddled with a heavy load of debt. The estates of landowners implicated in the rising were confiscated, and sold either to Spaniards or Cubans of known loyalty, or else to North American companies. The European market for Cuban sugar dwindled almost to nothing, even in Spain, as a result of the development of locally protected beet-sugar industries. The loss of these markets was balanced, it is true, by the rapid expansion of the North American market; but the distribution of sugar in the United States was increasingly controlled by big financial combines, culminating in the formation in 1888 of the Havemeyer group, which became the American Sugar Refining Company, or 'Sugar Trust', in 1890. For the next twenty years this vast concern supplied about 80 per cent of the refined sugar consumed in the United States. The effect of all these circumstances was a steady drop in the price of raw sugar to the Cuban producers, at a time when the industry was struggling to adjust itself to the abolition of slavery. The only remedy was the reduction of costs by greater efficiency, the separation of sugar-growing from manufacture, the concentration of manufacture in fewer and larger central factories, connected by private railways with the tributary plantations with supplied the cane. All this was achieved. The number of factories dropped from 1191 in 1877 to 470 in 1895: sugar production rose steadily, and reached 1 000 000 tons for the first time in 1894. But new railways and bigger factories required more capital, and capital in the required amount could only come from abroad. In general, British concerns financed and built the railways, while capital for new sugar factories was found in the United States, chiefly among people concerned with the marketing of sugar. At the same time, United States tariff policy sought to protect home refineries by heavy duties on refined sugar, and admitted only raw sugar duty-free from Cuba. The expansion and modernisation of the industry was achieved therefore at the price of the extension of foreign control and the subordination of the producer to the dealer. An analogous development took place in the tobacco industry. The production of tobacco leaf increased steadily in the last two decades of the century; but in order to escape the McKinley tariff (which gave the president power to suspend imports into the United States from any country which 'unreasonably' taxed American exports to it), a considerable number of Cubans engaged in the manufacture of cigars were obliged to move their operations to the United States. It was among the émigrés of Key West that Martí found his most devoted adherents.

Throughout all these changes the Cuban Junta in New York continued its propaganda and its conspiracy for Cuban independence of Spain. Its leadership had by now devolved upon the journalist and philosopher José Martí, one of the most magnetic personalities of West Indian history and a visionary of uncommon power. Martí did not belong to the class of landed creoles who had made the earlier insurrections. He was the son of a Spanish sergeant who had become a captain of rural police in Cuba. Cuban independence, not merely autonomy, was for him a matter of youthful conviction, for which he had duly served a prison sentence during the Ten Years War. From 1880 to 1895 he was in exile, mostly in New York, acquiring a great reputation as a journalist throughout the Americas. He possessed, in unusual combination with his other qualities, considerable tactical skill in politics. His selection of the moment to strike was as skilful as that of Céspedes had been ill-judged. His propaganda was a potent force in rallying American support for a Cuba believed to be groaning under an antiquated tyranny. Cubans, ground between the millstones of Spanish taxation and American tariff policy, came more and more to attribute both these troubles to their imperial connection, and to reflect that, were they independent, Spain could not tax them, and the United States would have no motive for discriminating against them. These reflections were given a sharper edge by the general depression of 1893, which especially afflicted primary producers such as Cuba; and by the Wilson tariff of 1894, which placed a new and crippling duty on raw, as well as refined, sugar. Poverty and hunger proved the best recruiting agents for the forces which the insurgents collected in the east of the island, where Martí raised the standard of revolt in 1895.

The horrors of this civil war surpassed all that went before. Martí, bent on seeing real action after years of campaigning with his pen, was killed in one of the first skirmishes, leaving the direction of the rising to old Máximo Gómez, and to the mulatto Maceo, who had won a considerable reputation as a *guerrillero* as a youth in the Ten Years War. The insurgents sought to drive the peasantry into their ranks, and to render Cuba valueless to Spain, by deliberate destruction of crops and holdings. Weyler, the captain-general, attempted to deny recruits to the enemy by the establishment of vast concentration camps, whose inmates he could not adequately house or feed. Atrocities occurred on both sides, and were greatly exaggerated, sometimes invented, by the North American press. Maceo was killed in 1896. Gómez, over seventy but vigorous and elusive still, fought on in the east, losing ground. He was saved by American public opinion, which vociferated against the camps and induced the Spanish government to recall Weyler and replace him with the less efficient and less ruthless Blanco. American property, as before, was suffering severe damage. In 1896 President Cleveland hinted at the possibility of intervention. McKinley, the following year, used stronger words, though disclaiming all thought of annexation. Two months later the United States battleship *Maine*, making what was termed a courtesy visit, was sunk by an external explosion in Havana harbour. Responsibility for the act was never fixed, but most Americans believed, or professed to believe, that it was deliberately planned by the Spaniards. McKinley, still negotiating vaguely to preserve peace, allowed himself in May 1898 to be pushed into war.

American victory was swift and complete; and the resulting American military government was conscientious and ruthlessly efficient. For three years American governors gave the Cubans aseptic treatment, whether they liked it or not. Their administration was honest, in that they endeavoured to punish those of their officials who plundered the public: a thing the Spaniards had rarely thought of doing. The starving were fed, ruined houses restored, roads repaired, schools founded, placemen ejected, drains disinfected. Above all, yellow fever was traced to its insect source and conquered. The intuition of Finlay, a Scot settled in Cuba, was brought to scientific certainty by devoted American and Cuban physicians; and so the Panama Canal became a possibility.

With all this, the United States government stuck to its promise not to annex Cuba, though both the Spanish government and many wealthy Cubans urged it to do so, as a guarantee of peace and property. It annexed Puerto Rico, which was much poorer, though strategically even more important; but in Cuba it encouraged the establishment of a convention, which framed a republican constitution and made an agreement with the United States, including the famous 'Platt Amendment'. By this instrument Cuba granted coaling or naval stations (later reduced to one at Guantánamo) to the United States, undertook not to contract any debt without adequate provision from the ordinary revenue, and consented that the United States 'may intervene for the preservation of Cuban independence (and) for the protection of life, property and individual liberty'. In December 1902 the American governor, Wood, handed over the administration to the first elected president, Estrada Palma. Thoughtful Cubans, looking back to the years of prosperity before the Ten Years War, and reflecting upon the Platt Amendment, the fact of the Sugar Trust and the possibility of the Panama Canal, might have wondered whether they had not exchanged King Log for King Stork; but in the enthusiasm for 'Cuba Libre' these chilling doubts were not expressed.

CHAPTER XVI

The British and French West Indies 1860–1918

The period from 1860 to 1870 forms a watershed in British West Indian history. The labour shortage in Trinidad and British Guiana was being made good; a satisfactory scheme of immigration had been devised, and a rising tide of Indian labour was flowing into the two colonies. By 1870 there were 28 500 Indians in Trinidad, and by 1883 the number had risen to 48 000 — about one-third of the island's population. In the same year there were 65 000 Indians in British Guiana out of a population of a quarter of a million. This steady supply of labour enabled the sugar estates to expand production and put the two colonies on the road to prosperity. At the same time conditions developed which encouraged peasants to settle on the land, and this led to an increase in the number of smallholders and in their economic importance. It will be remembered that after emancipation free villages had been established and a landed peasantry had come into existence, but that by 1870 the strength of the first impulse towards community development through ownership and education had lost its strength and the leadership had disappeared. The royal commission of 1882 described the change in these words: 'The first few years which followed [emancipation] saw great activity and a good deal of expenditure by the imperial government and the local governments as well as by private humanitarian organisations and by the churches. By the 'fifties and 'sixties of the nineteenth century the first burst of enthusiasm waned, and education fell into the doldrums . . . .' Knibb and the other missionary leaders of the emancipation period had carried through plans for land settlement and had aimed at educating the labourer technically and as a citizen. The former slaves were held together partly by affection for their missionary leaders and partly by the religious organisations to which they belonged; but by the middle of the century many of the leaders were dead and there was no permanent organisation to keep alive the dynamic of the early years. The pace of settlement slowed down, for the savings of the years of slavery and apprenticeship had been spent, and the price of land had been pushed up. The managers of estates tried to stop the flow of labour from the plantations on to Crown lands or purchased lands. Burnley tells how, in Trinidad, squatters had been encouraged before emancipaion to settle on Crown lands, but immediately after emancipation the planters tried to eject the squatters in order 'to condense and keep together the population in such a manner that it may always contain a due proportion of labourers'; and the government itself collaborated in this policy 'by diminishing the facilities of obtaining land...by fixing the price of fresh land so high as to place it above the reach of the poorest class of settlers'.

In the eighteen-sixties there was a change of policy. In British Guiana and in some of the islands the government divided portions of the Crown lands into small lots and sold them to peasants at low prices. This was done in British Guiana in 1868, and in the same year the governor of Trinidad, Sir H. H. Gordon, threw open some of the Crown lands to settlers. The Indian labourer enabled Trinidad to expand its sugar production from 20 000 tons in 1850 to 67 000 in 1879; and during the same period planters and smallholders trebled cacao production, pushing it from about 4 000 000 pounds to nearly 12 000 000. In Jamaica the banana trade began in 1870 when Captain L. D. Baker with a little 85-ton schooner stopped at Port Antonio on his way from Venezuela to New York and took a cargo of bananas. By 1890 the trade was fully established, and the banana became the main smallholder's crop. The combination of cheap land and of a profitable crop led to an increase in the number of smallholders in the island from one-sixth of the gainfully occupied population in 1881 to one-third in 1911. The emergence of the smallholder, his economic importance, and the adoption by governments of a policy of land settlement are among the most significant features of this period.

The best book about the West Indies of the eighteen-sixties is Sewell's *Ordeal of Free Labour in the West Indies*. He points to the difference between the other British territories and Jamaica. Barbados and Antigua were comparatively prosperous, and Trinidad, with a population of from 70 000 to 80 000, was at the beginning of its prosperity. St. Vincent was recovering from the recent depression, arrowroot production had been increased, and the sugar planters, being now assured of labour and freed of debts, looked forward to a time of 'revived and redoubled prosperity'. Grenada, Tobago and St. Lucia were in some difficulty, but their position was not critical. Of all the islands, Jamaica seemed in worst case. 'I know of no country in the world,' wrote Sewell, 'where prosperity, wealth, and a command-ing position have been so strangely subverted and destroyed, as they have been in Jamaica within the brief space of sixty years.' Kingston was shabby and impoverished: 'not a house in the city in decent repair...not a wharf in good order'; the people were in wretched plight: 'they perish miserably in country districts for want of medical aid; they are not instructed; they have no opportunities to improve themselves in agriculture or mechanics; every effort is made to check a spirit of independence'. What Sewell found was that 'while sugar cultivation in Jamaica has retrograded under a free system, in other colonies it has advanced', and that the country 'wanting nothing but capital and labour' was 'sparsely settled by small negro cultivators, who have been able to purchase their plots of land for £2 and £3 an acre'.

The reasons for the difference were clear. In Trinidad and British Guiana a steady supply of labour made it possible to expand sugar production, and Indian estate labourers provided a profitable market for the peasant who grew foodstuffs. In Jamaica the estates were short of labour. Immigration was negligible. Local labourers were often unwilling to work on estates, and even if they had been willing, the estates lacked the cash to pay them. Jamaican estates declined, therefore, both as sources of employment and as markets for pro-duce, instead of expanding, as they did in Trinidad. Meanwhile, the population was growing; it was 370 000 in 1844 and rose to 406 000 in 1871, in spite of the heavy death rate during the cholera epidemic of 1851. Subsistence agriculture was the only immediate solution. Consequently, as the peasant population grew, more and more people wanted land, and although there were Crown and estate lands lying idle, this land was not readily available to peasants because of the difficulty of transfer and because, sometimes, owners thought that if the peasant was able to buy land he would become too independent. The pressure of the expanding peasant population on the geographical economic and legal limits which confined it was one of the funda-mental causes of the Morant Bay rising. Nor was the labourer who remained on an estate in much better case. He had no security, his employment, and consequently his house and provision ground, depended upon the will of his employer, and when differences arose he could not be expected to feel much confidence in the justice dispensed by a planter magistracy.

By the beginning of 1865 the danger signs were clear, and were pointed out to the Secretary of State for the Colonies by Underhill, the secretary of the Baptist Missionary Society, who drew attention to the increase in petty convictions and in applications for poor relief, the low wages and irregular employment, the failure of crops because of drought and the existence of the truck system. Underhill did more than point to the inflammable material. He showed how it could be reduced by political and legislative reform so as to give fair representation and proper protection; by organising the production of food for export; by improving roads, and so on. The governor at the time, E. J. Eyre, was a second-rate official, obsessed as many such people then were by recollections of the Indian Mutiny; and characteristically he proceeded to court unrest in Jamaica. In his comments on Underhill's letter he told the Secretary of State that the evils complained of did exist but that the main reasons for the prevailing distress were the 'idleness, improvidence and vice of the people'. He made Underhill's letter a public issue by his attempts to refute it, and he later added to the mischief by giving island-wide publicity to the so-called 'Queen's Advice', which was a harshly worded reply from the Secretary of State to a group of poor peasants in the parish of St. Ann who set out their distress and asked for land which they planned to cultivate co-operatively. They were told that it was from 'their own industry and prudence' in dealing with what they had 'and not from any such schemes as have been suggested to them' that improvement would follow.

One of Eyre's chief opponents was George William Gordon, whose father had been attorney of several sugar estates and whose mother had been a slave. Gordon educated himself, became a landowner in St. Thomas, and soon became politically active. He stood as 'the people's candidate' for election to the House of Assembly, and he was a member of the parish vestry. He also founded an Independent Baptist Church and was a vehement and vigorous speaker. He had already clashed with Eyre, who had engineered his removal from the magistracy, and he attacked Eyre strongly during the controversy over the Underhill letter.

During the summer of 1865 matters went from bad to worse, what with the drought, the high prices due in part to the American Civil War, and the obstinacy of Eyre. In St. Thomas there were special grievances over land and over the maladministration of justice. On October 11 a crowd led by a local Baptist preacher named Bogle marched to Morant Bay, where rioting broke out, property was destroyed and twenty-one white and coloured persons and seven black rioters were killed. The measures taken to suppress the riot and to pacify the disaffected parish were effective but brutal. Gordon, suspected — without proof — of complicity, was taken from Kingston to Morant Bay, court-martialled and hanged. Five hundred and eighty men and women were killed, six hundred were flogged, and a thousand houses destroyed.

It has been the practice to see the Morant Bay uprising only as an event in the history of Jamaica, a practice that has its origins in geographic fragmentation, imposed imperial rivalries and educational systems that breed particularism. The dimensions are in fact Caribbean and American, for it was a significant event in the long series of the new world African's demand for freedom, justice and human rights. The wider perspective reveals links with earlier slave mutinies and rebellions, such as the use of magic and, later, of religion. The Maroon chieftainess Nanny, the rebel Tacky, Boukman in Haiti used magical powers and religious rites to inspire their followers. Sam Sharp and Paul Bogle were religious leaders, moved, like Martin Luther King and Bishop Tutu in our time, by a passion for human rights that draws its strength from justice, not from legality. Neither the abolition of the slave trade nor the emancipation of the slaves had broken the tyranny of unjust laws that sustained the oligarchic rule of a small privileged minority. In this respect the uprising belongs in the history of the rise of the Caribbean working class and of popular movements that led gradually and with bloodshed to adult suffrage and the involvement of 'the meanest he' in his country's political process. But no labour movement sprang out of the rising as it did out of the 1937 and 1938 disturbances, because neither West Indian nor Jamaican society was cohesive enough to produce a national leadership or a national movement, and because the wage-earning group was too small to be organised as a labour movement in the way that English labour was being organised.

But the West Indian see-saw was in motion again. Though other crops like nutmeg, cocoa, and limes were important, sugar was still the main support of most of the West Indian colonies. Jamaica was an exception. There the number of sugar estates in operation fell from 513 in 1848 to 211 in 1877 and to 77 in 1910. The labour requirements of the estates fell from about 30000 workers in 1860 to about 20000 in 1910. In the same fifty years the population of the island rose from 441000 to 832000. The period was one of comparative prosperity, however, because of the growing trade in bananas. The smallholder made a substantial contribution to this development. Cumper estimates that 'In 1867 there were about 500000 acres in cultivation...including land under holdings of less than 100 acres. Between 1867 and 1896 the cultivated area increased by 200000 acres, and only 14000 acres of this increase related to holdings of over 100 acres. Allowing for the higher proportion of grass and pasture on the larger properties, we are justified in supposing that by 1896 the holdings under 100 acres included more land under intensive cultivation than those of more than 100 acres. By 1910 the cultivated area had further increased to 895 000 acres.' These developments were greatly assisted by the road and railway-building activities of governors such as Sir John Peter Grant and his successors under the Crown colony dispensation; for the abolition of the Assembly had removed one of the brakes upon the raising and spending of money on public works.

While Jamaica was moving towards some measure of prosperity, Trinidad and British Guiana were again experiencing severe hardships. First there had been strong competition in the sugar market from Cuba, though the Cuban war of 1868–78 reduced this. While the front was being held against Cuba, competition came from a new and unexpected quarter. Europe began to increase its production of beet-sugar and to subsidise it for export. The West Indies could not compete, though sugar was their main support. In British Guiana, Trinidad, Barbados, and the Leeward Islands sugar represented 75 per cent of the total value of exports in 1896, whereas in Jamaica it had fallen to 18 per cent. Britain bought in the cheapest market, and her import of colonial sugar fell from 63 per cent in 1861 to 14 per cent in 1886 and 2.5 per cent in 1900. The selling price of sugar also fell from 29s. per cwt. in 1881 to 4s. 9d. in 1896. Subsidised beet-sugar drove colonial sugar out of the market. British Guiana gained some benefit from the discovery of gold in 1897, but when a royal commission under Sir Henry Norman visited the British Caribbean in that year it found that 'a very serious condition of things was rapidly approaching'. An account by the owner of Palmiste estate in Trinidad shows the effect on the West Indies of beet-sugar competition. The estate consisted of 2200 acres and up to 1883 had four factories using the old 'copper mill' process to make muscavado sugar, the cost of production being £14 2s. 7d. per ton. Falling prices compelled the owner to modernise his factory in order to cut production costs. He replaced the four factories by one central factory which was able to produce 15 to 20 tons of vacuum-pan sugar daily, and cut the production cost of sugar to £11 7s. 8d. per ton, but he was still unable to compete with the subsidised beet-sugar. The position was desperate, and the Norman Commission urged the abolition of the bounty system. As immediate measures they proposed that land settlement should be undertaken, minor industries encouraged, means of transport and communication improved, the fruit trade with the

United States encouraged, and production increased by harnessing science to agriculture, providing agricultural education, and by making it easier for planters to expand their cultivations through better systems of rural credit.

The Secretary of State for the Colonies at this time was Joseph Chamberlain, who looked on the colonial empire as a vast undeveloped estate and took energetic steps to develop it. There was a good deal of haggling about bounty-sugar with the European powers, with the result that in 1902 a sugar convention was signed by which the signatories gave up the payment of bounties on the production or export of sugar. This gave some relief to the West Indian sugar industry; but Chamberlain went further. He saw that West Indian agriculture needed scientific knowledge and brains even more than fertilisers and manure, and so the Imperial Department of Agriculture for the West Indies was founded in 1898, for teaching and research. Some governments had moved in this direction some years before. Sir Anthony Musgrave had reorganised the Jamaican Department of Agriculture in 1879 and British Guiana, Barbados, and Jamaica had already appointed government botanists. A botanic research station had been set up in Barbados and sugar-cane was successfully grown there from seed in 1888. Soon improved varieties of cane were being produced and cane planters were able to replace the old Bourbon canes by new and better varieties. This work was of vital importance to an island like Barbados which had to increase its yield, being unable to increase the land available, but it was also of special importance throughout the region since West Indian sugar had to compete on the world market. The white transparent and Bourbon canes gave way to better varieties, and when mosaic disease threatened to wipe out the industry a resistant South African variety, the Uba, was introduced. At the same time, factories were modernised, the *central* taking the place of a number of small and wastefully inefficient factories. The improvement in yield of sugar per acre was remarkable. In Jamaica, for example, the average yield in 1888 was 18 tons; in 1950 it was 32.4 tons.

The main flow of West Indian trade at this time was to Britain, the United States and Canada. West Indian sugar had a valuable market in the United States up to 1898, when the Spanish-Cuban war came to an end and the United States began its close trade relationships with Cuba. High preferences were given to sugar from Puerto Rico, Cuba and the Philippines while a tariff wall kept out British West Indian sugar. The Canadian market remained, however. In 1897 Canada gave British West Indian sugar a special preference of 25 per cent and in 1912 a trade agreement with Canada provided further benefits to West Indian products.

Such were some of the chief developments in trade and commerce. This was also the period of migration, when British West Indians began to go to other countries to settle. This was a new development. The population spilled over from the islands on to the mainland, establishing themselves in Central America. In the eighteen-sixties Jamaican labour went to Panama to help to build the railway; they went in the eighteen-eighties to work with de Lesseps on the canal; and when the United States set about building the Panama Canal in the nineteen-hundreds West Indians furnished the labour. To this day thousands of people of West Indian descent on the Isthmus keep their Barbados, Antigua, Grenada and Jamaica societies. Along the coastlands of the Central American republics West Indians settled, working on the banana and coffee plantations in Costa Rica and Honduras, setting up shops and homes in Port Limón and Cristóbal. They moved by the thousand to Cuba to work on the sugar estates and went further north to New York and the other cities of the United States and Canada, establishing themselves in the great industrial centres and playing a worthy and important part in many spheres of American life. The story of West Indian migration in search of wages and education at this time is an epic of courage and adventure.

The picture that West Indian society presents during this period is one in which different groupings begin to appear; a class structure with the possibility of upward or downward movement from one class to another. The social distances are still considerable, but they are less than they were in the post-emancipation period. The groups move a little closer to each other, but they are still separate; there is a wider distribution of money and of privilege but there is no pervading and dynamic feeling of national unity.

One way of measuring the growth of a community is by examining its social services. In the West Indies of 1850 these hardly existed. Before emancipation the estates had their own health services and provisions for the care of the sick; but on the whole people in the West Indies — and in Europe, too — knew and cared little about the principles of sanitation and public health, and still less about the causes of disease. Dysentery or the 'bloody flux', typhoid and typhus, cholera and smallpox, malaria and yellow fever, the dropsy and venereal disease killed their thousands and ten thousands. In 1741 the British army before Cartagena had lost two-thirds of its numbers from fever. In Haiti at the time of the war of independence the English troops were defeated by yellow fever. In 1851 cholera decimated the population of Barbados, Jamaica and the Bahamas. Meanwhile in 1848 the Public Health Act was passed in England, and health became the concern of the State. The Sanitary Commission of 1869 added years to the lives of people in England by insisting on the improvement of water supplies, and by enforcing precautions against bad food and epidemics. The West Indian governments set up medical services, with district medical officers and nurses; quarantine regulations were made, water supplies improved, and water-works and water-mains installed. Preventive medicine has wiped out yellow fever, and reduced the incidence of typhoid. The foundation work in public health was laid during these years.

Education is a better measuring rod for our purpose because it is an expression of social purpose and of the values which people accept. During the eighteenth century education had been left to the home and to charity; schools were founded by benefactors, and this tradition was continued in the West Indies. Christopher Codrington left two Barbados plantations and some slaves for founding a college to teach medicine and theology, and in 1735 Harrison College was founded for twenty-four indigent white boys. In 1728 a jeweller of Kingston, John Wolmer, left money for founding a free school, and other Jamaican schools like Manning's, Rusea's, and Beckford and Smith's owe their origin to similar bequests. These were all grammar schools, founded by bequest, and attended by a handful of children, for neither the scholar nor the school was highly esteemed in the materialistic West Indian society of the period. Leslie says that in Jamaica in the seventeen-forties the churches were atended only for funerals, and that learning and scholarship were despised.

Planters generally sent their children to school in England. Long judges that in 1770 about three-quarters of the children of the proprietors growing up in Jamaica went abroad for education. The consequences were that 'all the real interests of such students centred in England, which became home to them as it had to their elders. Therein lies the lamentable lack of local pride and feeling already noted, and also to a great degree the reason for the vicious system of absenteeism.' Some West Indians went to the North American mainland also for their education. Between 1650 and 1790 there were at least eighteen West Indian and Bermudian students in North American colleges like Harvard, William and Mary, the College of Philadelphia and King's College in New York, which later became Columbia University; and in 1720 a Jamaican-born Jew called Judah Morris was lecturer in Hebrew at Harvard. Of all these West Indian students, the best known is Alexander Hamilton of Nevis, who went to King's, New York, and later became Washington's chief of staff and one of the architects of the American constitution.

The enslaved part of the population went through an education of a sort. Newly arrived slaves had to be 'seasoned' — that is, they had to be given time to adjust themselves physically to their new environment. They learnt their work under the direction of a driver or from a creole slave, and the trades were taught by craftsmen brought out from England. The purpose of training was to get as much value as possible in labour from the slave, and the same purpose directed the training of the children through the 'pickney gang'. The only people who thought that slaves should be taught to read and write were the missionaries. The planters regarded literacy as a sort of social dynamite, but in 1760 the Moravians were allowed to begin the instruction of slaves in the Christian religion because they taught acceptance of the rule of the master. As the evangelical movement gained in strength in England the habit of reading the Bible spread, and out of this there sprung a mass movement in literacy in England in the early nineteenth century. At the same time in the West Indies the missionaries pressed forward with their efforts to christianise the slaves. In 1797 the Barbados Consolidated Slave Act made it the duty of every Anglican rector to set aside a time every Sunday for instructing the slaves in the doctrines of Christianity, but it was illegal to teach reading and writing.

One of the first statements of the purpose and aims of education in the period just after emancipation was given by Lord Grey, the Secretary of State for the Colonies, in 1838. He pointed out to Lord Harris, governor of Trinidad, that the people who had been freed should 'look to labour on the estates as their main dependence'. He proposed that schools should be set up which would have a curriculum that was largely industrial and would encourage 'a love of employment'. Lord Harris, however, had a more liberal conception and demanded in 1848 that the aim of British policy should be not merely to free a race but to form a society. He put forward proposals for the training of teachers and for free schools paid for out of local rates, with free secondary education for those who passed the necessary tests. Lord Harris's scheme for local government and for secular education broke down on the indifference of local board members.

The Church, and the British government, made an excellent beginning after emancipation and it was reported that in 1838 there were more than 73 000 pupils in day and Sunday schools. Barbados had the most comprehensive provision, largely because of Bishop Coleridge, while St. Lucia and Dominica lagged behind the other colonies.

Money came from Britain and from the churches. Two years after the British government gave its first grant for elementary education in England it gave £25 000 for the education of the West Indian people. The grant was increased to £30000 in 1836 and further grants were made up to 1846. The churches bore the main burden of organising education and establishing schools, and some of the West Indian governments assisted with small grants. A long step forward was taken by setting up colleges for training teachers, the money coming from the Lady/Mico Trust. The story is a romantic one. In 1670 Lady Mico left £1000 'for the redemption of poor Christian slaves in Barbary'. When there were no longer Christian slaves in Barbary to be redeemed the money accumulated until in 1827 it amounted to £120000. Sir Thomas Fowell Buxton formulated a scheme which the Court of Chancery accepted for using the money to promote 'education among the black and coloured population of British Guiana and the West Indies'. Schools were opened in Trinidad, Demerara, the Bahamas and St. Lucia and training colleges were founded in Jamaica and Antigua with money from the Mico Trust. Codrington College was completed in 1840 and this, with the Mico Colleges in Antigua and Jamaica, gave a permanent footing to education in the British West Indies. More schools and more teachers were needed. What had been done represented a beginning on a very modest scale, for Codrington started with few students, and the Mico College in Jamaica in its early years turned out only ten students a year. Herman Merivale of the Colonial Office saw that in building up colonial societies endowments for education should be put on a permanent basis, since these societies tended to take the short rather than the long view, and made laws to meet emergencies rather than for constructive action. What in fact happened was that when the United Kingdom grants ceased and the economic depression began very little money was provided by the governments for education. In 1861 Jamaica, which then had a population of nearly half a million, spent only £3700 of public money on education. From the eighteen-seventies, however, the State began to play a more active part. Neglect had produced its results in ignorance, for in Jamaica in 1883 only 22 000 blacks out of 250000 could write, and the 1891 census showed that about one-half of the people of the West Indies over five years of age were illiterate.

The difference, however, between what existed in 1860 and in 1900 was substantial. The number of pupils enrolled in 1868 in Trinidad was 2836; in St. Lucia, 2258; in Jamaica, 19 765. In 1809 the Trinidad figure had gone up to 24 866, while it stood at 6833 in St. Lucia and

97 091 in Jamaica. Figures like these represented substantial progress; but there were serious deficiencies in the quantity and content of education. Technical and vocational education were poor relations — an interesting contrast with the development of education in many of the states in the south after the American Civil War; there technical and vocational education flourished because they were considered safe for the black. In the West Indies the whole community depends for its very life on agriculture; but this means field work, which had been the lot of the slave under the old plantation system. The free man therefore wished his child to get as far away as possible from manual work. Those who became peasant farmers, it is true, found some fulfilment of aspirations, despite hard conditions, the inaccessibility of markets, and difficulties over tenure. In general, however, the way of the agricultural worker, subsisting on day labour and a backyard economy, seemed to offer neither dignity nor hope. Psychologically the land worker tended to reject his lot, and aspired to escape from it; consequently, he rejected also the idea that school should prepare children for the life which their parents had to lead. Instruction in such accomplishments as needlework, domestic science, handicrafts and horticulture, when introduced, was widely welcomed; but even in practical subjects the demand was — and to some extent still is — for training in techniques for ceremonial occasions rather than for daily life.

There is this further point, that the curriculum of the schools, and especially of the secondary schools, gave little place to the history of the West Indies and did not help the child to develop an interest or pride in its own environment or country. The elementary schools helped to bring about social cohesion. They increased social mobility by enabling men of any race or colour to take up professions like medicine or the law which gave prestige and security. They did not contribute as fully as they might have done to the development of a national outlook because they tended to neglect the environment and historical background of West Indian society. The primary-school teacher, however, furnished a leadership which was to make its influence felt in the nineteen-twenties and later, not only in teaching the three 'r's' but in all the social and economic activities of small rural communities. The primary-school teacher, at least in rural areas, still exercises an important role of leadership in the countries of the Commonwealth Caribbean.

Of the French West Indies, it would be an exaggeration to say, as one French historian put it, 'A partir de 1848 jusqu'à nos jours...la Martinique n'a plus d'histoire'. Politically speaking, however, from the restoration of representation in 1871 down to the period of the great world wars, the history of the islands was singularly uneventful. In form, government was representative on a wide franchise; in fact, the French governor was necessarily still the dominant power in government. Since French policy was made in Paris, and French economic help, especially the protected French market for sugar, was necessary for survival, the local elected general councils could not exercise truly responsible government; nor, as a rule, were the colonial representatives in the French assembly a significant force in the determination of colonial policy. The chief economic activities of the islands were still the making of sugar and the distillation of rum. The annual sugar export of Martinique fluctuated between 25 000 and 40 000 tons; it was 33 000-odd in 1860 and 32 000 in 1913, on the eve of war. The corresponding figures for Guadeloupe were 28 000 and 26 000. Neither the type of ownership nor the methods of the estates and their associated factories changed much during this period, though peasant smallholding increased more in Guadeloupe than in Martinique. Such things as primary education and social services hardly existed. Economically and socially the history of Martinique, and to a less extent of Guadeloupe, was one of somnolent stagnation punctuated by occasional riots or natural disasters. The most destructive of these cataclysms was the eruption of Mont Pélée in Martinique in 1903. It was far more disastrous in its effects than, for example, the earthquake which wrecked Kingston in 1907. The whole town of Saint-Pierre was engulfed in ash and lava, and almost all of its 30 000 inhabitants perished. Saint-Pierre was the chief centre of European wealth and culture in the island. It possessed the only secondary school of any reputation — the Lycée Saint-Pierre founded in 1882. The destruction of the town greatly accelerated the decline of European population and influence, and the transfer of social leadership to a coloured élite. Nevertheless, both Martinique and Guadeloupe remained — and remain — staunchly French in culture and outlook. Both islands accepted military conscription with enthusiasm on the eve of the First World War. Both sent considerable numbers of men to fight in Europe; as, indeed, did the British islands also, without the spur of conscription.

Wars have always had the effect of stimulating West Indian economies by sending up the prices of primary products. This happened again to some extent during the First World War. In the course of the war the price of sugar, despite controls, rose to nearly five times its 1914 level. The French islands were unable to take full advantage of the rise because of lack of shipping, but in most of the

British islands production rose sharply for the first time in eighty years. The value of cocoa, cotton, and copra was doubled, and the market for bananas held up well, allowing for shipping difficulties. The general economy of the region was strengthened also by the development of other crops and by the discovery of oil and other minerals. The East Indians on the Courantyne coast in British Guiana were extending their production of rice; the cultivation of sea-island cotton, which is the best long-staple cotton in the world, began again, after a lapse of nearly a century, in the Leeward Islands and St. Vincent; and Trinidad was busy expanding the export of oil and asphalt. The hopes of renewed and lasting economic prosperity encouraged by these developments proved premature, it is true, in so far as they related to agricultural produce; but at least there was hope to feed on. More important still, the war gave an impetus, as wars will, to West Indians' sense of their own community, and pride in their own place. The war record of the British West India Regiment was excellent. A combination of nascent nationalism, constitutional and administrative reform, and renewed economic initiative was to work startling changes in the following thirty years.

CHAPTER XVII

The United States and the Independent Caribbean 1900–1969

The international life of the area in the first half of the twentieth century was governed chiefly by four interrelated facts: the rapidly growing power of the United States, the diminishing power of the European colonising nations, the strategic importance of the island screen and Panama canal and the increasing impact of the Caribbean on the United States.

The Isthmian Canal project was taken over by the United States in 1903 and the canal opened to traffic in 1914. It provided an immensely valuable new line of communication in which the United States had a paramount and fundamental interest. The increasing sensitiveness of the American government with regard to the situation in the Caribbean, and the increasing determination which it displayed in preventing European intervention in that area, were closely related to the problems of the defence of the canal. There were three threats to be feared. The most obvious was an armed assault upon the Canal Zone, or its approaches, by a hostile power in time of war. To guard against this possibility the United States began to acquire bases at key points, beginning in the zone itself and in Cuba. Another potential source of danger would be the cession of colonies in the Caribbean, by a neutral power or one friendly to the United States, to another power less friendly. The weapons against this danger were diplomatic or (as in the case of the Virgin Islands) financial. A third and more likely possibility was the occurrence, in any Caribbean country not under European or American tutelage, of disorders involving damage to foreign property, or a major default upon foreign debt, which might entail intervention by one or more European powers to protect the interests of their nationals. Such a situation arose in Venezuela, for example, in 1902. It was largely to discourage future interventions of this kind that T. R. Roosevelt in 1904 enunciated his celebrated 'Corollary' to the Monroe Doctrine; a pronouncement which logically implied the intention to exercise, where necessary, a degree of supervision over the internal affairs of independent states.

The Roosevelt 'Corollary' not only expressed the understandable truculence of his own attitude, and that of his immediate successors, during the years when the canal was building; it also gave scope to the didactic purpose which has never been entirely absent from United States foreign policy. It confronted the State Department with a series of dilemmas. Successive United States governments have had to find ways of reconciling traditional respect for self-government and self-determination — both sacred words in the American vocabulary — with a desire to insist on good order and constitutional procedure, or else to establish United States control, in places dangerously close to vital strategic points. The issue has usually been complicated, moreover, by the presence of American business interests.

This problem of reconciling irreconcilables first presented itself in an acute form in Cuba, which is the nearest of all the islands to the United States and which experienced, in its early years of independence, the difficulty which revolted colonies often find in providing themselves with a stable administration. The United States government, true to its traditional principles, withdrew from Cuba in 1902, but safeguarded its freedom of action by the so-called Platt Amendment; an instrument which, by all the liberal rules, should have been as galling to Cuban pride as it was troubling to the American political conscience. In fact, the 'struggle' for freedom, self-government, and so forth, in many parts of the world has often proved to be a figment of the theorist's imagination. It exists, from time to time, in most places, but intermittently, not continuously. Peoples have had self-government thrust down their throats almost as often as they have struggled for it. In Cuba the first American invocation of the Platt Amendment was brought about deliberately by the Cubans, or by a group among them. In 1905 Estrada Palma, after his re-election as president, found himself faced with an armed revolt; attempts to reach a compromise agreement, by negotiation or through the efforts of American commissioners, having failed, the president and vice-president resigned, leaving the country without a government and with no alternative to anarchy but American intervention. This occupation lasted from the end of 1906 to the beginning of 1909, and ended with a general election under American supervision, followed by withdrawal.

After 1909 there were no more interventions in the strict sense of the word, and singularly little continuity in American policy towards Cuba. The Taft administration, whose Secretary of State was Philander Knox — 'a statesman', to quote Professor Dexter Perkins, 'distinguished for his limited knowledge of the psychology of the

Latin-American mind' — proffered unsolicited advice on a wide range
of topics, including the question of amnesty after the negro revolt of
1912, a contract for harbour development, and a concession for the
reclamation of the Zapata swamp. During the 1912 revolt United
States naval forces were sent to Cuba, and marines landed, in order to
protect American property; and the demands made upon the Cuban
government on behalf of resident Americans materially hampered
the government's efforts to suppress the revolt. The State Department
did not, however, regard this action as amounting to intervention,
and explicitly denied the intention to intervene. Obviously, so long
as American advice, backed by an implied threat of intervention,
was accepted, official intervention was unnecessary. Wilson's
administration showed a somewhat less open interest in Cuban
internal affairs, exerting its influence through its ambassador in
personal conversations rather than through minatory notes; but
Wilson also sent marines to Cuba in 1917. This was to protect
American lives and property believed to be threatened by a liberal
revolt against the administration of Menocal, a sugar magnate who
had been elected president in a notoriously corrupt election. The
American refusal to go behind the Cuban election results was entirely
proper, but had the effect, in this instance, of supporting the authority
of an extremely unpopular government. The United States was fast
drifting into war with Germany, and Cuba must be quiet. The State
Department communications with Cuba were at least frank: 'As the
Allied Powers and the United States must depend to a large extent
upon the sugar production of Cuba, all disturbances which interfere
with this production must be considered as hostile acts.'

Cuba was the first American country, after the United States, to
enter the First World War; and at the end Cuba sat at the conference
table at Versailles. The war brought Cuba an increased sense of
nationality, an opportunity to vindicate her international personality.
On the other hand, the end of war brought sudden wealth, equally
sudden financial collapse, and increased economic subjection. As
always, Cuban-American relations were governed by the state of the
sugar industry. The United States government feared — wrongly but
persistently — a sugar shortage, and endeavoured to stimulate home
production, while at the same time fixing prices to prevent profiteer-
ing. Cuba, in urgent need of food, coal and shipping — all controlled
by Americans —, was in no position to bargain, and accepted a price
fixed with reference to the figure at which the leading American beet-
sugar producers agreed to sell. As it worked out, the price, though less
than Cuba would have received in an uncontrolled market, was fair,

and allowed reasonable profit and rapid expansion. It was considerably increased the following year — again, indirectly, through the insistence of the beet-sugar producers and their farmer allies; and in September 1918 the newly established Sugar Equalisation Board contracted to buy the whole 1918–19 Cuban crop. This amounted to 4 000 000 tons — about 25 per cent of the world's supply. Ten years before, Cuba had produced 1 500 000 tons, or about 10 per cent of the world's supply. In 1909 sugar amounted to 54 per cent of Cuba's exports; in 1918, 89 per cent. Cuba had become even more dependent upon the market for her sugar than the world was dependent upon Cuba for its supplies. Expansion caused an acute demand for labour, and set in motion a steady stream of immigration, both from Europe and (for a time at least) from the rest of the West Indies. Jamaica, especially, profited indirectly by the temporary employment of some of its surplus population in the Cuban canefields.

Two months after the 1918 contract the war came to an end. The demand for sugar continued to rise. The Sugar Equalisation Board sold the 1918–19 Cuban crop at a profit of $42 000 000, to the accompaniment of growing protests from Cuban producers, and an epidemic of investigations in Washington. As a result, the 1919–20 crop was thrown upon the world free of controls. There ensued the wild scramble for the available sugar which Cuban journalists called the Dance of the Millions. The price, which had been fixed at $5\frac{1}{2}$ cents a pound at the end of the war, reached four times that figure, after many fluctuations, in May 1920. Before 1920, although the expansion of the sugar industry had depended upon the North American market and had been carried out, in part at least, with capital borrowed from North American banks or other investors, the actual production of sugar had remained largely in Cuban hands. Estates and mills had belonged mostly to Cubans, and the peculiarities of the *colono* system had ensured that small cane-farmers shared in the increased profits. Now, North American refiners, distillers, confectioners and others, seeking to safeguard their supplies of sugar, rushed to buy mills and estates in Cuba, offering unheard-of prices for all kinds of sugar property. Some fifty large factories changed hands during the boom; thousands of *colonos* sold their rights and their standing crops; and those who resisted the temptation to sell made immense profits, with sugar selling at 20 cents a pound.

But since the sugar shortage which caused the boom was largely imaginary, the boom itself was short-lived, the reaction swift and catastrophic. By October 1920 sugar was down to 7 cents and still falling, and many sugar producers, who had borrowed heavily to expand their business, were in serious difficulties. To add to their distress, the United States government in February 1921 introduced an Emergency Tariff Bill raising the duty on Cuban sugar by about 60 per cent: a tribute levied upon Cuban producers at the moment when they could least afford to pay. More and more mills and estates fell into North American hands, now through forced sale or foreclosure. The Havana banks, which had vied in lending money on sugar, mills and standing cane, now found themselves faced with disastrous withdrawals. They begged government for a moratorium, and when it was granted closed their doors. Most of them failed early in the spring of 1921. Government, heavily indebted, and pledged to an elaborate public works programme, found its revenues dwindling and its treasury almost empty. Only foreign assistance on a large scale, it seemed, could save the republic itself from bankruptcy.

The solution of the financial crisis was made more difficult by the fact that Cuba experienced a serious political crisis at the same time. As usual, the trouble arose from a disputed election, in which the 'government' candidate, General Zayas, was elected president, and his predecessor, Menocal, was accused by the Liberal opposition of rigging the polls. It was partly the entreaties of the Cuban Liberals, and partly the outcry of American bankers and merchants, who were prevented by Menocal's moratorium from collecting their debts, which induced the United States government, early in 1921, to send General Crowder 'to confer with President Menocal with respect to the political and financial condition of Cuba'. Crowder — in the words of Leland H. Jenks, a severe critic of his country's policy in Cuba — was 'the personification of that aggressive altruism which has given the world its great proconsuls'. He knew Cuba well, and had twice before been employed to advise the Cubans about electoral arrangements; but he spoke no Spanish. Crowder's arrival — in a battleship, unheralded and uninvited — began an intervention, in fact if not in name, which lasted for three years. Briefly, Crowder used the urgent Cuban need for a North American loan to compel the judicial tribunals to make decisions on the election results, in order to obviate the need of American intervention, and then to induce President Zayas to retrench government spending, to reform his administration, to expel from public office a large number of expectant political adherents, and to appoint a cabinet whose competence and honesty conformed to Crowder's own exacting standards. In the autumn of 1922 a 5 per cent loan was negotiated with J. P. Morgan and Company, and appropriate taxation imposed for meeting the interest and amortization payments. To that extent, Crowder's mission was a success, however unwelcome his authority may have been to some Cubans, and however disillusioning the ultimate results to his own idealism. He left Cuba in 1923, to return shortly afterwards as the first United States ambassador — a friendly gesture. The price of sugar, and with it the economic health of Cuba, improved markedly in 1923. Public revenues increased again, and the year ended, almost miraculously, with a budget surplus. Zayas, president now in fact as well as in name, lost no time in dismissing Crowder's 'honest' cabinet and replacing a number of its members by others, reputed to be equally honest, but unembarrassed by the stamp of Crowder's public approval. Politics returned to normal.

The ultimate result of war, crisis and intervention was to concentrate the economic control of the island more firmly in the hands of a relatively small group of New York financiers, both through the increased part played by the sugar industry in Cuban economic life and the increased part played by foreign capital in the Cuban sugar industry. Jenks estimated that of the 1926–27 crop — some 4 400 000 tons — $62\frac{1}{2}$ per cent was made by American-owned mills, 8 per cent by mills jointly owned by Cubans and Americans, and 4 per cent by Canadian-owned mills. Most mills, both native and foreign owned, were in debt to American bankers and sugar merchants for short-term loans. The total value of American permanent investment in the Cuban sugar industry was about $600 000 000; of such investment in all industries in Cuba, including railways, public utilities, tobacco and so forth, about $1 150 000 000. This great volume of investment involved a steady increase in production, a constant pressure to reduce unit cost of production, and a continued tendency to increase the size of factories. For the Cuban countryman it meant higher wages, regular payment, improved housing, living conditions, and facilities for recreation. At the same time the unbalanced condition of the Cuban economy, the increasing amount of food, clothing and amenities which had to be imported, made — and still make — the cost of living extremely high. Moreover, the economic freedom of the peasant was largely destroyed. Unless he happened to possess a *vega* in one of the favoured tobacco areas he was more and more caught up in the machinery of industrial enterprise, in vassalage to a foreign giant.

Paradoxically, the war, the Dance of the Millions, and the Crowder mission produced, or fostered, a greatly strengthened sense of Cuban nationalism, a new willingness to subordinate family and faction to nation, a new reluctance to seek foreign backing for the sake of party advantage. This change of feeling became apparent in Zayas' time, particularly over the dismissal of Crowder's cabinet. It accounted partly for the support given to the brutal but businesslike dictatorship of Zayas' successor Machado. As if in response, there grew in the United States a new determination to respect Cuban feelings and to refrain from political meddling. After 1923 even veiled interventions ceased. Possibly political purists in Washington shared with Crowder a sense of disillusion over the results of intervention. It is unlikely that, twenty years earlier, the United States government would have tolerated a Machado in Cuba. With all the patriotism and vigorous competence of his early administration, Machado's methods were those of a small-scale Mussolini. They included imprisonments without trial, torture of prisoners, political assassinations, and all the highly developed modern apparatus for preventing the expression of opinion. During the hard years of the depression discontent was met by the employment of hired gangs of gunmen. For two years the University of Havana, a notable centre of learning with roots in Spanish times — it had been founded in 1721 — was closed for fear of student demonstrations. Through all this Washington held its hand and Machado ran his course until armed mutiny and revolution turned him out in 1933. The United States government did not recognise the short-lived revolutionary government which succeeded Machado, but it extended prompt recognition to the administration formed in 1934 by the scholarly and respected Mendieta, and — more important still — in the same year it gave public evidence of the permanence of its policy by the formal abrogation of the Platt Amendment and the voluntary renunciation of all right to intervene in Cuba. It is true that tolerance and respect for Cuban interests were less evident in the economic field; in 1930 the United States dealt the Cuban sugar industry one of the hardest blows it had ever suffered — the Hawley-Smoot Tariff — at a time when the Cubans were least able to bear pressure. Even this, however, was brought to negotiation in 1934; the rate of duty was lowered, by mutual agreement, from 2.5 cents a pound to .9 cent, and a fixed quota of Cuban sugar guaranteed admission to the United States. Both the United States and Cuba had travelled a long way, in political maturity and mutual respect, since the days of the 'big stick'.

The other two independent republics of the West Indies have differed from Cuba in the present century in that they have been much less dependent economically upon the United States, whether as a market or as a source of capital. Being somewhat more free in that respect, they are both — but especially Haiti — poorer. The population of Haiti, except for a small group in the towns educated in French, consists of black peasants. The country has some industry but its most considerable export is coffee. Its rural economy is largely one of direct subsistence. The Dominican Republic has a considerable sugar industry, but its economic life is more diversified, and sugar is relatively less important there than in Cuba. A considerable amount of the sugar crop, moreover, is sold outside the United States. American capital did not enter the country, except in very small amounts, until the occupation by American troops. Bankers and financiers in New York were understandably reluctant, in the first decades of the century, to invest in these disorderly little states; when they did so, it was partly at the insistent urging of their own government. While it is true that the history of both countries, from 1900 to 1936, was largely the history of American interventions, it is also true that those interventions were not made at the behest of American investors. The motives were principally political and strategic.

The murder of Heureaux left the Dominican Republic in a state of political and financial chaos, and there was a real possibility of European governments seizing custom-houses and other sources of income, on behalf of creditors who were their nationals. In 1905 the United States government, to forestall this possibility, negotiated — or demanded — an arrangement for the collection of the customs by American officers. This arrangement, and a second one which followed in 1907, were from an administrative point of view highly successful. Similar but more comprehensive suggestions were made a few years later in Haiti, but several presidents, who followed one another in rapid succession at the time, refused to consider the proposal. Knox, however, while Secretary of State, pursuing a policy of transferring the foreign indebtedness of Caribbean countries from European to American creditors, had persuaded the National City Bank of New York to take a part of the stock of the Haitian Bank. Thus the United States government had financial excuses for intervention both in Haiti and the Dominican Republic. During the First World War anxiety over the intentions of Germany in the Caribbean, and chronic disorder in both republics, combined to alarm the State Department, and armed intervention in both countries was the result. In Haiti the occasion was an incident in 1915 in which a Haitian president, who had been driven from office by revolution and had sought refuge in the French legation, was seized, dismembered, and his mutilated body paraded through the streets of Port-au-Prince. In the Dominican Republic the occasion was a disorderly interregnum in 1916, when President Jiménez, pressed to accept a greater degree of American control, refused, resigned, and left the country without a government.

The occupations brought with them great advantages to both countries, of which the most important, perhaps, were the maintenance of order and the reorganization of finances. In each case arrangements were made for the service of the public debt, and measures taken for the adjudication, and inevitably the reduction, of foreign claims against the governments. These arrangments were of more immediate benefit, perhaps, to the foreign investor than to the Haitian peasant or Dominican cane-cutter; but the development of any country must depend upon the soundness of its credit, and to that end United States help has been highly effective, especially in the Dominican Republic. Other physical improvements have been the construction of motor roads (which in Haiti hardly existed); the organisation of public health services, water supply, and sewage disposal; and the provision of schools. This last endeavour, with the aid of educated local people, achieved considerable success in the Dominican Republic. It was less effective in Haiti, owing to the twin difficulties of finding prospective teachers among an illiterate peasantry, and persuading members of the 'élite' group to take an interest in peasant schooling; but the efforts made were not entirely wasted, and have continued since the American withdrawal.

In making these considerable (if unsolicited) gifts the United States discovered the truth of a remark which an observant student of imperialism — Kipling — made, years earlier, about a not entirely dissimilar situation in the Sudan: 'It is a hard law, but an old one — Rome died learning it, as our western civilisations may die — that if you give any man anything that he has not painfully earned for himself, you infallibly make him or his descendants your devoted enemies.' The occupations were deeply resented. In the Dominican Republic persons described by the American Press as bandits put up considerable resistance, and in 1917 and 1918 the military government undertook extensive operations against them, especially in Seibo and Macoris provinces. Inevitably, unauthorised acts of violence were committed by the occupying troops, and acts of repression by the government. The trial of the poet Fabio Fiallo for making some indiscreet remarks about the occupation caused a considerable stir. Full use of such incidents was made by the enemies of the United States in Latin America, who at that time were many. In Haiti feeling was even worse. American officials, having failed to secure the effective co-operation of social or political leaders, encroached more and more upon the powers of the Haitian administration. Also, in order to hasten road construction and relieve unemployment, the old *corvée*, which was still lawful but which had not been enforced within living memory, was revived in 1916. The manner of its enforcement led in 1918 to an armed rising led by an irreconcilable *caco* chief, Charlemagne Péralte, which dragged on throughout 1919 and into 1920. Some two thousand Haitians, seven U.S. marines and twenty-seven *gendarmes* were killed in this fighting.

A permanent policy of intervention, with its implication of bullying, was no more popular in the United States than in the occupied countries, and in the nineteen-thirties the strategic necessity for it was past. The government was anxious to be rid of an expensive and unpopular responsibility; but it would have been highly irresponsible to have abandoned a task of reconstruction half completed, because of a change of political circumstances. The Americans naturally, and rightly, wanted some assurance that their efforts would not be wasted, that the work they had initiated would be continued after their withdrawal, and above all that just debts would be paid. All this meant careful and patient negotiation. In the Dominican Republic the negotiations between Mr. Sumner Welles, General Vásquez, and other political leaders were successful, and in 1924 the American occupying forces were withdrawn. Only one outward mark of tutelage remained: the customs of the island were left under American administration. In Haiti the required assurances were more difficult to obtain. It was not until after the Havana Conference of 1929 had revealed the almost universal unpopularity of the United States in Latin America that negotiations for withdrawal were begun. The occupation — though not, once again, the control of the customs — ended in 1934. By that time the 'Roosevelt Corollary' had been explicitly disavowed; the United States had embraced the policy associated with F. D. Roosevelt and described by him as that of a 'good neighbour'.

The ending of North American control left a political vacuum in the Dominican Republic which was capably and brutally filled by General Rafael Trujillo. From 1930 to 1961 the country was governed by a dictatorship — under various titles — which made no pretence of lip-service to representative, scarcely even to constitutional, practice, and which was probably the most efficiently ruthless government, in both foreign and domestic politics, that the country had ever had. Trujillo's first major task was the rebuilding of the ancient capital — founded in Columbus's time and famous for four and a half centuries by the name of Santo Domingo — which in 1930 was partly destroyed by a hurricane. After the rebuilding, Trujillo renamed the city in commemoration of himself. His activities were not confined, however, to public window-dressing and repression. Improved communications, land colonisation, the encouragement of rice and corn growing (by bounties and protection) and modest advances in social legislation were among the features of Trujillo's administration. Thanks to these efforts, and perhaps even more to the expansion of the sugar industry and the influx of North American capital, the country was relatively prosperous by Caribbean standards. A large share of its increased wealth went to swell the private fortunes of the Trujillo family and their immediate associates; but enough remained in peasant hands to keep the mass of the people reasonably contented. Opposition — repressed by an extremely brutal secret police — came chiefly from an urban middle class denied any part in political life, and, in the dictator's last years, from the Church.

The Dominican Republic in Trujillo's day maintained an army and an air force extremely formidable in relation to the size and resources of the country. These forces both served the purpose of internal repression and supported an aggressive interference in the affairs of neighbouring states. Ciudad Trujillo was an open asylum for exiled dictators and provided a base for their conspiratorial activities. For such dangerous meddling — specifically for supporting an assassination plot in Venezuela — the Dominican Republic was indicted in 1960 by the Organisation of American States and subjected to damaging economic sanctions. Its relations with its neighbour Haiti had been consistently bad. Haiti has an area of 10 714 square miles as against the 18 811 square miles of the Dominican Republic. It was overcrowded, with a population density of 415 to the square mile. In contrast the Dominican Republic had 177 people to the square mile. The Haitian people, whose trade was in value one-fourth that of their neighbour, were in the habit of spilling over the frontier, which runs through wild mountain country and is sparsely inhabited. Some wandered across to find work on the sugar estates, others to settle in remote valleys as squatters. The Dominican Republic was resolutely opposed to Haitian immigration in any form, and in 1937 Trujillo, with characteristic savagery, had the Haitian squatters rounded up and massacred. The number of those who were murdered is not accurately known; some estimates put it as high as 10 000. An international tribunal assessed the amount to be paid as indemnity. This was eventually paid but the resulting hatreds remained as another potential danger to peace in the Caribbean.

Trujillo's assassination, long awaited in other American capitals, took place in 1961. The problem of an alternative government was an intractable one. Newly formed political parties abounded, but Trujillo had wiped out his political opponents with great thoroughness and there were few men with administrative experience left alive who were not assoicated with his régime. Eventually, early in 1962, a Council of State was set up under the Presidency of Dr. Rafael Bonnelly. With United States approval, and substantial United States credit, the Council of States set about leading the country back to some kind of legally constituted government.

The enormity of the task soon became apparent. On December 20 Professor Juan Bosch was elected President in the first free elections held in the country in forty years. After his installation in February 1963 he instituted an austerity programme in order to repair and strengthen the economy; but there was insufficient support in the country for measures such as a pay-pause and the devaluation of the currency and he was overthrown by the Army in September. A three-man civilian junta superseded the military, an administration was formed, martial law imposed and new elections promised for the following year. Towards the end of 1963 the United States, which had suspended diplomatic relations and withdrawn aid at the time of the *coup*, recognised the new régime. It handed out no money, however.

A period of instability set in, the eighth change of government coming on April 25 1965 when the Government of Señor Donald Cabral was overthrown by supporters of Juan Bosch. Cabral had lost support by trying, as Bosch had done in 1963, to impose an austerity programme. A 'constitutional' régime ruled for three days and then was turned out by the Army under General Wessin y Wessin. The situation rapidly deteriorated, and President Johnson despatched United States forces into the country, an action that provoked strong criticism throughout Latin America. In an attempt to remedy the situation the United States force, which then numbered some 20 000 men, was made part of a force sponsored by the Organisation of American States, to which Brazil contributed 1250 men, and Paraguay, Costa Rica and Honduras small contingents. The United States gave its support to a provisional government under General Antonio Imbert, who had been a leader in the conspiracy to assassinate Trujillo. Quiet was finally enforced after four months of fighting between the 'constitutionalists' and the supporters of Imbert, and the loss of about 3000 lives. In September a provisional government was set up under Dr. Héctor Garcia Godoy, to run the country until June 1966, the date for which presidential elections were promised.

The revolt and the troubles of the year were disastrous for the economy. The central bank had no funds and the sugar crop fell sharply. The United States bolstered the economy with substantial financial aid. Relative quiet followed the Presidential elections of June 1966 when Joaquin Balaguer defeated Juan Bosch. The American peace-keeping force withdrew, yet another austerity programme was instituted, and the economic condition of the country gradually improved. Balaguer retained power in the 1970 elections, defeating yet again his rival, Juan Bosch.

While the Dominican Republic struggled to establish and maintain a democratic system of government, Haiti remained in the firm grip of Dr. Francois Duvalier. In 1957 he succeeded the junta which overthrew Magloire in 1956, and in 1963 he succeeded himself without troubling about such a formality as an election. In the following year he had himself made President for life. They year 1963 had been one of crisis for himself and his country. A diplomatic quarrel erupted between Venezuela and Haiti over the grant of safe passes to Haitians who took refuge in the Venezuelan Embassy; and at the same time the Dominican Republic, incensed at the Haitian Government's invasion of its embassy, moved its forces into battle positions on the frontier, which at one point was little more than forty miles from Port-au-Prince. United States and British warships hovered off-shore and there was some talk in the United States Senate about intervention. A Committee appointed by the Organisation of American States persuaded the Dominicans to withdraw their forces from the frontier and secured Duvalier's agreement to the granting of safe passes. Those who had expected Duvalier to fall were mistaken. He emerged as the man who had 'stood up' to the Dominicans and the United States when it cut off aid in 1962. The invasions inspired by General Léon Cantave in 1963 and 1964 came to nothing. So did an attempt from Florida by refugee Haitians and Cubans in 1967. Projecting himself as 'Le Rénovateur de la République', symbolising the triumph of the black peasantry over the privileged mulatto caste that most hated him, suppressing all opposition with his brutal private army the *tonton macoutes*, and making shrewd use of voodooism, Duvalier kept control of his police state. With its tottering economy, its censorship of press and radio, and 90 per cent of its people illiterate and outside a cash economy, Haiti remained a tragic figure in the group of Caribbean nations until the overthrow of Duvalier's son in 1986. There has been a significant growth of Haitian nationalism of an African type, distinct from the European culture of the 'elite' group. This nationalism tends to prefer créole French to the French of France, and Voodoo cults to Catholic Christianity; and one of its features is the growth of a primitive and vigorous school of local painting.

Nationalism in all its forms became an increasingly prominent feature of the Caribbean scene. Even in Cuba, by far the largest and richest of the islands, the consciousness of economic dependence and relative powerlessness imparted a shrill emphasis to outward expressions of national pride and exclusiveness. The hardships of the great depression accentuated the tendency. From 1931, legislation placed increasing difficulties in the way of immigration, and of the employment of foreigners in many industries. The chief victims of this policy were West Indians, who competed for rural jobs at a time when chronic unemployment was general, and who were regarded in some quarters as a 'cultural liability'. During the 'thirties a considerable number of Jamaicans and Haitians were rounded up and deported.

The general lines of Cuban economic development seemed firmly established. The Second World War, however, damaged the tobacco trade by cutting off the Cuban cigar-maker from his European customers, especially in England and in Spain. Great upheavals must always hurt an industry which exists to supply products of high excellent to a discriminating market, and the trade in fine cigars never fully recovered from the ravages of war. On the other hand, war once again encouraged an increase in sugar production; but this was achieved rather by a more efficient use of existing machinery than by any radical change in the structure of the industry. The peak year was 1946, with a production of 5 225 000 tons. There was also a significant increase in mining. Cuba has considerable deposits of iron and manganese; but as it lacks fuel, the presence of these minerals had not led to any great industrial development. The product of the Cuban mines, like the product of the sugar mills, was exported, until 1960, to the United States.

In political affairs, the *Machadato*, and the spontaneous violence of the revolution which brought it to an end, revealed in the Cubans an unsuspected depth of hatred for arbitary rule. On the whole, the Cubans throughout their history have been long-suffering people, prepared to accept from their rulers a great deal of incompetence, of personal dishonesty, of unconstitutional procedure, for the sake of peace. In these respects the first decades of the republic probably did not differ much from the Spanish régime in the nineteenth century, except that more of the proceeds of graft stayed in the country. In their reaction to Machado, however, the Cubans demonstrated with remarkable unanimity the limits of their tolerance. They would not endure brutal repression and senseless cruelty. The rising of 1933 had no previous parallel in Cuban history. It was followed by a return to elected government and, for a time, by an improvement in the competence, the honesty and the scope of administration. This was a

Cuban achievement. The United States government scrupulously observed its undertakings, both explicit and implied, not to meddle in the interal affairs of Cuba; though probably no administration which Cubans were likely to accept could command the entire approbation of North American doctrinaires. Cuba already had a Communist movement — probably the only serious organized Communist movement in the West Indies — apparently imported by Spanish immigrants in the 'twenties. The avowed Communists were not very numerous; but the left-wing government of Dr. Grau San Martin secured office in 1944 with the support — among other parties — of the Partido Social Democrático, which was described by foreign observers as 'frankly Communist', and which certainly contained some Communists. The Partido polled some 122 000 votes in 1944. It was well represented in trade-union circles, especially in the Confederation of Cuban Workers which, like many West Indian trade unions, had become a powerful factor in national politics.

At the other end of the effective political scale from Grau San Martin stood the remarkable figure of Sergeant — later President — Batista, the chief architect of revolutionary success in 1933–34, with his skill in organizing the non-commissioned-officer element in the army for political ends. He remained the power behind the scenes until elected in his own right in 1940. He had a tolerable — even genial — rule until 1944. Batista's political strategy was both opportunist and flexible. He even accepted, for a time, a working arrangement with the Communists. Throughout this period, however, he never repudiated the political principles of his revolutionary days. His influence did not prevent the adoption of an orthodox liberal constitution in 1940. In 1944 he went into a voluntary and strategic exile, and in 1952 stood constitutionally for election as president. When the election seemed likely to go against him, however, he resorted to a military *coup*, which inaugurated a new period of personal dictatorship. During this period Batista, like many other dictators, was chiefly concerned to maintain himself in office as long as possible, and to secure his own private fortune against the danger of revolution. The rapacity of the leadership, the brutality of the police, the corruption of the government and its indifference to demands for social services and economic opportunity, all recalled the last years of Machado. When Dr. Fidel Castro collected his irregular army in the Sierra Maestra and proclaimed an armed revolution, Batista, with his professional army, was able for many months to resist the threat; but his civil support behind the lines crumbled rapidly, and at the end of 1958 he was driven from office. Like other exiled dictators, he fled to the

Dominican Republic, leaving the field to Dr. Castro and a group of revolutionary enthusiasts totally inexperienced in the task of government.

The proclaimed objects of the Castro revolution had included traditional liberal items — the restoration of the constitution of 1940 and the electoral code of 1943 — and land reform. After victory, the constitutional objects were quickly forgotten. Like many other successful revolutionaries, Dr. Castro found it necessary to govern by propaganda police, to shoot large numbers of his political opponents and to imprison many who had supported him against Batista but subsequently differed from his policies. The Communists in his *entourage* — semi-professional revolutionaries in a crowd of amateurs — rapidly extended their influence, monopolising the instruments of mass propaganda and using them incessantly, insisting upon a strict revolutionary orthodoxy in all public speech. The treatment of universities is usually a reliable measure of the tolerance and the self-confidence of a government. The University of Havana had been closed for considerable periods by both Machado and Batista. Under Dr. Castro it was bullied into conformity, in teaching and writing, with the current official doctrine and jargon. Some two-thirds of its staff went into exile.

The economic objects of the revolution, on the other hand, were pursued with great vigour. Confiscation of large properties and distribution of land to peasant co-operatives began on a scale without precedent in the Caribbean, and work was started on impressive schemes for rural housing, rural education and medical services. These radical departures won for the government the enthusiastic support of a peasantry long accustomed to poverty and hopeless economic dependence. They went to the root of rural discontent, and once made they were irrevocable. They entailed, on the other hand, heavy expense and diplomatic and military hazards. Much of the confiscated property belonged to North American concerns; an understandable resentment in the United States against the confiscations was quickened to shrill fury by reports of the Communist sympathies of the confiscators. Such a reaction was understood and expected — indeed positively welcomed — by the more extreme of Dr. Castro's advisers. Anti-American nationalism, an emotional rejection of dependence, was latent in the revolution from the beginning. To maintain the momenturm of a revolution which had neither a party organization nor a clear-cut programme, it was necessary to represent the United States not only as a past oppressor but as a present enemy. The United States government had virtually earned this rôle by the assistance it gave to an inept counter-revolutionary landing at Cochinos Bay in 1961; and its attempt — which met with only limited success — to arraign Cuba before the Organisation of American States as a danger to the peace of the hemisphere. More it could not do, without eating thirty years of protestations of respect for Latin-American sovereignties; and without incurring the risk of a war which might spread far beyond the boundaries of Cuba. Cuba, therefore, was not immediately attacked; but the economic consequences both of American displeasure and prodigal internal spending were serious. Sugar exports to the United States ceased; the tourist trade disappeared; debts mounted; and shortages of imported commodities, including food, became acute enough by 1962 to necessitate rigorous rationing. Inevitably, the Cuban government turned to Russia. From that quarter, help was quickly forthcoming: purchases of Cuban sugar, credits to buy Russian goods, the services of technical, possibly military advisers, proposals to build a Russian fishing harbour on the Cuban coast within ninety miles of Guantánamo. So the Cold War, with its competition in conferring suspect favours, entered the American hemisphere through the internal disorders of a small Caribbean state.

The situation became highly explosive in October 1962 when U-2 photographs taken by the United States Air Force revealed that missile sites were being erected in Cuba. At the same time President Kennedy learnt that a number of Soviet ships were on the way to the island with offensive weapons. The President thereupon imposed a quarantine on all offensive military equipment under shipment to Cuba, and declared that missiles launched from Cuba against the United States would be regarded as an attack by the Soviet Union, calling for immediate and full retaliation by the United States. On October 28 Khrushchev offered to stop work on the missile sites and withdraw the offensive weapons to Russia. Castro was bitter at this agreement and Cuban-Russian relations deteriorated for a time, during which China gave its support to Cuba. In November 1962 the Soviet First Deputy Premier Mikoyan visited Havana in an effort to repair the breach.

China was a valuable counterpoise to Russia, and Chinese Marxism with its emphasis on violent revolution was attractive to many of the Cuban leaders, notably Ché Guevara. Cuba's attempt to support revolutionary movements in some of the Latin American countries led to her indictment in 1964 by the Organisation of American States for aggression against Venezuela. During the latter half of that year all Latin American countries with the exception of Mexico broke off diplomatic relations with Cuba.

Though Castro had shown considerable skill in playing off China against Russia, China had neither the resources nor the expertise he needed for the economic development of his country. Russia was the major trading partner, accounting for 45 per cent of Cuba's foreign trade during the first half of the 1960's, as against China's 10 per cent. Castro's position was difficult. His purpose was to preserve the complete sovereignty of Cuba. He had repeated his theme in an interview with *Pravda* in Moscow in 1963, affirming that the most important result of the Cuban revolution had been gaining independence from the United States. Alignment with China would have given him a partner on whom he was not economically dependent; but because of Cuba's economic circumstances Russia's influence grew, while China's diminished. The change may have been assisted by the disappearance of Ché Guevera in 1965. A breach came in 1966 when China declined to take an agreed 800 000 tons of sugar and sold the rice that was to have gone to Cuba. The Cuban-Russian trading agreement of 1966 was a comprehensive one, with Russia undertaking to supply Cuba with petroleum, wheat, fertilisers, raw material and mechanical equipment in return for sugar, tobacco and minerals. Another trading agreement was made in 1968.

In the face of formidable difficulties and recurring crises Castro consolidated the Cuban revolution in the decade of the 1960's. In the first years of power, relations between the Cuban communist parties had been strained — especially between the Partido Socialisto Popular with leaders such as Anibal Escalante, and Castro's group. Late in 1965 Castro organised the Partido Unida de la Revolución as the official Cuban Communist Party, with the leadership firmly in the hands of his men. There followed the trial of eleven of the 'Old Guard', including Escalante, in 1968. The charge was treason, the punishment imprisonment. In 1969 Castro appeared to be even more firmly established than he had been in the years immediately after his triumphal march from the Sierra Maestre to Havana in 1958. To a remarkable degree he had achieved this by force of personality. A pragmatist rather than a rigid theoretician, ready to change policy if it seemed in the interest of Cuba to do so, charismatic, voluble, with a capacity for winning and retaining the affection of the masses of the Cuban people, he remained the embodiment of the revolution.

Certain aspects of the Cuban revolution are of special interest to the new West Indian nations. Cuba, with its 44 164 square miles, is as large as the rest of the archipelago. It easily accommodates its population of 7.8 million people, the density being 164 to the square mile — a sharp contrast to the figure of 1415 in Barbados. Unlike most of the islands, it has large tracts of level land. Almost three-fourths of the island is a gentle rolling plain. In many parts its soil is fertile. It is not plagued with the problem of size, as are smaller countries like Jamaica, Trinidad, or, at the extereme, Antigua and St. Kitts. At the same time Cuba, like the Commonwealth countries, had experienced the cramping effects of colonialism, has a mixed population and is a sugar-plantation island. Its efforts therefore at economic development, at the diversification of its agriculture, the promotion of literacy and expansion of education have relevance for the countries of the region.

In 1963 the Junta Central de Planificacion urged the development of heavy industry, the expansion of thermo-electric energy, the development of mineral industries based on Cuba's nickel, the development of a large chemical industry based on by-products of the sugar-refining industry, and the substitution of Cuban-made goods for imported consumer goods. The plan required, for its implementation, industrial equipment of a kind produced by Western European countries such as France; and Cuba thereupon set about developing her trade with these countries. Since foreign exchange was needed, plans were made for increasing sugar production, which in 1963 had fallen to 3.8 million tons, the lowest on record.

By the close of 1964 it became clear that a drastic change had taken place, the emphasis being on agriculture and not on heavy industry. In particular, more sugar was to be produced and 1965 saw the production of 6.5 million tons. The target set for 1969, the 'Year of the Decisive Effort' in Castro's phrase, was 10 million tons. The target was not reached but production stood at a record figure of 8.5 million tons.

The goals that were set in economic development led inevitably to greater economic dependence on Russia, and the question therefore arises for other parts of the West Indies as to the extent to which political independence and national sovereignty can be accompanied by economic independence.

The intense effort to lift sugar production drew attention away from the considerable progress that had been made in diversifying agricultural production in a variety of ways: by the cultivation of rice; of gandules, which are a type of bean suitable for food and also for cattle fodder; of coffee; by the planting of large quantities of forest trees; and by the expansion of the livestock industry. The programme in agriculture is supported by the development of technical institutes and training schools. An outstanding example is the relatively new Institute of Animal Science near Havana. Another important development was the growth of a well-equipped fishing fleet, serviced by machine shops at the harbour of Havana.

Reports on the work done in teacher-training and in the promotion of literacy are impressive. In the years before the revolution about one-fourth of the children over the age of ten never attended school. About one-fifth of the population was illiterate. A UNESCO report published in 1965 indicated the remarkable extent to which Castro's government had overcome illiteracy and expanded its school system. The effects have been to increase the levels of competence of Cuban labour, and to involve the masses more closely in the revolution, since there were no free elections and no free press.

CHAPTER XVIII

The Caribbean Colonies 1918–1960

In the middle period of the century the Caribbean colonies were transformed. Puerto Rico entered into a special relationship with the United States, the French Antilles were integrated into France, the Dutch West Indies became part of the Kingdom of the Netherlands, the larger countries of the Commonwealth Caribbean became sovereign nations, and the smaller islands became Associated States of the United Kingdom. Many forces brought about these radical changes. One was the emergence of local nationalisms in communities that for more than three centuries had been closely linked with their metropolitan powers. Another was that after two world wars in defence of democracy the metropolitan powers no longer had the will for empire. Colonialism had become a bad word. European hegemony in the Caribbean belonged to a past century. The urgent question was whether a small Caribbean community with limited resources could reject colonialism and remain economically viable.

This problem was posed in its most acute form in the island of Puerto Rico. Puerto Rico had been one of the poorest and least considered of the Spanish colonies. Its value had lain chiefly in the great fortresses at San Juan. At the end of the nineteenth century it differed from most West Indian islands in that it had never developed extensive slave-worked plantations and its population was also largely Spanish. The island did not rebel against Spain, but nevertheless was ceded to the United States by the Treaty of Paris in 1898, and so lost the autonomy which the Spanish government had tardily conceded in 1897. It again became, like most of the British islands at that time, a colonial possession; but, unlike them, it differed profoundly in language and traditions from its new metropolitan rulers. In the first Organic Act of 1900 Congress created a system of government resembling that of some British Crown colonies; power was to reside chiefly in a governor and officials appointed in Washington; there was to be a legislature, with a nominated upper house and an elected lower house; and a supreme court, also appointed in Washington.

These arrangements caused considerable disappointment among those Puerto Ricans who had hoped for admission to the United States, or, pending such admission, for the restoration of an autonomous government such as that of 1897. Their disappointment was not counter-balanced by any obvious or immediate economic gain; for though the inclusion of Puerto Rico within the tariff wall of the United States brought rapid expansion and great wealth to the sugar industry, the industry itself came under the control of three or four American corporations, which acquired in a few years — despite legislation forbidding such concentrations — more than half of the land suitable for cane-growing in the island. The remaining sugar lands belonged mostly to small cane-farmers, who depended on selling their canes to the American-owned mills. A big sugar corporation was in many ways a state within the state. The benefits of economic union with the United States were largely lost to the people of the island. The first enthusiasm for incorporation in the United States quickly evaporated, to be succeeded in the minds of many by vague aspirations to complete independence.

Public opinion in the United States also — when it considered the matter at all — was uneasy about the situation in Puerto Rico. The island was of little direct value to the United States as a possession, except in the negative sense that its use as a potential naval base must be denied to other major powers. Imperial responsibility was a new experience for Americans, whose thinking on the subject still commonly found expression in the concepts of 1776. Elected officials, for example, were associated, somewhat uncritically, with liberty; appointed officials with repression. These considerations affected the amendments to the original Organic Act, enacted by Congress in 1917, creating an elected senate and depriving the governor's executive council of its powers of legislation. Puerto Ricans were declared to be United States citizens, though obviously they could not exercise the full rights of citizenship unless they resided in the continental United States. The constitutional position of Puerto Rico still depended upon legislation by Congress, and the more senior officials continued to be appointed in Washington. These cautious enactments failed to satisfy either Puerto Rican pride or American conscience. The only possible escapes from an uneasy relationship seemed to be either formal independence — which, in the economic and geographical circumstances, might be largely illusory — or else statehood within the Union, attainment of which depended upon a complex array of political factors, many of which had nothing to do directly with Puerto Rico.

No further constitutional changes of importance were made in the next thirty years; and during that time it became clear that neither of the two ready-made solutions provided exactly what the Puerto Ricans, or at least their leaders, really wanted. The reasons for this were mainly economic. The Puerto Rican sugar industry, which had been of minor importance in Spanish times, grew rapidly under the directing force of the United States tariff and United States capital, until it dominated the entire economy. Not only did it provide the main outlet for employment and investment; it gave the impetus also for the development of a network of ancillary institutions — transport, communications, power, banking, and so forth. Within the limits of this growing monoculture, total output and income grew rapidly under American rule; but population grew more rapidly still. Sanitation and medical services, though not good enough to prevent the prevalence of debilitating diseases, were sufficient to keep the death-rate surprisingly low, considering the economic conditions. The gains in total income were largely absorbed by the increase in the number of consumers; and in the sugar industry, the backbone of the economy, expansion of total income was in any case limited, internally by the amount of land available, externally by the international sugar quota system. The economic situation, never very favourable, deteriorated greatly as a result of the great depression, and throughout the nineteen-thirties most Puerto Ricans suffered serious distress. The federal government did its best to remedy the situation, both through the efforts of the Puerto Rico Reconstruction Administration, and through relief grants and loans which, from 1933 to 1941, amounted to some $230 000 000; but even these large sums only alleviated distress, without doing much to strengthen the foundations of the economy. Federal initiative received relatively little spontaneous support from the Puerto Rican public, among whom the prevailing feelings in the 'thirties seemed to be apatheic dependence and hopelessness.

It was the peculiar merit of the Popular Democratic Party, in making its first bid for office in 1940, that it bravely abandoned the traditional legal-constitutional-political grounds of party difference and set out to rally public support for a programme of economic and social reform. The party's achievement, both political and administrative, in this direction proved to be remarkable. Its policy embraced three main features. The first was what may broadly be termed 'social reform', and included the acquisition of land for smallholdings and 'proportional benefit' farms; the strengthening and regulation of the position of trade unions — usually of weak and tardy growth in a sugar economy; and the beginnings of a social security system. The second feature was the improvement of the public services and facilities, both to lay the foundations of economic expansion and to encourage social progress. Electricity supply, transport, water supply, and sewerage were all made the concern of separate governmental 'authorities', and the facilities were greatly improved and expanded. Much money was spent on education and health services, and large-scale slum clearance and public housing schemes also made notable progress.

The third, and boldest, sector of the programme aimed at the direct promotion of economic development. In the face of the reluctance of private enterprise to take risks in untried fields, the insular government in 1942 created an Industrial Development Company for the purpost of opening up new manufacturing opportunities, and established a Development Bank to provide long-term investment credit. The earlier policy of promoting industrial development through the activities of government-built and -operated factories gave way, soon after the Second World War, to attempts to attract mainland industries and capital to the island by means of tax exemption, industrial services, loans, provision of buildings, and other forms of assistance. A large number of manufacturing concerns of various sizes have been established in this way in Puerto Rico, mostly in the textile or clothing fields, or in assembly. Attempts were made also to promote agricultural development by means of research, land reclamation, the introduction of new crops, and so on; these attempts were less successful, but some progress was made. All in all, the Puerto Rican economy made great gains. Production of goods and services increased greatly; and the material level of living of the average Puerto Rican was much higher than it had ever been.

All this represented a remarkable achievement; and the most remarkable of all, perhaps, is the evidence which it afforded of the administrative competence of the island government, and the extraordinary corporate enthusiasm among all classes of Puerto Ricans which soon replaced the apathy of the 'thirties. It represents, among other things, a striking tribute to leadership. Elected politicans who can combine high administrative ability with great political magnetism, and with transparent integrity, are rare indeed. Luis Muñoz Marín would be an eminent figure on a much larger stage; his willingness to accept administrative responsibility as well as political leadership was Puerto Rico's good fortune. Other parts of the West Indies have suffered much from politicians who would not, or could not, administer. Nevertheless, in comparing the development of

Puerto Rico with that of other West Indian colonies it must be remembered that external circumstances were then extremely favourable to Puerto Rico. The high level of economic activity in the United States after the Second World War was 'a crucial factor. A strong continental demand kept up the prices of Puerto Rican agricultural products; high taxes and high wages in the United States supplied a powerful inducement to American industry to set up factories in Puerto Rico; and — most important of all, perhaps — several hundred thousand Puerto Ricans found employment in the United States. Air travel is easy and rapid, and the island government has done all in its power to make it cheap. Year by year, over the last 35 years, emigration has drawn off between one-half and four-fifths of the natural increase in population. Emigration has been of vital help to an overcrowded island not only demographically, in reducing the pressure of population upon resources, but economically also, because the emigrants send large sums of money back to Puerto Rico. Without the safety-valve of emigration the industrial and agricultural developments which took place would have been little more than palliatives. Too little had been done by the government to limit population increase, chiefly because of opposition from the Catholic Church. The population density, 734 to the square mile, was the highest in the islands after Barbados. The situation could grow worse, for recent studies indicate that the island was receiving more Puerto Ricans from the mainland than it exports. Important oil refineries and chemical plants have been established but the farming industry has languished and Puerto Rico imports much of its food. The comment has been made with justice that like many colonial peoples they continue to produce what they do not consume and consume what they do not produce.

These economic considerations go far to explain the peculiarities of the constitutional history of Puerto Rico. In such circumstances complete political independance appeared impracticable. There is, it is true, a nationalist party, some members of which, in the spring of 1954, made their way into the House of Representatives in Washington and shot five Congressmen. The comparative indifference with which this news was received by the Amercian public contrasted sharply with the shocked horror which it caused in Puerto Rico. Among Puerto Ricans the nationalists were then mostly a discredited band of fanatics. The traditional alternative to independence was, of course, statehood. Other areas which the United States had at various times annexed from its neighbours had become states after a period of tutelage as 'territories', and this seemed to many Americans an obvious aspiration for the Puerto Ricans. It did not, however, command the support of a majority of the people of Puerto Rico in those years. They saw that statehood would mean federal taxation, the loss of the peculiarly favoured position enjoyed by the island, under the Foraker Act, since 1900. A decision to enter the Union as a state, moreover, would establish a frame of relations — as Amercian history has abundantly demonstrated — both rigid and irrevocable. Puerto Rican leaders sought a new political form which would avoid these disadvantages, while permitting local self-government and self-respect.

In 1947 the governorship of Puerto Rico was made elective. This step, which in other places has so often produced either popular dictatorship, or administrative mediocrity, had a fortunate outcome in Puerto Rico. Muñoz Marín, the first elected governor, and his associates in government, found a way of avoiding the political dilemma by means of a 'Commonwealth' — *Estado libre asociado* — and induced Congress in 1950 to accept it. The concept itself was both ingenious and workable, and ingenious devices were used to give a special symbolic significance to its introduction: referenda in the island, and a revocable 'compact' with the Congress of the United States. The relation so created by Law 600 and the corresponding Federal Relations Statute bore a superficial similarity to the British concept of 'Dominion status'; but the similarity is misleading. The British Dominions are associated but independent kingdoms (or, more likely today, republics). Puerto Rico is not independent. It is self-governing in all local matters, but its defence and foreign relations are handled by the United States. The federal government, in its normal sphere of activity, operates alongside the island government, as it does in the states of the Union. Puerto Rico, on the other hand, pays no federal taxes, and all customs duties collected in the island, or on Puerto Rican goods entering the continental states, are refunded to the island treasury. In some ways the constitutional arrangements are nearer to those of the French than to those of the British Caribbean; but whereas the French islands send delegates to the National Assembly in Paris, Puerto Rico — on the principle of no representation without taxation — has no voting representatives in Congress. The *Estado libre asociado* was, in fact, unique. It was a notable example of wisdom and ingenuity, in devising constitutional machinery to suit a difficult social and economic situation.

But the very transformation, the bustling new urban areas, the Miami-style resort hotels, the multiplication of off-shore industries, the growth of entrepreneurship, the expanding middle class, the

improved levels of education, the prosperity of the 1960s, produced a
new climate of opinion in which the leaders of the Popular Democratic Party became grand old men of the state with eyes fixed on the
past, and the Commonwealth relationship itself came under suspicion
as colonialism in disguise. Young Puerto Ricans wished to have a face
of their own, or to have statehood instead of an ambiguous
relationship. An increasingly large number of people considered
that the Popular Democratic Party had been in power too long;
others, that the New Progressive Party, which was in favour of statehood, had been out of power for too long. A plebiscite taken
in 1967 confirmed the country's wish that the Commonwealth
relationship should continue, but it also revealed the growing strength
of the pro-statehood party. In the general elections held at the close
of 1968 Luis Ferré's New Progressive Party defeated the Popular
Demorcratic Party and came into power. It was significant that the
new governor promised to respect the existing political status, and
emphasised the need for further economic development by pledging
that the south-western third of the island would be industrialised and
that sugar industry would be reorganised so as to produce a million
tons a years.

The French Antilles sought viability through assimilation. In March
1946 the General Councils of Martinique, Guadeloupe and French
Guiana voted unanimously that these colonies should become
overseas departments of France. The symbol of colonial rule, the
governor, gave way to the agent of highly centralised authority, the
Prefect. He had all the powers of a Prefect of a department in France,
and in addition, because of distance from Paris, control of the local
armed forces and the power of declare martial law without first having
to obtain permission from France. There was an elected General
Council, which in principle concerned itself only with administrative
activities, and was forbidden to express any political desires. This
restriction was not acceptable in the Antilles, and when a riot broke
out in Fort de France in December 1959, arising out of an incident
between a white man and a black man, the Council protested against
the brutality of the Republican Security Forces, against the arrogance
of some white Frenchmen, against large-scale unemployment, heavy
texes and low wages. France heeded the protest and in April 1960
enlarged the powers of the General Council and of the Prefects.

The chief advocates of autonomy were the Communist Party and
Aimé Césaire's Parti Progressiste de la Martinique. In a referendum in
October 1962 the majority of the voters in the Antilles voted in favour
of de Gaulle and against a change of status. The Communist Party,

which has a substantial following in Martinique and Guadeloupe, was not supported on the issue of autonomy. The P.P.M. sought enough autonomy to allow the islands to conduct their local affairs within the French constitutional structure. Césaire's welcome speech to General de Gaulle in 1966 expressed the dilemma that faced many of the West Indian islands:

'We can no longer avoid facing a problem that obsesses our youth: the problem of the necessary remodelling of our institutions (I refer to our local institutions) so that they will be better suited to our Antillean conditions; ...so that we may no longer have the feeling, the most depressing feeling, that a group of poor but proud men can experience, the feeling that they helplessly look upon the unfolding of their own history, the feeling that they submit to history instead of making it; in short the feeling of being frustrated about their own future.'

As far as the masses of the people were concerned, however, they have remained largely passive, treasuring their long attachment to France, wanting to be French, unwilling to give up the economic benefits that they enjoy through assimilation as part of the European Common Market.

The autonomy Césaire advocated, and more, was granted to the Dutch Antilles under the Charter of the Kingdom of the Netherlands which was proclaimed by Queen Juliana on 29 December 1954. It had been promised by Queen Wilhelmina during the Second World War at a time when the only land under the effective control of the Dutch sovereign was in the Caribbean. From her place of exile in London the Queen promised the formation of a new Kingdom in which the overseas territories would participate on an equal footing with Holland.

The Caribbean countries concerned were vastly different. They included six islands with a total area of 394 square miles, and the mainland state of Surinam. Of the six islands, two, Curaçao and Aruba, had 63 per cent of the land area and 94 per cent of the population. In contrast Surinam on the South American mainland has an area of 55 174 square miles, much of it jungle-covered, and a population of just under 300 000, about a third of whom lived in the capital city Paramaribo. The population of the islands was predominantly black whereas Surinam had Africans, East Indians, Indonesians and small numbers of Amerindians, Europeans and people from the Middle East. In this heterogeneous population political parties have been organised largely on racial lines — the Creole Party drawing most of its support from Negroes, the Hindustani Party from East Indians, and the Indonesian Party. As a result in Surinam the voice of nationalism had racial undertones. The chief problems in these diverse countries have been economic, as the riots that broke out in Curaçao in 1969 indicated.

Thus far we have considered the solutions adopted by Puerto Rico, the French Antilles and the Netherlands Antilles in their search for economic viability and autonomy. In the rest of this chapter we shall trace in greater detail the course followed by the countries formerly grouped together as the British West Indies, up to the collapse of the Federation of the West Indies in 1961. In the following chapter we shall describe the events of the decade of Independence (1960–70).

The solution that aroused most interest among West Indian leaders was that adopted by Puerto Rico. They recognised that Martinique and Guadeloupe were much nearer, culturally and in their political attitudes, to Paris than to the Caribbean, and their own long association with Britain had not anglicised them to the extent that they wished for assimilation. Nor did the concept of partnership as expressed in the Charter of the Kingdom of the Netherlands appear at any time a practical solution. But the vigour with which Puerto Rican leaders set about transforming their country, the qualities of leadership that they showed, the practicality of the economic programmes, and the essential conservatism of the Puerto Rican approach indicated what might be attempted. They saw that the difference between the Puerto Rican situation and their own was considerable. Their countries were widely scattered through the archipelago. One island, Jamaica, was comparable in size and population with Puerto Rico, but the others ranged in size from Trinidad and Dominica to St. Kitts and Montserrat. They varied greatly among themselves. They were at a great distance from Britain. They were not a part of a vast internal market nor would British aid ever approach within measurable distance the massive federal subsidies that Puerto Rico received.

These were considerable differences, but there were also under-lying similarities in the two stories. The English-speaking Caribbean communities had experienced hopelessness and resentment in the 'thirties, hope and constructive activity in the 'fifties. Their external circumstances had been much less favourable but, as in Puerto Rico, leaders were emerging who inspired hope and who were prepared to press for radical political change. New sources of financial and technical assistance were available, and apathy gave way to purpose. Some islands had valuable mineral resources. Trinidad's oil and asphalt made it relatively well off. In Guiana and Jamaica the development of the bauxite industry added substantially to the national income. Every country pushed industrialisation as fast and as far as it could, so that tax holidays and incentive legislation became the fashion. A range of local industries was established, especially in Jamaica, Trinidad and Guiana. Less spectacular but still substantial innovations were made in agriculture. A notable one in Jamaica was the development of stable local breeds of tropically adapted milk and beef cattle, a development which coincided most happily with the decline in the demand for draught animals. British Honduras, long neglected, began to stir under its own leadership, its declared aim being to establish an independent republic once it had put its economy on a sound footing.

Some of the initiative and much of the capital for these developments in the 'forties and 'fifties came from outside sources, public and private. The Colonial Development and Welfare Acts of 1940, 1945 and 1949 provided funds for the colonial empire as a whole; but a special Comptroller for Development and Welfare, with a technical and research staff, was appointed in 1940 for the West Indies, not to spend the money voted, but to assist governments in framing projects which, when approved by the Secretary of State for the Colonies, would be eligible for grants. Up to 1950 the West Indies had received, in grants and loans, some £18 700 000 out of a total £76 400 000 granted or lent to the colonial empire as a whole. Private capital investment from outside sources had also been considerable. But a great deal of initiative and a surprising amount of 'risk' capital had been found within the West Indies. Governments had been generous in tax concessions to pioneer industries, and vigorous in encouraging enterprise. In Jamaica the Industrial and Agricultural Development Corporations, established in 1952, had quickly demonstrated their value as centres for collaboration between business and government, and as agencies for intelligent and imaginative economic planning.

Meanwhile, one ineluctable fact remained: the central position of the sugar industry. The price of sugar was still the barometer of West Indian prosperity. It had been high in England during the First World War, and mounted higher still after 1920, when price control was abandoned; but it began to fall in 1923, and fell catastrophically after 1929 to reach the lowest figure in its history — less than £5 per ton — in 1934. Lord Olivier, in his report of 1930, urged a substantial increase in preferential protection, but this was not granted until the eleventh hour, in 1934. The industry, meanwhile, strove to set its own house in order and to offset low prices by increased production. It did this by amalgamating factories, by closing small and inefficient units, by reducing the cost of production in field and factory, and, especially in Jamaica, by irrigation, which brought much virgin but arid land into cultivation on the south side. The Moyne Commission in 1939 remarked on the increase of production, from 370 000 tons in 1928 to 620 000 tons in 1938, and added that 'the preferential assistance which the industry had received has been a vital factor'. Limits were set to the increase, however, by the International Sugar Regulation of 1937, which, in a not very successful attempt to raise prices, apportioned world production on a quota basis. In these circumstances increased efficiency combined with preference was not enough to guarantee the prosperity of the industry; certainly not enough to guarantee a living wage to those employed in the canefields — a fact to be borne in mind in discussing the riots and disturbances of 1935–38.

As had often happened before, war brought a reprieve. Demand increased and quantitative control was abondoned. The Ministry of Food became in 1939 the sole importer of sugar for the United Kingdom, and remained so until the end of 1952. It became also the agent for supplying Canada and other Commonwealth countries. The price, negotiated from year to year, was increased as costs of production rose, reaching a peak of £42 6s. 8d. per ton (c.i.f. U.K.) in 1953. By that time, however, quantitative controls had been re-established. The Commonwealth Sugar Agreement of December 1951, and the International Sugar Agreement of October 1953, prescribed quotas for the sugar-exporting countries. In the negotiations in 1950–51 the West Indian producers, who were then exporting some 740 000 tons annually, asked for a quota of 1 100 000 tons in the British market. The United Kingdom government in the end agreed to buy 925 000 tons of West Indian sugar, at prices guaranteed to be reasonably remunerative. This was considerably less than the West Indies could produce, given increased guarantees and encouragement; but the neo-mercantilist age could not be expected to last for ever. The agreed arrangements were to last until 1960.

Long-term contracts gave a measure of security to the industry and so to the community. They were essential — as the Moyne Commission pointed out — because 'there is a radical difference between the economic difficulties that face the West Indies today, and those they had to encounter in the nineteenth century. Then the world demand for almost every tropical product was increasing so rapidly as to outstrip...the available supply...but the development of new productive areas has been carried so far that the productive capacity seems now to be greatly in excess. . . .' The war-time and post-war arrangements placed the British West Indian industry in a much stronger position than before. It was much more closely organised. During the war, to safeguard the future of the industry and ensure that war-time arrears in maintenance of capital equipment would be made good, mutually agreed reserve funds were established by legislation in the Commonwealth exporting countries concerned. The funds were built up by the payment of a specified contribution in respect of each ton of sugar exported. They were to be used for price stabilisation, capital rehabilitation and labour welfare. At the same times, associations of sugar manufacturers were formed to negotiate prices, pool resources, provide for scientific research, use modern techniques, and act on a regional basis in the interests of the industry.

The tendency towards common action appeared even earlier in the banana industry in Jamaica, which also faced grave difficulties during this period. Though sugar was the predominant industry in the West Indies, bananas were the principal crop in Jamaica. Sugar is mostly a plantation crop, but banana cultivation could be — and was — undertaken by a large number of smallholders. Moreover, unlike sugar, which offers only seasonal employment to the majority of those engaged in its production, bananas can be harvested throughout the year. Bananas were essential to the well-being of rural Jamaica, In 1929 the Banana Producers' Association of Jamaica was formed to consolidate the producers into one body for protection and co-operative action. This organisation has proved, on the whole, a notable success. Certain local factors helped to counteract monopolistic tendencies and to protect the independence of the banana planters and of the people as a whole. First among these influences was the authority of the government, which ensured stable conditions and respect for law, and rendered the island less vulnerable than the 'banana republics' to coercion by foreign corporations. The United Fruit Company, which had usually taken at least half of the Jamaica crop, nevertheless failed to secure, by threatening to cut its passenger service, monopolistic privileges such as the exclusive use of a new pier and control over a railway. Having good roads and railways, Jamaica was never dependent on a railway run by a fruit company. Having satisfactory retail shops, it was not balked by the problem of company commissaries competing against local business. With no one company dominating the chief ports, competing companies were able to enter the banana trade. Alone among the banana-exporting countries, Jamaica produced a body of specialised banana buyers who knew the country and were prepared to organise purchase and collection on behalf of any company which cared to employ them. These men served the Association well. By 1931 it handled one-third of the total output and with government assistance it ran a regular shipping service and did its own marketing. The structure of the Association was changed in 1936, when it was transformed into a private trading company; but the company worked closely with the All Island Banana Growers' Association, which was itself another example of the growth of primary producer organisations. The value of the Association lay not only in its own marketing activities but in the fact that it maintained a state of competitive buying, so that other fruit companies normally paid considerably higher prices in Jamaica than in countries where they held monopolies. An interesting, but quite unforseen, outcome of this competition was the discussion between Mr. Norman Manley, as legal representative of the Association, and Mr. Samuel Zemurray, as president of the United Fruit Company, which led to the gift by the company of one cent for every stem exported for the cultural development of the island and its peasantry. This was the origin of Jamaica Welfare Ltd., whose activities and methods won wide recognition within and outside the Caribbean area.

The Jamaican banana industry showed an astonishing resilience in the face of recurrent adversity. The Second World War, which brought prosperity to sugar growers, brought banana growers near to ruin. Shipments to Great Britain stopped in 1940 and were not resumed until after the war. Disease also — leaf spot (which can be controlled) and Panama disease (which cannot) — entered the island from Central America and caused great losses. The damage due to disease has since been very greatly reduced by spraying and by the introduction of resistant varieties; and after the war exports to Great Britain again mounted rapidly. In 1951, however, a severe hurricane destroyed more than three-quarters of the crop. Once again the industry recovered. A government-sponsored scheme for insurance and rehabilitation kept planters on their feet. The British Ministry of Food agreed to take 85 per cent of the exportable surplus, at least until the end of 1954; and the production of bananas in 1954 already approached the peak years of the 'thirties.

The coming together of primary producers was characteristic of the period throughout the British West Indies. The Nutmeg Growers' Association of Grenada, the associations of cotton and rice growers, of coconut and citrus producers, of cane-farmers, and many others, all illustrate the general tendency to form groups to defend common interests and to secure common benefits. Their importance is social as well as economic; and they were not, for the most part, associations of the poor against the rich, of the peasant against the big planter or factory owner, for among the cane farmers, the coconut growers and the banana growers large and small producers have been able to make common cause. It was not unusual in Jamaica to find the manager of of big sugar factory taking a prominent and helpful part in the affairs of the local cane farmers' association. Allied with the producers' associations were the co-operative groups. A Trinidad Co-operative Citrus Growers' Association was formed in 1931, and within five years was handling over 60 000 crates of grapefruit annually. Tobago formed a lime-growers' co-operative in 1931. The Jamaica Citrus Growers' Association ran its own canning factory. The inevitable needs of these groups for credit was met in part by the development of co-operative credit societies. A survey in 1950 revealed the existence in the British Caribbean of 350 savings unions, 207 credit unions, 279 agricultural credit societies, 158 consumer societies and about 30 marketing societies. Almost all were of relatively recent growth; their numbers and their influence were steadily increasing. different in kind from the blinder discontents which in the nineteenth century also led occasionally to disaster.' Further, the population of the British West Indies had increased from 1 719 000 in 1896 to 2 514 000 in 1936, and there were no outlets for emigrants. The 1941 Constitution of the Republic of Panama forbade the immigration of 'the negro race, whose native language is not Spanish, the yellow race and the native races of India, Asia Minor and North Africa'; in 1942 the United States government promised, in recruiting labour for the Canal Zone, to 'co-operate to the extent feasible under present circumstances in meeting the expressed policy of Panama in this matter'. Costa Rica, Cuba and the United States similarly had all either closed the door completely to the West Indian or left only a small space for a few to enter.

Discontent erupted first in St. Kitts, the powderkeg of the West Indies, in 1935, when sugar workers struck for more wages. Some months later the tension mounted in St. Vincent, and the St. Vincent Workingmen's Association was formed to press for land settlement and a new constitution. In Castries there were strikes among the coal-heavers, but no violence. It was in the Trinidad oilfields that blood was shed. There Uriah 'Buzz' Butler became the leader of a great mass of workers, and arms had to be used to quell the disturbance and to restore order. Soon after, rioting broke out in Barbados over the deportation of Clement Payne, who had gone to the island from Trinidad to persuade the sugar workers to organise.

Finally in June 1938 there were serious disorders in Guiana and in Jamaica originating in economic and in political grievances fomented by inflammatory speeches and sensational journalism.

Out of these disorders there emerged the first enduring labour organisations of the British West Indies. Trade unions sprang up overnight, and some unions became also political parties. In Antigua the unions soon claimed a membership of 12 000, or approximately one-quarter of the population. In Jamaica the 1089 trade unionists of 1938 had grown to 57 700 in 1947 and 67 000 in 1950. In all the West Indian territories the trade-union movement grew and flourished, and the leaders became important political figures in the community. After 1938 this growth was encouraged by governments. Between 1939 and 1945 some sixty-five trade unions were formed and legislation was passed setting up departments of labour and providing machinery for regulating labour disputes.

The rise of labour to political power soon proved to be as dramatic as the rise of trade unions. The leaders who emerged from the period of the riots were capable of formulating the demands of labour, and pressed for political reform as well as for increased wages. Bradshaw in St. Kitts, Bird in Antigua, Grantley Adams in Barbados, Bustamante and Manley in Jamaica, were foremost among those who made labour an organised and powerful political force. The sustained and wide-spread nature of the agitation which preceded the disorders pointed to a growth of political consciousness that made these risings different in kind from earlier disorders, and that expressed itself in a demand for increased political responsibility. There had been dissatisfaction in the nineteen-twenties over Crown colony government, and constitutional changes had been made in Guiana and Jamaica which gave rather more power to the elected members and a little less to the governor, but now the leaders of the new nationalist movement sought the abolition of Crown colony government and the granting of new constitutions and responsible government.

The tendency to express economic dissatisfaction in terms of political reform reflected the remarkable speed of social integration in the West Indies in this period. Trade unions, producers' associations, co-operative societies and professional societies all played a part in this process and they took action both in local matters and on a regional basis. In each territory the community was becoming organised within itself, and at the same time all the territories made common cause and acted together when need arose. The dynamic after emancipation was evangelical and philanthropic, and it had manifested itself not only in action to gain security and independence but also in missionary effort, by sending teachers from Jamaica to West Africa. The dynamic in the West Indies of the 'forties was political, springing from the identification of oneself as a citizen of a particular country.

Racial considerations played a part in the national movement. One of its best-known exponents was Marcus Garvey, who, though born in Jamaica, became celebrated more as an international champion of the negro race than as a West Indian. Garvey left Jamaica, as a youth, for the United States, where he came under the influence of Booker T. Washington, and launched the 'Universal Negro Improvement Association' to improve the conditions of negroes everywhere, and to establish a government of negroes in Africa. Garvey did much to create a feeling of racial pride and unity among blacks in the United States and the West Indies. His return to Jamaica was occasioned by his deportation from the United States, after serving a prison sentence for fraud in connection with his celebrated Black Star Steamship Line. Garvey was a powerful and picturesque figure. His emotional hold over many West Indians was extra-ordinarily strong. The Garvey cult of the 'thirties showed what power could be acquired by an orator who identified himself with the mass of the people and preserved his emotional links with them. More recent political leaders have not failed to profit by the lesson.

Parallel with the mass appeal of men like Garvey was a different but related factor — the discovery of the West Indies by the West Indian intellectual, of whatever race or colour, and his growing wish and ability to identify himself with the community.

Factors such as these coloured and influenced the social protests and disturbances of the nineteen-thirties and helped to bring about conditions in which professional men — lawyers like Manley and Adams — seeing the potentialities of trade unions as sources of political power, defied the restrictions which social convention placed upon their class and became labour leaders. They campaigned for constitutional reform, and in 1944 a political change of the first magnitude was made by the grant to Jamaica of a new constitution in which the House of Representatives was to be elected by full adult suffrage. Up to 1944 the majority of people in the British West Indies had been without a vote. It is true that from time to time the franchise has been extended under Crown colony government, but as late as 1934 in Trinidad only 25 000 out of 400 000 people had the vote, and in Barbados in 1937 only 5000 had the right to vote out of a population of nearly 200 000. Now the Colonial Office publicly announced a

policy leading towards self-government for the West Indies, the abolition of Crown colony administration and the adoption everywhere of
adult suffrage.

Representative government, as West Indian history has repeatedly
demonstrated, can produce only frustration and deadlock if it is not
accompanied by corresponding responsibility. The constitutions
promulgated in several of the British West Indian colonies in the
nineteen-fifties provided, in varying degrees, for systems of ministerial responsibility. The most complete was that inaugurated in
Jamaica in 1953 with Mr. (later Sir Alexander) Bustamante as chief
minister. Foreign relations and defence remained the responsibility of
the United Kingdom; the courts and the civil service establishment (as
in England) and the police were excluded from the control of political
ministers. Otherwise, the whole range of government departments,
including the all-important financial departments, fell within the
authority of five ministries, each headed by a minister, advised and
assisted by a permanent secretary. The ministers were all elected
members of the majority party in the House of Representatives, and
were responsible to the House. They formed a majority in Executive
Council, where they sat with the colonial secretary, the financial
secretary and the attorney-general, under the chairmanship of the
governor. Somewhat similar arrangements were introduced in
Trinidad, Barbados, British Guiana and (with some misgivings)
British Honduras. In British Guiana ministerial administration broke
down after a few months, and the colony was threatened with financial chaos and serious disorder. In 1954 the constitution was suspended, and an interim government set up with wide emergency
powers in the hands of the governor. Elsewhere, the system worked
with reasonable efficiency, and afforded a period of preparation for
the political independence eventually proposed.

It was clear, however, that the smaller British territories — and
perhaps some of the larger ones — could not by themselves support
the cost and the responsibility of complete independence. The idea of
a West Indian federation was not new, though in the past it had been
extremely unpopular. The Leeward Islands were formed into a federal
group, against much local opposition, in 1871. Attempts to federate
the Windward Islands were unsuccessful. In 1876 Barbadians
rioted against proposals to include their island in such a federation. In
1921 E. F. Wood reported that proposals for federation were so
unpopular as to be impracticable. As late as 1936 a commission from
the United Kingdom considered the possibility of a closer union
between Trinidad and the Leeward and Windward Islands, and

reported unfavourably. After the Second World War, however, opinions and attitudes became less hostile to the idea. Many factors contributed to the change — the growth of West Indian national feeling; the spread and inter-connection of labour movements (a labour congress in British Guiana in 1938 urged federation); and the insistent urging of a few respected leaders, notably T. A. Marryshow in Grenada. Encouragement from the United Kingdom also played a part. The establishment of the Development and Welfare organisation — though the initiative for it came from London — was a response to a felt need for regional rather than purely local planning. The Colonial Office, anxious to create a self-reliant state which would take over all British West Indian responsibilities, promoted and supported proposals for a political federation, it being understood that it could be successfully created only by the efforts of the West Indian governments themselves.

The first conference on British West Indian federation was held at Montego Bay in 1947. By a majority vote it accepted the principle of political federation and set up a Standing Closer-Association Committee to study the possibility of federation and to draft a federal constitution. The Committee produced a report, notable both for wisdom and for ingenuity, which in 1953 was submitted to a second conference in London and accepted, with modifications, for embodiment in the conference's recommendations. It then went back to the individual governments for acceptance. The two mainland territories, British Guiana and British Honduras, had both announced beforehand that they would not accept. In both territories there was widespread fear of a flood of immigrants from the over-populated islands, and the 'East Indians' of British Guiana disliked the prospect of joining a large community, with a population chiefly African in origin, in which they would be a relatively small minority. The mainland attitude robbed the federal project of much of its attraction; nevertheless, Jamaica and the other islands accepted the proposals. A period of administrative preparation ensued, during which reports were prepared on federal finance, the future federal public service, and allied matters. A third conference on federation met in London in 1956, and the final decision was then made to federate the island territories and to leave the way open for the admission of British Guiana and British Honduras at a later date. The following year, after long and stubborn argument, it was agreed that the federal capital — to be built with the help of £1 000 000 contributed by the Government of the United Kingdom — should be in Trinidad. Lord Hailes was appointed Governor-General of the

Federation. The first federal elections were held early in 1958; the federalist party — supported by Sir Grantley Adams, Mr. Manley and Dr. Eric Williams, premiers of Barbados, Jamaica and Trinidad respectively — secured a small majority in the house of representatives, and Sir Grantley Adams became the first prime minister.

Enthusiasm for federation had always been strongest in the small islands. In the larger islands opinion was divided. In Jamaica especially, many people feared that they were being asked to support the poorer territories, and that their progress in local self-government might be delayed by association with less 'advanced' groups. Jamaica, heavily dependent on customs duties for its revenue, refused to consider a customs union; Trinidad as resolutely opposed free movement of population, which Barbados considered to be essential for a federation. To these differences were added traditional insular prejudices and the personal jealousies of political leaders. In consequence, the federal government set up in 1957 was extremely weak. It had no power to raise taxes. Its revenue, derived from 'unit' contributions, was only about £2 000 000 a year. Federal 'subjects' of government were few and in concurrent 'subjects' the federal government was unable, both for financial and political reasons, to take the initiative. Foreign affairs, while awaiting final independence, were to be conducted through London. Apart from functions concerned with its own maintenance, therefore, the principal activities of the federal government were the distribution of grants under Colonial Development and Welfare Acts, the administration of the West India Regiment and the support of what was then the University College of the West Indies.

The Federation lasted only three years. Its end was caused by the defection of Jamaica. Support in that island which holds half the population of the Commonwealth Caribbean was confined to a relatively small number of educated people, and Sir Alexander Bustamante, in Opposition, was able to persuade an unsophisticated though shrewd electorate that they were being exploited in the interests of remote and indigent islands in the Eastern Caribbean. The government put the question to a referendum in 1961. The vote went in favour of secession and as a result Jamaica sought independence on its own.

The real causes for the collapse of the Federation went deep. They were rooted in the imperial rivalries and colonial particularism that characterised the Caribbean for three and a half centuries. The debates in the local legislatures and at the London Conference of 1956 showed that there was no strong West Indian national sentiment. For

West Indians the island remained the most compelling area symbol. This resulted from the sharing-up of the islands between a number of distant powers, and their long attachment as separate units to the metropolitan administration. Another difficulty lay in the fact that Jamaica, the largest unit, was 1200 miles away from the federal capital in Port of Spain. The Jamaicans had little connection with or fellow feeling for the people of the islands in the Eastern Caribbean. They were accustomed to going north to New York and Montreal, and across the Atlantic to London; few ever thought of going east to Barbados and Trinidad.

Also the disproportion between two of the units in the Federation, Jamaica and Trinidad, was extreme. These two had 83 per cent of the total land area, 77 per cent of the population, and three-quarters of the wealth. In both these countries the Opposition party in the Federal Government won majorities, so that most of the Cabinet seats went to the smaller units. The imbalance was made greater by the swifter pace of economic development in the two large islands. They had made good progress in their economic development and every step forward widened the gap between them and the smaller islands, 'the Eight'. Each was sensitive about any attempt to lessen its power to direct this drive for industrialisation, and about any attempt to add to already formidable problems by the freedom of movement from other islands. Trinidad in particular viewed this with apprehension. Since the political leaders of the two large units refused to go to the centre, knowing full well where political power lay, there was little chance of resolving these and other difficulties within the Federal Cabinet; and the Federal Government was so lacking in control and weak in resources that it could do little. Further, Jamaica and Trinidad suspected London of trying to pass on its economic burdens to them, as far as the small islands were concerned. Resentment was added to suspicion when the Imperial Parliament passed a Commonwealth Immigrants Act to control immigration from Commonwealth countries. Following on this came Britain's decision to seek membership of the European Common Market. West Indians whose banana and sugar industries depended on Commonwealth Preference agreements saw themselves being left with an ineffective Federal Government at a period of crisis. The larger countries decided to press forward to independence separately, and the smaller countries were left to make the best arrangements they could with Britain.

Of the smaller groups of non-British dependent territories in the Caribbean, one, the Danish Virgin Islands, was purchased by the United States in 1917 to prevent the possibility of German seizure. The administration has been a disillusioning experience. The total population is about 25 000. Most of the sugar plantations ground to a standstill many years ago. Apart from relief expenditure from the United States — which has been on a fantastic scale by normal West Indian standards — the islands live mainly by the tourist trade, specialising, until very recently, in catering for visitors seeking easy divorces. The St. Thomas hotels feed these birds of passage largely on provisions grown by the hard-working peasant population of the British Virgin Islands, and brought in schooners down Sir Francis Drake's channel.

CHAPTER XIX

New Caribbean Nations and States 1962–1972

Historical forces are numerous and observe no calendar. There are times, however, when they combine to bring about radical change within a relatively short span of time. We have already noted two of these climactic periods in recent West Indian history, when established economic and social structures collapsed and new directions were set. The first of these was the decade of freedom, 1830–40, in which the Act of Emancipation was passed by the Parliament of the United Kingdom, the system of apprenticeship was terminated, and a black peasantry emerged. The second was the liberation decade of the 1930s, in which the West Indian people began to reject traditional attitudes and to develop new concepts of themselves and of their society. The emergence of the masses of the people as a dominant political force, the dynamism created by the national movement and new cohesive forces that began to unify the segmented society of the islands, make this a decade of decisive change. The third was the independence decade of the 1960s, which saw the break-up of the British Empire in the Caribbean, the achievement of independence by four former British colonies and the passing of political power to preponderantly black and brown communities. The far-reaching consequences of this transfer of power have manifested themselves in changed social attitudes and values and in a certain measure of de-Europeanisation.

The decisions made by the various West Indian colonies in their search for autonomy and viability varied according to their size and circumstances. The order of events, after the Parliament of the United Kingdom dissolved the Federation of the West Indies in May 1962, can be stated briefly. After the dissolution, Jamaica and Trinidad and Tobago moved forward without delay into independence. Jamaica became a sovereign state on 6 August 1962, Trinidad and Tobago on the last day of the same month. The eight remaining states of the defunct Federation entered into negotiations with the United Kingdom about setting up a mini-Federation. The negotiations, which were spread over three years, proved fruitless and were abandoned in 1965. Barbados achieved independence in November 1966. The remaining seven island units had an offer of unitary statehood with Trinidad and Tobago. They preferred to negotiate with the United Kindom about a constitutional arrangement that would give them self-government but leave them grant-aided. A formula was found. In the course of discussions with the United Kingdom during 1966 it was agreed that Antigua with Barbuda and Redonda, St. Kitts-Nevis-Anguilla, Dominica, Grenada, St. Lucia and St. Vincent would each enter into a free and voluntary association with Britain as an Associated State. The arrangement could be terminated by either country at any time. Each island-state was to be fully self-governing in all its internal affairs. The constitution provided for a Parliament consisting of the Sovereign, a Senate, and an elected House of Representatives; for a Premier and Cabinet and for their collective responsibility to Parliament; for Public Service and Police Serivce Commissions; and for the protection of the fundamental rights and privileges of the citizens, as these are understood in the democratic system. The responsibility for defence and foreign affairs rested with the United Kingdom. Provision was also made for the Associated States to share one Supreme Court. Self-government to a more limited extent was granted to the smaller island communities of Montserrat and the British Virgin Islands. In British Honduras full internal self-government came into effect on I January 1964. Under the leadership of Premier George Price, founder and head of the People's United Party, the country moved steadily toward its twin objectives of economic viability and of independence as a republic.

The other large mainland colony, British Guiana, passed through a period of turbulence before achieving independence. As a result of the General Election of 1961, held after the grant of full internal self-government, Dr. Jagan's People's Progressive Party gained power, defeating Mr. Forbes Burnham's People's National Congress and Mr. Peter d'Aguiar's United Force. The three years that followed were marked by bitter political conflict and racial hatred. The government's proposals for a drastic austerity budget and for unaccustomed tax measures added fuel to already inflammable material; and on 9 February 1962, while Georgetown was filled with protesting crowds, several buildings were set on fire and the centre of the city destroyed. In the following year the government introduced controversial labour legislation and, in opposition, the British Guiana Trade Union Council called a general strike, which lasted for eighty days. Violence broke out, then a state of emergency was declared, and British troops were sent to British Guiana. During this period a reconvened constitutional conference in London, including representatives from the three parties, failed to agree on proposals and asked the British government to find the answers for them. A solution proposed and accepted was for direct election by proportional representation, the purpose being to discourage the development of political parties on racial lines by treating the whole country as a single constituency. Dissension continued, and spread from the towns to the countryside when, in February 1964, the Guiana Agricultural Workers' Union, which was linked politically with Dr. Jagan's party, called a strike. This lasted until July. In the course of the five months of conflict a state of emergency was declared, British troops were again flown in, numbers of East Indians were evacuated from their villages, and 159 people were killed. The latter half of the year passed quietly. Calm prevailed during the general elections which were held in December, with a turnout of more than 90 per cent of the electorate. Dr. Jagan's party gained 24 seats, Mr. Burnham's 20, Mr. d'Aguiar's 7. Mr. Burnham and Mr. d'Aguiar combined to form a coalition government. The new government gave first priority to obtaining independence; and in May 1966 the country, under the name of Guyana, became independent. The alliance between Mr. Burnham and Mr. d'Aguiar was an uneasy one, and did not last for long. In general elections held at the close of 1968 Mr. Burnham retained power, gaining 30 of the 53 seats in the Assembly.

But Guyana was not through with disturbances. No sooner had the country become independent than two of her neighbours pressed their claims for about 70 per cent of her territory. Surinam claimed a triangle, 6000 square miles in area, between the Courentyne River and New River, reportedly rich in bauxite, iron ore and nickel, and with potential for hydro-electric power. Shooting very nearly started when a detachment of the Guyanese Defence Force drove from the area some Surinamese who were setting up a camp and laying out an airstrip. The crisis was defused by The Hague, which made diplomatic gestures, and by Mr. Burnham's emphasis on his preference for negotiation.

Venezuela, in making her claim to rather more than one-half of Guyana, questioned the validity of an arbitration tribunal's award of the territory to Britain. Guyanese-Venezuelan relationships became strained when the President of Venezuela issued a decree in 1968 annexing a nine-mile belt of sea extending to within three miles of Guyana's Essequibo coast. Rumour said that oil lay beneath the troubled waters. Then, in January 1969, Georgetown was set astir by news of a rising in the Rupununi Savannahs. It was said that Venezuela was aiding the rebels, who failed in an attempt to win over the Amerindians. When the Guyanese Defence Force flew in, the disaffected ranchers took refuge in Venezuela, and Guyana sealed off its frontier. The atmosphere cleared noticeably after the new President of Venezuela, Dr. Caldera, took office. He turned to negotiation instead of sabre-rattling.

It is appropriate to consider some constitutional points of general interest before turning to the search for economic viability. The constitutions of the four new Caribbean nations were modelled on that of the United Kingdom. They contain provisions that reflect the anxieties and aspirations of the states concerned. Jamaica, for example, in an effort to preserve and strengthen the two-party system, gave certain specific functions to the Leader of the Opposition. One-third of the members of the Senate were to be appointed by the Governor-General on the nomination of the Leader of the Opposition. Also, though some appointments, such as that of the Chief Justice, were to be made by the Governor-General on the nomination of the Prime Minister, it was the duty of the Prime Minister to consult first with the Leader of the Opposition, who had the further right to make his views known to the Governor-General. Another feature of the Jamaican constitution was the inclusion of a Bill of Rights based largely on the Declaration of Human Rights of the United Nations. The constitution of Guyana differed in significant ways from that of its three sister nations and from the United Kingdom model. Thus, it was provided in 1969 that the Guyana Parliament could by a majority establish a republic modelled on the Parliamentary system. Guyana took this step in 1969 and was declared a republic on 23 February 1970. Further, whereas the other constitutions provided for a bicameral legislature made up of an elected Lower House and a nominated Upper House, the Guyana constitution provided for a unicameral legislature, a National Assembly. One possibility offered by the bicameral structure was that of appointing one or more ministers from the nominated House. The Guyana constitution provided for the appointment, on the advice of the Prime Minister, of four ministers who were not elected members and who had the right to sit as non-voting members of the Assembly. It also provided for the appointment of an Ombudsman by the Prime Minister after consultation with the Leader of the Opposition.

Constitutions in themselves are not enough to safeguard or sustain independence. Each government, faced with heavy additional expenses, and knowing that it now stood alone, put almost feverish urgency into strengthening its economy. The drive for economic development had its origins in the national movements of the 1930s and 1940s, and it was furthered by grants and technical aid from the Colonial Development and Welfare Organisation. The chief objective in the first years had been to remedy the deficiencies so extensively catalogued and described by the Moyne Commission. When the various governments became internally self-governing they began to exercise greater initiative in planning development so that it would meet national needs and express national purposes more adequately. Planning units and planning departments were set up, Puerto Rico-style incentive legislation passed, Industrial Development Corporations established. Independence added new dimensions, opened up new perspectives, raised new questions about the meaning of viability, about employment and fiscal policies, about the extent to which political independence could have meaning without economic independence.

In the first place the institutions essential for carrying out national fiscal policy were established: the Banks of Barbados, Jamaica, Trinidad and Tobago, and Guyana. National Export Commissions were founded. Jamaica established a Development Bank. Legislation was passed and, in some countries, work permits instituted, in order to secure and safeguard the employment opportunities of citizens.

It is not possible to do more here than review briefly some of the results: In Jamaica, years of effort combined with the happy discovery of bauxite had transformed the economy from one dominated by plantation agriculture to one far more complex, far more diversified, with new sources of revenue from bauxite, gypsum and an expanding tourist industry. The island's trade had grown from £11$\frac{1}{2}$ million in 1938, the year of the Frome riots, to £200 million in 1969. Bauxite and alumina made up almost one-half of the total exports. Investors had been attracted by a wide range of tax concessions and other incentives. The signs of development and industrialisation were written in the landscape, in the bauxite works of five companies, in new shipping and docking facilities at Newport West and Montego Bay, in Montego Bay's Freeport, in new urban complexes at Ocho Rios and around Mandeville, in the development of the Kingston waterfront and in hotel resorts along the north coast. In Barbados, still heavily dependent on its sugar industry, tourism had become a substantial revenue-earner, and the government's support of a family planning programme coupled with emigration had held the population increase to 1 per cent per annum, a significant matter for an island with a population density of almost 1500 to the square mile.

The traditional dependence on estate crops had not been characteristic of Trinidad and Tobago where for half a century oil and asphalt, along with sugar and cacao, had made the island relatively prosperous. Tourism had developed, especially in Tobago. The inflow of investment had increased. The garment industry had expanded, and new manufacturing plants had been established, such as those for making fertilisers and motor-car tyres and for assembling motor-cars.

At the same time, under the pressure of rising levels of unemployment and of the high rate of population increase which eroded many areas of progress, governments passed budgets to expand their schooling systems, spent more on vocational and technical education, promoted training programmes in industry, introduced National Insurance schemes and sought new markets for their products. One of the factors limiting productive capacity was the fequency of labour disputes and strikes. In 1965 the government of Trinidad and Tobago passed an Industrial Stabilisation Act which forbade, under heavy penalty, strikes and lock-outs except where there had been adequate notice to the Minister of Labour, who could refer the dispute to an Industrial Court constituted under the Act. The Court's decision was final, subject only to a limited right of appeal.

The effect of the tourist industry on a small island was seen most clearly in Antigua in the first half of the 1960s. The island had depended for long on two crops, sea-island cotton and sugar. When the cost of production increased, the sugar industry became marginal. Cotton production was affected by disease and by a fall in prices on the world market. Tourism changed the picture. Modern hotels were established, the airport enlarged, a deep-water harbour finally completed, some secondary industries established. In the first half of the decade the per capita income in Antigua rose to a higher level than in the other islands of comparable size.

Generally, manufacturing and mining expanded whereas agriculture lagged, and concern grew about the future of the two chief export crops, bananas and sugar. These found their chief market in the United Kingdom. In view of Britain's wish to enter the European Common Market, the West Indian governments combined to send a mission to the capitals of Western Europe in October 1969 to urge that the interests of the Commonwealth Caribbean should be protected, since existing commodity agreements, such as those for Commonwealth sugar and for the marketing of bananas, were vital for the West Indian economy.

There were good reasons for concern. Toward the close of the decade banana production fell. In 1967 Jamaica, Dominica, Grenada,

St. Lucia and St. Vincent exported 337000 tons of bananas to Britain. The total dropped to 328000 tons in 1968. In Jamaica the industry fell into such disarray that the government, forced to take drastic steps to reorganise, it, abolished the Banana Board, set up a new authority, subsidised a banana replanting programme and designated a special Commissioner for marketing Jamaican bananas in Britain.

The issues were more complicated in the case of sugar. In 1968 the sugar-producing countries of the Commonwealth Caribbean had produced 1 125 000 tons. Jamaica was the largest producer in that year, with 445 000 tons. In 1969 Guyana and Trinidad increased their output but in Barbados the total crop declined to 137000 tons, the lowest figure in twenty years, and in Jamaica a state of crisis developed and manufacturers closed down five factories. Sugar manufacturers and estate owners pressed for the mechanisation of the industry in order to cut production costs. The government of Jamaica hesitated because of the high level of unemployment. It appeared, however, that few of the unemployed were seeking work on the estates. Industrial diversification had opened up new possibilities for permanent rather than seasonal employment. Labour was drifting away from the estates. Cutting cane is hard work and the worker in the canefield has low social status; so alongside a shortage of labour there was a good deal of voluntary underemployment.

The search for viability led, of necessity, to regional economic co-operation and to links with the larger American community as well as with Latin America. It was natural that the years immediately after the break-up of the Federation should have been marked by an assertive local nationalism, the new nations and states being preoccupied with affirming and establishing their powers as sovereign states. Regionalism became a bad word. By 1968, however, they began to define areas where national needs could best be met by regional co-operation. A first step toward this objective was taken in 1968, when the countries of the Commonwealth Caribbean agreed to set up a Caribbean Free Trade Area (CARIFTA). The agreement provided for the immediate removal of customs duties from most of the items of trade between member countries. Some items were placed on a reserve list, customs duties on them being phased out over a five-year period in the more developed countries and over a ten-year period in the others. CARIFTA was a beginning. In itself the agreement was not enough to bring about basic changes in the economy of the region, for only about 6 per cent of the total trade of the Commonwealth Caribbean was between Caribbean countries. Another forward step was taken in 1969 when a Caribbean Development Bank was established, with its headquarters in Bridgetown, to provide a structure for financing development in member countries, and perhaps also some means of co-ordinating production. It was too early, at the close of the decade, to say to what extent the CARIFTA agreement was proving effective, though there were encouraging sings that the larger market it provided had begun to stimulate production and increase regional trade. As far as the countries of the Americas were concerned, the new nations were admitted to membership in the Organisation of American States and in the Inter-American Development Bank.

The search for viability required new legislation and new institutions, and these in turn required trained manpower at various levels. This had been recognised in the late 1940s when some of the Commonwealth Caribbean countries became self-governing. Many of the problems that beset them then were not primarily political but administrative. Political leaders emerged naturally and quickly as national consciousness grew; but not trained administrators and competent civil servants. A reserve had to be created of specialists and of well-educated people qualified to man the public services, to advise political leaders on the formulation of policy and to see that policy was carried effectively into action. This meant higher education within the West Indies. Only through the establishment of a university could the need be met for teachers, doctors, engineers, chemists and so forth, West Indians trained within the region, aware of its needs and circumstances, committed to its development. West Indians saw that one of the most potent agents in the development of Puerto Rico had been the University of Puerto Rico. The West Indian governments and the United Kingdom together established a University College of the West Indies in Jamaica. It grew up in a special relationship with the University of London; but on the approach of independence the purposes and structure of the University were changed. The concept of a highly centralised university was abandoned in favour of one that remained a unitary institution, but with its facilities decentralised. A second campus was established at St. Augustine in Trinidad in 1960, when the former Imperial College of Tropical Agriculture was merged with what was then the University College of the West Indies, and a third at Cave Hill in Barbados in 1963. A start was made at setting up University Centres in island territories that supported the University but had no campus. The range of teaching was widened, and faculties of agriculture and engineering and the social sciences established. Less restrictive policies were adopted with regard to entry and residence. In 1970 the number of day and evening students stood at over 4000 as against 700 in 1960. Even so, it was clear that the output of graduates was not enough to meet the demands of the developing countries. The University, which became an autonomous institution in 1962, the teacher-training colleges and the technical colleges could function effectively only if the secondary-school system were expanded, and so large sums of money were spent on building junior secondary and secondary schools, these programmes being financed in some instances by loans from international agencies such as the World Bank and the Inter-Amercian Development Bank.

While these things were being done, a series of disturbances occurred that highlighted critical areas of stress in the countries of the Commonwealth Caribbean. In October 1966 the government of Jamaica had to declare a state of emergency in order to quell disorder and check violence in West Kingston. A combined force of soldiers and police carried out a house-to-house search for arms, took a number of persons into custody and clamped down on disorder. Order was soon restored. Trouble broke out again in 1968. A rise in the cost of living had followed the devaluation of the Jamaican pound. Consequent on the devaluation of the British pound, unemployment had increased, and there had been serious deterioration in such public utilities as the telephone service, light and power. Two years of drought had reduced the island's water supply and crippled small farmers who produced vegetables and root crops for the local market. Tension increased in West Kingston, the island's powder-keg. It was fanned by the teaching of militant Black Power advocates. General discontent erupted in October 1968, when riots were sparked by an orderly but illegal march of University students protesting at a government exclusion order against a member of the University staff, Dr. Walter Rodney. Three lives were lost in the rioting that followed and heavy damage was done to property before the military restored order.

In 1969 rioting broke out in Willemstad, the capital of Curaçao, an island that seemed one of the most stable and orderly in the Caribbean. Dutch paratroopers were flown in at the request of the Premier, Ciro Kroon, and calm was imposed, but not before the heart of the famous shopping centre had been destroyed, the streets littered with plate glass, discarded display cases, cameras, and the relics of looting. The immediate cause was a dispute over the disparity in wages paid by a plumbing company associated with the Shell Refinery. In sympathy with the plumbers other workers joined in a demonstration on the morning of 30 May in front of the Shell building. When the marchers moved on towards Willemstad the police were waiting for them. Several men were shot. By the time the streets were cleared the centre of the capital was ablaze. The flames illumined the unemployment and poverty that had been hidden by the facade of crowded duty-free shops and resort hotels.

In the spring of 1970 disorders broke out in Trinidad, one of the most prosperous countries of the Commonwealth Caribbean. There were marches of unemployed in Port of Spain, organised and led by militant Black Power leaders. A section of the Army mutinied. For a brief period government itself seemed in danger of being overthrown. The loyal section of the Army, the coastguard and the police restored order while the men of the fire brigade worked night and day to control arson. A state of emergency was declared, curfew imposed, and most of the mutineers were placed under arrest.

A fourth area of turbulence developed in the north-eastern Caribbean during 1967. This differed from the troubles in Jamaica, Curaçao and Trinidad in that it raised important constitutional problems for the Commonwealth as a whole. Angered by what they regarded as victimisation by Premier Bradshaw's government in St. Kitts, the residents of Anguilla, 35 square miles in area, seceded from the Associated State of St. Kitts-Nevis-Anguilla. After two years of negotiation, during which Anguilla refused to return to the St. Kitts fold, events took a more serious turn with the island's unilateral declaration of independence as a republic under the rule of 'President' Ronald Webster. British paratroopers were flown in and the Anguilla dispute submitted to a specially appointed Commission. The Anguilla case had evoked considerable sympathy in the Commonwealth Caribbean but much of this was lost with Anguilla's declaration of independence. Reports of support for the new republic from dubious elements in the United States further alienated public opinion.

The Anguilla affair raised large issues. For Britain, they included the question of what to do about the secession of small black Anguilla bearing in mind the secession of large white-dominated Rhodesia. The Commonwealth Caribbean was concerned about the intrusion of undesirable foreign elements that could eventually affect their own security. In international politics the issues had to do with international law, fragmentation, regional co-operation, alien domination or exploitation of small states and military intervention.

The disorders in Jamaica, Curaçao and Trinidad served as hurricane signals to the new states and nations, which notwithstanding all their efforts faced grave difficulties, some of which were the products of development. There was more money in circulation and there was more unemployment. There were more jobs for the skilled, fewer jobs for the increasing number of unskilled and partially educated people. The gap was widening between those with high incomes and those with little or nothing, and the disparity was displayed for all to see in new residential suburbs with luxury houses and in the festering slums of West Kingston. Dependence on foreign markets left the agricultural producers of export crops with a feeling of insecurity. Inflation and steep increases in the cost of living wiped out the benefits that might otherwise have come from increases in salaries and wages. The inflow of foreign capital and the grant of special incentives to investors roused suspicions that the country was being sold out, that its capacity to make its own fiscal decisions was being weakened. These were among the most serious causes of social discontent. In addition, race became openly a dominant factor in Caribbean politics.

We have seen in what circumstances the two largest racial groups in the former British colonies came to the Caribbean: the African brought for life, with no hope of a return to his homeland, the East Indian for a limited period with the possibility of return to India if he wished; the African torn from family and tribe and forced to adapt as an individual to a creole culture, the East Indian able to retain his language, many of his customs, his tight-knit family structure and his religion. African and East Indian laboured in a society dominated by a small white or near-white elite, which held political and financial power, made and administered the law, set the social values. Black, brown, white — each was, in the words of a West Indian poet, 'manacled in skin, in race'. Personal ability, character and social standing were ascribed on the basis of colour. The kind of world that resulted was described by George Lamming in his first novel, *In the Castle of My Skin.* We have seen the significance of Garvey, and noted the effect of the introduction of universal adult suffrage which put political power in the hands of a non-European majority.

We have seen also how it came about that East Indian indentured labour was employed on a larger scale in Trinidad and Guyana than in other British colonies. In these two countries during the period of responsible government, as well as in the period of independence, voting was largely on racial lines, a large majority of the East Indians of Guyana supporting Dr. Jagan, an East Indian, and a large majority of the East Indians of Trinidad supporting the Democratic Labour Party, which was East Indian-dominated. In the other islands of the Commonwealth Caribbean by far the largest part of the population was black. In all these, as in Guyana and Trinidad, the achievement of independence, the widening of educational opportunity and greater social mobility combined to change attitudes and to enlarge the African presence. External forces encouraged the growth of stronger and at times bitter racial feeling: the racial policies of South Africa, the assumption of power by a white minority in Rhodesia, Britain's immigration policy, the support given by many people in Britain to Powellism, the discrimination and injustices to which black people were subject in the United States. West Indians also found an increase of racial prejudice in Canada, long a haven and refuge for their students and for those seeking advancement. The militant Black Power movement in the United States, led among others by Trinidad-born Stokeley Carmichael, encouraged a more articulate and positive assertion of blackness, of black dignity, of the right of black people everywhere to equality before the law and to equal opportunities of employment. The American movement was the protest of a minority group; that in the Caribbean was a claim by the majority group to economic as well as political power. The Black Power militants of the United States were convinced that only self-contempt and discrimination shut them off from a share of the good things in American life that they saw white Americans enjoying. The West Indians had black power through universal adult suffrage; almost all who symbolised political authority, whether Governors-General or Prime Ministers, were black; but they began to ask whether this meant financial independence and also a shift away from the assentially authoritarian attitudes of a colonial administration. West Indian society had always had its political nonconformists and radicals: Edward Jordan as a young man, William George Gordon, Bogle, Henry Alcazar, Cipriani and others. These had been powerful but relatively lonely voices. Garvey had attacked the social and political system of the West Indies and the United States, but the law had been used against him in the United States and in Jamaica. The 1940s witnessed the rise to power of radicals who attacked the colonial system and claimed independence: Manley, Bustamante, Adams, Williams and others. Up to that time the political nonconformist and radical attacked power that was centred elsewhere. Self-government and independence meant that the system under criticism and attack was now centred within each independent country. To what extent was it possible for countries that are small and insecure to tolerate and come to terms with their political nonconformists and radicals? And how far was the expanding middle class able or willing to understand that other world in West Indian society, the world of partially educated and insecure people, out of whom came the explosions of the 1930s? The 1960s saw the emergence of new Caribbean nations and states. It was also a decade in which the West Indian's vision of the world and his concept of himself were being changed by the external and internal pressures that we have outlined.

In response, governments pointed to their very substantial achievements. Some political leaders went further and defined both the goals and the principles that guided their search for viability. Dr. Eric Williams described the Trinidad and Tobago model of development as less totalitarian and more democratic than that of Cuba, more autonomous and self-reliant than that of Puerto Rico, with reliance on outside investment but also with increasing control over 'the commanding heights of the economy'. Mr. Forbes Burnham described a model of another kind, that of the co-operative republic of Guyana in which development was the result of a three-pronged effort by the public, private and co-operative sectors. He asserted that this differed from collectivism because it rested on persuasion, and he stated that there was no intention to confiscate private property.

Another aspect of recent West Indian history that deserves attention is the growth of the North American influence, which was greatly increased during the Second World War by the establishment of United States bases in the islands and in Guyana. The noise of the bulldozer at work on new airports echoed round the islands, from Beef Island and the Caymans to Anguilla and Exuma. The bauxite industry also changed trading patterns and industrialisation increased the demand for heavy equipment from the United States and Canada. Radio and TV put American personalities and American events inside West Indian homes. The trade figures for Jamaica illustrated the change. Traditionally the island had been chiefly a British market, but between 1960 and 1964, whereas exports from the island to England increased by 22 per cent, from £18 million to £22 million, those to the United States increased by 66 per cent, from £15 million to £25 million. The United States took more bauxite, an increasing quantity of sugar and light manufactures, especially textiles, and it increased its sales to Jamaica even though Britain enjoyed a tariff preference. West Indians knew that they had moved out of the orbit of Britain into that of the United States, and there was an obvious ambivalence in their attitude toward the cultural and economic influences exercised by so powerful a neighbour. They admired the egalitarian principles enshrined in the American constitution and they deplored the racial discrimination that still existed. They were impressed and attracted by the brilliant scientific and technological achievements of the United States, but they had no wish to become merely satellites. They liked Americans and they made a great effort to attract them to their countries, but they were not prepared to accept the establishment of hotels that in any way discriminated against their own people. They admired American wealth and business efficiency and they shared the American conviction that educational opportunity up to university level should be available to anyone, but they were often apprehensive about American aid programmes with their heavy emphasis on the use of American expertise and American equipment.

Towards the close of the decade, the West Indian community in the Caribbean and overseas suffered a series of heavy losses. Early in 1968 Sir Alexander Bustamante, at the time Prime Minister of Jamaica, retired from active politics. For thirty years he had shaped the political life of his country and had been one of the foremost architects of its independence. He had built up a strong trade union and a powerful political party and had promoted the interest of Jamaica on the international scene. He was succeeded by Mr. Donald Sangster, later Sir Donald, whose ability as a Minister of Finance, skill as a politician and personal loyalty to Sir Alexander had gained him respect throughout the Commonwealth Caribbean. He died a month after taking office as Prime Minister. Mr. Hugh Shearer succeeded him as Prime Minister and Leader of the Jamaica Labour Party.

Mr. Norman Manley died on 2 September 1969. A lawyer of the highest distinction, he had entered politics at the close of the 1930s and had founded Jamaica's first modern political party, the People's National Party. He established many of the institutions that are required by a country moving out of colonial status into independence, and had devoted his many gifts of intellect and of character to establishing and maintaining his country's independence.

No account of the recent history of the Commonwealth Caribbean would be complete without a reference, however brief, to the art movement which was inspired by, and grew out of, the national movement of the 1930s. The discovery of one's community and one's self exercised a powerful liberating influence, and led in turn to an attempt to portray the West Indian way of life and the beauty of the West Indian landscape. There had been instances of creative work before 1930; but these were isolated, the work of pioneers without the stimulus of public interest or the companionship of other artists. The following decade saw an extraordinary flowering of artistic ability at many different levels, in many different moods and through a wide variety of media. There came into existence vigorous schools of painting and national dance companies that were rooted in the rhythms of the folk, novelists, poets, sculptors. The rich variety of artistic expression and its power was almost bewildering, whether we

Basic Indicators for the West Indian Islands

	Population millions mid-1982	Area 1000's sq. km.	Density per square mile[2] 1974	GNP per Capita Dollars 1982	Av. annual growth rate %[1] 1960-70	1960-82
St. Vincent and the Grenadines	0.1	(.)	612	620	4.0	0.6
Guyana	0.8	215	9	670	2.4	1.7
Dominica	0.1	1	247	710	3.8	-0.8
St. Lucia	0.1	1	456	720	3.6	3.4
St. Kitts/Nevis	0.1	(.)	439	750	5.5	1.1
Grenada	0.1	(.)	732	760	3.4	1.6
Belize	0.2	23	15	1,080	3.4	3.4
Antigua and Barbuda	0.1	(.)	412	1,740	3.1	-0.2
Barbados	0.3	(.)	1,429	2,900	2.3	4.5
Bahamas	0.2	14		3,830	3.4	-0.4
Jamaica	2.0	11	457	2,398	3.8	
Trinidad/Tobago	1.2	5	498	6,106	3.2	
Cuba[3]	9.8	115	85	810	1.2	
Dominican Republic	5.7	49	116	1,330	2.1	8.8
Haiti	5.2	28	185	300	4.0	9.2

Sources:
1 The World Bank, World Development Report, (New York: Oxford University Press, 1984).
2 The World Bank, The Commonwealth Caribbean, (Baltimore: The Johns Hopkins University Press, 1978).
3 World Bank, Poverty and Human Development (New York, Oxford University Press, 1980), p. 69.

consider the novels of V. S. Naipaul and his younger brother, the late Shiva Naipaul, George Lamming, John Hearne, E. R. Brathwaite, Wilson Harris, or the poetry of Derek Walcott, Edward Brathwaite and Michael Smith. From the Spanish-speaking areas, the novels of Gabriel Garcia Marquez describe life on Colombia's Caribbean coast, so close in the culture to the rest of the Caribbean; in Costa Rica Quince Duncan's novels describe the trials, tribulations and joys of his West Indian forefathers who built that nation's railroads. In Cuba and the Dominican Republic there is renewed interest in their African heritages in all spheres of life.

The musical richness of the area continued to grow, from the Afro-Cuban rhythms such as the son, the mambo, the rumba, to Puerto Rico's salsa, to the Dominican-Haitian merengue, to the cadence of the patois-speaking peoples of Guadeloupe and Dominica in the Eastern Caribbean. Everywhere the basic instruments, the counterpoint between rhythms, the spontaneity in the blending of melodies, all indicate African origins. In Trinidad and Guyana the complex arrangements of Indian Hindu rhythms continue to be performed as are the staccato rhythms of the Muslim 'tassa' drums.

There are the carnivals of Santiago, Cuba and of Trinidad where the costumes, dancing and marching bands all reflect their common Mediterranean Catholic origins; and then there are the original and unique art forms: the Trinidad steel band of World War II vintage, the calypso with its imaginative political critiques especially when sung by the likes of the Mighty Sparrow, and Jamaica's reggae which reflects the adaptation of new electronic instruments to the social and political commentary of singers like the late Bob Marley. In the plastic arts there is the originality of Rastafarian sculpture and painting and the distinguished sculpture and drawing of Edna Manley.

These artistic interpretations had their counterpart in the historiography of the area. Historians such as Jamaica's Elsa Goveia, Trinidad's Eric Williams, Cuba's Manuel Moreno Fraginals, the Dominican Republic's Frank Moya Pons, all contributed to the rapidly growing identification of the Caribbean intellectuals with their own communities and with the past of their own people as well as of the region.

These artists and historians describe and interpret the way of life of people who belong to the Caribbean archipelago; and since all art is both local and universal, they portray also the essential unity of the larger archipelago of mankind with its deep dividing tides of nationality, colour, race.

CHAPTER XX

The Politics of
Post-Independence

There can be no doubt that the existence of particular 'generations' of leaders who have shared experiences and have a compatibility of political ideology can have a significant impact on decision-making and, as a consequence, on a region's political milieu.

In the Caribbean the British colonies had — upon independence — became members of a community with longstanding social and political conflicts. Caribbean leaders' reactions to these conflicts tended to take the form of generational responses. One such response was that of Venezuela's Rómulo Betancourt, Costa Rica's José Figueres, Puerto Rico's Luis Muñoz Marin and Colombia's Luis Alberto Camargo. These Latin American leaders had a considerable early involvement with one of the region's most dramatic events, the Cuban revolution; they would later respond negatively to many acts of that revolution. This was less the case with early leaders of West Indian independence whose Fabian-type socialism and Eurocentric vision did not have events in Cuba at its center. That generation's concern was the political decolonization process first and secondly, a concern over the unity of these territories.

In the West Indies, Norman Manley, Eric Williams, Grantly Adams and many of the leaders of the Eastern Caribbean, formed something of a 'club': their association and relationship went beyond state-oriented instrumentalism and involved a commitment to some form of 'regionalism'. It was, however, a regionalism of the English-speaking areas; the Hispanic Caribbean was still very much a world apart. It is clear that by the 1970's even this regionalism of the English-speaking area — expressed first in the Federation, then in Caribbean Free Trade Area (CARIFTA) and later in the Caribbean Common Market (CARICOM) — was not working smoothly. And yet, these early West Indian leaders had legated a pride in the achievements of their small nations not the least of which were functioning parliamentary democracies where respect for human rights reigned supreme. They had also legated a tradition of democratic succession political authority which in turn created a stability in leadership. The post-independence West Indian leaders were sometimes the same ones who led their nations into independence; such was the case of Eric Williams of Trinidad who governed from 1956 until his death in 1983. Others were the children of leaders of independence: Jamaica's Michael Manley and Barbados' Tom Adams followed in their fathers' footsteps.

But the region was changing and a large number of forces were pushing for even faster change. The question raised in the previous chapter had become crucial in this post-independence period: to what extent was it possible for countries which are small and insecure to come to terms with their political non-conformists and radicals? The question was made all the more urgent by the significant changes occuring in the area.

The number of independent states in the island Caribbean had gone from three in 1958 to 16 by the 1970's. With that change in numbers came changes in the nature of the area's politics, for the small as well as the major actors. Since foreign policy is a necessary activity of all modern states — no matter how small — both Cuba and the United States, for instance had a fourfold increase in the points of diplomatic contact in the area. Equally important, however, were three other changes which had been in process in the area since the late 1970's: (1) its internationalization which made for greater linkages with other regions as well as augmenting the total number of actors in the area; (2) the changing cartography and thus geopolitical definition of the area to include the circum-Caribbean states; (3) the dramatic structural crisis in the economic base of the area as a whole.

Interestingly, this tendency of the interaction of these three forces to generate conflict in certain parts of the Caribbean tended also to encourage a particular type of consensus, of concerted action, in other parts of the area. In either case, a dramatically different environment had evolved in the post-independence era and both the United States and Cuba as well as the newly independent smaller states had to deal with it.

For the Cubans the task was not an easy one and that fact made Cuba a centre of attention in the post-1960 decades. It was not only that this traditionally had been a North American sphere of influence with Cuba in the role of 'outsider' within that sphere, it was also that the new nations in the area had political cultures which tended to support the United States' view of Cuba as an outsider. This did not mean, however, that Cuba had been completely outside the broader political game. Events in the area since the 1970's had shown that it was in the game. For one, none of the major West Indian States participated in the diplomatic isolation of Cuba; since 1970 Guyana, Jamaica, Trinidad and Tobago and Barbados had diplomatic relations with Cuba. In fact Jamaica, chiefly because of the large Jamaican population still resident in Cuba, had long exchanged consulates with Cuba and even as conservative a leader as Alexander Bustamante had (in the early 1960's) refused to go along with the policy of isolating Cuba emphasized by the United States and all Latin American countries except Mexico.

These formal West Indian diplomatic links, however, were not enough to overcome a variety of obstacles to a closer West Indies-Cuba relationship, obstacles which reflected major realities of Caribbean life, and which were not eliminated by formal political, state-to-state relations. There were linguistic, cultural and even racial obstacles which had not been overcome in the Cuba-West Indies relationship and which often exacerbated the obvious ideological and political system differences between these nations. Additionally there were fundamental economic factors involved: to a large extent Cuba and the West Indies had compatible rather than complementary economies. The integration of Cuba into the socialist bloc of nations (COMECOM) and of the West Indies into the European and North American markets further illustrated the divergent paths taken by these Caribbean states.

All these factors contributed to a certain level of conflict in the area; they were certainly not the only ones. Other factors which made international relations in the Caribbean in the post-independence era increasingly conflictive were the exogenous factors. West Indian leaders would probably have disagreed among themselves on the particular weight that should have been attached to each of these factors but they would have agreed that in the post-independence period at least the following had been present and influential:

1 The shift from an Euro-centric orientation in most things of life (education, defence, culture, recreation, commerce) to a United States-centred one. With this shift came, of course, all the perceptions and definitions of the United States of its vital interests. It is obvious that even though the USA's conflict with Cuba, for instance, preceded the entry into independence of all the new Caribbean states, it slowly but surely became an integral part of the concerns of these small states during the post-independence era.

2 The entry into the area of other factors, the so-called 'middle power', Venezuela, Brazil, Mexico; the international transnational actors representing ideological interests (Marxist-Leninists,

Christian Democrats, Social Democrats, trade union 'federations') as well as transnational corporations. It is important to note, however, that the traditional and historical openness of the area continued so that very often the presence of these actors was more invited than imposed. This included the Cubans whose presence was often used as leverage at various levels of politics as well as the United States and the Europeans whose financial assistance was not insignificant to these economically strapped islands.

It is evident that it is not possible to address the problems and concerns of the region in the post-independence period without dealing with Cuban actions. That island had experienced the most revolutionary internal change of any Caribbean country since the independence of Haiti. Its international relations necessarily tended to reflect those structural changes and it was through these international relations that Cuba made its presence in the Caribbean most felt. The isolation within which the independence leaders of the rest of the Caribbean had operated was a luxury the post-independence leaders no longer enjoyed. Even as an 'outsider' the Cuban revolution had created a new Caribbean-wide international relations context. The analysis of two crucial watersheds in the history of the Cuban revolution will illustrate.

The first watershed came during the years 1960–1963 and affected the rest of the Caribbean in an indirect fashion. Three critical developments in Cuba illustrated these indirect Caribbean-wide impacts. First the economic break with the United States led to a reallocation of the Cuban sugar quota to such producers as the Dominican Republic, Guatemala, Costa Rica, and to a lesser extent the smaller islands. Because Cuba was now off limits to United States tourists and investments, other islands — quite importantly Puerto Rico and Jamaica — picked up the North American markets in these areas. Since West Indian leadership had already decided to follow the Puerto Rican model of development, the embargo on Cuba channelled new opportunities in their direction.

The missile crisis of October 1962 was fundamentally a confrontation between the USA and USSR. It demonstrated again what the Caribbean had known since the 16th Century: this was still an area of Great Power rivalry and conflict. Similarly the Bay of Pigs invasion illustrated how easily third parties could be drawn into conflicts in this relatively small sea.

In Cuba itself it was clear that these events had direct impacts and contributed to bringing anti-Americanism to fever pitch. But during these years, Cuba was not held out as a model to the non-Hispanic

Caribbean islands. The Cuban leadership was widely perceived to be communist; in a region where ideologies tended towards the conservative end of the political spectrum this leadership was given a cool reception at best. Despite these perceptions there was no uniform and coherent ideology emanating from Cuba during those years. Notwithstanding the harsh Cuban rhetoric surrounding the break with the United States market dominance, the essential argument and justifications given by Cuba still had an eclectic ring to them. There was perhaps more of the nationalism of the Raoul Prebisch and Economic Commission for Latin America (ECLA) 'centre-periphery' type arguments than Marxist ones. And even after the Bay of Pigs invasion, Cuba was unwilling to state expressly that they were Marxist-Leninists. An example is the speech in the United Nations by Raul Roa, quoted in *The New York Times* (January 5, 1961):

> It has been stated falsely that Cuba is the satellite of international communism, but the truth is different. Cuba has ceased forever to be a satellite of American imperialism, and it is for this reason that we are accused of being communists.

The period up to 1963 showed a Cuban leadership engaged in much strategic manoeuvering and characterized by relatively little ideological dogmatism. They first attempted to institutionalize the party into something called the Organization of Revolutionary Institutions (ORI). This organization, however, was dominated by orthodox Marxists-Leninists of the old Communist party (the Partido Socialista Popular) and they were purged in 1963. Something called the Party of the Socialist Revolution (PURS) was then created under the direct leadership of Fidel Castro and his 26 of July movement followers. Similarly, Castro's stance on revolutionary internationalism also shifted as necessary. A much more ideologically focused period of the Cuban revolution came after 1964 and it was after that year that Cuban influences began to be felt in the other islands. There radical circles began blending Cuban Marxism with Black Power sentiments emanating from the USA and Great Britain into a powerful anti-establishment ideology. And, yet, in Cuba the shift responded as much to internal dynamics as it did to the now more clearly defined Marxist-Leninist orientation of the revolutionary leadership. Those internal dynamics had given shape to a strong undercurrent of Cuban nationalism. Critical in understanding this particularly Cuban revolutionary style was the role of Eduardo Chibás, an important reformist leader of the 1950's. In his youth Fidel

Castro had been a member of Chibás' party, the Partido Ortodoxo. Chibás' favourite political saying was 'verguenza contra dinero' ('Shame against money'). In a way it expressed a latent hostility, very Catholic and very Spanish, against capitalism in its North American shape. To be sure, this was a love-hate relationship because Cubans, especially in the last decade before the revolution, were proving to be quite adept at capitalism. It was, however, that latent vein of anti-capitalism which Fidel Castro tapped during this period. He was strongly assisted by his Argentinean colleague, Ché Guevara. Guevara advocated a socialist 'New Man' — a revolutionary man, motivated by moral and collective drives rather than material and individualistic ones. In order to accomplish this the Cuban leadership had virtually, by definition, to transform the entire social order. A new political culture, i.e., a new system of empirical beliefs, expressive symbols and values which form the context of political action, had to be generated.

This Cuban search for an original version of socialist man had an appeal to intellectuals in the wider Caribbean area. These however were very definitely in a minority. The more representative view in the rest of the Caribbean was that the Cuban model was far from being a success, hardly something for the other islands to emulate. This was especially so in the late 1960's when the Puerto Rican model of development seemed to be paying significant dividends to the other islands. Jamaica, Trinidad, Barbados, the Dominican Republic and the nations of the Central American Common Market were achieving good rates of economic growth during these years. In Cuba, the revolutionary leadership attempted to bring about the cultural changes necessary for the creation of the new man through various massive mobilizations of the citizenry. Each mobilization involved enormous sacrifices for the common man; clearly the Cuban revolution was not a painless process. The first mobilization was the Campaign Against Illiteracy which like many others was initiated in late 1969. In a country where 42% of the rural population and 12% of the urban was illiterate (1953 figures) such a campaign was urgent enough. But the proportions of that campaign, with one out of every four adult Cuban participating actively in literacy work, indicated that to the revolutionary leadership the importance of that massive mobilization went beyond the question of literacy, In fact, in a fundamental way the campaign to eradicate illiteracy served as a testing ground for many of the ideas, tactics, and organizational devices later incorporated into the revolutionary style of that governance.

This style of politics was equally apparent in the origin and functions of the Committees for Defence of the Revolution and the Schools of Revolutionary Instruction. There was nothing in the Caribbean — where the emphasis had always been on individualism or on cooperation among small groups — equivalent to this type of social-political action. Additionally, these great experimental attempts at creating the 'new man' were both of questionable Marxist origin. They depended on 'voluntarism' (the human will to do something) and other idealistic efforts. The reform of the schooling system — especially the creation of the *circulos infantiles* — were intended to change human nature enough to liberate the Cuban woman from exploitation and chauvinism; and to create the 'new man' by combating what Cubans called the 'historical pathology' and 'diseased' previous system. Orthodox Marxists were severely critical of such measures noting that 'moral' incentives had already been tried unsuccessfully elsewhere.

The goals of the Cuban revolution were lofty and as such could appeal in a very general way to those dissatisfied with their systems. But the actual programs and policies of the revolution were hardly exportable, especially as they did not seem to be paying off in Cuba itself. The Prime Minister of Trinidad and Tobago, Eric Williams, spoke for many in the Caribbean when in his book *From Columbus to Castro* (1970) he expressed a sympathy for the Cuban efforts but rejected their model as 'totalitarian' and unproductive. The difficulties the Cubans were having became evident in 1970, a watershed year in Cuban as well as Caribbean history. It should be remembered that in 1969 and in 1970 major social upheavals occurred in Curaçao and Trinidad. At the same time that much of the Caribbean was experiencing major difficulties of the post-independence era, in Cuba there was a dramatic shift in governance style and emphasis taking place. One economist called 1970 the period of the 'termination of Cuba's unique formula for the construction of communism'. Fidel Castro's July 26, 1970 speech is a Cuban and Caribbean landmark; it set the tone for this period in which the following critical developments were crucial:

1 Castro's explanations of the failure of
  (a) the moral incentives initiative,
  (b) the industrialization programme,
  (c) initiatives in agriculture and the resultant increase in dependence on the USSR.
2 The increasing presence of the military in the government: six of the seven new vice-premiers created in late 1972 were military men.
3 The failure of the Cuban originated 'foco' theory of guerrilla

warfare throughout Latin America and the death of Ché Guevara in Bolivia.

The years after the victorious entry of Fidel Castro into Havana, the Cuban leader was honestly facing up to the failures of his many revolutionary initiatives, from agriculture to promoting revolution abroad. Since 1969-1970 were years when discontent leading to mass protests swept many of the other Caribbean islands, 1970 can truly be called a watershed year for the region, the beginning of the post-independence era.

In the case of Cuba, it appeared to certain authors that by 1970 the '*fidelista* phenomenom', the charisma of Fidel, had perhaps reached its limit. This conclusion was premature but it is evident that major changes were taking place on the island.

For one, the presence of the military in the society, already highlighted in the works of K.S. Karol, R. Dumont, and H. Thomas, appeared more evident than ever before. Accompanying this was the fact that reliance upon the 'new man' morality for achieving economic growth had been abandoned as impractical and idealistic. The changed was summed up by a Canadian economist: 'Indeed, Premier Castro's conception of human nature underwent a significant change. Prior to July 1970 the Premier continuously spoke of the perfectability of man and of the advisability of restructuring society on the assumption that man was motivated by altruism and patriotism.' Absenteeism, falling productivity, growth of black markets, the proliferation of *amiguismo* (special privileges to the élite), and increasing recourse to regimentation and coercion (militarization) all led to a fundamental change. After July 1970 Premier Castro adopted what was in effect the Stalinist formula for the distribution of income — 'to each according to his work' — though he phrased his new position more tactfully and elegantly: 'Society must do most for those who do most for society.' The phase of idealism in the Cuban revolution had passed.

There is no evidence that this transition caused any major trauma initially in the leadership or the society. Again, Castro was able to switch metaphors and do so fairly smoothly given the stakes involved.

Whatever the metaphors used for internal consumption, Cuba's impact on the rest of the Caribbean was reduced by its inability to deal with a critical issue central to Caribbean concerns: the problem of economic dependency. Between 1959 and 1978 there was a complete change in the direction and nature of Cuban trade but the essential statistics were startlingly similar: in 1959 98.6% of Cuba's total trade was with market economies, and of that 68.7% was with the United

States. By 1978, 82.3% of Cuba's trade was with the Socialist bloc and of that 69% was with the Soviet Union. Additionally, this dependency was accompanied by two other trends: increasing trade deficits and increasing dependence on Soviet price supports for both sugar and oil. In 1976 Cuba received from the Soviet Union 15.2 US cents more than the world price per pound 'for its sugar, and bought Soviet oil at US $6.37 per barrel less than the world price. These terms of trade continued into the 1980's and clearly had nothing to do with economics and everything to do with politics. It was not a model other Caribbean islands could want to emulate. Combatting economic dependence had already become a major challenge to Caribbean leaders everwhere. But, Cuba was part of the region and in the late 1970's a series of events would make it a matter of direct concern to the post-independence leadership of the West Indies. In fact, three different Cuban involvements in the Caribbean brought that island into centre stage while at the same time revealing the fact that the Caribbean had entered a new phase in it international relations. Much of the subsequent West Indian perceptions that developed about the area's geopolitical and geostrategic situation were shaped by these events.

First was the airlift, through Barbados initially and Guyana later, of a division of Cuban troops for Angola. Eric Williams of Trinidad was particularly put out by the discovery of what an old Cuban hand called 'this...sensational development in hemispheric history.' And, this led to the first discussions on mutual security assistance between Trinidad and Barbados.

It should be clear that the objection of the West Indies was not to Cuban actions against South Africa, this latter country and its abhorrent system of *apartheid* has no sympathisers in the islands. The objection was to violations of their sovereignty by an action which demonstrated Cuban audacity and logistical capabilities while at the same time showing how easily these small states could unknowingly be drawn into an East-West tangle.

It was in the context of this dramatic act by Cuba that West Indian apprehensions escalated in the months after a coup d'état toppled the government of Eric Gairy in Grenada in 1979. While the movement against the increasingly eccentric and incompetent Gairy had wide support it was actually led by a small group of middle class radicals called The New Jewel Movement. Their leader was a charismatic young lawyer, Maurice Bishop, whose Marxist ideology was not revealed to the Grenadians until after the coup d'état, but whose wide appeal and popularity was undisputed. Such was the unpopularity of

Gairy in the other West Indian islands that the initial shock at this first violent overthrow of an elected independent West Indian government was followed by some relief. The West Indian government leaders were not as sanguine but eventually they also adopted a stance of cautious and suspicious neutrality *vis-à-vis* the People's Revolutionary Government which the Grenadian leadership installed. There was no neutrality on Cuba's part nor on the part of the United States. They quite rapidly made Grenada part of their ongoing conflict in the region. Cuba almost immediately had the only resident ambassador on the island, who soon presided over a growing Cuban presence. It seemed to replicate the situation in Guyana, where the Cuban mission took up nearly half a city block and where Cuba's multiple involvements had long been the talk of Georgetown. Some 15 Cuban doctors arrived; so did fishing trawlers and instructors. On November 18, 1979 Prime Minister Maurice Bishop told a rally that he expected 250 Cubans to start building a new international airport.

Eventually there would be 700 Cuban workers. There would also be a full Soviet embassy staffed by a diplomat whose previous post was Ambassador to Argentina, the Soviets most important trading partner in Latin America. Not since World War II with the building of the US military bases had the area seen such activity and certainly never since the conflict in British Guiana in 1953 had these former British colonies been in the midst of such an East-West conflict. This, in the final analysis, is what it was; a supra-national international relations fray much more than national ones. Again, as on previous occasions throughout the centuries and most recently with the Cuban missile crisis of 1963, the Caribbean was converted into an arena of Major Power politics as the United States focused on the airport as a major military threat. Whatever private apprehensions West Indian leaders had about the ultimate use of this airport, they kept their counsel to themselves, noting publicly that the Grenadian runaway was no longer than four others already in service in various West Indian islands.

The assassination of Prime Minister Maurice Bishop and several of his closest advisors on October 19, 1983 by a small ultra-Leninist clique within the regime brought down the first West Indian attempt at creating a socialist state closely allied to Cuba. It also led to the invasion of Grenada by the USA and small units of soldiers from Jamaica and police from the Eastern Caribbean.

It should be evident that Cuba had gone, in a very short space of time, from being an 'outsider' (both politically and culturally) to being virtually the major player in important parts of the West Indies, certainly in Grenada but also in Jamaica where the 'democratic socialism' of Michael Manley (1972–1980) developed very close ties with Fidel Castro's regime.

By the early 1980's West Indian leaders had little doubt about Cuban military capabilities and every incident involving the Cubans contributed to the perception of a threat, even those which were not so intended. A good illustration of this was an incident in the Bahamas in 1980. A Cuban MIG aircraft sank one of the Bahamas' three gun boats and strafed the sailors while in the water. Cuban military helicopters later landed on Bahamian territory. Although the incident appeared to result from a genuine case of mistaken identity (the Bahamians were thought to be Cuban exiled 'pirates') and apologies and reparations were eventually made, the harm was already done. A poll taken in the Bahamas showed that 85.9 per cent believed that the attack had been deliberate and not a mistake and that 73.3 per cent believed that Cuba still posed a threat to the islands. As a writer in Nassau put it, Cuba had attacked a 'defenceless neighbouring, friendly country'. But even more important than this, he continued, it had attacked 'a black developing nation at the same time that it purported to enjoy wide international prestige as a leader of the non-aligned movement.' The cultural and racial gulf between Cuba and the small islands in the Caribbean were still being utilized to sustain political and ideological differences. The deep divisions inherited from their various colonial pasts had been carried over into the post-independence era, divisions aggravated by ideological differences. A defensive attitude began to develop very rapidly. By the early 1980's, for instance, the nations of the Eastern Caribbean were ready to do something positive about their security. What developed was a set of ideas increasingly called the 'Adams Doctrine', after Barbados Prime Minister Tom Adams. This doctrine was premised on the belief that threats to their small democracies would not come from external forces directly but from the critically timed assistance these external forces might give to the small groups at home who would subvert democracy. The need then was for a small but mobile force which counted speed as its most effective asset.

The Adams doctrine was as much a product of the thinking of the Ronald Reagan administration in the USA as it was Tom Adams' own geopolitical views and of events which unfolded in the area during the late 1970's. It is important to know, therefore, that the first use of Adams doctrine was not in Grenada, October 1983 but in Union Island, St. Vincent (97 miles due East of Barbados) early December 1979. An invasion of alleged Rastafarians from the Grenadian island of Carriacou led to a St. Vincent request for assistance. Elements of the Barbadian defence forces intervened to help put down the movement. This was the first intervention in the name of collective security in the young history of Eastern Caribbean sovereignty. It was this incident and the suspicion that the revolutionary government in Grenada was training others for similar acts, which led eventually to the signing of a formal collective security understanding in September 1982. The 'Memorandum of Understanding' regarding security and military co-operation was signed by Barbados and all the independent states of the Organization of Eastern Caribbean States (OECS), except Grenada. It is one of those ironies of history that it should have been the fear of one of their own which led these islands to shape their first collective security agreement. The Western Hemisphere's collective security treaties, from the Act of Chapultepec (Mexico, 1945) to the Pact of Rio de Janeiro (1947) and finally the charter of the Organization of American States (Bogota, 1948), had been directed at outside forces, the Axis powers and later Soviet communism. The independent West Indian islands had created what they thought was additional protection to what these treaties already granted.

Clearly an operation such as that which took place in Grenada in October 1983 was quite beyond the collective capabilities of the signatories; nevertheless, that operation, once it came, was within their contingency plans and harmonious with their intentions. As distinct from so many other US interventions in the Caribbean, this one had truly been a collective enterprise even though its legality under international law continued in the mid-1980's to be a matter of debate. What was clear was that there had been a coincidence of West Indian views with US desires and means to make advantage of a situation created by the Grenadian leadership themselves.

Right after the Grenada intervention the idea of the Regional Security Pact contained in the Memorandum of Understanding of 1982 began to take shape. On November 17, 1983 the Barbadian Minister for Parliamentary Affairs told the House of Assembly that there would be a new force headquartered in Barbados with permanent units stationed in each island. The US, he said, would train and 'partially equip' the new force. By mid-1986 there had been no implementation of this Security Pact. The reasons for this were various including the death in early 1985 of its major proponent Tom Adams. More importantly, however, was the opposition of many leaders of the West Indian democracies. That opposition reflected a built-in distrust of military structures and a belief that the best defence of democracy is social and economic development. In the words of

St. Christopher-Nevis Prime Minister Kennedy Simmons, 'Security cannot be won by force of arms.' Son Mitchell, Prime Minister of St. Vincent was even more adamant on the subject: 'The age old lesson,' he noted, 'is if you live by the sword, you perish by the sword.'

The post-independence leadership of the Caribbean mini-states inherited some long-standing regional conflicts not the least of which was the Cuba-United States one. They were properly concerned with their national security but did not appear willing to threaten their budding democracies with military structures. They have uniformly pinned their hopes on the capacity of their societies to develop and sustain a decent standard of living for all as the strongest underpinning any democracy could have. And yet, there was no escaping the international relations realities the post-independence Caribbean leaders faced. The move to create an Eastern Caribbean collective security system was one small step in achieving a system which Gordon K. Lewis in his monumental *Puerto Rico: Freedom and Power in the Caribbean* (1963) hoped would be 'A real federal alliance, founded on the membership of really independent units which would gradually create an Antillean Community capable of asserting the Caribbean presence. . . .' It is an old Caribbean aspiration, far from being achieved but still burning in the hearts of many citizens of the region.

CHAPTER XXI

'Widening the United States' Sphere of Influence'

This book has covered three 'climactic periods': Emancipation in the 1930's, the 'liberation decade' of the 1930's and the period of independence of the 1960's. Everything indicates that history will record the 1980's as a fourth climactic period, not only because of the dramatically changing geopolitical factors outlined in the previous chapter, but also because the 1980's has once again shown the tenousness of Caribbean economies. The ever present search for economic viability reached a critical stage in the 1980's and so did the search for an economic system which would assure it. But this search has never been a smooth process, certainly not in the contemporary world. This is in part due to the fact that it is one of the ironies of contemporary world history that two apparently contrary trends are operating simultaneously. On the one hand there is the accelerating push towards independent statehood even among the smallest and least populated of territories. The driving forces behind this trend are often primordial ones such as ethnicity or similar sacred sentiments which encourage national exclusivism. Running in what might appear to be a contrary direction is the other trend, more secular in character: the perceived need to promote regional integration movements, from free trade zones to common market arrangements and, then, so goes the hope, some form of political integration. In some cases, even the search for membership in the sphere of influence of a major power can coexist with intense nationalism. Awareness of the constant economic pressures on small economies lead the same proponents of nationalism to press for regionalism in some form. The Jamaican nationalist leader Norman Manley encapsulated in 1947 this fear of insularity and consequent weakness:

> I say we must create a large enough area, small although it may be in the face of the colossi who bestride the world today, but large enough to give us a voice, and pull and power over those international affairs which in the long run determine the peace and

prosperity and the opportunity for happiness of the three million people of these lands.'

Since statesmen such as Manley gave up neither sentiment, the forces of insularism and those of regionalism were kept in constant and unresolved tension. In terms of the operation of this dialectic, the insular Caribbean was no different from many other regions of the world where the two trends have manifested themselves. The Caribbean has been unique, however, in the range of its experiments with a wide variety of regional attempts, stretching over a long period of history, each with its own peculiar political and sociological characteristics. In fact, certain well studied cases — such as the Puerto Rican model of integration into the North American economy and polity through the Associated Commonwealth or the thorough integration in 1946 of the French territories as Overseas Departments — have become 'models' for analysis and implementation elsewhere.

The price paid by those states of the area which have chosen — or had forced on them — isolated development (autarky) has been heavy. No Caribbean country illustrates this fact more dramatically than Haiti, the first black republic in the world and the second nation to declare its independence in the Western Hemisphere. Long isolated on purely racial grounds by the nations of Europe and the Americas, Haiti eventually had to purchase its recognition from France at a heavy cost to its economy. It was the destruction of the economic base during the wars of independence which turned that island into what we termed above, a tragic figure in the group of Caribbean nations.

Historically, the underlying problems of Haiti went beyond the political areas. They resulted from the great poverty of the country and the fierce competition for control of the state machinery, the only source of steady income. And that poverty has been getting worse. In the words of a sociologist, 'The Haitian peasant sector is caught in a downward spiral of circular and cumulative causation which slowly depresses the standard of living among the peasants.' Put differently, the man/land ratio in Haiti has deteriorated rapidly through population growth coupled with soil erosion and exhaustion.

Haiti is one of the few places in the Hemisphere where the number of farms is actually increasing: from 580 000 in 1959 to 616 710 in 1971.

It is a terrible commentary on the Haitian's desire to own his little plot of land that subsistence agriculture contributes substantially more to soil erosion than modern cultivation because of the primitive cultivation methods used. Additionally, soil erosion on the island also results from another characteristic of underdevelopment: the extensive use of wood, in house building, boat building and, most disastrous of all, firewood and charcoal. The black peasant protagonist in Haiti's most acclaimed novel, Jacques Roumain's *Masters of the Dew* (1944) painted a vivid picture of the 'gullies where erosion had undressed long strata of rock and bled the earth to the bone.' Roumain knew where the problem lay: 'They had been wrong to cut down the trees that once grew thick up there. But they had burned the woods to plant Congo beans on the plateau and corn on the hillside.'

When we add to this economic dimension a socio-cultural one we begin to complete a picture that explains in part the despair previously mentioned. That socio-cultural dimension is the Haitian's historical love of land. Land is such a valuable commodity to the Haitian peasant, as Melville J. Herskovits (*Life in a Haitian Valley*) noted in 1937, that 'there are few, among the peasants at least, who do not seek by all means to add to their heritage. . . . The drive to obtain property is an obsession with the Haitian peasants.' Four decades later that obsession can only have grown.

This poverty and pressure on the land has led Haitians to seek opportunities abroad. In Haiti — as in the rest of the Caribbean — migration became an acceptable option which, once exercised, carried both individual and collective responsibilities. The latter involved remitting monies to the folks back home and when possible giving a hand to others who will follow in the migratory path. Just as West Indians migrated to Panama and Central America to build the Canal then to build ports and railroads, so Haitians sought work in the plantations in Cuba and the Dominican Republic. Often these hardworking migrants experienced a cruel fate.

In the 1930's the Cubans expelled them in large numbers and in the most cruel fashion. In 1937 Dominican Republic dictator, Rafael Trujillo, sent his army to massacre between 5000 and 15 000 Haitian peasants who had settled in the fertile but under-populated Dominican side of the border. Already in 1941 James Leyburn could exclaim: 'In the world at the present time there seems to be no haven for penniless migrants, particularly illiterate blacks.' Leyburn's plaint was not totally accurate: by the 1960's there were an estimated 400 000 Haitians settled in the United States and in the 1950's and 1960's they were eagerly sought as construction workers in the then booming tourist industry of the Bahamas. Three events caused a shift in the destination of Haitians from the Bahamas to South Florida, in the United States: the decline in the Bahamas construction industry, the economic boom in South Florida brought about largely by the new Cuban refugees who settled there, and, third, the increasing political repression of the Haitian dictator Francois (Papa Doc) Duvalier. The tyranny of François' son, Jean Claude, was brought to an end in early 1986 but the origins and source of support of that dictatorship does not make one optimistic about that island's future. It was in the historical atmosphere of colour animosity between the 10 per cent who constitute the coloured bourgeoisie (*mulâtres*) and the 90 per cent who are blacks (*noirs*) that Duvalier came to power in 1957 in the first election ever held under direct adult universal suffrage on the island.

As Bernard Dietrich and Al Burt put it in their vehemently anti-Duvalier book, *Papa Doc* (1969), the question in 1957 seemed to be whether Haitians preferred a self-styled black idealist, Dr. François Duvalier, or a haughty mulatto patrician Louis Dejoie. The latter, they noted, seemed to have the support of the United States Embassy, United States and Haitian business interests and significant elements in the military. The vote, however, was for Papa Doc: Duvalier 679 884; Dejoie 266 993.

Rather than being due totally to fraud, the Duvalier victory appeared to have been the culmination of a populist movement of black intellectuals (noirisme) that had two crucial stages: The first was, the Les Griots movement of the 1930's led by a new class of black professionals and bureaucrats created by the United States Marine occupation (1915–1934) and against which they reacted. This type of nationalistic reaction had been typical in those Caribbean countries which had experienced United States interventions, as the cases of Mexico, Cuba, Nicaragua, Dominican Republic illustrate. Duvalier a medical doctor from a humble background was such a nationalist and an important member of Les Griots. Like the rest of the group he was an *authentique*, that is opposed to the Roman Catholic Church, the French language and culture, and a partisan of Voodoo and of the Creole language. Politically, this nationalism represented a 'revolution' of Haitienisme against what they considered was the politics of *doublure*, the traditional rule of the mulatre elite occasionally with a black president who was no more than a puppet manipulated by them.

The second stage in the emergence of this black élite was the coming to power of Dumarsais Estimé (1946–1949). As the Heinls put it, 'Estimé's politics...amounted to a kind of peasant populism tinged with...anti-foreignism and with fierce *mangeur-mulâtre* [mulatre-eating] black racism.' That this racial populism was not intended to help the masses could be seen in some of Estimé's nationalistic measures. Various nationalizations of businesses really had as their goal the creation or enrichment of a new black bourgeoisie to counter the mulâtres. It was this newly strengthened urban black middle class that later became one source of support for the Duvaliers. Their aim became the control of the state, as vital a prize in Haiti as it was in the rest of the Caribbean; it was that control which determined who were the 'ins' and who the 'outs'. This noir-mulâtre conflict, with its elements of both colour and class had its counterparts in many Caribbean islands but hardly anywhere with the intensity evident in Haiti.

One could not understand, therefore, the duration of the Duvalier rule unless one also understands that a major source of support of the regime had been the black rural 'mediating class'. In a country which was 80% rural, the potential significance of this class in controlling the mass of the peasantry becomes clear.

The official element in this mediating class was traditionally the *chef de section* (the section chief). The section is the purely rural administrative unit literally controlled by a chief. The section chiefs go back to the days of the liberation of the slaves and traditionally represented black civilian power against mulatre elite control of the military. It is crucial to know that these chiefs are referred to as *leta* (creole for 'the state') by the peasants. With intimate knowledge of his rural environment and its inhabitants, this chief can be a precious political ally or formidable enemy. It was Duvalier's political skill that converted them into his staunch supporters. With the vast rural sector secure, Duvalier had a free hand to deal with the urban 20 per cent where most of his enemies were. But race and class hatreds were not the only weapons available to Duvalier. He also had raw military force.

The need for a better equipped and controlled rural force became evident during the early stages of the Duvalier regime. There were some six anti-Duvalier invasions from Cuba, the United States or the Dominican Republic, all attempting to start 'guerrilla' warfare à la Cuba. There is no known case of significant peasant support of these largely mulâtre-led invasions. The reasons might lie in the very nature of this newly recognized intermediate class, many of whom by then now formed part of the VSN (*Volontaires de la Securité Nationale*). As the Heinls described them, its rural platoons in every village 'wore the red sashes of Ogun and big straw hats of the old Cacos, whose latest descendants they were, and were meant by Duvalier to be.'

Together with the section chiefs these VSN militias formed a formidable armed counterforce to the professional military that had heretofore been the makers and unmakers of Haitian governments.

We see here, therefore, the fundamental natively Haitian bases of the power of the Duvaliers: a traditional network of powerful black peasants, newly recognized and rewarded; the skillful integration of the symbolism of 'black' Haiti (the black and red flag instead of the mulâtre blue and red one) and of the folk religion: Ogun is the Voodoo god of war; the integration of a powerful historical symbol, the Cacos: the black peasant guerillas who fought both the mulâtres and the United States Marines during their occupation (1915–1934). For the first time since the disarming carried out by the Marines, partisan groups of Haitian peasants were armed. Clearly the presence of this rural network made it much more likely that any change of regime would take place through urban action or a 'palace coup' rather than from any invasion or military campaign, whether supported by the United States or not. The change of regime occurred in early 1986. With young people protesting bad economic circumstances and human rights violations, eventually the revolt spread in the way it always had: from the Northern city of Cap Haitien to the middle city of Gonaïve and then to Port-au-Prince. In that capital city, the centre of power but also the location of thousands of impoverished migrants from the rural areas, a distinct political force had been latent since the 1940's: the explosive force of the unemployed. In the 1940's and 50's they called it the *rouleau compresseur* (literally, steamroller): masses of slum-dwellers smashing and looting and in such numbers than even military repression became useless.

This phenomenom (on a much smaller scale) was present in Curaçao in 1969 and Trinidad in 1970; it is latent in virtually all the Caribbean islands which have high rates of unemployment especially among the young. It is the combination of these phenomena — urban youth and unemployment — which led the Prime Minister of St. Vincent to say in 1984 that 'we are in a race against time.' It is the fear that none of these fragile economies can deal with this phenomena in isolation which leads sincere nationalists to search for some form of multilateral — be it regional or extraregional — economic arrangement. The pragmatism of their motives has been evident for decades and, yet, the vital question in West Indian history remains: can the various units of an area where as is stated above, the island is the 'most compelling area symbol', work in concert even for the most pragmatic of reasons? Is not the isolation, the autarky, of a Haiti more of a probable future trend? The facts are both encouraging and discouraging as one looks at contemporary attempts at working together.

On the economic side, the prospects of Great Britain's entry into the European Common Market (EEC) had stimulated the creation of CARIFTA. When that British move finally took place the West Indians perceived a need to join the African and pacific countries' agreement with the EEC and this in turn stimulated the establishment of the Caribbean Common Market (CARICOM). It was a pragmatic need which led to quick agreement on the common external tariff and the common protective policy which are the central features of CARICOM. As one observer put it, CARICOM was called for 'as much by the necessity to deal with the EEC negotiators as by the desire, in itself, to deepen the integration movement'. Through the Lômé Convention, the Caribbean now became part of the APC countries: the former European colonies in Africa, the Pacific and the Caribbean. Worldwide decolonization had led to new and much more equitable forms of economic association.

Despite the pragmatic auspices of its birth, CARICOM — established by the treaty of Chaguaramas, Trinidad on July 4, 1973 — was expected to be more than a common market, indeed it was supposed to offer the outside world, and fundamentally the EEC, the idea that there were dealing with a West Indian 'community'. But was there really such a community? Did the move to create a common market reflect a social and cultural propensity towards integration? Would the West Indies at least avoid the pitfalls and dangers of isolation in a region which — as argued in the previous chapter — had already become an arena of East vs. West and North vs. South battles? The idea that CARICOM — by providing substantial assistance to the smaller, weaker islands — showed an incipient sense of community was held by some including William Demas, a past Secretary General of CARICOM. The objective economic realities, however, pointed towards an opposite conclusion and tended to support those scholars who saw CARICOM as relatively successful economically but who had serious reservations about making this judgement in terms of conventional social and political integration theory. To quote Anthony Payne: 'It is simply not concerned with integration in that sense. . . if integration is considered to have anything to do with the emergence of a new and separate community into which previous identities are submerged.'

Individualistic action was encouraged by a series of factors. To start, the disparities in size and resources in the area were too great. Jamaica and Trinidad/Tobago alone had 75% of CARICOM's G.D.P. and controlled 75% of its intra-regional trade. Not even the fact that by 1977, 66% of the loans made by the Caribbean

Development Bank and gone to the LDC's could compensate for this imbalance. Trinidad/Tobago, for instance, consistently showed a favourable balance of intra-regional trade with the less developed countries (LDC's) while these small islands had yet to post a single year of favourable balances in the decades since CARIFTA and CARICOM had been in existence. Not surprisingly, these small LDC's tended to look beyond CARICOM and towards other bilateral and multilateral arrangements. There was also a flagging of personal commitments in the post-independence era.

In regional movements good intentions are not enough, yet, without them regionalism would get nowhere. Ideals appear, thus, to be necessary but not sufficient causes for successful integration and in the 1980's the level of leadership commitment to the ideal of regionalism weakened. Commenting on the history of regionalism from the days of the West Indies Federation onwards, Trinidad's Eric Williams noted in 1980 that Federation had been replaced by something 'more indigenous but equally unstable, CARICOM' and even that organisation, he continued, 'is on its last legs.... Such as it is, this Caribbean Community is deeply divided among its members and the Treaty setting it up has been honoured more in the breach than the observance.' Views such as these by the leader of the financial center of CARICOM, did not give encouragement. Weakened commitments, however, appeared to be as much a consequence as they were a cause of the crisis in the West Indian integration movement. In the final analysis the basic cause was structural: a fundamental change in the nature of the economies to which the Caribbean as a whole was linked and, consequently, a basic crisis in the traditional Caribbean economies. These economic changes brought in turn changes in international political relationships which were reflected in the commitments and attitudes of the leaders.

This deep structural crisis in the economy of the Caribbean has come about in stages. The first stage was the disappearance of the traditional markets and economic links provided by colonialism. Even as the Lômé Convention helped ameliorate the economic costs of decolonization, Lômé affected only the traditional exports, those agricultural commodities such as sugar whose future was already in doubt. The new sectors such as oil, bauxite, tourism and, increasingly, international services such as off-shore banking were not covered. This has meant that the Caribbean economies have had to reorient themselves to new markets and new sources of finance for the development of these new sectors. This changing relationship was evidenced in the English-speaking Caribbean exports to the EEC —

which at 43% of their total have shown a moderate, though steady, decline — but especially in their imports: by 1977 a mere 10% of West Indian imports came from the EEC.

But the crisis evident in the 1980's went beyond the capacity of Lômé to reverse the decline. To be sure, it was a crisis of Caribbean production costs and world prices for their traditional products. The Caribbean-wide crisis in sugar illustrates this. In 1983 the privately owned Barbados industry had its lowest tonnage in 35 years and this was also the case with state-owned Caroni in Trinidad. Even Cuba, with 75% of its arable land in sugar and with an advanced state of mechanization, was throughout the early 1980's continuously short of production targets and forced in to the market to buy up to 150 000 tons in order to meet commitments to the International Sugar Organization. While the reasons for such low productivity vary, the price of 8 US cents a pound in 1986 — down from 78 US cents in 1980 — hardly provides an incentive to Caribbean producers. Meanwhile wages throughout the Caribbean kept rising regardless of market prices. To some countries these trends were devastating. With 41% of its exports earnings coming from sugar, the Dominican Republic for example was particularly hard hit by the price drop in 1982, its real GNP growth went from 5.8% in 1980 to 1.5% in 1982.

Similar situations existed in other traditional products such as cocoa and citrus. Together they represented the first stage in the deep crisis of the 1980's. But there was a second stage: the crisis in the non-traditional sectors of the economy, precisely those sectors in which these new nations had placed their hopes for economic development. At the same time in 1985 that the major sugar refiner in the Dominican Republic, Gulf and Western Corporation, was selling its interests in that country, many of the bauxite companies were also moving out of Jamaica. It was a question of world prices and thus profitability. There were world gluts in both sugar and bauxite and worse, cheaper substitutes were already available.

In the case of Jamaica, the closing, in mid-1984, of the Reynolds bauxite mines badly affected an already hurting fiscal budget by an estimated US$100 million which was equal to 40% of the receipts from the tourist industry for 1981. A revealing example of the bargaining weakness of the individual small state was given when Jamaican Prime Minister Edward Seaga told the press that Reynolds took the decision to leave the island without any prior consultation or even informing the Jamaican government. Decisions were being made at headquarters in the metropoli and tended to respond to general changes in the economies of those metropoli. Gulf and Western moved completely out of agriculture and into high technology information services and the Dominican Republic did not figure in these new plans.

And so, in the 1980's, foreign owned major industries abandoned the region in large numbers. In Aruba, where Esso once operated the world's largest oil refinery, they shut it down completely in 1985. In Curaçao, Royal Dutch Shell sold the refinery to the government of the Netherlands Antilles which managed to keep it functioning through Venezuela's offer to rent it for six years starting in 1985. Hess Petroleum shut down its transshipment terminals in St. Lucia and the British Virgin Islands. In Trinidad, where the government had already purchased British Petroleum and Shell, they were forced to buy out Texaco in order to save thousands of jobs.

The structural nature of the crisis indicated that in the 1980's the issue was not the nature of ownership but of prices and markets. The case of Guyana illustrates this. There the state-owned bauxite company Guymine, had to go on a three-day work week in 1983, this reflected a 30% decline in production in the mining sector, a major factor in the 9.1% decline in Guyanese GDP for 1982. With mining, a critical part of the 80% of total production in government hands, and with private investments stagnant, it became difficult in the mid-1980's to estimate how Guyana would repay its external debt, service on which was 34% of total exports by 1984.

Thus, it was not only that each and every island economy was hurting, it was also that the crises transcended both the type of economic system of individual nations as well as the collective schemes so carefully constructed to minimize the impact of declining world prices.

In the 1980's the Caribbean was learning that success at the economic level stimulated the idea of integration; failure undermined that idea. Legitimacy did not last long without some degree of economic effectiveness. If the path to development was perceived to be through integration then clearly failures in the process of integration were set backs to development.

All this came at a time when the turmoil created by economic recession was being compounded by political dissension. This is exactly what happened following the October 1983 invasion of Grenada by the United States and some West Indian nations, a move strongly condemned by CARICOM members Trinidad, Belize, Bahamas, and Guyana. There were bitter recriminations between the leaders of Guyana and Barbados especially and these contributed to a paralysis in the machinery of CARICOM. The passing away during the mid-1980's of three of the region's most dynamic (and strong-willed) leaders, Eric Williams, Tom Adams and Forbes Burnham, removed some of the personal animosities in CARICOM but none of the economic difficulties.

The point is, of course, that in addition to economic forces there were also political and ideological considerations determining intra-Caribbean co-operation. It was along international economic as well as political-ideological planes that events in the Caribbean moved with dramatic swiftness in the 1980's, slowly but surely turning the whole area into a definite United States sphere of influence. Economics, mass communication of culture and, most definitely, geopolitics all played their parts.

It is clear that with the decline in Caribbean trade with the EEC had come a decline in overall EEC influence. This fact was quite evident when events in Suriname and Grenada showed Holland and the United Kingdom unable to seriously affect events. In Suriname, a military coup led by Desi Bouterse overthrew a corrupt but never-theless elected government. The subsequent murder of 17 of the regime's most outspoken opponents led to a Dutch suspension of financial assistance but it was the United States' invasion of Grenada in 1983 and constant Brazilian pressure which led to a moderation of the regime's behaviour. Similarly, the case of Grenada demostrated the incapacity of the British to influence events there, much less act decisively; the fact was that the only. effectives Britain had left in the Caribbean was a batallion of Ghurka troops stationed in Belize. From a geopolitical point of view neither Holland nor Britain were any longer powers in the area.

It is in the context that one has to analyse the 1982 Caribbean Basin Initiative (CBI), the main initiative of the United States under the Ronald Reagan administration in the Caribbean. With provisions covering duty free Caribbean exports to the United States, incentives to investors as well as increased foreign aid it was by far the most comprehensive US economic programme ever enacted for the Caribbean, even after a protectionist Congress had a go at it. While it is too early to make any overall assessment of the historical impact of the CBI, there might be some benefit derived from analysing some already (by 1986) evident impacts on US — insular Caribbean relations. First of all, the CBI initiatives barely had an impact on the small islands of the Caribbean, especially those of the Eastern Caribbean. The fact is that by 1986 these islands — considered politically vital by the United States — had received a mere 2.48% of the CBI investments and 4.8% of the jobs created. Three countries,

Costa Rica, Jamaica and the Dominican Republic, had received 65%
of the CBI investments representing 53% of the jobs created.

Contrary to the old colonial economic relationships and the
multilaterally negotiated Lômé convention, the new relationship with
the United States carried no guarantees. This fact was evident from an
analysis of the forces in the United States which opposed a more
generous CBI. One was the US Congress' unwillingness to provide tax
credits for those firms investing in the Caribbean. This was a direct
result of organized labour's objection to the 'exporting of American
jobs'. Contributing to this was the growing protectionism in the
United States which led to the placing of increasing obstacles to the
duty-free importation of Caribbean goods.

Despite all these barriers, the CBI was one of the few avenues open
to the Caribbean nations whose economic options in the 1980's
appeared to be narrowing. As such, and given these characteristics of
the CBI it should be evident that the United States' presence and
predominance in the area could only augment. And on this score
events in the Caribbean in the post-independence era carried a lesson
for much of the ex-colonial areas of the world.

One of the weaknesses in the argument against 'sphere of influence'
thinking is that it has tended to assume that there is only one actor
involved, the stronger power. In fact, spheres of influence are often
desired by weaker states which throught fear for their security or
legitimacy share an ideological position with the stronger nation
and/or wish to derive material benefits from it. When various of these
factors operate at the same moment in history — as they were doing in
the Caribbean in the 1980's — then the trend carries considerable
force. The stronger power thus is often as much invited as inviting
itself. This appeared to have been the case with the Grenadian PRG
elite's dealings with Cuba, the Soviet Union and other members of the
socialist bloc. They were very much invited in; the 'outsider' is made
an 'insider' not by any aggressive intervention but rather at best an
aggressive acceptance of an intervention. The local élites have their
own ideological and practical political reasons for making the
'outsider' a major player.

It certainly has been the case with the evolution of the West Indies
and most of the Caribbean into an explicitly United States sphere of
influence. The late Barbadian Prime Minister, Tom Adams, could not
have been more candid or accurate than when he told the Royal
Commonwealth Society in London on December 9, 1983 that that
year was the 'watershed' year in which the influence of the United
States, willy-willy, came observably to replace that of Great Britain.

The term 'willy-willy' might be a cavalier way of describing such a momentous event but it in no way modifies the historical certainty of its occurance.

In the 1980's, the Caribbean was facing a new watershed, a fourth climactic period. Certainly, the trend towards independent action would lead to a wide range of responses on the part of the region's leaders. But the history of the Caribbean peoples' responses to the three previous climactic periods leave the observer optimistic. The region's peoples acted with initiative and courage in the face of past crises. There is no reason to doubt their capacity and determination to deal with equal imagination and tenacity with the structural crisis of the 1980's. The peoples of these small nations have learned to heed the words of the Caribbean poet:

> ... Should you
> shatter the door
> and walk
> in the morning
> fully aware
> of the future
> to come?
> There is no
> turning back.

Suggestions for Further Reading

Chapter I. Discovery

T. A. Joyce, *Central American and West Indian Archaeology.* London, 1916.

S. Loven, *Origins of the Tainan Culture, West Indies.* Göteborg, 1935.

S. E. Morison, *Admiral of the Ocean Sea.* Boston, 1942.

Columbus, *Journal of Christopher Columbus*, trans. Lane, ed. Vignoras. Blond and Brian Press, London.

Chapter II. The Spanish Indies

C. H. Haring, *The Spanish Empire in America.* New York, 1947. *Trade and Navigation between Spain and the Indies in the Time of the Hapsburgs.* Cambridge, Mass., 1918.

A. P. Newton, *The European Nations in the West Indies.* London, 1933.

I. Wright, *The Early History of Cuba.* New York, 1916.

J. H. Parry, *The Spanish Theory of Empire in the Sixteenth Century.* Cambridge, 1940.

L. Hanke, *The First Social Experiments in America.* Cambridge, Mass., 1935.

Chapter III. The Challenge to Spain

Sir J. S. Corbett, *Drake and the Tudor Navy.* 2 vols. London, 1898.

J. A. Williamson, *Maritime Enterprise 1485–1588.* Oxford, 1913. *Sir John Hawkins, the Time and the Man.* Oxford, 1927.

R. Hakluyt, *The Principal Navigations, Voyages, Traffiques and Discoveries of the English Nation* (1589). 12 vols. Glasgow, 1903–5.

C. Fernández Duro, *La Armada Española desde la Unión de los Reinos de Castilla y León*. 9 vols. Madrid, 1895–1903.
C. B. de la Roncière, *Histoire de la Marine Française*. Paris, 1899.

Chapter IV. The Settlement of the Outer Islands

C. M. Andrews, *The Colonial Period of American History*. 4 vols. New Haven, 1934–38.
J. A. Williamson, *The Caribbee Islands under the Proprietary Patents*. Oxford, 1925.
V. T. Harlow, *History of Barbados, 1625–85*. Oxford, 1926. *Christopher Codrington*, 1668–1710. Oxford, 1928.
C. S. S. Higham, *The Development of the Leeward Islands under the Restoration*. Cambridge, 1920.
G. Debien, *'Les Engagés pour les Antilles'*, in *Revue d'Histoire des Colonies*. Paris, 1951.
E. Sluiter, 'Dutch-Spanish rivalry in the Caribbean area, 1594–1609', *Hispanic American Historical Review*, vol. 28 (1948), pp. 165–196.
A. E. Smith, *Colonists in Bondage*. Chapel Hill, N. C., 1947.
Père J-B. Du Tertre, *Histoire Générale des Antilles*. 3 vols. Paris. 1667–71.

Chapter V. The Sugar Revolution

R. Ligon, *A True and Exact History of the Island of Barbados*. London, 1657.
N. M. Crouse, *The French Struggle for the West Indies, 1665–1713* New York, 1943.
E. Williams, *Capitalism and Slavery*. Chapel Hill, N. C., 1944.
G. L. Beer, *The Old Colonial System, 1660–1754*. 2 vols. New York. 1912.
M. Herskovits, *The Myth of the Negro Past*. New York, 1941.
C. A. Banbuck, *Histoire de la Martinique*. Paris, 1935.
M. Satineau, *Histoire de la Guadeloup sous l'Ancien Régime*. Paris, 1928.
A. Whitson, *The Constitutional Development of Jamaica*. Manchester, 1929.
E. Dunn, *Sugar and the rise of the planter class in the English West Indies*. North Carolina Press, 1972.

Chapter VI. The Buccaneers

Colonizing Activities of the English Puritans. New Haven, 1914.
C. H. Haring, *The Buccaneers in the West Indies in the Seventeenth Century.* London, 1910.
Père P-F-X. Charlcvoix, *Histoire de l'Isle Espagnole ou de Saint-Domingue.* 2 vols. Paris, 1730–31.

Chapter VII. The Atlantic Slave Trade

Gaston-Martin, *Historie de l'Esclavage dans les Colonies Francaises.* Paris, 1948.
G. Scelle, *La Traite négrière aux Indes de Castille.* 2 vols. Paris, 1906.
R. Pares, *War and Trade in the West Indies, 1739–63.* Oxford, 1936.
F. W. Pitman, *The Development of the British West Indies, 1700–63.* New Haven, 1917.
Père Labat, *Nouveau Voyage aux Isles de l'Amérique.* 6 vols. Paris, 1722.
J. Walvin, ed., *Slavery and British Society.* Macmillan, London.
E. Donnan, ed., *Documents illustrative of the Slave Trade in America,* 4 vols. Washington, DC, 1930–1931.
Equiano, *Equiano's Travels 1789,* (ed. Paul Edwards). Heinemann, London, 1967.
R. Price (ed.) *Maroon Societies, Rebel Slave Communities in the Americas.* Anchor Books edition, USA, 1973.
M. Craton, *Testing the Chains; Resistance to Slavery in the British West Indies.* Cornell, 1983.
P. Curtin, *The Atlantic Slave Trade; a census.* Madison, University of Wisconsin, 1969.
O. Patterson, *The Sociology of Slavery.* McGibbon and Kee, London, 1967, reprinted 1979.

Chapter VIII. Commerce and War, 1739–63

A. Morales Carrión, *Puerto Rico and the Non-Hispanic Caribbean.* Rio Piedras, P. R., 1952.
L. M. Penson, *The Colonial Agents of the British West Indies,* London, 1924.
G. L. Beer, *British Colonial Policy 1754–65.* New York, 1907.

Chapter IX. Reorganisation, Rebellion and War, 1763–83

L. J. Ragatz, *The Fall of the Planter Class in the British Caribbean.* Washington, D. C., 1928.

F. Armytage, *The Free Port System in the British West Indies*. London, 1953.

H. T. Manning, *British Colonial Government after the American Revolution*. New Haven, 1933.

R. Pares, *Yankees and Creoles*. London, 1956.

C. Rossiter, *The First American Revolution*. Harcourt Brace, Harvest Books, New York, 1953.

H. Commager and S. Morrison, *Growth of the American Republic*, Harper, New York.

Chapter X. A House Divided Against Itself

E. Goveia, Slave *Society in the British Leeward Islands at the end of the Eighteenth Century*. Yale, New Haven, 1965.

R. Pares, *A West India Fortune*. London, 1950.

J. Saintoyant, *La Colonisation Française sous l'Ancien Régime*. 2 vols. Paris, 1932.

P. de Vaissière, *Saint-Domingue 1629–1789*. Paris, 1909.

M. L. E. Moreau de Saint-Méry, *Description de la Partie Française de Saint-Domingue*. 2 vols. Philadelphia, 1797.

Description de la Partie Espagnole de l'Isle Saint-Domingue, Philadelphis, 1799.

B. Edwards, *History, Civil and Commerical, of the British Colonies in the West Indies* (1794 — many editions).

D. Parsons, *Voyage of the Plant Nursery, HMS Providence, 1791–1793*. Institute of Jamaica, 1973.

Chapter XI. The Second American War of Independence

J. G. Leyburn, *The Haitian People*. New Haven, 1941.

T. Lothrop Stoddard, *The French Revolution in San Domingo*. New York, 1914.

J. Saintoyant, *La Colonisation Française pendant la Révolution*. 2 vols. Paris, 1930.

La Colonisation Française pendant la Période Napoléonienne. Paris, 1931.

R. W. Logan, *Diplomatic relations of the United States with Haiti, 1766–1891*. Chapel Hill, 1941.

C. L. R. James, *The Black Jacobins*, 2nd ed. New York, 1963.

Chapter XII.   Freedom Without National Identity

W. L. Burn, *Emancipation and Apprenticeship in the British West Indies*. London, 1937.

T. Clarkson, *The History of the Rise, Progress and Accomplishment of the Abolition of the African Slave Trade*. 2 vols. London, 1808.

W. L. Mathieson, *British Slavery and its Abolition, 1823–38*. London, 1926.

D. H. Hall, 'The Apprenticeship Period in Jamaica', *Caribbean Quarterly*, December, 1953.

V. Schoelcher, ed. A. Césaire, *Esclavage et Colonisation*. Paris, 1948.

R. Coupland, *Wilberforce*. Collins, London, 1923.

W. Green, *British Slave Emancipation, the Sugar Colonies and the Great Experiment*. Oxford, 1976.

J. Burns, *Vineyard of Liberty, the American experiment*. Knopf, New York, 1982.

A. de Tocqueville, *Democracy in America*.

H. Campbell, *The Dynamics of Change in a Slave Society, a Socio-political History of the Free Coloureds*. Fairleigh Dickenson University Press, 1976.

E. Brathwaite, *The Development of Creole Society in Jamaica 1770–1820*. Clarendon Press, 1971.

M. Craton and G. Greenland, *Searching for the Invisible Man: Slaves and Plantation Life in Jamaica*. Cambridge, Harvard University, 1978.

B. Higman, *Slave Population and Economy in Jamaica 1807–1834*. Cambridge University Press, 1976.

Chapter XIII.   'The Best and Worst of Times'

P. D. Curtin, *Two Jamaicas: The Role of Ideas in a Tropical Colony, 1830–1865*: Cambridge, Mass., 1955.

W. L. Mathieson, *British Slave Emancipation 1838–49*. London, 1932.

J. Davy, *The West Indies before and after Slave Emancipation*. London, 1854.

W. Sewell, *The Ordeal of Free Labour in the West Indies*. New York, 1861.

A. Caldecott, *The Church in the West Indies*. London, 1898.

H. Schuler, *'Alas, Alas, Kongo', A Social History of Indentured African Immigration into Jamaica, 1841–1865*. Johns Hopkins, Baltimore, 1980.

Chapter XIV. Patterns of Colonial Government

H. T. Manning, *op. cit.*

H. Wrong, *Government of the West Indies*. Oxford, 1923.

K. N. Bell and W. P. Morrell, *Select Documents on British Colonial Policy*. Oxford, 1928.

Sir C. Clementi, *The Consitutional History of British Guiana*. London, 1937.

Report of the Jamaica Royal Commission, 1886.

Chapter XV. The United States and the Hisponic Caribbean

S. Welles, *Naboth's Vineyard*. 2 vols. New York, 1928.

R. Guerra y Sánchez, *Manual de Historia de Cuba*. Havana, 1938. *Azúcar y Población en las Antillas*. Havana, 1944.

F. Ortiz, *Cuban Counter-point*. New York, 1947.

H. H. S. Aimes, *A History of Slavery in Cuba*. New York, 1907.

H. E. Friedländer, *Historia Económica de Cuba*. Havana, 1944.

H. F. Guggenheim, *The United States and Cuba*. New York, 1934.

L. M. Diaz Soler, *Historia de la Esclavitud Negra en Puerto Rico 1493–1890*. Madrid, 1953.

J. M. Sanromá, *Puerto Rico y su Hacienda*. Madrid, 1873.

R. W. Logan, *op. cit.*

Chapter XVI. The British and French West Indies, 1860–1918

Lord Olivier, *The Myth of Governor Eyre*. London, 1933.

W. L. Mathieson, *The Sugar Colonies and Governor Eyre 1849–66*. London, 1936.

C. D. Kepner and J. H. Soothill, *The Banana Empire*. New York, 1935.

G. Cumper, 'Labour Demand and Supply in the Jamaican Sugar Industry 1830–1950', *Social and Economic Studies*, vol. ii, no. 4. Kingston, 1954.

Report of the Royal Commission appointed 1882.

D. Nath, *A History of Indians in British Guiana*. London, 1950.

I. M. Cumpston, *Indians overseas in British territories 1835–1865*. Oxford, 1953.

E. Underhill, *The Tragedy of Morant Bay*. Alexander and Shephearde, London, Reprinted, Books for Libraries Press, New York, 1971.

Chapter XVII. The United States and the Independent Caribbean 1900–1969

L. H. Jenks, *Our Cuban Colony*. New York, 1928.
R. L. Buell and others, *Problems of the New Cuba*. New York, 1935.
R. Fitzgibbons, *Cuba and the United States*. Menasha, Wis., 1935.
L. L. Montague, *Haiti and the United States*, 1714–1938. Durham, N. C., 1940.
C. Lloyd Jones, *The Caribbean since 1900*. New York, 1936.
Dexter Perkins, *The United States and the Caribbean*. Cambridge, Mass., 1947.

Chapter XVIII. The Caribbean Colonies, 1918–60

Chapter XIX. New Caribbean Nations and States, 1962–1972

M. Ayearst, *The British West Indies*. New York, 1960.
E. Clarke, *My Mother Who Fathered Me*. London, 1957.
E. Williams, *The Negro in the Caribbean*. New York, 1942.
G. K. Lewis, *The Growth of the Modern West Indies*. London, 1968.
J. Mordecai, *The West Indies: The Federal Negotiations*. London, 1968.
P. Blanshard, *Democracy and Empire in the Caribbean*. New York, 1947.
Sir F. Stockdale, 'The Work of the Caribbean Commission', *International Affairs*, vol. xxiii, no. 2. April 1947.
M. Proudfoot, *Britain and the U.S.A. in the Caribbean*. London, 1954.
C. O'Loughlin, *Economic and Political Change in the Leeward and Windward Islands*. London, 1968.
F. Hoyos, *Grantley Adams and the Social Revolution*. Macmillan, London.
P. Sherlock, *Norman Manley*. Macmillan, London, 1980.
R. Hill, ed., *Marcus Garvey and Universal Negro Improvement Association Papers*. University of California Press, 1983.
E. Williams, *Inward Hunger, The Education of a Prime Minister*. Deutsch, London, 1969
P. Sherlock, *West Indian Nations*, Kingston, Jamaica Publishing House. 1973.
G. Coulthard, *Race and Colour in Caribbean Literature*. Oxford, 1962.

L. Barrett, *The Rastafarians, The Dreadlocks of Jamaica.* Heinemann, London, 1977.

G. Roberts, *The Population of Jamaica.* Cambridge, 1957.

D. Waddell, *British Honduras.* Oxford, 1961.

Earlier Works

Sir R. Schomburgk, *History of Barbados.* London, 1848.

W. J. Gardner, *A History of Jamaica.* London, 1909.

E. Long, *History of Jamaica.* 3 vols. London, 1774.

H. Breen, *St. Lucia.* London, 1844.

S. L. Caiger, *British Honduras, Past and Present.* London, 1951.

R. Guerra y Sánchez, J. M. Pérez Cabrera, J. J. Remos, E. S. Santovenia, eds., *Historia de la Nación Cubana.* 10 vols. Havana, 1952.

Chapter XX.   Politics of Post Independence

Chapter XXI.   Widening the United States' Sphere of Influence

Histories of Individual Countries

Gordon, K. Lewis, *Puerto Rico, Freedom and Power in the Caribbean.* Monthly Review Press, New York, 1963.

Sidney W. Mintz, *Sweetness and Power, The Place of Sugar in Modern History.* Elisabeth Sifton Books, New York, Viking, 1985.

Trinidad

Selwyn Ryan, *Race and Nationalism in Trinidad and Tobago.* University of Toronto Press, Toronto, 1972.

Jamaica

Carl Stone, *Democracy and Clientelism in Jamaica.* Transaction Books, New Brunswick, New Jersey, 1980.

Guyana

Leo A. Despres, *Cultural Pluralism and Nationalist Politics in British Guiana.* Rand McNally & Co., Chicago, 1967.

V. Daly, *Short History of the Guyanese People.* Macmillan, London.

C. Thomas, *Plantations, Peasants and State.* Centre for Afro-American Studies University of California and Institute of Social and   Economic Research, Kingston.

Grenada
Tony Thorndike, *Grenada: Politics, Economics and Society*. Frances Pinter Ltd., London, 1985.

Dominican Republic
Pierro Gleijeses, *The Dominican Crisis: The 1965 Constitutionalist Revolt and American Intervention*. The Johns Hopkins University Press, Baltimore, 1975, translated by Lawrence Lipson.

Haiti
Mats Lundahl, *Peasants and Poverty: A Study of Haiti*. St. Martin's Press, New York, 1979.
David Nicholls, *From Dessalines to Duvalier. Race, Colour and National Independence in Haiti*. Cambridge University Press, Cambridge 1979.

Cuba
Jorge I. Dominguez, *Cuba: Order and Revolution*. The Belknap Press of Harvard University Press, Cambridge Mass., 1978
Carmelo Mesa-Lago, *The Economy of Socialist Cuba, A Two-Decade Appraisal*. University of New Mexico Press, Alburquerque, New Mexico 1981.

Panama
David McCullough, *The Path Between the Seas. The Creation of the Panama Canal, 1870–1914*. Simon and Schuster, New York, 1977.

Barbados
F. A. Hoyos, *Barbados*: *A History from the Amerindians to Independence*, Macmillan, London
West Indies
Gordon K. Lewis, *The Growth of the Modern West Indies*. Modern Reader Paperbacks, New York, 1968.

West Africa
E. Isichei, *History of West Africa Since 1800*. Macmillan, London, 1986.

General Works
G. K. Lewis, *Mainstreams of Caribbean Thought*. John Hopkins, Baltimore, 1985.

D. Lowenthal, *West Indian Societes*. Oxford, 1972.

G. Simpson, *Black Religions in the New World*. Columbia University Press, New York, 1978.

F. Cassidy, *Jamaica Talk*. Macmillan, London, 1961, 1971.

Some Recent British Official Publications on the West India
Report of Royal Commission appointed 1938. (1945. Cmd. 6607.)

Statement of Action Taken on the Recommendations of the West Indies Royal Commission. (1945. Cmd. 6656.)

The Colonial Empire, 1939–47. (1947. Cmd. 7167.)

The Colonial Empire 1947–48. (1948. Cmd. 7433.)

Report of the West Indies Committee of the Commission on Higher Education in the Colonies. (1945. Cmd. 6654.)

Closer Association of the British West Indian Colonies. (1947. Cmd. 7120.) (Montego Bay) Conference on Closer Association. Part I, Report. (1948. Cmd. 7291.) Part 2, Proceedings. (1948. Colonial No. 218.) Report of the British Caribbean Standing Closer Association Committee 1948–9. (1950. Colonial No.255.)

Report of the Commission on the Unification of the Public Services in the British Caribbean Area 1948–49 (the Holmes Report). (1950. Colonial No. 25.)

Report of the Commission on the Establishment of a Customs Union in the British Caribbean Area 1948–50. (1951. Colonial No. 268.)

Report by the Conference on West Indian Federation held in London in April 1953. (1953. Cmd. 8837.)

The Plan for a British Caribbean Federation, agreed by the Conference on West Indian Federation held in London in April 1953. (1953. Cmd. 8895.)

Report of the Fiscal Commissioner (Cmd. 9618, December 1955).

Report of the Civil Service Commissioner (Cmd. 9619, December 1955).

Report of the Judicial Commissioner (Cmd. 9620, December 1955).

Report of the Conference on movement of persons within a British Caribbean Federation, Port of Spain, 1955.

Industrial Development in Jamaica, Trinidad, Barbados and British Guiana. Report of Mission of U.K. Industrialists, Oct.–Nov. 1952. (1953. Colonial No. 294.)

Comptrollers' Reports on Development and Welfare in the West Indies.

(i) 1940–2. Sir Frank Stockdale. (1943. Colonial No. 184.)

(ii) 1943–4. Sir Frank Stoçkdale. (1945. Colonial No. 189.)

(iii) 1945–6. Sir John Macpherson. (1947. Colonial No. 212.)
(iv) 1947–9. Sir Hubert Rance. (1950. Colonial No. 264.)
 (v) 1950.   (1951. Colonial No. 269.)
(vi) 1951. Sir George Seel. (1952. Colonial No. 282.)
(vii) 1952. Sir George Seel. (1953. Colonial No* 291.)
      Etc.

Report by the Conference on British Caribbean Federation held in London in February 1956. (Cmd. 9733, March 1956).

Report of the Tripartite Economic Survey of the Eastern Caribbean, January–April 1956. (H.M.S.O., London, 1967.)

Index